Struggle for Synthesis

D1542915

Struggle for Synthesis

The Seventeenth Century
Background of Leibniz's
Synthesis of Order
and Freedom

LEROY E. LOEMKER

Harvard University Press
Cambridge, Massachusetts
1972

© Copyright 1972 by the President and Fellows of Harvard College
All rights reserved
Library of Congress Catalog Card Number 72-79308
SBN 674-84545-5
Printed in the United States of America

Preface

This study grew from a conviction that the systematic thinkers of the seventeenth century, confronted by wars, contentions, and the disorders occasioned by the rise of new institutions (which make their age so much like our own), come closer to defining the ideals which must guide the establishing of an adequate, more comprehensive order and to defining the conditions needed for its creation than did those of the centuries which followed them. They did this on the basis of an enlarged version of Neoplatonism, particularly the Christian Neoplatonism of St. Augustine, though they differed greatly on details.

At the heart of this effort lay the issue of the nature of human freedom. The paradox of freedom rests upon a conflict between two equally valid convictions: that established order interferes with the individual's freedom, but that on the other hand, his freedom is impossible without established order. The practical resolution, it would seem, must be an order so enlarged that it is capable of absorbing the effects of individual creativity. Yet the paradox invites two opposing patterns of thought and life, to which I have given names common in the seventeenth century—names with a Roman origin which had received new meanings in the revival of ancient learning. The libertine, descended from the Roman *libertus*, or freed man, finds freedom in escape from bondage to authority, whether civil, religious, or ethical; the man of *honestas*, or *l'homme honnête*, on the other hand, finds freedom and fulfillment in the Stoic virtue of honestas, that is, in loyal conformity to a superior order or rule by which he governs his life.

Both of these moral ideals, however, are supported by larger patterns of thought and action, and it is with the opposition between these two thought patterns and the enlarged Platonic systems which struggled for their synthesis that the book is concerned.

This is therefore a study in intellectual history, narrow in its limitation to one dialectic issue, though an important one, but broad in its choice of thinkers illustrating one aspect or another of this dialectic. These examples take the form of brief studies in the history of ideas, which together, I hope, present a converging and coherent argument for the idealistic synthesis, but also point to certain weaknesses which reopen the way for libertinism. In the first part these ideas are drawn from aspects of social order; in the second they are more narrowly philosophical.

Thus the work is not intended to be a closely drawn history of the seventeenth century or of its intellectual life. It contains no ordered history or systematic exposition of Christian humanism, Reformation theology, Renaissance individualism, posttridentine Scholasticism, literary styles, or the philosophy of the physical sciences—though it draws materials from all of these fields. The thinkers discussed are not treated systematically; they are chosen (at least in most cases) not for their importance or direct influence, but because aspects of their thought illustrate the argument at some point.

The figure of Leibniz may well be judged an exception to this statement. The centrality of his thought in the argument is not due alone to my own interest in him, however, or to the fact that I am better informed or more enthusiastic about him than about others. His thought, and the great projects for which it was to serve as foundation and stimulus to men of good will (the *hommes honnêtes*), and which, I am convinced, were more important to him than the perfection of his own philosophy, inevitably make him, more than any other man in the century, the focal point upon which resolutions of the tensions and conflicts of his age converge.

I have used much material not well known or available in English, some of it perhaps justifiably neglected. Except where I have acknowledged the source of the translations, they are my own. I have given the original terms or phrases in parentheses only when some doubt may arise about my rendering or when their effectiveness is lost in English.

Much already well-beaten and winnowed straw has no doubt been rethreshed in the pages that follow. Yet I hope that certain fresh interpretations will be found, supported by the "congruence" or "consent" of widely spread sources, and that the argument of the book itself will be found timely (however indirectly) in view of the repudiation of absolutes and the widespread epidemic of irrationalism of our time—the nadir of a negative libertinism. The perhaps too obvious conviction underlying my work is that if a viable social and cultural harmony is to be restored, it must be through a growing commitment to an ideal of rationality which goes beyond the mere understanding of experienced facts and the determination of means for achieving accepted ends, to undertake once more a definition of the valid goals of human freedom, and to win people to a reasoned cooperation in using the scientific discoveries of our age to achieve these goals.

I have received help from so many sources, and over so long a time, that adequate acknowledgments and thanks are impossible. A John Simon Guggenheim Memorial Fellowship awarded in 1958-59 and supplemented by a Fulbright Research Fellowship enabled me to break ground in European libraries and to write first drafts of some of the chapters. I hope that I have given recognition to the many sources of which I have made use in my documentation and bibliography. To the officers and staffs of these libraries I am deeply indebted for their courtesy and helpfulness, notably the British Museum, the Universitätsbibliothek and Westdeutsche Bibliothek in Marburg Lahn, and the Widener Library of Harvard University. Occasional grants of leave from Emory University were necessary complements to these aids.

The selection on page 3 from Saint Augustine, *On Free Will*, translated by John H. S. Burleigh, is printed by permission of the Westminster Press, Philadelphia, Pa.; that on page 224 from Pico della Mirandola's *Oration on the Dignity of Man* is used by permission of the University of Chicago Press. I am also indebted to the D. Reidel Publishing Company of Dortrecht, Holland, for permission to print several translations of my own from Gottfried Wilhelm Leibniz, *The Philosophical Papers and Letters*, revised edition, Dortrecht, 1961.

My indebtedness to colleagues and students is also great; had I been able to live up to their advice and expectations my book would have been better. Dean Charles T. Lester of the School of Graduate Studies has encouraged me with secretarial aid through the research funds of the University. From my colleagues Ivor Leclerc and Gregor Sebba, and from the Reverend Edward Connelly, who have read the manuscript in various stages, I have received valuable criticisms and suggestions. In addition to the gracious and always helpful editorial staff of the Harvard University Press, I must acknowledge gratefully the assistance of Elsa Mauger and Cris Caravacci in putting much of the text, and the index, in legible form, and that of Margaret Wood, who worked carefully and patiently in preparing the index.

To these, and to the other students who have contributed to my education through many decades, I should like to dedicate this book.

Contents

Part I.
Cultural Aspects
of Revolt and Synthesis

1 The Vision
of Dynamic Unity

The will, therefore, which cleaves to the unchangeable good that is common to all, obtains man's first and best good things, though it is itself only an intermediate good. But the will which turns from the unchangeable and common good and turns to its own private good, or to anything exterior or inferior, sins. It turns to its own private good when it wills to be governed by its own authority; to what is exterior, when it is eager to know what belongs to others and not to itself; to inferior things, when it loves bodily pleasures . . . That "aversion" and "conversion" is voluntary and is not coerced. Therefore it is followed by the deserved and just penalty of unhappiness.

[St. Augustine, *On Free Will*, II, xxi, 53. From *Augustine: Earlier Writings*, trans. and ed. J. H. S. Burleigh (Philadelphia, Westminster Press, 1953). Used by permission.]

It is credible that there are natural laws, but they are lost in us; this fine human reason everywhere so insinuating itself to govern and command, as to shuffle and confound the face of things according to its own vanity and inconstancy . . . Thus reason finds appearance for divers effects. 'Tis a pot with two ears, that a man may take by the right or left.

[Michael de Montaigne, "The Apology for Raymond of Sebonde," *Essays*, trans. Charles Cotton. 2 vols. London, n.d., p. 491.]

You never enjoy the world aright, till the sea itself floweth in your veins, till you are clothed with the heavens, and crowned with the stars: and perceive yourself to be the sole heir of the whole world, and more than so, because men are in it who are every one sole heirs as well as you. Till you can sing and rejoice and delight in God, as misers do in gold, and kings in sceptres, you never enjoy the world.

[Thomas Traherne, *Centuries of Meditations*. Edited by Bertram Dobell (London, 1948). Century 1, sec. 29.]

The Seventeenth Century Background

Viewed from the perspective of the twentieth century, the greatest paradox of the seventeenth seems to be that an age so torn by destructive forces and so disrupted by cultural innovations should give expression to so many absolutes. The exuberance of Traherne's conviction of the unity of man's life with the world of nature and of his fellows, and his faith that this whole can be encompassed by a rational order of meaning, seems to us strangely implausible in the face of a Europe devastated by the Thirty Years' War and the sequence of lesser wars which followed it,[1] by an Empire in decline and impotent against the rise of new independent states, and a Christian church torn apart by radical reforms and captured by the new "national" political units.

It was a century in which absolutisms—political, ecclesiastical, and intellectual—had their strongest defenders, yet were also most effectively challenged by the rapidity with which the failures of old ways were revealed, and accomodations to the new were demanded.

In its feeling for change, power, action, and violence, the seventeenth century was much like the twentieth. But in its faith in reason it stood at the antipodes of our own lapses into undisciplined feeling and impulse. It may well have been a historical misfortune that in a century in which science and mathematics made available both new forms of power and new ways of controlling this power, and when Renaissance individualism was rapidly dispersing authority and freedom from restricted classes to lesser orders of gentry, merchants, and citizens, modern nationalism and colonialism also began to formulate their most convincing myths and ideologies. Our most pressing problems now seem to have arisen out of that century's projects and failures.

Yet historical failures may not always be the best perspective from which to evaluate men's efforts to progress. And this is true of the endeavor made then to achieve an enlarged rational ordering of human understanding, action, and taste, which should absorb the freedoms discovered through individual and group revolts against the classical traditions of the past, thus preparing the way for a new, unified, religiously oriented harmony of loyalties. This was the problem of which the thinkers of the seventeenth century showed an awareness.

The result was a polarization between doubt and revolt, on

the one hand, and a constructive effort to set up more universal principles for a more general and stable order. Such tensions have characterized most warlike ages, for the harsh realities of conflict and the rapidity with which the conditions of life change collapse old certainties and rob old absolutes of their power. Skepticism and the exploration of new possibilities are both intensified, and each attitude serves as corrective or regulative of the other.

In fifth century Athens, for example, the defeat of the Persians, followed by internal frustration and dissent over outworn political forms, gave rise to new educational, political, and aesthetic endeavors, and eventually to the logical disciplines of Socrates and the great intellectual systems which have since set directions for Western culture. The decline of the Roman Empire, its republican ideals of justice perverted by power, in danger from internal corruption and the intrusion of barbarian peoples, evoked the great Christian synthesis of St. Augustine, in which the changing values of history were contrasted with the abiding values of the Eternal City. Later, out of the crisis of the feudal order which eventually followed the Dark Ages, and the rise of city republics (or tyrannies) which freed themselves from it, a revived interest in Rome and the ancient classics of literature and thought was generalized and transformed into a new creative ideal of civic and individual humanism.[2] It is with a similar dialectic of polarity and synthesis in the seventeenth century, in which protest and skepticism are opposed by a vigorous effort to determine a new ideal of order and culture, that the present work is concerned.

The Dialectic of Struggle and Synthesis

The seventeenth century has been characterized in many very revealing ways; it has been called the glorious century (and "glory" expresses one of its distinctive values), the century of genius, the scientific Renaissance (though the new science was surely already a healthy youngster at its beginning), the baroque age, and the "age of the death of tragedy."[3] Taking a hint from Daniel Defoe's "Essay of Projects" but anticipating his dates by many decades, one might appropriately name it the "age of projecting."[4] I have chosen René Wellek's perceptive description of the baroque as "the struggle for synthesis" to stand for the opposition and dialectic relationship of these two ideal types of personal and social reaction. They had a common source in earlier centuries, but were used in wider perspectives as Renaissance humanism passed into its late intellectualistic phase. To use Montaigne's figure, Reason now proved indeed to be "a pot with two ears, that a man may take by the right or left." One type was the *libertine*,[5] skeptical of preestablished order and untrammeled by it; the other that of *honnêteté*[6]—the old Stoic virtue of *honestas*—seeking freedom in the discovery of, and obedience to, the order or law on which the world is grounded. It is the unifying assumption of the present work that the synthesis sought was an enlarged humanism enriched by the free inventions of the libertine and absorbing them into more universal principles of order.

To grasp even incompletely the complexity of this opposition and synthesis, it is important to examine the confusions and conflicts of the century somewhat more fully. The collapse of established orders can appropriately be discussed in three aspects—the destruction of religious unity through the schisms of the Church; the disintegration of the Empire, accelerated by the rise of new and powerful nation-states and new federations of smaller states for their security, and the widespread repudiation of the intellectual authority of Scholasticism and its version of Aristotle. Never very effective, the two swords, sacred and secular, upon which European order had been based, had been broken by open revolt, and the unified intellectual foundation destroyed by a new respect for facts and freedom.

To these negative historical developments must be added the effects of certain physical forces. A prominent one was the plague (as well as epidemics of other diseases, including the venereal) which swept Europe at intervals throughout the century, raising deep problems for faith and revealing the impotence of medical science. But beyond these natural causes, there were important historical ones, the underlying one, inherited from the Renaissance, being a fresh appreciation of the centrality of the individual and his values. As the same rights and freedoms that noble and courtly classes enjoyed were demanded by mercantile and professional classes and the citizens of free cities, social rigidities and absolutes were relativized. In the wars of the century new political and economic forces engaged each other under religious as well as national banners. The concept of a state church was firmly established by the treaties ending the Thirty Years' War, but at the same time in England, its corollary, the divine right of kings, after being vigorously defended by the first Stuart, was dramatically destroyed by the execution of the second Stuart. Islam was no stranger to Europe, but having been long since expelled from the South, it had once more pushed in from the East even to the gates of Vienna, the last capital of the Empire. Geographic discoveries had destroyed European insularity, but had also revived the crusading spirit of Christianity and at the same time stimulated an appetite for the new wealth which was uncovered. Through the missionary enterprises of the Jesuits in China and India, and explorations and colonies in the New World, entirely new cultures, some of them built upon nature rather than human art (in Aristotle's sense of the terms) were brought to play upon European life.

In a century of such changes, the dialectic of tradition, revolt, and synthesis must appear in many particular forms, which will be discussed in this chapter and those that follow. In relation to aesthetic styles, it appeared in the sixteenth century as the manneristic reaction to classical order, and the baroque synthesis, and was continued with variations into the seventeenth. In literature the old theme of the conflict between ancient and modern, a perduring subject, was given a content fitting the quarrels of the time; in late Scholasticism the controversies over the *via antiqua* and the *via moderna* took place between Scotists and Ockhamists, with the *Novantiqui* seeking a synthesis. Now it became one between late Scholasticism and the Cartesians, with the Scholastic Cartesians combining them. Viewed from the perspective of the problem of knowledge, the issue was drawn between the tradition of erudition and the new turn toward factuality and directness. Francis Bacon, thoroughly erudite in his own literary habits, at least pointed to the need of synthesizing both in his *Advancement of Learning*. The deeper logical issue, however, concerned the old argument about universals—Platonic and Aristotelian realism, challenged by the nominalism of libertines and atomists, evoked a revived synthesis of Augustinian conceptualism.

In religious and theological questions the quarrels were far more bitter and divisive. Harshest of all were the charges and countercharges resulting from the Protestant Reformation and the Counter-Reformation of the Church, and the further divisions between Lutheran and Reformed churches among Protestants, and between Jansenists and Jesuits in the Catholic church. Luther was Antichrist for the Romans, and all Protestant leaders were heretics and "politici." But Pope, and sometimes Emperor, were Antichrist on the other. Yet in contrast to the bitter controversy over the schism of the churches three very different movements encouraged a new unity. The entire Christian tradition faced the threat of "atheism" and sought to combat it (as well as heathenism) with new apologetic efforts. There were also limited efforts made, from both sides, to bring about a reunification of the churches through agreement on doctrine. Then, too, the changes of the times convinced Christians of all persuasions that the prophesied return of Christ was at hand; there was a widespread revival of eschatological hopes and predictions.

Such are the issues about which the struggle and synthesis of thought and culture turned. But deeper were the metaphysical issues implicit in them, some of which are the subject of the second part of this work. They emerged in the great systems of philosophy in close relation to the problem of the nature of universals. The epistemological triad is that of rationalism, empiricism, and their syntheses in intuitionalism and in an enlarged rationalism. The antithesis of perfection and imperfection is resolved eventually in the concept of progress, to which the eschatology of the century makes an indirect contribution. Order challenged by revolt leads to a quest for a new order supported by science and by new Christian conceptions of justice and of the interdependence of persons. An enlarged conception of the law of nature, Platonic rather than Aristotelian, binds the individual more intimately to the physical and the moral order.

The remainder of this chapter will explore some of the analogies between the opposing personal ideals in the struggle and their aesthetic expressions, and specify some of the new qualities of experience which render the synthesis fruitful. In Chapters 2, 3, and 4, certain developments illustrating the dialectic in three different fields of culture—the world of letters, the world of religion, and the cultural impact of the emerging scientific knowledge—will be examined.

Christian Neoplatonism as Synthesis: Some Seventeenth Century Emphases

Among the earlier intellectual syntheses in European culture, the most important one, for the purpose of this study, was a Christian Platonism which had shown itself capable of absorbing elements of Stoicism, Neoplatonism, and Aristotelianism into a new intellectual basis for thought, art, and public order—as well as for theology, psychology, and ethical ideals. Renaissance humanism in its development from Nicholas of Cusa and the Florentine Academy to the later thought of Giordano Bruno and Tommaso Campanella had shown its creative force. The Augustinian doctrines of the divine sovereignty, of infinite degrees of goodness in the hierarchical orders of creation (in particular the human order of freedom and the physical order of law), and of the origin of evil in man's freedom and his pride and its justification in the plan of Providence, had furnished a broad doctrinal support for the social order of the cities and courts, for ethical and literary reflection, and for the widespread flowering of creative individual powers.

Implicit in this eclectic Platonism were the two differing ideals of personality and of the good with which we are concerned. In part these depended upon one's notions of the scope of human freedom and of reason. Theologians like Blaise Pascal would relate them to man in a state of nature and in a state of grace—but Pascal had already experienced the terror evoked by the new state of nature. In the much earlier fruitful revival of the negative theology by Nicholas of Cusa, a beginning of both ideals can be traced: on the one hand there is the cosmos of *order*, expressing the explication and corresponding implication of the creative thought of God, reflected uniquely in its scope but not in its perfection in each individual microcosm. But on the other hand there is "learned ignorance," a limitation of the intellect keeping it from grasping the ultimate unity in which all oppositions are resolved.

In Nicholas this latter path was by no means the ultimate skepticism of the *libertine* who, unable to discern—or at least to accept as authoritative—any superior order commanding his allegiance, acts freely on the basis of his own feelings and best perceptions. It is rather a skepticism determined by the limits of the finite mind—a critical skepticism which Plato inherited from the questioning Socrates and developed into a rational criterion for the distinction between appearance and reality. It was applied to Christian doctrine by St. Augustine and became effective again with the revival of logical studies in the late Renaissance, to be applied as a method and criterion (notably by René Descartes, implicitly by Thomas Hobbes and others) for attaining clarity and distinctness in human thought. Such skepticism is the condition of right reason, essential to the scientific attitude.

In this sense the *homo honestatis* of the seventeenth century, affected by the mathematical ideal of knowledge which had purged Platonism of spiritistic and animistic explanations, used skepticism as a tool for rejecting indistinct and inadequate notions.[7]

Both views—that of the doubting libertine and the skeptical man seeking a better order—recognized the uniqueness of the individual, but the libertine denied that each individual, from his unique point of view, can reflect a common overarching order of being within which he must find his place; so far as he can know, he can detect only an order relative to his own experience and is free to accept, reject, or alter it. *Honestas*, on the other hand, rested upon the Neoplatonic-Stoic doctrine of the *Logos* with the correlated conviction that each man, though unique, is a microcosm reflecting, from his point of view, the greater macrocosm, and therefore is bound to his fellows through their participation in a common rational order.

It is the argument of this study that the ideal of *honnêteté*, used to describe the courtier in earlier literature, was given an enlarged interpretation in the seventeenth century commensurate with the great changes taking place in European culture, and that this new interpretation strove to absorb into itself many of the rightful values of the libertine position. To achieve this synthesis was an ideal of the great systems of the century, whose success must be measured in part at least by the adequacy of the program which they supported for European order and human freedom. In this sense George Lukács was right in referring to these systems as "philosophic diplomacy."[8] They were apologetic and strategic in character.

In the new and enlarged contexts of life and the greater pluralization and incoherence of culture into which Europe was now thrown, certain old *idées-forces* emerged with new power. The individualistic spirit of the earlier Renaissance was retained, but in the enlarged context of the new nationalistic absolutisms with their corollaries of colonialism, a new concern for freedom and rights, the new conception of nature implicit in the growth of science and technology, and a new philosophical eclecticism largely Platonic in pattern.

Among the traditional convictions which were given a new emphasis and enlarged application, six are of particular importance for the issues dividing the libertine and the man of *honestas*. They are: (1) a new growth of *self-consciousness* combined with a new sense of its importance as revealing meaning; (2) a new awareness, implicit in the microcosm-macrocosm conviction, of the dependence of each person upon society, and the tendency to use this relation of social dependence and conformity in interpreting both human relations and the cosmic order; (3) a new consciousness of *power* and its role in culture; (4) a new appreciation of *reason* in the solution of both theoretical and practical problems; (5) a new sense of the urgency of achieving certainty in knowledge and understanding; and (6) a widened and more socialized sense of *freedom.* In each of these new convictions there are decisive points of agreement and difference between libertine and authoritarian ideals.

Like any age with new problems which demand new solutions, the century grew in self-consciousness and in its recognition of the importance of this self-consciousness for its thought. It did not discover self-consciousness; Socrates had done this through his demand for self-knowledge; and his discovery, systematized and built into Western thought as a ground for philosophical insights by Plato and Aristotle, was pushed into the center of religious life and of metaphysical issues as well by St. Augustine.

In the seventeenth century, however, self-consciousness became the key, not merely to new metaphysical systems but to new orders of human value and relations. Both Reformation and Counter-Reformation had turned to it for a criterion of individual certainty of redemption, but had also helped to universalize, secularize, and socialize it, since redemption is available to all. Philosophically there was widespread agreement that self-awareness is the necessary basis of both memory and (through memory) imagination, and that both of these are the precondition of reason and therefore (for many thinkers) of freedom.

The libertine agreed with his opposite on the significance of self-awareness for the individual—save on the issue of freedom, to which the libertine found a more direct self-conscious access. Pascal alone seems to have seen most clearly the two contrary interpretations which self-consciousness could be given in an age in which the new had overwhelmed the old. It is man's awareness of himself which throws him into despair at his situation; yet it is this same understanding which is challenged to greater commitment by the reasons of the heart. The confidence which the man of the classical revival had in the objectivity of his values and purposes either collapses into the self-reflection of the skeptic or is converted into a confidence in the power of reason to give solutions to man's new problems. The empirical basis for the decision must be discovered in self-consciousness itself; either man finds within himself the basis of loyalty to a universal order of reason and law with which his own thought and will is continuous, or he finds by inner examination that order, at least in so far as it can be known, is relative to his feeling, desire, and will. The issue had been drawn by the Scholastics, especially in the Ockhamist tradition. In the Italian city-states the individualistic ideal of the courtier had encouraged both the restricted loyalty of the courtier and his freedom from other orders. But now, when the conflicts of political and religious loyalty had become too conspicuous to be overlooked, the need of a single all-encompassing rational unity of order and purpose was once more recognized, though the possibility of finding grounds for defining such an order was also widely challenged.

The inwardness and uniqueness of personal life as revealed by self-consciousness was balanced, however, by a new sense of social interdependence. This is implicit in the microcosm-macrocosm theory, for since each individual, however unique, represents the order of the whole, all must have that order imbedded in their experience as a common ground for reason and communication. Such a view is, of course, excluded from the libertine position. But the philosophy of *honestas* pursues it further in the interest of social order. There is a new interest in seeking a universal language based on logical order, and communication becomes the model for the interpretation of the unity of a plurality of beings. Evidences of this will appear in later chapters in the discussion of Bacon's suggestion, which he seems not to have developed further, that the relations between all things might be understood in terms of actual or virtual perceptions, and its further development into a theory of *symbiosis* by the Calvinist theologians of Herborn.

A similar division of convictions was shown about the other traditional problems. A new awareness of power accompanied the century's growing sense of dynamism and change, and the problem of the control of absolute political power became particularly acute during a period in which wars were fought on supposedly religious grounds and the authority of a universal religious faith had disintegrated. To this was added an intensified sense of power in nature; Bacon's teaching that science is power was to receive dramatic justification in the new bombs constructed by the Sun King's military genius, the Marquis de

Vauban, the awful effects of which Leibniz celebrated by a widely read ode.

For the man of *honestas*, all power, both physical and social, rests on nature, and nature itself is an expression of the divine. As potency (*potentia*), power had been an important philosophical category since Aristotle and his Scholastic interpreters. In the humanistic revival, however, it had been discussed in more empirical contexts—political power by Niccolò Machiavelli and Jean Bodin, physical power more vaguely by the writers on physical matters before Galileo in connection with their analysis of motion through impetuses or conatuses. Influenced by Bernardino Telesio, Thomas Campanella introduced the century to a new conception of the trinity in his doctrine of the "primalities"—God must be understood as *power* manifesting itself in the parallel attributes of *wisdom* and *love*, which are therefore basic throughout creation as well. In physical theory the Aristotelian analysis of things into form and matter was superseded by a concept of force manifested in active striving and passive mass.

The question which is as old as the Platonic Socrates thus became acute—how can power be exercised in harmonious and orderly ways, or in the social field, how can it be rendered just. The great systematizers of the century followed the Augustinian clues in basing the normative unity of force and order, power and justice, upon the unity of power and thought in God—who is the source of all power and all wisdom. Thus the ideas, which are the archetypes of existence in God's mind, are themselves dynamic—as Leibniz said, they have a striving, an exigency, for existence—and are therefore the assurance of the possibility of a just order in the world.

This was the faith of the man of *honestas*. For the libertine, in contrast, who distrusted any confusion of words with objective order and was skeptical about the real reference of words beyond sensory things, power resides in the will of man; or (in the physical world) power is an abstraction from the motion of atoms; divine power is unknowable.[9]

To the difference of opinion about the status of power there corresponded a disagreement about the nature and basis of *reason*. For the man of the revived Stoic virtue of *honestas*, the place of reason was the eternal *Logos*, always present for human reason to find and obey, or to reject; or in Christian terms, reason was identical with the divine intellect, providing the order of nature for man's use if he finds this reason, and supplying also the principles of thought which man must obey if he is to discover this order and to act accordingly.

For the libertine, on the other hand, human reason lacked such an objective norm, but must limit itself to the experiences of men which are certain, notably those relative to his senses and feelings. Reason was for him the logical act by which the mind establishes its own order within experience.

It follows that next to the metaphysical problem of the reality of order, the problem of the scope of human knowledge and the degree of certainty which it can achieve is of importance in the dialectic between the two ideals of human life. It is in this context that the philosophers of the century were forced to examine the matter of degrees of probability in knowledge and the possibility of its adequacy.

The most concrete of the problems at issue between the two camps, however, was the problem of human freedom, since questions of human power and its conditions, of the relation of will to intellect, and of the nature and knowledge of good and evil depend for their answers upon this problem. Again, for the man of *honestas*, freedom is an achievement of that individual who, through reason and loyal obedience to the sovereign order of the universe, finds this order fully reflected in his own thought and commitments; his relation to God, like that of the earthly courtier to his prince, is both the condition and the actualization of his possibilities of perfection and fulfillment. The libertine, on the other hand, recognizes no knowledge of an overlord, nor indeed of any sovereign or source of order but himself. For him, freedom is the natural power of man "to do what he wills" or to determine, in not fully determined situations, the action most desirable for him.

Thus the two ideals imply two distinct sets of conclusions about individual man and his good, about God as the source of order and power, and about the conditions of knowledge. From these opposites it will be seen that others follow, including the priority of eternity to time or of time to eternity, of the changing to the changeless, the role of the subjective in knowledge and valuation, and the relation of ethics to metaphysics. More pertinent, however, is the question of which alternative possesses the adaptability and force to assimilate within it the truth of the other. In the great metaphysical systems of the seventeenth century the valid points of libertinism were absorbed with some success (as valid mannerist innovations were absorbed by the baroque). But by the end of the century, strains in the inner unity of these systems appeared, and the so-called Enlightenment is marked by a distinct victory of the libertine spirit, and the restriction of reason to the limits of human purposes.

Libertinism and Honestas: Possibilities of Synthesis

It will be useful to examine the opposition between the two ideal types of individual in terms of certain cognate concepts.

In Nicholas Malebranche's first response to Antoine Arnauld's attack upon his *Treatise of Nature and of Grace* (1683), he gave a clear definition of the two opposing views in relation to positions associated with them. He described his own work as an effort to refute libertinism, and charged Arnauld with encouraging it. Both the Oratorian Malebranche and the Jansenist leader Arnauld were obviously on the side of the *homo honestatis*, and libertinism was obviously a term of offense for both, promising grave evils for their world.

> I have proved in the *Recherche de La Vérité* that we see in God all things of which we have clear ideas, that is to say, in an immutable nature, in the eternal wisdom, in universal Reason. I have proved that all spirits have a common good, Reason, which illumines all men and by which alone they can have a true society and a communion of thoughts and actions among themselves and also with God. In a word, I have proved . . . that if it were not the Wisdom of God himself which enlightens us, if we did not all, when we return within ourselves, have the idea of an order so immutable by nature that God himself cannot change it and fail to follow its laws, because he loves his wisdom invincibly and cannot contradict himself, there could no longer be a demonstrative proof of morality and religion, nor even any veritable science.
>
> For how could you prove to a libertine that nature is out of order, if there were no immutable and necessary order whatever? He would only have to reply impudently that God has made spirits for bodies, to drink, to eat, and calmly to enjoy sensible things. How prove to him that God will reward good actions and punish crimes, and even that justice and injustice are not at all a phantom which one uses to bring fear in the credulous? The libertine has only to say boldly and churlishly that the Wisdom or Reason of God is

far different from ours, and that it seems just to us to reward what one calls good works, but that what seems just really is not, or at least is not from the viewpoint of God, who is the absolute Master of his creatures.[10]

The libertine was thus regarded by Malebranche not as a theoretical atheist, but as one who regards himself as free in thought and act from any regulation through a divinely ordered set of laws. Libertinage is thus primarily an intellectual state, but may also, derivatively, be a moral state in which inclinations and desires, undisciplined by order, determine actions. It is this intellectual libertinism, contrary to later usage but already confused with it, with which the argument here is concerned. It is closely related to *atheism*, also a deep concern in the century, as Chapter 3 will show, but it conforms rather to the practical atheism which Plato described in the Laws, Book X—the atheism which recognizes God but denies that he influences human life. Libertinism therefore has more kinship with *skepticism* than with theoretical atheism. The revival of interest in Sextus Empiricus and the more direct influence of Montaigne and other skeptics is closely traceable in its rise. Like Montaigne and the skeptics whom he defended, the libertine may admit that there is a universal order, but hold that this order cannot be known without subjectifying it. To say further that the libertine adhered to the nominalistic tradition is valid, if nominalism is taken in the negative sense of denying that the reality of universals or forms, even if they are real, can be known by us. Thus libertinism, unlike skepticism, cannot have affinities with religious *fideism*, since the fideist still subjects himself to higher authority; for the authority of universal reason he substitutes the authority of religious tradition. However, it is noteworthy that there were distinct efforts among the supporters of the ideal of *honestas* either to prove that revelation is identical to, or at least compatible with, reason, or to show that the reasonable grasp of this authoritative order may be *instinctive* (Herbert of Cherbury) or *intuitive* in some more explicitly intellectual sense (Spinoza).

The core of libertinism is thus to be found in the release of the individual from all outer authority. This was a product of the Renaissance, when the creativity of the individual artist, the rise of subjective or unconventional literary innovations such as the essay and the imaginative tale, the introduction of fresh, arresting details in classical art, and even less strained than these, the willfulness of condottieri, princes, and dictators (compare the popular figure of the Emperor Frederick II) conspired to create an atmosphere in which freedom from established restraints combined with the urgency of action to encourage willfulness and arbitrariness. That the century regarded the libertine as suspect not merely on intellectual but on moral grounds, is shown in Malebranche's ascription to him of such qualities as "impudence," "boldness," and "churlishness."[11]

The man of *honnêteté*, by contrast, came into prominence, as I have already said, in the Renaissance ideal of the courtier, who achieved his freedom through respectful obedience to the higher order of the master or the court which he served.

In Baldassare Castiglione's *Book of the Courtier*, Canossa speaks for the Italian courtier as follows:

> Besides goodness, our true and spiritual grace I believe to be letters, though the French recognize nobility only in arms and think nothing of all the rest; indeed, they not only do not appreciate letters, they detest them and hold all lettered man in abject contempt; and they think it the worst affront in the world to call one a clerk.[12]

This ideal convention was one capable of being universalized and extended to new professional and civic classes through virtues and their basis in objective reason—whether this is conceived as the Stoic Logos, the Platonic Idea of the Good, or the Augustinian trinity of power, wisdom, and love. Thus there was alive in the Renaissance an ideal of the nobleman—well rounded, possessing an internal harmony which reflected the unity of the moral ideal, combining courage in warfare, grace in social accomplishments, and good taste in arts and letters. Grace implies wit, but short of satire. In the small courts of Renaissance Italy, the imitation of the Greek city-state and the Roman Republic seems to have provided models for societies of companionable and jointly responsible individuals, each of whom finds his unique self-fulfillment in concert with his peers and in obedience to the orders established by his prince.

Both dimensions of *honestas*—the concert of peers and the obedience to the law and its power—were thus pushed to universal scope in the seventeenth century, even though claims to absolutism in the newly unified states and the divided churches were threatened by national rivalries and religious quarrels, and the old universals of Roman law and of feudal order were being displaced by new civic structures. Francis Bacon reflected this new universalism in his discussion of the ethical principle that man's individual good is subordinate to and is controlled by the good of the social group which determines his duties.[13] The new science seemed to reveal a new order of nature which physical events obeyed and which revealed the reasonableness of natural power. The imaginative yet critical thought of the century revived the Classical-Christian conception of a law of nature and identified it with divine law—an all-inclusive order of law, in obedience to which nature serves man, and the wise man—the courageous, well-lettered, socially sensitive, and cultured man—finds fulfillment for himself and peace and order in the universal commonwealth, that is, the Kingdom of God.

In this socializing and universalizing of the ideal of the *homo honestatis*, the more enlightened courts often assumed a leadership which the churches, divided and hardened in their dogmas and disagreements, and the universities, hampered by an excessive traditionalism, were in danger of losing (although the founding of the Society of Jesus was a perfect example of the adoption of the ideal in the Roman church). Thus Bacon, Hobbes, Descartes, Spinoza, and Leibniz, all of them moved by aspects of this new ideal, avoided university life, though for different reasons, and all sought, though in different ways, to find an intellectual basis for religious peace, a united moral effort to further the growth of science, and a common spirit of harmony that would provide a standard for European well-being.

The thinkers of the century thus formulated a new explication of *honestas* in terms of such virtues as obedience (*pietas*), courage (*fortitudo*), consensus (*equitas*), wisdom, and love (*caritas*). In his emphasis upon understanding, Malebranche stressed the virtue of *curiosité* (a new corollary to wisdom). Spinoza described *honestas* in the *Ethics* in a complex relation to benevolence, piety, and friendship, defining all of these, consistent with his theory of affections as motives to action, in terms of desires, that is, inner drives to action based on clear and distinct notions of the good.

> The desire of doing good (*bene faciendi*) which is inbred in us from the fact that we live by the guidance of reason, I call *pietas*. Finally, the desire by which the man who lives by the guidance of reason is held to bind others to himself

in friendship (*amicitia*) I call *honestas*, and that is *honestum* which men who are thus led to praise, and in contrast, that is *turpe* which conflicts with the conciliation of friends.[14]

Leibniz converted the virtue of *generosité*, by which Descartes proposed to withstand the passions, into a similar combination of *wisdom* and *love*, in terms of which he defined the most sweeping social virtue—*justice*—as the love of the wise man. Enthusiastic about the new ethics of the moral affections propounded by the third Earl of Shaftesbury, Leibniz nevertheless warned him of the dangers of "raillery" (or satire), which breeds bitterness and thus threatens the harmony for which the man of honor strives.[15]

The ideal courtier, therefore, must have a character reflecting, from the point of view of his unique situation and gifts, the universal classical virtues—but in a form revised to fit the religious, political, and human conditions of the century.

It will be useful to summarize some of the main positions of the eclectic philosophical tradition in terms of which this universalization of authority through reason and this redefinition of the virtues in *honestas* were developed.

The logical issue which is the immediate ground for the opposite contentions of the libertine and the man of *honestas* is that of the reality and status of universals. The libertine acts on the assumption that there is no real order of universal meanings which we can know and which must be regarded as a norm of our thoughts and actions. Nominalism is the name often given, loosely, to this position. The opposite position may be called Platonism, though the conviction that there is a real pattern of universal meanings which man can know and should accept as norm in his thought and action is shared in various ways by Stoics, Aristotelians, and the Hebrew-Christian tradition as well.

The ideal of *honestas* therefore demands a refutation of skepticism. Complete skepticism is rare and impossible, practically, to sustain. But skepticism about knowledge of a real world order independent of our subjective processes of knowledge lies near the surface of all thought, and its constant challenge of common sense views of knowledge has been very productive philosophically. In particular the question of whether the independently real existence of universals can be known or whether they are merely thought processes is pressing in the seventeenth century. It is an important part of the task of the intellectual apologist of *honnêteté* to establish the objective validity of reason beyond the limits of what can be sensed, and to build increasingly "clear, distinct, and adequate" knowledge of a real order of being which shall demand and fulfill our thought and guide our action. In the seventeenth century the defender of absolutes, encouraged by the apparent certainty and infallibility of mathematical and scientific reasoning, undertook a new justification of the old Scholastic notion of clear and distinct knowledge as the *adequatio intellectus ad rem* ("the adequation of understanding to thing.")

The completion of these logical, ethical, and epistemological ideals must be sought in metaphysics. As a skeptic the libertine distrusts metaphysics; in practice unable to avoid it in a century in which science is formulating its first principles and primary concepts (the very possibility of these is at stake in the argument), the libertine is negatively, atheistically disposed, and positively, a champion of atomism or some other materialism. (Most of the atomists of the century, however, exempt God and the human soul from their atomic hypothesis).

The defense of *honestas*, on the other hand, found an eclectic metaphysical argument ready at hand, deriving from two distinct historical currents. The theological arguments arising from Reformation and Counter-Reformation rested upon a renewal of Aristotelian and Scholastic metaphysics, the preeminent example being the *Metaphysical Disputations* of the Jesuit Francisco Suarez, which was studied at most of the universities, Catholic or Protestant, taught to Descartes at La Fleche, read by Leibniz as a boy as if it were a novel (so he says), and which is still one of the great treatises on difficult points in metaphysics.

The other current is that of Christian Platonism, sustained by a no-less theological but more strongly humanistic current, contributed to by Franciscan Scholastics like Bonaventura and John Duns Scotus, Nicholas of Cusa, the Italian Platonists, and toward the end of the Renaissance by Tommaso Campanella (in his prison cell) and Giordano Bruno (whose manneristic style was already embodied in a light and darkness metaphysics, and who carried the new Platonism to Geneva, London, Paris, and the German universities). A general distrust of Aristotle in the seventeenth century made this second tradition more effective than the other, so that the Logos and its reflection in every particular center of finite being was once more given a theological elaboration in the doctrine that God's perfections are not only "univocal" with the attributes of his finite creations, but are, with finite limitations, identical with them. Thus God's trinitarian nature, conceived as power expressing itself in thought (the Logos) and love, operates through the dynamic qualities of the Ideas which strive from possibility to existence, so that every individual creature in its immanent being, "participates" in the reality of the Divine being.

This metaphysical synthesis was also expressed in a wide range of metaphors which provided structure to the arts and the general tone of the culture. The hierarchy of beings between the One and nothing was symbolized in Bruno's philosophy of light and darkness, and much later, by Leibniz in the binary number system. The microcosm-macrocosm correspondence[16] found analogical expression as harmonious sound and its echo, or as the mirroring image (in a spherical or parabolic mirror) of the All, or (as in Shakespeare) the representation of life on a stage (or in a dream). Thus many manneristic and baroque motives have their origin in this philosophical model.

More difficult was the adjustment and revision undergone by the metaphysical categories, themselves old, which was needed to explicate this enlarged philosophical vision. The old Aristotelian theory of causality was gradually revised to fit not only the new science with its mathematical and empirical presuppositions, but also this metaphysics of universal harmony. Both science and philosophy called for a more rigorous formulation of the principles of sufficient and necessary reasons. The extension of mathematical theory into transcendental functions and the analysis of the continuities of change led to paradoxes involving the continuum and the limits of discrete series, which were as old as Zeno, but now demanded a new logical precision. The problem of the infinite, whether beyond or within the finite, became acute in astronomy and physical theory, and the priority of permanence (whether as substance or law) over the changing (whether modal qualities or instances of a universal) was pushed into the center of metaphysics. Though these were problems proper to philosophy, they were not merely philosophical in origin but arose in mathematics, law, theology, and the arts as well. But the systematic development of these and other categories in an enlarged metaphysics served the ideal of a theoretical unity underlying the "struggle for synthesis" in the century.

Tension and Synthesis in the Styles of Art

I have argued that the ideal of *honestas* in its generalized application implied an extension of reason to cover new aspects of life which the classical conception failed to unify—inadequacies which had been uncovered in the course of individual criticisms and innovations. Libertine revolt and the new freedoms were thus to be absorbed into a new enlarged unity and harmony, providing more play for the uniqueness of the individual, the freedom of imagination, and the revival of religious devotion which resulted from the great schism.

This parallelism between the historical synthesis of the ethical ideals of Renaissance courtier and libertine in a universalized ideal of the *homme honnête* on the one hand and the development of classicism, mannerism, and the baroque as aesthetic styles of art on the other is suggestive but loose; yet common characteristics can be pointed out which justify the analogy. It has become a commonplace to apply the adjective "baroque" to the systems of men like Spinoza, whose thought and affections spiral upward to God like the columns in Giovanni Lorenzo Bernini's baldachin in St. Peter's, or like Leibniz, who conceives of the creation of the world as a vast calculation of maxima through the calculus of infinites, and expands the ideal of a codification of European laws under the model of ancient Rome into a philosophy for the new spiritual nobility of Europe.[17] The analogy serves a propaedeutic purpose, if one universalizes the underlying characteristics of the three art forms, raising them to more general philosophical categories.

That the two sets of ideal forms—the ethical of the courtier and the aesthetic of classicism—have principles in common can be seen if one considers that the differences among the three modes within each and the continuities of their development turn about the same themes: (1) the nature of the individual and his freedom, whether as obedience or as personal inclination; (2) the ability (or inability) of reason to extend its ordering activity into new areas of experience—cognitive, affective, and active; and (3) the defense (or rejection) of an independent reality of order and harmony. Classicism and the baroque agree in their emphasis upon objective order and its normative role in experience but disagree in their demands for the clarity and simplicity of the forms which define this order. Here the baroque has learned from mannerism to make order less distinct, less complete within itself, more dynamic, and more involved in that which lies beyond the limits of present sight or hearing.

Mannerism began as an individual protest against the classical orders in the interest of personal virtuosity and inventiveness;[18] it grew into unexpected, impulsive distortion, the free play of fancy about the obscure, the grotesque, the unaccepted. Classicism and the baroque both presuppose the reality of universals; mannerism is consistent with the nominalistic reduction of universals to language or signs (released from rigid rules of grammar and rhetoric). But in the baroque the universal is incomplete, remote, but fruitful as an intellectual instrument for deeper intuitive insights. In Kantian terms, it serves regulatively more than constitutively. It is therefore capable of absorbing manneristic deviations as individualistic approaches into intuitive but incomplete grasps of an enlarged, no longer sharply defined unity. When the baroque succeeds, a greater harmony is achieved, or at least suggested, in which old disharmonies are redeemed. The baroque is a leap beyond the classical, yet achieves a continuity with it and with eccentricities as well, as a circle is expanded into an ellipse and eventually into a parabola or even a hyperbola through the separation of two foci and the extention of one focus to the finite. Just as the parabola and the ellipse reveal freer, more general formulas for conic sections, of which those for the circle are a simpler special case, so the baroque offers greater freedom of forms which remove the specific restrictions of the classical and admit the eccentric. Manneristic protest has brought new life and enlarged expressiveness to the baroque—what is inert comes to life, the static becomes dynamic, sharp discriminations become vague and tend to disappear in a flux which exceeds finite frames or rules.

Although it is true that Heinrich Wölfflin's enumeration of the four characteristics which distinguish the baroque from the classical have been partly superseded by later analyses, they may still serve to explicate some of its enlarged, freer characteristics. The first three of these characteristics serve to distinguish the baroque from classical; the fourth also distinguishes it from the manneristic.[19]

1. The baroque, according to Wölfflin, stresses the "painterly" (das *Malerische*) as opposed to the linear. The indefiniteness of physical contours was specifically taught by the new atomists, and later by Christian Huygens and by Leibniz in their efforts to correct Aristotle's physics, particularly his notion that the coinciding boundaries of things define the spatial order. This removal of exact contours is in turn a special case of the principle of continuity to which Leibniz gave a clear and adequate mathematical definition. On another level of order, just as the circle is a simple, specified case of a continuing order of conic sections, so concrete existence becomes a particular deter-

mination of an infinite continuum of possibilities. The function of mathematical parameters is to demonstrate that particulars are definable in terms of universal classes.

2. Closely related to this "painterly" quality is Wölfflin's contrast of baroque unclarity as against classical clarity. The dramatic mystery implicit in natural and human forms is here suggested, particularly the blurring effect of motion and the dynamic. Wölfflin does not include in his characterization, but does later discuss, the baroque effect of power bursting the forms imposed upon it and creating its own new forms. The baroque expresses the secretive, cryptogrammatic aspect of experience. Levels of meaning are increased and deepened. The labyrinth (but also Ariadne's thread) is a favorite manneristic and baroque device. We have mentioned the play of light and shadow as a basic philosophic metaphor in thinkers like Bruno and the Florentine Platonists. The distinction between the classical and the baroque use of light and shadow in revealing individuals in their apartness sharing a common experience, and individuals tied into a whole (including the dynamic dimensions of past and future) in a moment of experience, is perceptively described by Georg Simmel in his contrast of Leonardo da Vinci with Rembrandt.[20] Philosophically this category of dynamism appears in the importance of unclear, confused, and inadequate ideas and the limits of their perfectibility through reason (for example, in Leibniz's analysis of truths of fact).

3. The baroque uses open forms in contrast to the closed forms of classicism. With Bruno the concept of the infinite enters cosmology to stay. The new developments in mathematics required an infinite continuity, not merely of series but of operations. For later thinkers in the century, infinity, in combination with continuity, played a significant role both in metaphysics and in the theory of knowledge. Basic was the conception that the infinite is the "not de-fined" context within which all finite experience is to be delimited, and conversely, that all finite experience possesses a wider symbolic quality which refers beyond itself. The extension of architectural forms beyond the classical dependence upon the rectangular and circular, to include all of the conic sections and many transcendental curves such as the spirals and cycloids as well, illustrates this distinction. The subsumption of all conic sections under a single formula by which each is determined by assigning specific values, varying from zero to infinity, to each of its parameters, is an important model for the philosophical thinking of the century.

4. The fourth of Wölfflin's characteristics involves the balance of multiplicity and unity. This is fundamental, for as we have seen, classicism sought a perfect balance between the two, and the multiplicity of individual deviations which marks mannerism induced a rupture of the classical unities. But in the baroque there is a new ideal of unity not completely explicated in the finite experience, but suggested by its vitality and its incompleteness, which impels the imagination outward beyond bounds. The mathematical model for the new microcosm-macrocosm conception is that of the infinite sphere whose center is everywhere—a metaphor arising in German mysticism and found in Nicholas of Cusa, the Italian Platonists, Bruno, Pascal, and elsewhere.[21] The Renaissance theory of a unity of perspectives becomes one in which the unperceived source and unity of all creation is given only in a multitude of finite perspectives, but reveals itself not merely in each individually but in the lesser harmonies of their symbiotic relations.[22] Diverse variations on the same basic musical theme, the contrapuntal play of polyphonic music, concave mirrors which draw together dispersed rays at a point, are further figures symbolizing this new relationship of the one and the many. The problem of the function and place, not merely of each individual but of lesser physical and social unities within the ultimate One, becomes a central philosophical issue, with new implications not only for metaphysics but for the theory of knowledge and for ethics.

Whatever their detailed differences in interpreting the meaning of mannerism and baroque, many critics have noted the fundamental opposition and dialectic development of the three forms. Identifying the classical as "the striving for absolute clarity of forms in detail as well as in the whole," André Chastel points to a growing tendency, after 1485, toward a "sentimental realism" in its perfect representative, Sandro Botticelli. A spirit of "newfangledness" intrudes into his style. Passing in several phases from individual revolt to a new academization, this new spirit brings in a new tradition of "lumenism" which plays upon space and time, using distorted but revealing forms, and such imaginary orders as the three-dimensional foreshortening of figures, the use of new curves, and symbols such as masks, grotesques, grottoes, labyrinths, monsters of phantasy, expressions of violence, natural cataclysms. The trend is conspicuous in such great but different geniuses as Leonardo and Michelangelo.

Therefore no comprehensive formula can be found for mannerism. It is a mode of individual revolt and invention which seizes upon new experiences and new discoveries to stimulate the observer to reject or at least to overcome traditional orders. A brief examination of the publications of men like Erhard Weigel and in a much more grandiose vein though not more fantastic, the Jesuit Athanasius Kircher, whose magnificent folios appeared under Imperial patronage, shows clearly that mannerism is not merely a sensory aesthetic phenomenon, but also a matter of the unfettered intellectual imagination.[23] This is not subjectivism, but rather an exploration of the possibility of new combinations on the vague, unruled, and unexplored boundaries of experience. To the mannerist, the symbolic use of forms is a constant temptation. Thus, both in motivation and mode of expression, its corresponds, though not within precise limits, with the mood of the libertine.

A similar argument can be offered for affinities of the baroque with the goals of *honnêteté*. According to Chastel, the origins of the baroque may be found in the advanced techniques of Roman neoclassicism, especially those of Raphael and Michelangelo, who accept but transcend the mannerist exaggeration of the particular and corporeal and its "strange, restless instability," through a new sense of the dynamic harmony of spatial order (Raphael) and of the magnificence and power of the human body (Michelangelo). These origins led to a movement which sought to recover a felt unity in forms which regressed into the infinite—the dynamic, spatial outreach of Tintoretto, the architectural triumphs of Giovanni Lorenzo Bernini and Francesco Borromini, the ceilings of Giovanni Battista Tiepolo and his school, imply types of feeling and modes of perception relevant for the understanding of both the resplendent "glory" of a Sun King whose radiance induced so much creativity in science, literature, art, and diplomacy, and the "glory" of his enemy, the great Eugene of Savoy, the very type of *homme honnête*. Intellectually and morally, the essence of this spirit is the transformation of man's imaginative self-determination from the free play of fancy about new sensible forms, and new opportunities for individual action, into an enlarged, secularized kind of Christian obedience through the disciplines inhering in an overarching order of meaning, itself not fully revealed in experience, but manifested in the binding authority of law, justice, harmony, and love.

The philosophical ground for this formation is a Christian Platonism which has absorbed a fresh interpretation of Neoplatonism. Involved in it are a fresh affirmation of the coextensiveness of faith with a reason, newly given wider range through achievements in mathematics. Within it the new science, a hope for religious and political unity, a new sense of the relevance for the entire world of a European culture, in short, the striving for a universal reasonableness, come into being.

Thus the triad—Platonic realism, nominalism, conceptualism with a universalized and unifying principle of reason—provides the philosophical foundation; the triad—classicism, mannerism, baroque—provides the aesthetic cultural ideals; and the triad— courtier, libertine, and *homo honestatis*—provides the moral ideal of the "struggle for (rational) synthesis" at the heart of the century's life.

In this chapter I have tried to establish the fact of a dialectic between two opposing ideals of human life and the conditions of its fulfillment, and the effort to synthesize them through enlarged perspectives of thought. The examination of this effort as it affected several aspects of the culture will be the subject of the following chapters.

This, however, is but one thesis of the book. The other, largely undeveloped here but surely to be read between the lines, concerns the failure of the century to achieve that synthesis. It was the *libertine* tradition which prevailed and which dominated so much of the "Enlightenment" in the century which followed—pragmatic, empirical, distrustful of universals, atomistic in its individualism. And to carry this theme further, the continued growth of this spirit of intellectual libertinism, through and beyond the romanticism, naturalism, and positivism of the nineteenth century has reached an extremity of irrationalism, anticonceptualism, subjectivism, and undisciplined voluntarism in our own times. *Honestas* and its intellectual justification have become for the present implausible, remote from our lonely individualism, our coerced opinions, and our material preoccupations.

2 Crisis in the Republic of Letters

"It is through application and magnanimity that the kingdom of letters is to be achieved and preserved, whose soul is Virtue and the pursuit of Truth, not conspiracies through flattery and factions by which others are torn in different directions and Wisdom itself, which was in the middle, is mangled."

This present age would bring forth fewer tumultuous talents, less supercilious judgments, fewer innovators, if everyone would turn over in his mind, frequently and repeatedly, this most elegant thought.

[Julius Caesar Scaliger, quoted with a comment by John Henry Alsted, *Logicae systema harmonicum*, Herborn, 1614. *Praefatio ad lectorem*, 1-2.]

I esteem everything that pulls us out of our ignorance. It is good that the soil of the country of the Republic of Letters should be well cultivated throughout, and I hold that M. Bayle obligates us no less in the execution of this grand design, than if he continues to give forth[1] the beautiful thoughts which one well sees that he has on philosophy and other matters.

[Leibniz, on Bayle's *Dictionary*, 1697, Gerhardt VI, 19-20]

The Character of the Republic of Letters

The high moral demands which Julius Caesar Scaliger made of the Republic of Letters (of which he himself was a distinguished but contentious member), and Alsted's impassioned attempt to recall it to its high task, suggest that all was not well with the letters and learned arts at the beginning of the seventeenth century. Both men acknowledged "conspiracies," factionalism, the mangling of wisdom, and such apparent misfortunes to learning as "tumultuous talents," "supercilious judgments," and "innovators." Libertinism seems already to have been at work. Similar laments can be found later in the youthful writings of Leibniz, who feared the "shipwreck of atheism" and who esteemed Bodin's *Colloquium Heptaplomeres* as more dangerous than the dialogues of Julius Caesar Vanini, which "are child's play compared with it."[2] In his maturer writings, however, Leibniz found the literature of the day more reassuring, though his words in justification of Bayle's new *Dictionary* suggest also that the conception of a Republic of Letters may itself have changed somewhat in the half century which had passed.

It is to the strains to which this Republic was subjected by the excessive individualism of the century, manifesting itself in quarrels, arguments, and satires, and to the intensification of critical intellectual concerns about method, order, and scientific objectivity which resulted in reaction that this chapter is addressed.

The signs of unrest and change which disturbed Scaliger and Alsted and the young Leibniz were not confined to their times. Nowhere, in fact, is the significance of that period for the twentieth century more apparent than in what was happening in the face of religious conflict, political and social change, and new scientific insights to the overlapping interests of literature, education, and the philosophical quest for wisdom. These were the concerns of the Republic of Letters.

The concept of a Republic of Letters was not new. The phrase seems to have been brought into being only with the development of printing, but the ideal was much older and had its roots in Cicero, in whose epistles such phrases as *ratio litterarum*, *studio litterarum*, and *litterae publicae* appear in various contexts.[3] In the later multiplication of specialized "republics" and "commonwealths" inspired by St. Augustine's distinction of the two cities, it is not surprising that the notion should have taken firmer shape as an order of literacy—a *res publica litterarum*. As Leonard Olschki has shown, the concept is explicit in the fourteenth century in Petrarch's *De sui ipsius et multorum ignorantia*, where the seriousness and moral character of the literary community is stressed in the context of its opposition to Aristotle and the Scholastics.[4] But it was only later in the Renaissance, when the humanistic ideal had become a more pervasive intellectual and cultural force through the revival of ancient ideas and their wider dissemination through printing, that the concept was brought into clear focus and the term became a commonplace in the prefatory remarks of authors to their "benevolent" and "learned" readers—or even to "unlearned" ones.[5]

As a new middle class emerged into leadership in the Renaissance and the moral ideals of *honestas* spread, the Republic of Letters underwent a similar process of socialization. Though essentially aristocratic in its citizenry (for printing was neither cheap nor widely disseminated), the Republic of Letters did not exclude any potentially literate person. Never clearly defined, it consisted of the intercommunication of those who wrote books or expressed their thought in writing, those who sponsored them, and those who read them. The bonds which held them all together were less the seven liberal arts as still taught in the trivial schools and the universities than the *studia humaniores.* Poetry, romances, and drama were admitted, as much by virtue of their classical forms as by their content, which tended to become didactic in aim. Members of the Republic were nobles and courtiers who patronized the arts and sometimes practiced them, and professors with a public following that extended beyond their students. It also included among its members all of the learned and the interested, not merely the creative and the critical but also the *curiosi* and the *virtuosi*—the amateurs— virtues which had been added in the Renaissance to the ideal of *honnêteté.*[6] A knowledge of the classical authors gave common content to its publications, and the continuing labor of recovering and providing printings of the best possible texts was a part of its tasks. The Republic of Letters had not yet achieved the state in which it was to find itself in the eighteenth century, when the new sciences had been separated from their humanistic context and the ideal of belles lettres predominated in it.[7] Nor had that breach developed which later separated a class of specialized writers from the proletariat of the Republic, so that the masses were captured by agencies of mass communication and taste, and creative artists and writers, having lost their wider public, created primarily for each other.

Yet the Republic of Letters was not a classless republic. This is shown by its currency, which is language itself. Since Dante and Petrarch had turned to the Italian language as the medium for much of their greatest poetry, two languages had served the Republic. Its universal character was expressed in Latin, its local, popular, national, intimate appeal was through the vernacular. Many books now began to appear in both languages, the folk language for consumption at home, Latin for use abroad. By the seventeenth century Latin was not merely the universal language for the Republic, it was also the language of logic and criticism, giving clarity if not always intuitive depth to the values of literature. But while Italian, French, Spanish, and

English had by now become standardized literary languages, the devastation of the long war, and the absence of unified national order, had left German corrupted by foreignisms and dialectal differences, and without the flexibility of a literary tongue.

This differentiation of languages was itself a sign of several shifts in the dominant functions of the Republic. In the first place, Latin supplied the structural basis for the analysis of the living languages, standardizing their vocabularies and word forms, and formalizing their syntax. More important, the linguistic interest led to a popularization of logic, the instrument, or the science, of valid thought. The most conspicuous example of this popularization was the logic of Peter Ramus, whose rhetoricized logic swept the Protestant countries of England, the Netherlands, and Germany.[8] The division of languages, moreover, corresponded to a separation of social roles within the Republic. The pattern of communication in the Republic involved three levels—the intellectual commerce between writers and thinkers; the communication of these with the wider membership of the Republic, who read their books and responded to their work; and the general cultural sharing and application, on this broader level, of the values imparted through the interchange.

Universities were only part, though an increasingly important part, of the system of letters; indeed, a German derivative of the term *"res publica litterarum," "die Gelehrtenrepublik,"* signifies a social fabric of scholarship, and it was this that the Republic of Letters tended increasingly to become around 1600.[9] By then the exchange of scholarly letters and, much later, the cultural journals,[10] provided a new and effective method for the dissemination of new thought and knowledge. At the courts and at certain centers of printing there developed an active commerce in ideas, with certain men functioning primarily as disseminators of the achievements of others— Descartes's friend Marin Mersenne in Paris, Samuel Hartlib in London, the Baron von Boineburg, and John Philipp of Schönborn, the Prince Bishop of Mainz were men who, though productive themselves, devoted much time to spreading information about the work of others. The scope of the network of letters which covered Europe in the seventeenth century will be appreciated by anyone who studies the list of people with whom Mersenne in Paris,[11] or Leibniz in Hanover, or Hartlib in London, or in a somewhat narrower circle, Herman Conring in Helmstedt corresponded. The traveling disseminators of literary and scholarly information—a tradition begun in the Middle Ages—included Desiderius Erasmus, Juan Luis Vives, Giordano Bruno, Tommaso Campanella, Paracelsus, John Amos Comenius and his friend John Dury, men stirred by publishing opportunities, by religious persecution, or by ideals of reform to travel from center to center arousing interest and spreading light.

Such was the structure of the Republic of Letters. It was complex, for it was already interwoven with the threads of many distinct motives and goals, as the written and spoken word entered the service of a variety of social and cultural ends and organizations. In the later Renaissance, St. Augustine's amplification of Plato's *polis* into the two cities—of God and of man— tended therefore to proliferate into subordinate Republics with more particularized concerns, laws of order, and goals. The concern of a Republic of Scholars, which was in part included in that of Letters but centered in the universities, was with learning, and increasingly, with learnedness. In his correspondence Mersenne speaks of Girard Desargues as "an adornment of the Republic of Geometry."[12] And with the growth of cooperative scientific research, some of whose founders were without university connections, the new order, that of the researchers into the secrets of nature, naturally assumed its place within the Republic of Letters at the side of the other humanistic arts.

More objectively, corresponding to the divine functions of Creation and Redemption, a distinction was made between a kingdom of nature and a kingdom of grace. Thus the two cities of St. Augustine—the temporal and the eternal—were translated into the two great and distinct concerns, the order of physical events and the order of Christian society. After reading the bitter controversy with Arnauld begun by Malebranche's *Treatise of Nature and of Grace* (1680), Leibniz incorporated the two commonwealths into his metaphysics as the two realms of law—physical and spiritual, or natural law (*mechanical*) and natural law (*judicial and religious*). But all of these new commonwealths were obviously entangled with the Republic of Letters, without which they would have lacked the discussion and critical evaluation needed for agreement.

The Educational Role of the Republic: Encyclopedism

In the late Renaissance the humanistic tradition had declined into an intellectualism which emphasized characteristics and objectives significant for the argument of this book. The humanistic ideal of the Republic of Letters may be said to have been the cultivation of the free, creative individual through the revival of ancient learning. From its Italian beginnings in Petrarch and Dante, education was thus a strong motive in the tradition, its aim being the cultivation of character through learning—the moral and aesthetic stimulation of the individual by means of his understanding. The reinterpretations by Renaissance thinkers of the classical Aristotelian psychology provided an empirical theory of learning based on sense, spurred on by the affections, and terminating in a practical wisdom whereby the total *ingenium* of the learner—his essential powers and character, as well as his understanding—is unfolded and perfected. Of all the early sixteenth-century humanists, Juan Luis Vives developed this psychology of learning most fully and was most influential in expressing its educational ideals. He discussed the grounds of learning (*De ratione discendi*) in terms of three concepts—doctrine, discipline, and *ingenium*—and stressed the continuity of feeling with sense, and of understanding with character.

> Doctrine is the transition (*traditio*) from those things which one knows to those which one does not know. Discipline is the acceptance of that transition, except that the mind is filled by passing on what it receives but is not emptied by it; indeed, erudition is increased by communication, as if by the motion and agitation of fire. For the *ingenium* is aroused and run through with those things which pertain to present problems.[13]

Consonant with the extension of humanistic aims to the rising middle classes and the strengthening of its didactic aims is a growing concern about beginners and the "untrained" (*rudes*). As early as the fourteenth century, Nicholas of Cusa addressed his books on the mind, on experiments in statics, and on wisdom, to the "layman" (*Idiota*). In the fifteenth, the great physician Jean Fernel addressed the *tyro*, or the *nimis docte*, in his dialogue on the hidden secrets of nature. In the opening of his work "On the Shadows of Ideas," Giordano Bruno appealed to all readers "whether unskilled (*rudis*) or erudite, since it can be known easily by all and becomes understandable through use."[14] And Descartes in his *Discourse on Method* proposed rules which should make discovery and judgment possible for all men, whether learned or ignorant. This faith in a "common sense," or natural *ingenium* characterizes most of the thinkers of the century.

The encyclopedist John Henry Alsted, who learned much psychology from Vives, closed the Preface to his *Philosophia digne restituta* with the cry: "*Usum, usum dice respexi tanquam cynosurum meae qualiscunque scriptonis*" (Use, use, I say I have regarded as the cynosure, as it were, of my every writing.")

By the end of the sixteenth century, however, this Socratic goal of learning had been partly superseded by the conception of *erudition* as an end in itself. Learnedness retained its pedagogical fervor but the spirit of *erudition* became widely eclectic, and education emphasized the transmission of the learned tradition. By 1600 erudition was aiming at the organization of learning for the purpose of discovering its gaps and making it more readily transmissible. Erudition fulfilled itself in Encyclopedism.

The most widely influential representative of this encyclopedic effort was, of course, Francis Bacon in *The Advancement of Learning* (1605; Latinized in a revised form as the *De Dignitate et Augmentiis scientiarum* in 1624). Bacon formulated an important pedagogical principle, repeated by many of his readers, that for the purpose of the growth of knowledge, learning was best transmitted by the same method by which it was first discovered.[15] The encyclopedic tradition, however, claimed a broader and earlier beginning than in Bacon. A list of encyclopedists drawn up by Leibniz in one of his own programs began with Pliny and Martianus Capella. But the incitement to the modern movement coincided with the swing of Renaissance humanism from its moral basis to erudition.[16] Encyclopedism was concerned with the ingathering of knowledge, in whatever state of organization it was found, and with the effort to achieve the unity of a system. The compendious work of John Henry Alsted, which did much to popularize the title of *Encyclopaedia*—a term involving a mannerist allusion to the great "circle" (*cyclos*) of being and knowledge involved in "*paedaea*" —provided an incomplete list of forerunners in the encyclopedic effort, including Peter Ramus, Jerome Cardan, Matthew Martini, Bartholomew Keckermann, Clement Timpler, Robert Fludd, and others, but strangely omitting Francis Bacon and Tommaso Campanella, both of whom he mentioned frequently elsewhere.[17]

Alsted's inclusion of Aristotelians in his list confirms the lack of unified order in the encyclopedic ideal, for in his influential discussions of method Giacomo Zabarella, the outstanding commentator on Aristotle in the late sixteenth century, had held that order must be restricted to individual disciplines, and could not be based upon any principles unifying the separate disciplines.[18]

The efforts of Amos Komenski (or Comenius), who studied under Alsted in the old University of Herborn in Nassau, are the outstanding example of the development of the ideal of erudition into a program of didactics, a process in which its character was changed remarkably in two new directions—the need to organize knowledge, and the need to ground it anew upon the experience of things rather than in the literary tradition. Though Comenius failed in both directions, as had Bacon before him, his influence on the reform of education throughout northern Europe was a stimulus to those who followed him.

Following the pattern of Vives's thought and Bacon's, Comenius's efforts to reform teaching were in the interest of pleasure, speed, naturalness, and thoroughness. This goal involved not merely the popularization of textbooks from which children were taught, but a grounding of learning upon observation, and a striving to make the scope of knowledge universal. Comenius himself had little interest in the physical sciences, but the writings of Bacon had convinced him that the process of learning is most natural when based on direct experience, and that there are very important gaps in knowledge which can be closed only through observation. The range of Comenius's influence was very wide, extending from Poland and Transylvania to Germany, the Netherlands, Sweden, and England, where his philosophically most interesting book, the *Prodromus Pansophiae* was published,[19] and where he was invited by Parliament in 1641 to complete his *Pansophia*, that is, the complete summarization of all knowledge and wisdom. This task, of course, he never succeeded in carrying out.[20]

Comenius's entire Platonic mode of thought, an elaboration of Bacon's analysis of learning, is built about the ideal of *harmony* as a key to knowledge and to character. Wisdom had until now failed because of prolixity, difficulty, the uncertainty of what is known—(*Tota res litteraria plena est dissentionum, contradictionum, pugnarum*, the old, oft repeated theme of reform)—and its meager usefulness for life. The twofold cure must be to abandon all "external testimony about things, that is, traditions, and to teach and learn things through themselves" and thus move toward the ideal of their unity—"things are so connected by a perpetual harmony that truth is as undissipable [i.e., as impossible to scatter apart] as the machine of the world itself."[21]

This dynamic urge toward education and the exhaustion of knowledge characterized most of the seventeenth century. In his *New Method for Teaching and Learning Jurisprudence* (1667), Leibniz borrowed some of Comenius's ideas, and his ideal of an encyclopedia and a *general science* continued the tradition which Comenius received from his teachers and expressed imperfectly in his *Pansophia.* But it differed from mere encyclopedism by requiring, in the spirit of Bacon, not merely the collection of known facts and their organization, but the development of a method for analyzing them to discover first principles, and for developing new fields and relations between knowledge and practice in terms of these principles.[22]

The Expansion of Literary Forms

The instance of Comenius has been used to exemplify several changes in the purpose of the Republic of Letters early in the seventeenth century, notably the shift from books to things which its educational aim involved, and the development of the encyclopedic ideal, first as an instrument of character education and then as an instrument of learnedness itself. The ideal of learning for use continued, but with this new aim at completeness and ultimacy, usefulness took on new applications. The implications of this expansion and shift of purposes were far reaching.

Erudition showed great adaptibility in adjusting its traditional literary forms to such changes. The old ideals of literary excellence, rhetorical skill, ease in improvisation, and eloquence in interpreting and applying the classics showed their enduring worth. Cicero and Seneca, for example, continued as foundations of literary excellence, though Vergil achieved some preeminence over them after the turn of the century. The old fusion of Platonic and Stoic ideals was presupposed in the educational principles of Vives and his followers, though a stronger activism began to pervade them. Even in urging the importance of seeking a knowledge of the physical world, Francis Bacon still wrote entirely in this tradition of literary erudition.

Both the dialogue form, derived from Plato, and the essay, whose ancestry must be sought in Hellenism and Rome, had shown themselves peculiarly fit for the individualistic pedagogical purposes of the Renaissance, and both continued to show their usefulness in explicating arguments and dressing dialectic in conversational form. Bodin, for example, used dialogue as a basic rhetorical device in his *Colloquium Heptaplomeres* for an exploration of religious agreement and dissent; Giordano Bruno used it for moral reform and metaphysical exploration, as did Lorenzo Valla in his dialogue On the Free Will. Galileo, also Platonically inspired, made use of the same form to expound the *Great World Systems* and the *Two New Sciences.*

Thus although literary forms remained the same, the content of learning shifted. It remained consciously concerned about use, but by the early seventeenth century the ideal of utility had been expanded beyond the simple humanistic ideal of character—the magnanimity and wisdom to which Julius Caesar Scaliger referred—to more theoretical applications, both scientific and speculative. The result was the revival of two old disciplines in new garb—*logic* to meet the demands of the new learnedness and of scientific exposition, and *metaphysics*, primarily to serve in the clarification of theological disputes.

The New Logic

Three new traditions in logic were particularly influential in the seventeenth century. In the order of time these were: first, the anti-Scholastic, rhetorical logic of Peter Ramus; then the refined Aristotelian realistic logic of Zabarella, continued by Keckermann, Joachim Jungius, and others; and finally, much later, the simplified Cartesian logic of Port Royal.[23]

The logician par excellence of erudition was Peter Ramus, who rejected the basic orientation of Aristotle for a simplified treatment of logical forms and their applications, which he readily related to the rhetoric of the new learning. Ramus defined logic as "the art of effective discourse," thus permitting it to intrude upon many traditional problems of rhetoric.[24] His *loci communes* (commonplaces) were designed to aid discovery of the meanings of terms and the structure of a "theme," and the technique he made possible was an elaborate system of analyzing problems subsumed under a theme by dichotomizing them into elaborately bracketed classes. His illustrations were drawn from Roman literature, particularly from Cicero and Seneca. From Aristotle he borrowed this thinker's fundamental but obscure principles for ordering meaning in propositions and syllogisms "according to all, to the individual (essence), to the universal" (*kata pantos, kath'auto, kath'olou,* or in Latin, *de omne, per se, universaliter*), which he broadened, however, beyond Aristotle's usage to apply to all discourse involved in learning.[25]

By the turn of the century, however, the interest in logic was already shifting from erudite learnedness and the rhetoric of disputation to the understanding of facts and the most useful methods for interpreting them. This shift marks the outstanding developments in logic which followed.

Bacon was critical of Ramus, though also influenced by him,[26] but seems rather to have followed Giacomo Zabarella, who applied logic not to discourse but to the disciplines of learning and their order. Zabarella's disagreement with Francesco Piccolomini on the nature of the method of analysis and synthesis was an important point in the formulation of the modern doctrine of causal analysis, which reappeared in Galileo, Hobbes, and other thinkers in the new objective vein. Agreeing with Ramus that logic is an art, not a science, Zabarella held, however, that it is an instrumental discipline whose goal is not *cognitio* but *operatio*, aiding the intellect to escape from the accidentals of sense to the "intelligible species" (or appearances) of objective order. In spite of errors and looseness of thought, Zabarella largely set the pattern for the development of logic in the coming century, and so opened the way for a logical analysis of scientific procedures which were shortly to become widely adopted. Joachim Jungius and the logicians of Port Royal presupposed his point of view.

As Chapter 7 will make clear, this shift from literary erudition to factuality required a corresponding change in the entire conception of method, one in which the role of logical theory was reinforced by the new interest in mathematics and its application to the understanding of nature. And this shift was guided by an adherence to the old Pythagorean-Platonic conception of *harmony*.

Sectarianism and the Quarrel Between the Ancients and Moderns

A great gap existed in the Republic of Letters, as in the City of God or the Republic of Grace which is its religious parallel, between the community as an ideal and the community as it really was. The evils which lurked in the scholarly and literary community were, as the opening statements of Scaliger and

Alsted show, evils of pride and individual aggressiveness. In his feuds with Erasmus and Cardan, Scaliger showed himself to be one of the most contentious. Such instances of violent individual dissent and ad hominem attacks obviously disregarded the classical canons of literary taste and general courtesy, and became expressions, often manneristic, of the libertine spirit of individualism.[27]

Two general aspects of this literary libertinism in the seventeenth century are worthy of further discussion. One of these was the spirit of philosophical sectarianism, a conspicuous instance of which was the well-known quarrel between the ancients and moderns. The other was the use of satire to discredit one's opponents or to strengthen one's own case.

The evils of learned sectarianism had been lamented long before Scaliger and Alsted. They were considered the scandal of philosophy and of all clear thinking. Aristotle, like Plato before him, had undertaken a synthesis of previous conflicting theories of *physis* or *arché*. Galen was said by Comenius to have condemned the addicts of sects for "becoming deaf and blind."[28] It was patent that in principle, philosophy could not tolerate sects, yet that previous philosophy had in the main (Platonism was often excluded from this generalization) produced sects. No factor was more important in driving scholars to direct observation than sectarianism, and none was more important in driving men with less confidence in facts to skepticism. Sectarianism was as inimical to truth as religious sectarianism was to salvation and the state of grace. Indeed, it might have been called (though it was not) the intellectual sin.

The revival of learning had brought with it an advocacy of ancient schools, and the first modern treatments of sectarianism were based on these ancients. Gerhard Johannes Vossius's *De Philosophia et Philosophorum Sectis Libri II*, which Paul Dibon has called the first history of philosophy to be written in the Netherlands,[29] undertook a brief description and evaluation of each and then proposed a method for achieving an eclectic synthesis—electicism itself being a philosophical tradition which, to the extent that it succeeded, was not sectarian. In the past, Vossius held, Aristotle and Plato had approached this ideal most closely, yet Aristotle "overshadows the light of those who preceded him in sharpness of genius and variety of doctrine, as the sun does that of the moon and the stars." It is true that in matters pertaining to God and to spiritual beings Plato is superior to him, but Plato's language is metaphorical and un-

suited to philosophy, and the Christian heresies have their beginnings in his thought. Aristotle admits nothing unsupported
by reason, avoids myths, and orders his thought logically, but is
deficient in matters pertaining to God, spiritual beings, and the
origin of the world.

Characteristically for his century, Vossius encouraged participation in none of these sects; his survey was intended to show
that "since no one is free from error, we ought to look, not at
who said something but at *what* someone said (*non quis aliquid
dixit, sed quod aliquis dixit).* " He proposed rather that, avoiding
the weeds, "We shall choose the flowers from all the sects and
weave a garland for our head; for the more adequately this
treats of the true and the good, the more beautiful and fragrant
it will be, and the less it will wither away." Unfortunately
Vossius's analysis of eclectic method did not take him far beyond this florid, baroque metaphor, though he did suggest that
one should "first see what each (sect) says, why it is said, what is
replied adversely against it, and (finally) whether both sides can
be reconciled."[30]

The long history of philosophical sectarianism cannot be discussed here. The growing conflict of intellectual opinions
brought with it an awareness of its absurdity and dangers, and
the great efforts of the century toward an intellectual synthesis
aimed to overcome it.[31] But before this could be done, the
eclecticism proposed by Vossius and other historians of thought
had to be supplemented with an analysis and examination of
the presuppositions of the sectarian positions and their reduction to first principles. Eclecticism can achieve systematic unity
only when guided by some regulative ideal of harmony, and by
a method of analysis and synthesis which can serve to discover
the primary concepts and first principles implicit in the sects.[32]

The most obvious and prolonged expression of these quarrels
within the Republic, however, was the controversy between
advocates of the ancients and the moderns—a quarrel best
known through the debate between Charles Perrault and
Nicholas Boileau in France at the end of the century, and a
little later by Jonathan Swift's bitter satires in England.

The battle between ancients and moderns is much older than
the seventeenth century, however; indeed it is a perennial one
between the justifiers of tradition, whether in literature and
thought or in social and political affairs, and the innovators and
advocates of the new who reject established ways. The argument is recurrent because it rests upon the enduring antithesis

between tradition and originality or even creativity. In the Middle Ages, the Brethren of the Common Life established the *devotio moderna*, their settlements and schools breathing the breath of spiritual and human revival into such men as Nicholas of Cusa and Erasmus. Later the Ockhamists were known as innovators in philosophy, freeing the will of the individual and bringing Aristotle's logic and physics into closer relation to observation; the Thomists and Scotists with their traditional adjustments of reason to authority were the *Veteres*.[33] An issue in the Renaissance was between the "vulgar philosophy of the schools" and a revival of rhetorical humanism. Bacon's works contain frequent allusions to the quarrel in this sense.[34] In Peter Ramus and Marius Nizolius, the new was the simplistic reduction of logic to discussion as opposed to the detailed formalism of the Aristotelian logic. In 1624, the same year in which the Parliament of Paris forbad "à peine de vie, de tenir ni enseigner aucune maxime contre les auteurs anciens et approuvés" (that is, Aristotle and the Scholastics), Pierre Gassendi published his *Exercitationes paradoxicae adversus Aristoteleos.*

By the time of Gassendi, however, the most conspicuous debate had become one between the new mathematico-empirical approach to truth and the old erudite accumulation of book learning. As for the clarification of literary style and form, the contrast between Bacon's traditional erudite florescence and Hobbes's crisp factual simplicity marks the line between the old and the new. By the time of Descartes the erudite were becoming the defenders of the old against the new tradition of empirical economy of utterance and mathematical precision of thought—the new, concealed Platonism of mathematics and the revival of Aristotelian logic (from Padua) against both the traditional Platonism and Aristotelianism of the Scholastics and the hermetic, animistic, and theosophic Platonism of the sixteenth century.

In spite of his alchemical and astrological interests, it would be hard to overestimate the extent to which Paracelsus's strong emphasis upon observation and experiment influenced the gradual replacement of dependence upon Galen and the tradition by a more empirical approach to medicine. Later, Galileo's treatment of the nonquantifiable qualities of things as mental, followed by Descartes's emphasis upon self-awareness as the essential ground for certainty, encouraged a conviction that human experience is subjective and self-contained, yet also compatible with an objective interpretation of scientific knowledge of the natural order. In spite of the efforts of Nicholas Male-branche and other Cartesians, Descartes came to be understood as the source of the "new way of ideas" in opposition to the old.[35] This problem and the added difficulty of reconciling sci-entific mechanism with a telic world order which supports human faith and values became the issues on which science, following Descartes's lead, finally was separated from the literary-humanistic tradition. Thus the stage was set for the metaphysical controversies about scientific knowledge which reached a crisis in the Locke-Newton-Leibniz discussions at the end of the century.

The quarrel between ancients and moderns, however, survived the separation of the physical sciences from the more humanis-tic aspects of letters. By 1688 Charles Perrault, though himself actively concerned with mathematical problems, could limit his argument for the superiority of the moderns to arts, letters, and morals,[36] and Swift's bitter attack on the moderns in the *Battle of the Books* centered in questions of literary criticism. By the eighteenth century the triumph of *curiosité* over *eruditio* was complete, and science had been freed from the realm of erudite discourse.[37]

Satire in the Republic of Letters

It is at this controversy between ancients and moderns that much satire of the seventeenth century is directed in defense both of the old and the new. Satire is a manneristic, libertine phenomenon. As an excessive individual deviation it is a product of the Renaissance. It violates the existing, objective order which is satirized by pretending to understand and sympathize with it, but its purpose now becomes to change, sometimes to annihilate it through ridicule. Its psychological roots lie deep in the nature of the satirist. It is often "sick" humor, pretending the goodness of evil, the normalcy of the pathological. Its master, Jonathan Swift, stands at the end of this brief account of satires on the Republic of Letters.

Humor appeared only infrequently in the Republic. There had been satires of much literary merit in the late Renaissance—Francois Rabelais, Giordano Bruno, Miguel de Cervantes, the Pasquinades of Aretino, and Erasmus's *Praise of Folly* are ex-amples. But in general the Republic took itself seriously as com-mitted to learning, reform, and education for character, even in its controversies and growing diversity of interests; such wit as was shown by Vives, Cardan, Bacon, Alsted, and even Descartes (all of whom showed manneristic inclinations) was incidental and not intended to disturb the earnest objectives of the harmonious commonwealth. Leibniz, who possessed great skill as a satirist and used it ably for political purposes, as his attack on the warlike policies of the great Sun King in the *Mars Christianissimus* (1683) shows, still distrusted the motives and effects of satire. Upon receiving from the third Earl of Shaftesbury a copy of his *Characteristics of Men, Manners, and Opinions* (1710), he at once commented at some length with excited approval. But with the opening *Letter on Enthusiasm*, which repeated sentiments of Shaftesbury *On Raillery*, he expressed some misgivings:

> I believe that raillery is good protection against this vice (enthusiasm), but I do not find it suitable for curing people of it. On the contrary, the contempt which is clothed in raillery will be taken by them as affliction and persecution . . . I am not sure that the use of ridicule is a good touchstone of error, since the best and most important matters can be turned to ridicule, and it is not always certain that truth will have those who laugh on its side, since it is most often hidden from vulgar eyes. I have already said that all raillery includes a little contempt, and it is unjust to try to make contemptible what does not deserve it. But it is good always to be in good humor, so that joy rather than irritation will be apparent in our conversation and writing.[38]

As a virtue, *honestas* frowns upon satire, which is divisive and destructive of harmony. But satire was alive within the Republic, and served to bring to light the weaknesses and failures in its work and the decline of its influence.

In 1606, Robert Burton, later author of the *Anatomy of Melancholy*, wrote a Latin comedy, *Philosophaster*, which, as the title suggests, satirized the philosophical sects.[39] In altered form it was performed in Christ College, Oxford, in 1617. Among the characters were Polypragmaticus, a Jesuit; Aequivocus, his servant; Pantometer, a mathematician; Pantomagus, an alchemist and physician; Simon Actus, a Sophist; Theanus, a theologaster; Pedanus, a grammarian; and Amphimacer, a poetaster. Beyond what is implicit in these names, the point of the satire may be inferred from one exchange. Eubulus asks Polypragmaticus: "You who are first: what science do you profess? Whence do you come, from the Peripatetics or the Stoa? Of whom are you a sectary; Plato or Aristotle? Scotist, Thomist, realist, nominalist or whom?" Polypragmaticus answers: "Nullius et omnium [Of none and of all]."

In 1655 there was published posthumously a book by Diego de Saavedra-Fajardo entitled *La Republica Literaria;* anonymous translations into English appeared in 1705 and 1727, but a French one had been published in Paris in 1670 (two years before Leibniz began his sojourn in that city, where he began a Satire on the Republic of Letters intended to reach the ears of Louis XIV).[40] Saavedra's account of the walled city of letters is largely fun without malice, though his remarks about grammarians, critics, rhetoricians, historians, and philosophers are aimed at the triviality and self-inverted effectiveness of arts and letters. Modern critics disfigure ancient classics: Erasmus falls from his tightrope; Ovid is robbed of his nose by Scaliger, of his teeth by Tibullus, of his arm by Claudian. The poets' quarters have handsome facades which hide the absence of dwellings behind them. Fields of hellebore surround the city, to guard against "distempers of the brain" and to improve the memory, though this remedy is found also to impair the judgment. The moat is of ink, the fortifications are quills, and bales of paper are fired against enemies. The German tapestry weavers work beneath their looms, without seeing the design of their work: "Which gave me further occasion to reflect in how much the same manner but with a vastly different degree of success, do Princes, with their Instrument of State, sign and order to be done things brought before them, of which they see but the wrong side, and know little or nothing or?" (Saavedra was a statesman who had represented Spain at the signing of the Treaty of Westphalia). The activities of the Republic center in protecting and nurturing the goddess Glory, and the Virtues defend her against the attacks of the Stoic philosophers. The whole is as much moralizing allegory as satire.

Leibniz, however, wrote his satire for another purpose. It is possible that he had read Saavedra, for Glory is the theme of his Satire too, but this glory is not a goddess but a gas. The Republic of Letters is the New World colony of Europe; and Glory is its one product, a rare intangible smoke like tobacco. The colony is not self-supporting, but depends upon the home country for sustenance. Leibniz's aim was to enlist the colony in the new scientific enterprise—to build a new Salomon's House, so to speak—and to secure from the sovereign the support necessary to this end, to his own everlasting Glory. The satirical component may be a bit weak, since the entire purpose of the allegory is constructive.[41]

The full force of satire, however, was directed at the quarrelsomeness and sectarianism of the Republic, and particularly at "the quarrel between ancient and moderns." This is best known in literature through Swift's defense of the ancients in the *Battle of the Books*, and the equally well-known debate between Charles Perrault and Boileau, already referred to, where an old argument was renewed and given literary standing at a time when the cultural decision had already been made in the interest of progress. Perrault in particular revived and underscored an old quantitative argument found in Bacon (which history has itself since challenged)—that the new must be better than the old since it has inherited the best of the old and created something more (and better) in addition!

Eclecticism, the New Metaphysics,
and the Ideal of Harmony

To summarize briefly, the conflict which threatened the ideal of a Republic of Letters was, as Vossius showed, to be countered by an eclectic procedure, an important result of which was the effort to gather exhaustive accounts of what is known in an encyclopedic order useful for teaching and learning. Furthermore, disagreements among the members about particulars drove scholars from a merely literary ideal of erudition to a consideration of what is actually the case—a shift essential to the grounding of both the sciences and philosophy in generally confirmable observations.

Two questions became important in this change. The first was whether the two distinct aims of *encyclopedism* are compatible—orderly and comprehensive *unity*, and *utility* for learning; in itself eclecticism assured neither. The second was the related question of the unity of the Republic itself: could the new sciences, as they developed their own literature, also relate this literature constructively to the larger purposes—educational, social, and cultural—which were demanded by European order? Could the Renaissance ideal of a character-building goal in letters be made to encompass the innovations of the rising sciences and the new expressions of political and technological forces?

To resolve these problems a new formulation of method was

needed—one upon which first principles and primary concepts could be built which should provide the needed unity of truth and action. Also needed were regulative ideas which should give direction to thought and action; among these the most important was the ideal of *harmony*—the notion which impelled thinkers to move beyond mere eclecticism and encyclopedism to a "general science" and a metaphysics.

Most frequently, though not always, the efforts at eclecticism were made with Platonic presuppositions. The fresh insights of Nicholas of Cusa had rested on a Christian Platonism with strong affiliations with Platonic skepticism ("learned ignorance") and Neoplatonic mysticism. The uncompleted efforts of Ficino and Pico della Mirandola to reconcile Aristotle and Plato were matched by the efforts of Aristotelians in the Renaissance, Scaliger and others, to enliven the scientific spirit of their tradition with some Platonic spiritism.

It must be admitted that John Clauberg was justified in comparing the eclectics of his day to bees that gather promiscuously what is in books, yet produce no honey. Yet eclecticism was an important phase in the revival of the quest for the *philosophia perennis* which engaged seventeenth century thinkers, and particularly in the development of a new rational metaphysics. For it presupposed that there exists a single harmony which makes possible the agreement of experience, understanding, and faith, and that to the extent that any one of these digresses from the ideal which this harmony imposes, it is in danger of error. The basis of harmony may be sought in Christian faith, as in Augustinus Steuchius of Gubbio, who revived the idea of a perennial philosophy, or in an expanded Neoplatonism, or in some other concurrence of ideas which could support a synthesis.[42]

Encyclopedism anticipated this demand for harmony by its need for principles of organization. Bacon, for instance, opened his exploration of the order and gaps in human knowledge with the sketch of a Neoplatonic order of spirits and values, which he promptly supplemented with a psychological basis for distinctions in learning based on the three human faculties: *memoria, imaginatio, intellectus.*[43] But for Bacon organization and method were external to the detailed summarizing of the erudition of the present, and no unity of meaning is apparent within his program itself. Nor can more be said for Alsted's scheme for the structure of knowledge, which carried out in an astronomic figure the metaphor of the new term *"Encyclopaedia."* The circle of knowledge and arts, being not merely intellectual but educational in its purpose, has as its center, as sun and moon, metaphysics and logic. These two sciences, which provide the principles of being and of method respectively, must underly the general truths in all of the circumferential sciences and arts.[44] Thus metaphysics is not, for Alsted, the crown of philosophy but its a priori source of principles; nor is its "satellite," logic, merely an art but it is also a science of subordinate principles, whereas philosophy is expanded into its full concreteness by the inclusion of not only all the sciences and the applied arts, but of the higher disciplines of law, medicine, and theology as well. (Even the new healing art of tabacology was assigned a chapter in Alsted's work.)

An underlying harmony of determinative first principles was thus sought in metaphysics and logic as the goal of the encyclopedic exhaustion of knowledge, although, following the devices of Ramus, these principles were at first regarded chiefly as principles of classification. At the same time, Alsted was one of the revivers and commentators on the old *Ars Magna* of Raymundus Lullus, who in the thirteenth century had proposed a program for the rapid exposition of all possible knowledge through the mathematical combination of a limited number of primary concepts.[45] A more fundamental ideal of harmony was suggested by Alsted's son-in-law and follower, John Bisterfeld, who theorized that the method of discovering, applying, and teaching knowledge operates within a living, interharmonious order in which everything is vitally connected with every other thing. To this logical and purposive monism he applied the term *symbiosis*, which must be regarded as an adaptation of the role of love and of harmony, in the Platonic tradition, to the context of encyclopedism. These strongly manneristic approaches of Alsted, Comenius, and Bisterfeld to the problem of unity and harmony in knowledge are anticipations of the enlarged Platonic context in which the later systems of the century attempt to operate.[46]

The restoration of metaphysics from its neglect in the Renaissance is one of the arresting features of erudition in the last decades of the sixteenth century. Several reasons can be given for this revival. Ernst Lewalter has found the grounds for it in the conflicts in theology which arose within the Protestant Reformation, and which could be resolved only by means of metaphysical categories.[47] Though his argument is convincing, it may be extended in two ways. In the first place, the formulations of the Council of Trent likewise required, and received, metaphysical justification and interpretation, particularly by the group of Spanish and Portuguese Jesuits and Dominicans who turned their attention to metaphysical problems. In particular, the *Metaphysical Disputations* of Francisco Suarez, a great feat of electicism, served students in both Catholic and Protestant universities as a definitive and constructive compendium of metaphysical disagreements. In the second place, however, a new spirit of zeal in spreading the Christian gospel and convincing man of its truth came alive in this century, and some thinkers found in metaphysics an aid in this newly emphasized apologetic task. Thus strong religious and social interests, and the need for a structural ground for the unified organization of knowledge, combined to revive and restore metaphysics to a central place in the Republic of Letters. By 1600 fairly standardized texts and disputations on metaphysics were appearing in most universities, and theses which challenged (but usually ended in justifying) Aristotelian and Scholastic theories were disputed along with theses from the *Physics* and *logical* writings which had become prominent in the later Middle Ages and the Renaissance.[48] Slowly but clearly, however, the new concerns of the Renaissance, such as the nature of the individual and his good, the problems of truth and certainty, and the empirical study of nature, forced metaphysics to seek new values in sense experience, and to recognize a greater convergence in thought of sense, reason, and intuition. Vives, Telesio, and Campanella were cited in disputations and books, their theories of knowledge providing a stronger basis than Aristotle's more cautious analysis for the apologetic and dogmatic role which new concerns demanded of philosophy.

Erudition and the New Sciences

Eclecticism, encyclopedism, and the new metaphysics thus all supported, in different ways, an appeal to direct experience and facts to correct the manneristic quarrelsomeness of the erudite tradition. Thinkers from Vives to Bacon had stressed the need for a look at nature to close the gaps and remove the errors of human knowledge, and had intruded corrections based upon both external and internal observation, as Vives's psychology shows. There had been experimenters and interpreters of experience in the sixteenth century: Paracelsus and others in medicine, the alchemists in chemistry, and Nicolaus Copernicus, Tycho Brahe, and Johannes Kepler in astronomy. That the undisciplined gathering of facts and their interpretation in an erudite style was continued in the seventeenth century is shown by the amazing productivity of the German Jesuit Athanasius Kircher, who is remembered chiefly for the handsomely engraved and printed quarto editions of his writings, in which he undertook to give the true explanation of Lullus's *Ars Magna*, decipher Egyptian hieroglyphics, reconstruct the temple of Solomon, show the scientific possibility of Noah's ark, solve perverse optical problems, and develop a universal scientific language which should correct the damage done by the Tower of Babel—all in the most mannerist spirit and within the erudite tradition of the Republic.

The most influential prophet of the scientific movement, Francis Bacon, rightly regarded learning as comprised of two parts—the gathering together of existing knowledge to organize and disseminate it through books and other agencies of communication, and the discovery of new knowledge through experience, indeed, through experiment. Not only was Francis Bacon erudite and learned in the old Renaissance sense of using a style adorned with classical allusions and quotations, he sought erudition in the new sense as well in his demand for the intellectual organization and completion of knowledge. Dividing all knowledge into two classes—that based on speech and argument, and that grounded on invention or discovery, he found that though the former had not been neglected, the latter had been largely ignored. It was his purpose to devise methods and modes of cooperative effort by which this neglect could rapidly be remedied. In his utopian vision of the New Atlantis, the storehouses of learning were as important as the laboratories or workshops—an emphasis which twentieth century scientific methodologies sometimes fail to recognize, but cannot neglect in practice. Thus Bacon thought in terms of a continuity between the traditions of erudition and the new interest in observed facts and their use. The notion of a separation of science from the Republic of Letters, not to mention the idea of a new scientific culture completely detached from literary erudition, was alien to his thoughts.

This is true also of the men whose discoveries in physics and astronomy justified the new scientific approach which explained empirical facts through mathematical order. Copernicus, Kepler, and Galileo, like their earlier empirical predecessors in medicine, Fernel and Paracelsus, thought of their scientific writings as still a part of the tradition of learning. The Platonic foundation for the thought of all of these men has been pointed out too often to be repeated here. But Galileo (whose father was an early modern theorist in musical harmony) explicitly described his method of reasoning (and not merely his literary use of the dialogue form) as analogous to that of Socrates in the *Meno.*

In the second half of the seventeenth century, the divorce between science and literature had not yet taken place, although Descartes's dualism may have prepared ground for it. Like Bacon, Robert Boyle revealed his erudition in his writings, the best known of which, addressed to "the Christian Virtuoso" and popularly known as the "Essay on Seraphic Love," hailed science as a hymn to the Creator. Somewhat like Pascal, however, Boyle distinguished between knowledge as science and the reasons of the heart.

In Leibniz, however, the lines were more sharply drawn. Leibniz's esteem for the new science was greater, perhaps, than Boyle's; at least he assigned to scientific investigation a higher place than to art in human activities. To Thomas Burnet he wrote in 1698: "I am distressed at the destruction of Holbein's pictures which were burned at Whitehall; yet I share a little the sentiment of the Czar of Muscovy, who, I have been told, admired certain ingenious machines more than all of the pictures which he was shown in the royal palace."[49]

Leibniz's notion of the erudite man does reveal, however, that the emphasis on experience for its own sake stood low in his conception of scientific method. In a letter of March 1679 to Pierre Daniel Huet he defined the new conception of a scientifically oriented erudition in the course of some personal flattery:

By an erudite man I understand one like yourself (for what example could be found more fitting to the question before us); one who has carried out the highest achievements in the known world which the memory of man has touched. In this matter it is a fact that no one can easily stand over against you. Thus he excels in erudition who holds in readiness the admirable phenomena of heaven and earth, the history of nature and of art, the migrations of peoples and the changes of languages and empires, the present state of the earth, and in a word, whatever cannot be discovered out of the mind itself but is to be learned from things and men themselves. Philosophy thus differs from that which is factual.[50]

Surely a left-handed compliment! For by separating philosophy, Leibniz seems to have reduced erudition or learnedness to versatility in the collection and use of facts—a possible starting point for science and philosophy, but achieving neither an understanding of the order of reality nor a perception of the right and reasonable.

The disintegration of the Republic of Letters into distinct domains began, and the Age of Reason developed as an age of cultural pluralism. In the *Introduction* to his youthful *Treatise on Human Nature* in the next century, David Hume proposed to restore the unity of this Republic of Letters by attacking "the capital or center in human nature," (not in Divine Order) at its heart, rather than "the castles or villages on the frontier."[51] Thus he foresaw a new age in which the hoped-for unity and harmony will be sought not in God but in man. Literature became an end in itself, while the content and goals of literature—educational, scientific, and philosophical— were treated as disciplines apart. Through a dominant concern with matters of the intellect, the Republic helped to produce realms of concern which, for reasons to be found in human nature, developed in independence of it. And thereby it itself also surrendered to others some of the sense of moral purpose and of human development which gave it its initial goals and justification. The harmonious inclusiveness of the Republic, for which the earlier centuries struggled, was shattered and the libertine victory in modern thought—and in the modern curriculum—was brought nearer.

Conclusion

The impoverishment of the Republic of Letters by the expulsion of the sciences, and then of metaphysics and the classical moralists, was reflected and perhaps accelerated by the satirical criticism of the Republic. The gap which divided the inclusive context within which Vives, Scaliger, and Campanella labored, and which Saavedra's satire still acknowledged, from the narrower belles-lettristic perspective of Perrault and Swift is a measure of the failure of the Republic of Letters to achieve its enlarged harmonizing and ordering goal. Meanwhile the tradition of erudition may be credited with providing certain advantages for the rising sciences, some of which are now lost but which might serve as an ideal for a restoration of a degree of cultural unity.

1. The erudite tradition involved a definite effort, from the sixteenth century on, to hold the interest of the educated layman in the new science, and to encourage his understanding and his participation in it. The dialogues in which such early scientists as William Harvey, William Gilbert, Galileo, and Mersenne presented their findings are evidence of this aim. In keeping in the forefront of thought the ideal of a unity of human knowledge and its central role in a unity of faith and culture, the eclectics and the systematizers who followed them gave the sciences wider human meaning.

2. At the same time, erudite learning opened the way for the new sciences to enter the universities and the liberal arts tradition.

3. The older tradition of learning created and enlisted literary channels of communication which served the dissemination and exchange of scientific knowledge. In its academies it provided prototypes for modern scientifically oriented universities and research centers, and indeed assured a literary and philosophical concern within them.

4. By setting literary standards and by stressing the interrelations and human worth of scientific knowledge, the tradition of learning served to sustain a balanced view of the scientific enterprise, to prevent narrow overspecialization, and to call attention to the complexity of scientific endeavor, to encourage the organization and conservation of its results in a useful form, and thus to assure its place in a realistic world view which may be not only theoretically fruitful but strong enough to prevent the split between scientist and humanist in education and between scientist and layman in life.

All of this was still a living possibility at the beginning of the seventeenth century, and was regarded as self-evident by its best minds, but by the end of the century it had become improbable.

3 The Kingdom of Grace and the World

This age of ours, indeed, which has much science yet little conscience, is divided not only by a disturbed religion which disturbs government, but also by the abominable separations within each part (of religion).

There are those who do great harm through their teaching, and those who do so through their living. By their teaching many bring about great divisions among their learners; but by living badly, many more demonstrate the break between life and profession. *O tempora, O mores!* It is not enough that the new Ariomanites of today work hard to attack and to shatter the articles of our faith, as if with catapults in open battle against the world of Christians. Not finding it enough, lightly to shake them, they grasp in particular for the jugular and the head of our faith, and tear from its central place the most sacred merit and satisfaction of our Savior and Advocate, Jesus Christ. To defend the integrity of the faith against these, I declare the fullest satisfaction of sacrifice and atonement for us, carried out by our High Priest, Christ. For these, Christ indeed, but alas! Without the reward of redemption and satisfaction.

We see many Pseudo-Evangelicals and others who rattle off many things about God, Christ, and the Gospel with their mouths, but who live lives than which nothing is less worthy of God, Christ, and the Gospel. These latter simulate Christ but live a Satanalia. The former, indeed, are plunderers of grace. But the latter are enemies carrying out an impious warfare against the holy Christian life, even if they are meanwhile great trumpeters of the name of Christian. To the end of cultivating the integrity of the Christian life against these, I press and urge the sanctity of the Christian virtues, so that Christ may indeed be the Savior by doctrine and example, merit and efficacy, and thus our Christianity may be restored to us in its integrity. These two things I propose in this book.

[Otto Casmann, *Christianismi integras adversus pseudo-evangelicos, eius mutilatores.* Frankfurt, 1607.]

The Two Kingdoms

The manneristic intensity of Casmann's preface to his defense of Christian integrity conveys the fervent concern shared by many Christians at the beginning of the seventeenth century about the two-fold threat to the unity of the faith—confusion of doctrine and a morally decadent formalism within, and disbelief without. It conveys also the fundamental faith which Christian apologists and evangelists had—a faith alien to our own, antirational century—in the understanding as an instrument of restoring Christian unity and power.

Like the Republic of Letters, the Kingdom of God (or the Commonwealth of Grace; whether Kingdom or Commonwealth, its order was ascribed to a supreme Sovereign) implied an ideal of unity and perfection. But the tattered remnants of that "seamless robe of Christ," the church, left after the Reformation and Counter-Reformation in the preceding century, evoked bitterness and hatreds far deeper than any controversies in the field of letters. The devil was still very much alive, and disagreement was heresy, and heresy, possession by the evil one. Soldiers of the cross were agents of inquisition; from opposing camps popes, emperors, and reformers were proclaimed to be Antichrist. Heretics were burned and savages slaughtered in the name of the Kingdom. Romanists were condemned as idolaters by Protestants, and Protestants, by Romanists, as heretics and "politici," that is, politically motivated destroyers of religious authority—a position given support in England by the record of Henry VIII and his successors, and by political motives in the Thirty Years' War and the ecclesiastical effects of the treaty of Westphalia on the Continent.

Yet, also unlike the Republic of Letters, the Realm of Grace, however badly torn apart, found these deep, violent antagonisms gradually moderated through reason. By the seventeenth century, many of its leaders were working diligently to restore the unity of the churches. It anticipated the attainment of perfection in the future, many of its members, in the sixteenth and early seventeenth centuries, regarding that coming perfection as imminent. Their rejoicings at the prospect were interlarded with confirmations of the growing signs of the end, and with resolutions to work with zeal and to strengthen these signs and so to hasten this end.

In their concern for truth and its utility for character, therefore, the two Republics complemented each other almost perfectly. Both were torn between an ideal of harmonious unity and the radical conflict and confusion of purposes and convictions into which they had fallen. Both confronted internal and external enmities, although internal dissenters in each regarded themselves rather as liberators than as enemies. Men could, indeed, belong to the one realm and not to the other. In spite of his eloquence and his expressive Bible translation and religious hymns, Martin Luther was not widely regarded as a leader in the Republic of Letters, though other Reformers—Erasmus, John Calvin, Ulrich Zwingli, Martin Bucer, and Philipp Melanchthon —brought their membership in the Republic with them as armor in their warfare for the faith.

At the beginning of the century the two thus depended upon each other. At its narrowest, the Kingdom of Grace could burn books—not to speak of people. On the other hand, the Republic of Letters could become a closed circle of mutual appreciation, excluding from its vision the vital springs of new creativity. But in their widest scope the two supplemented each other. Each could absorb into itself whole interests and loyalties of man; the field of letters could encompass all knowledge and wisdom, and the field of faith could vitalize all individual and social enterprises and thoughts. Religious faith and thought were still the life of the Republic of Letters. Without the literate Republic however, the growth and clarification of faith would have been impossible; both Reformation and Counter-Reformation relied upon their power to communicate, persuade, and refute. Though the boundaries of the two orders did not coincide, both were involved in a struggle to restore a lost unity; both had a solid foundation of faith in reason; and both, in some dependence upon each other, eventually lost that binding faith, and with it the struggle.

Universality of the Kingdom of Grace

The ideal of a Kingdom of God, like that of the Republic of Letters, was ancient in origin—a Biblical conception with striking ethical content which was soon found to sustain a Platonic framework of thought, and which was developed by Saint Augustine after the Sack of Rome (the City of Man) into a theistic version of Christian ethics and Christian order.

It may be said that Augustine's vision of the two cities dominated Western thought beyond the Middle Ages and into the seventeenth century. In the effort to expand the Renaissance ideal of the courtly virtues into a universal ethical formula for European order, however, his vision was reinterpreted to fit various political changes, even though its universal ethical basis in the nature of God and his Providence remained constant. The divine attributes of power, wisdom, love, and justice provided a metaphysical foundation for such a kingdom, and the scriptural accounts of God's covenants with man provided a theory of history which offered the possibility of a just social order. Yet there was disagreement about the extent of the Kingdom, its earthly, historical status, and the conditions of its membership.

Thomas Hobbes, for example, writing about the conditions of a Christian commonwealth in the early years of the Rebellion, and distinguishing sharply between the basis of government in contract or convenant, and the life of the spirit, held that: "With the second coming not yet being, the Kingdom of God is not yet come, and we are not now under any other kings by pact, but our civil sovereigns; saving only that Christian men are already in the Kingdom of Grace, in as much as they have already the promise of being received at his coming again."[1] Hobbes thus limited the kingdom of grace to "the godly," "those to whom God had given the grace to be his disciples;" it is an interim union of believers, "an earnest of the Kingdom of God which is to come" on Christ's return as King.[2]

In contrast to Hobbes, Francis Bacon, though distrustful of the authority of tradition, had clung to the essentials of the Augustinian conception of the Church as an order of laws based on God's new convenant with men in Christ, and had derived these laws from their ground in scriptural revelation, mediated through sermons (he valued particularly the English sermons of the last decades of the sixteenth century), and other more enduring intellectual theological dissertations.[3]

In spite of their differences over the historical presence of the *civitas dei*, however, both Bacon and Hobbes recognized the mysteries of faith and limited the religious role of reason strictly to the explication of what is given in revelation. It is only after a wider interpretation of the role of reason and the light of nature was accepted that the kingdom of grace (Hobbes's term) was applied again, as Augustine had applied it, to a metaphysical order of personal relations and values which should serve as a norm for all social organization—God being the source of all the natural conditions for human association and well-being, and the supreme end in relation to whom all natural bonds and ends are given eternal, and therefore reasonable significance.

This transition to a universal Kingdom of God is explicit in

Leibniz's early criticism of Hobbes's state of nature. To Hobbes himself he wrote in July 1670, "assuming a ruler of the world, there can be no purely natural state of man which would place him beyond the pale of any community, since God is the common monarch of all."[4] A beginning of this extension of the concept may be traced in Bacon's discussion of the two senses in which the light of nature is used—the one using reason in relation to the senses, the other the law of conscience as an inward instinct, a "sparkle of the purity of (man's) first estate."[5] Taken in connection with the christologically centered eschatology of *The New Atlantis*, in which the ideal of a scientific organization of society is presented in an apocalyptic vision, this places Bacon among the forerunners of the enlarged theological rationalism of the century.

The full elevation of the concept of a kingdom of grace to a universal order of moral law was found only when Malebranche, undertaking to resolve the problems of Cartesianism, brought the natural light in religion from its previous state as reason in the clouded and indistinct form of instinct[6] into the clarity and adequacy of an effective ideal within which the moral, psychological, and metaphysical implications of the doctrine of the Logos can be clearly explicated. For Malebranche undertook to unite Descartes's dual metaphysical insights—into the importance of man's inward experience and the validity of a mechanistic theory of nature—by absorbing both into the relationship between man and God, the Logos as reason and the Spirit as love.[7] In his development of the two kingdoms of nature and of grace, Leibniz clearly followed Malebranche's lead, with certain important epistemological and logical modifications. The kingdom of grace was enlarged to include all men, for no matter how far their life is removed from the Supreme Good, their very being is constituted by the essential attributes of the divine nature, and the possession of the power of self-consciousness assures the possibility of their discovering this, their true nature and good. Leibniz appropriated also Malebranche's doctrine of justice as the absolute expression of love, but elaborated it to cover the traditional aspects of legal justice.[8]

Thus the kingdom of grace appeared in the seventeenth century in its Augustinian theocratic form, but generalized into an ideal of human society which contains sin as well as virtue; it stood in contrast not with the kingdom of man (which it was intended to absorb) but with the kingdom of nature, which is itself ordained of God and serves, by his providence, to increase the divine glory and (as in Bacon) the well-being of man. The kingdom of grace thus became a metaphysically warranted ideal of human order and relations, including science as well as government and religion, criminals as well as saints, the controls of society as well as the grounds for its values.

It must be pointed out that in Malebranche and Leibniz, and in a secular sense in Spinoza, this universal kingdom of grace is justified through a metaphysics inspired by Platonism which must also provide an explanation, through its doctrine of degrees of privation in the existing order, for both disbelief and immorality. The disbeliever, whether atheist or skeptic, questions the existence of a meaningful universal order in conformity to which man is perfected; in this sense he is nominalistically oriented. The task of restoring him to faith is therefore essentially a metaphysical one, that of absorbing this nominalistic denial into a metaphysical conviction to which it can be assimilated. Christian philosophy thus assumes an apologetic role—the (intellectual) conversion of unbelievers.

Philosophy as Apologetic

The apologetic role of philosophy in the seventeenth century thus consisted of the defense of this kingdom against its enemies, and the persuading of men of character and self-awareness to become active in propagating the faith on which the kingdom rests. Its enemies were attacked under the common term of *atheism*. The refutation of atheists is a common theme of Western philosophy beginning with Plato's *Laws* (Book X); that it had long been a perpetual concern of believers but changed with the intellectual currents of the times is suggested by the range of writings on the subject, which include Cicero on the nature of the Gods, Lucius Caelius Lactantius's *de falsa Religione* and *de Ira Dei*, and Thomas Aquinas's *Summa contra Gentiles*. From Nicholas of Cusa's writings through the Renaissance, and into the seventeenth century, many outstanding thinkers wrote apologetic threatises. Among them were such characteristic titles as Juan Luis Vives's *De veritate fidei Christianae libri V, contra Ethnicos, Judaeos, Agarenos, et perverse Christianos* (Cologne, 1568, a late edition), and Jean Cousin (Johannes Cognatus) *Fundamenta Religionis . . . adversus politicorum, seu atheorum errores* (Douay, 1636); the list could be greatly extended to include works by Marin Mersenne,

Joseph Glanvill, Henry More, Robert Boyle, Theophilus Spizel, Richard Bentley, and even men like Bodin, Vanini, and later Spinoza, who were themselves accused of atheism.[9]

A brief examination of these writings shows, on the one hand, that atheism was interpreted broadly to apply to all those who resisted the truth of religion (the standard of faith being that of the writer) and that it had many strange associates—heathen religions, skeptics, "politici," and so forth. The title of Marin Mersenne's second apologetic work, *L'impieté des deistes, athées, et libertines combattué et renversée* (Paris, 1624) illustrates the ambiguity and range of atheism. On the other hand, the earlier refutations, beginning with Vives's moving appeals to harmony, to the roots of faith in feeling, and to the wholeness of man were supplanted in the seventeenth century by intellectual arguments about the nature of God, the goodness of his providence, and the immortality of the soul.

It is not too much to claim that the great thought systems of the seventeenth century were a part of this apologetic program, absorbing into it insights provided by the new sciences and the ideal of universal dynamic harmony. In the letter to the Sorbonne with which Descartes prefaced his *Meditations* he expressed his apologetic purpose, which twentieth century critics are more inclined than their nineteenth century predecessors to take at face value; he sought to rewin skeptics and atheists to the faith on grounds which they themselves accepted. If one reads Spinoza's *Ethics* in the context of his earlier *Essay on the Emendation of the Intellect*, his purpose is clearly seen as an attempt to lead men from false commitments to the single-mindedness of an *amor intellectualis dei*, which is a part of God's self-love, and is based on distinct and adequate ideas. Thus Spinoza writes a defense of an objectively grounded faith lying beyond all historical cults, but retaining the truth and value of the most ethical ones. Like Robert Boyle, Pascal, and Pierre Daniel Huet, Leibniz undertook to write a harmonizing and persuasive Christian apologetic[10] (though the four men differed fundamentally on the issue of the spiritual relevance of modern science), and like Malebranche, he considered his entire philosophy as an argument, addressed to modern man, for the Christian faith. The great so-called "rationalistic" systems illustrate what is true more generally of the apologetic enterprise of the period—the atheists to whom they were directed varied widely in their opinions and were by no means in agreement among themselves. But all were regarded as harmful to the faith and to personal salvation, and since their attack was intellectual, a response by reasoning and constructive argument was called for. The apologetic role of philosophy was an important aspect of the pedagogical task recognized by members of the Republic of Letters.

Atheism: Its Scope

The relation of atheism to libertinism is clear from the denial by both, either explicitly or as implied in conduct, of the existence of a divine being demanding obedience. Both therefore also implied the rejection of immortality. But the charge of atheism was also directed variously at heretics, skeptics, fideists who distrusted reason, and rationalists who demanded the submission of faith to rational criticism, or in short, dissent from any particular orthodoxy. The term was in danger of the same indiscriminate use which has been made of "Communism" in the twentieth century.

Decisions based on political expediency and opinions which followed the Reformations were involved. In 1597, Jean Cousin undertook to justify "the natural cognition of God, the immortality of the soul and a divine justice" against "the errors of the politicians (*politicorum*) or atheists." He did not name these specificially, but in his dedication to the Archbishop of Cambrai spoke of the Lutherans as "of most evil doctrine and heretical minds," and described the Sacramentarians, Calvinists, and Anabaptists as "far more degenerate" than atheists.[11] The link between politicians and atheists is frequent in Catholic and Protestant discussions alike. In the dedication of his *Atheismus Triumphatus* to Louis XIII, Tommaso Campanella, the most widely known champion of a European Catholic theocracy in the early century, attacked Protestantism, condemning Martin Luther, "Prince of Heresiarchs," for destroying the unity of the Church by denying its visible head and encouraging the princes to think themselves gods, thereby multiplying sects (as foreseen in Proverbs 28: 1-3).[12]

Campanella himself was widely followed by Protestant authors who adopted his theory of the original unity and rationality of man, but not his demand for a single visible head of the Church. Theophilus Spizel, Lutheran pastor in Augsburg, agreed with him in condemning as atheists "those who reduce all religion to political arts," using as examples Thomas Hobbes and (with particular emphasis) Hugo Grotius, "who first adhered to the religion of the reformers, then began to embellish Socinian dogmas (which he had once attacked in his writings), and who had disseminated the opinions of various sects in different nations—French, Swedish, English, not even abhorring the Jewish, and was wooed for Rome by the Jesuit Petavius on the ground that there was little alien to Rome in his writings."[13] Spizel, however, charged also that Campanella was himself "infected with the poison of atheism" since he proposed a new method for converting atheists based on a counsel like Vanini's—that is, arguing for a natural basis for religion in all men, in the form of three primalities or preeminences—power, wisdom, and love—in all three of which there inheres an *"ens primum essentiarum."*

The charge of atheism spread much more widely, however, than such intra-Christian exchanges. In the first edition of his *Questiones celeberrimae in Genesim* (Paris, 1623), Mersenne had charged that there were fifty-thousand atheists in Paris alone—an incredible number by definition, but certainly reaching beyond merely theological disagreements and intended to include all practical as well as theoretical disbelievers, skeptics, and libertines. Erasmus had warned that atheism was supported by skepticism; its kinship with libertinism was no less apparent. Machiavelli served as prototype of many alleged atheists. Among the Machiavellisti, who denied the "histories of the Gospels and the Apostles," were frequently named Geoffroi Vallée, author of the *Ars nihil credendi*, who was burned in Paris in 1574,[14] and Julius Caesar Vanini, burned and quartered in Toulouse in 1619 (though, as I have already noted, he himself had written a refutation of atheism which borrowed much from Scaliger and repeated the Averroistic proof of the existence of God based on motion).[15] In his youth Leibniz lamented the "shipwreck of atheism which now threatens us," shuddering to think, in spite of his slight and recent acquaintance with scholars, how many brilliant thinkers he had already met who were atheists. In his letter to Jacob Thomasius, he grouped together atheists, Socinians, naturalists, and skeptics, and judged Jean Bodin to be a greater atheist than Vanini himself, because of the *Colloquium Heptaplomeres de abditis rerum sublimium arcanis*, a dialogue on religious tolerence which was widely circulated in the century, but whose publication was prevented.[16] But by Leibniz's time, all of these alleged enemies of the faith had already been superseded by the two great "atheists" of the century (both of whom, however, he eagerly sought to engage in correspondence)—Hobbes and Spinoza—Hobbes condemned for his extreme nominalism, his materialism, and his political absolutism, Spinoza for his political toleration, his identification of God with nature, and his denial of teleology.

In short, although the philosophical apologists for Christianity based their arguments upon the adequacy of reason (in one of several different senses of the term), anyone who did not recognize the superiority of Christian revelation to all other patterns of belief, including that in reason itself, was in danger of facing the charge of atheism. The new scientists themselves were not exempt from this danger, and Joseph Glanvill used his gall-dipped pen in their defense in his *Plus Ultra* (1668):

> About it (atheism) I take notice, that Philosophical Men are usually dealt with by the zealous, as the great Patrons of the *Protestant* Cause are by the Sects. For as the Bishops and other learned Persons who have most strongly oppugned the *Romish Faith* have had the ill luck to be accused of *Popery* themselves; in like manner it happens to the humblest and deepest Inquisitors into the *works* of God, who have the *most* and *fullest* Arguments of his *Existence*, have raised *impregnable Ramparts* with much *industry* and *pious pains* against the *Atheists*, and are the *only men* that can with success serve *Religion* against the Godless Rout; These, *Superstitious Ignorance* hath always made the loudest outcry against as if themselves were guilty of *that* which they have most happily *oppugned* and *defeated*.[17]

Glanvill thus called attention to the limits of the *orthodox* appeal to reason as a defense against atheism; mixed too closely with experience and experiment, it was itself suspect. Against the real atheists, however, the "Saducees," whose disbelief was rooted in the rejection of revelation, Glanvill's satire was more vitriolic:

> These wits, as they are taken to be [also, "the small Philosophick Sir Foplings of this present Age" and "the coarse-grained philosophers as those Hobbians and Spinozians and the rest of that Rabble"] are so jealous, forsooth, and so sagacious, that whatsoever is offered to them by way of established Religion, is suspected for a piece of politick circumvention; which is as silly notwithstanding, and as childish, as that conceit of a Friend of

yours when he was a schoolboy in the lowest form of a Country-Grammar-School, who could not believe scarce that there were any such men as Cato, and Aesop, and Ovid, and Vergil, and Tully, much less that they wrote any such Books, but that it was a trick of our parents to keep us from the enjoyment of our innocent pastime in the open air.[18]

The Natural Light of Reason

The defense of Christianity against its modern enemies took many forms: the death penalty, imprisonment, raillery, charges of political motivation. But the chief weapon of the intellectual defense was a new appropriation of the doctrine of the natural light. While the power of reason, viewed as a natural light, was the most effective instrument of Christian apologists against atheists (who could not be reached by arguments from revelation), it was also clear that this reasonable light which lighteth all peoples could not safely be divorced from the more general parts of the Christian revelation without itself reviving the old charge of unbelief. In the sixteenth and seventeenth centuries several factors nevertheless served to modify and strengthen this old doctrine of the light of nature and to adapt it more adequately to the new circumstances of the age.

The confrontation with hitherto unknown cultures through exploration, colonization, and missionary endeavor had intensified and expanded the search for such a rational ground for religious belief beyond the three theistic religions generally recognized in Europe. Nicholas of Cusa, and before him Raymundus Lullus, had undertaken to win the Moslems to Christianity; in the newer centuries people seemed not to be sure whether Moslems should be evangelized or exterminated. Jesuit missionaries in China were reporting on the wonderful moral and intellectual quality of its natural religion, and Jesuits and others were giving similar (though not entirely unqualified) reports about the theistic and political implications of the natural religion of American Indians. The result was a new ambivalence with respect to the relationship of Christian revelation to the natural light of reason in religion. On the one hand, natural reason could be used as Paul had used it in writing to the Romans (Romans, 1 and 2) and as had Peter in his letters, and Aquinas and others in later times, as a universal ground for the conversion of heathen as well as atheist to the Christian faith. On the other hand, if the people of the earth already possess a natural insight into the teachings of Christianity, would this not rob Christianity of its claim of uniqueness—may not what remains in revelation be unnecessary "enthusiasm," needlessly divisive of the peoples of the earth?

It remained, of course, for thinkers of the eighteenth century to feel the full force of the second alternative. If it was not grasped in the late Renaissance, this is because of the Augustinian conviction of the rationality of the Christian revelation and the incompleteness and unclarity of human reason without it. The kingdom of grace may be universally extended, but for the peoples beyond the reach of the Christian revelation, the natural basis of faith was still clouded by the fall. The conclusion was that the principles of religion based on reason appear to these people not as logically self-evident principles but as "instincts" or as blind intuitions. They are *felt* with vague but general conviction. Only Christianity, therefore, is the true philosophy, rendering in clear and distinct teachings the rationality of faith.

This doctrine of natural religion and the fall of man was characteristic of Reformed (Covenant) theology and of Roman Catholic theology alike. According to Luis Vives, who had a deep influence upon Protestant humanism as well as on such later rationalistically inclined thinkers as Campanella and Herbert of Cherbury, the diversity of religions was due to the fall of man, which turned his corrupted will from the love of God to the vain and empty things of this world, and his intellect to incredulity, suspicion, lapses of faith, and bondage to sense. Yet truth did enter men's minds in a general revelation, though only through the mercy of God. Thus although men differ in what they worship, they all agree that there is a being worthy of worship. The testimony of Paul to the Romans and of Peter was now confirmed by the evidence of explorers and adventurers. Vives wrote: "Our men have discovered many peoples who have lived all their lives without letters, without laws, without king, without government (*res publica*), without arts, but not, however, without religion; so that it would appear that by nature religion is more true than are the other arts and inventions of men."[19] The natural truth of religion was thus established on the ground of consensus. Vives further reasoned that the natural light imparts the principle of reason to all men, but in the form of customs and traditions. Religion is natural in *genus* or kind, but the *species* are forms or qualities of men. Thus, after Noah, men were led to venerate God as the Lord of Nature, but their rudity and crassness was such that "led by their senses, yet also grasping intuitively what was beautiful and admirable and useful in the earth, they took this for God." And in the process of being passed from parents to children, this error grew so that the sun, moon, stars, and elements, and even brute animals or men from whom some goods were secured, earned divine honors. Abraham, who worshipped in this way in Chaldea, was the first to discover the Author and Rector of the universe, and to worship him not merely through sacrifices but "in love and faith."[20]

Vives proceeded from this point to trace the history of the plan of salvation, first through the covenant with Abraham's children and then through the universal covenant of grace. The doctrine of the Incarnation which he outlined in this context is put psychologically: the eternal nature of God, which is manifested in a duality of acts, *cognitio* and *amor*, necessarily gives rise to the Son, the principle involved being that perfect love arises from perfect knowledge. Later, in the dialogues between Christian, Jew, and Moslem which Vives included in his *De Veritate*, Books II and III, he consistently confirmed the superiority of the Christian faith on the ground of its Christology, according to which Christ mediates the Father's perfect-knowledge-becoming-perfect-love to the Holy Spirit. Thus the principle of natural religion was developed into a conception of the history of divine providence and an unusual argument for the superiority of Christianity. And since the later founders of the Covenant theology were readers of Vives, it may be said that he stands at the head of that development of Protestant apologetics which makes use of a philosophy of history and an Augustinian, psychological approach to the Trinity. His emphasis upon the intuitive role of the intellect in grasping religious truth worked effectively in the great systems of the seventeenth century, and his emphasis upon action and use as the criterion of truth directly influenced the Puritan theologians, and even much later, Jonathan Edwards.

Although Vives may have been the first to comment upon the religion of the New World inhabitants, such comments became more frequent in later versions of natural religion and the light of nature. Campanella, whose theory of the "primalities" (power, wisdom, love) shows the influence of Vives, reported on the American Indians in a section of his *Atheismus Triumphatus* entitled *De Cultu Americanorum* (1630), acknowledging that their rites serve Satan, but holding nevertheless that "they use confession of sins—the people to the princes, the princes to the king, the king to the sun, but the sun to God, as they think. And they eat bread as if it were eucharistic, forming an idol of blood and dough and distributing and communing through it with one whom they called in the name of the God— thus emulating a Christian rite in the magistry of the devil."[21] Thus Campanella too recognized an unclearly intuited general rational principle in the irrational pagan rites of uncivilized groups.

It was the Baron de la Hontan, however, whose fresh observations of the Iroquois Federation spread this conviction in the last years of the seventeenth century.[22]

This psychological reduction of universal truths of reason to unclear and indistinct instincts or feelings borne upon customs and traditions not only involved a significant shift in attitudes toward paganism and atheism, it was also to have a strong influence upon the great rationalistic systems of the seventeenth century. Herbert of Cherbury, the center about whom the arguments about natural religion turned later in the century, concluded that there are no true atheists, although some men who have been taught "false and horrendous attributes by certain people have preferred to believe, rather than there is such a Numen, that there is none."[23] In the "natural instincts" imbedded in all religions there are implicit five common notions according to Lord Herbert; with respect to these, Christianity is in no way distinguished from the rest. He provided six criteria for the recognition of such "natural instincts" as those upon which religion rests: they are recognized by their priority (over the faculties involved in the perception of particular truths); by their independence (from more particular instinctive assents which depend upon them); by their universality; by their certitude; by their necessity (this turns out to be a utilitarian consideration: they all serve the conservation of man); and by the mode of their mutual conformation. In contrast to Vives, who developed a rational basis for showing, within the universal light of reason, the supremacy of Christianity, Herbert reduced the natural light to a common denominator of all religions. The intuitive or instinctive grasp of reason, however confused, has moved to center and pushed cultural and credal details to the periphery, leaving no atheists to convert, even though its principles allow for an abundance of sinners and demand their punishment, here and hereafter.

With Lord Herbert, therefore, three significant changes have taken place within the task of delineating a religion of nature or of reason. (1) The Realm of Grace has been expanded to include all rational beings, regardless of differences in revealed faith. (2) The role of reason has been extended from that of supporting revelation to that of transcending and serving as a critic of revelation. (Here the Covenant theology, which regarded revelation as made necessary by man's fall and sin, served as a transition.) (3) The natural light manifests itself, however, to man in his present state not in logically self-evident propositions, but indistinctly in customs, unclear intuitions, and, in short, in the affections and the appetitive, motival nature of man.

Several significant consequences of this conception of the doctrine of the natural light of reason, as revealed in the nonrational aspects of man's nature, must be noted.

1. A new life, and a new task, are given to the discipline of logic, that is, to serve as an instrument of teaching and learning for those who feel truth darkly through instinct or intuition. Late Scholastic texts in logic had followed a traditional plan derived from Aristotle: Part I, Invention (that is, discovery), or the logic of concepts; Part II, Judgment, or the logic of inference; Part III, Method, or the logic of communication, instruction, or action. Aristotle's definition of logic as an instrument, or as his modern commentators put it, an art, naturally suggested an emphasis upon its applications. This ordering for use was retained by such a new Aristotelian logician as Zabarella, by the anti-Aristotelian, rhetorically oriented Peter Ramus, by the mediating anti-Ramist Keckermann,[24] and even in the alleged "subjectivization" of logic in the Port Royal logic of Arnauld and Nicole. But the mode and the object to which logic was to be applied varied with different circumstances.

Applied to the conversion of atheists it could not be a logic of pure reason; such a logic was available only to the redeemed, in whom the rational powers, the image of God, had been restored in its pristine clarity. For the unsaved, in whom the light of reason was dimmed in the darkness of feelings and instincts, reason could still be effective without the illumination of grace, but it must be a reason adjusted to the unclear and inadequate imbeddedness of principles in the experiences and habits of man. This was, of course, not new; it was implicit in Thomas Aquinas's approach to theology through the natural reason. But it now gave new life to logic. Vives himself, and following him, Ramus, devised a logic for fallen men, simple enough to be grasped by them and adequate, by its sharp cutting loci and dichotomies and its emphasis upon dialectics, to elevate him from the confusion of unbelief to an adequacy of understanding with respect to "the reasonableness of Christianity." The way of faith is thus, in any case, through reason. It is not surprising that as the literary humanism of the Renaissance moved toward learnedness and erudition, the religious interest of man was intellectualized as well.

2. The widening breach between faith and reason opened in the late middle Ages and Renaissance by Ockhamists and so-called Averroists was thus once more closed, and the mutual compatibility of reason and faith once more widely accepted. The revived doctrine of a natural light of reason was, in fact, only one factor in this restoration of reason to the center of religious thought; this restoration presupposed also an experiential conception of faith itself, the result of Protestantism and the Counter-Reformation. It required also a widening interpretation of the usefulness and the applicability of reason, when properly adapted to the subject matter at hand. In this more inclusive rational unification of interests, the Platonists, again, were influential, and their intellectualization of faith, which involved a Neoplatonic metaphysics of light and darkness and of degrees of perfection, was expanded by Bruno and Campanella. In Campanella's writings the doctrine already explicated in the Preface to Vives's *De Veritate Fidei Christianae* was amplified into an argument that there is a unitary truth to which sense, reason, and revelation make separate but consistent and mutually confirming approaches. Campanella, and his forerunner Telesio, from whom he learned this fusion of the three, were therefore widely quoted in the seventeenth century, notably by the Reformed theologians of Germany, England, and the Low Countries. This view of the unity of experience, reason, and revelation was to be fundamental in the great rationalistic systems of the century.

The trinitarian unity of experience, reason, and revelation, however, needed careful qualification. Sense cannot confirm revelation except with the aid of a doctrine of signs in which natural events are given a spiritual significance beyond their ordinary perceptual meaning. And even in scientific knowledge, sense and reason do not play parallel roles, but rather the complementary and mutually dependent roles of a posteriori and a priori components in truth, providing content and form respectively. In matters of faith it once more became clear that reason must either presuppose revelation, or judge it on a nonrevelatory, perhaps a moral, basis, or be judged and perhaps condemned by it.

Spinoza's friend Lodewijk Meyer, taking seriously Paul's injunction to the Thessalonians to "try all things and hold fast to what is good"—the quotation in Greek appeared on the title page of his book—published his *Philosophia Scripturae Interpres* in 1666.[25] Appealing to the natural light (suffused with "acumen, study, sedulity, and attention to observation") as the basis of sound philosophy, he applied Cartesianism, along with other sources such as Keckermann, Alsted, and Philippe de Mornay, to prove that the Reformed interpretations of doctrine were accurate, while those by Romanists and Lutherans were in error. Surely a commendable, even if sectarian, service to the faith, which he applied with a literalness exceeding that of Locke's thirty years later. He admitted that a test case, the doctrine of creation *ex nihilo*, is not sound philosophy, but showed it to be scripturally unsound theology as well, since it appears only in 2 Maccabees 7:28, which most Christians do not regard as revealed. Theologians did not, however, welcome this honest appeal to reason, and the work was condemned—not as harshly as Spinoza's, but along with it—as atheistic.

An emphasis upon natural reason as itself sound revelation thus forced Christian apologetics into a dilemma—either to be willing to change scriptural interpretation to fit reason when it spoke apodictically, or to abandon reason for an unsupported fideism, that is, with an ultimately libertine view of faith. It is this dilemma, already stated by Campanella,[26] which the rationalistic metaphysicians escaped by affirming as a first principle of all being the principle of sufficient reason, which applies in all thinking, whether within the scope of sense and the Aristotelian categories, or beyond them. Thus a unity of knowledge and faith, of truth and value could be established. This was their reaffirmation of the traditional doctrine of the convertibility of the transcendentals.

3. Yet there remained, after all of the efforts to retain a unity of reason and faith, the problem of what reason could do in support of faith. For the Reformation had put forward a deepened conception of faith, one which preserved and humanized the Protestant conception of the sufficiency of the individual's faith, and the vital efficacy of God, to achieve a state of grace. It is to the humanist Vives that we are indebted for the first influential modern theory of the affections and

their role as motives to action.[27] Faith is confirmed and established by reason, but it is fulfilled when understanding is transformed into love. And love develops in the affective, not the merely cognitive, nature of man. According to Vives, the Holy Spirit hovers above all reasons, nor can reason itself simulate the effects of the Spirit. In the eloquent Preface to his *De Veritate Fidei Christianae*, he warned the reader not to expect the gift of grace as the result of reading his book.

> Let no one fear that the merit of faith will be bestowed forth if he reads through this, our book, for it does not offer reasons of the kind which adduce sensory experiences. Nevertheless some among them are most efficacious, for there is more merit in faith and charity than in faith alone.[28]

Reasons may therefore bear fruit in love, but only if the Grace of God, through the Holy Spirit, is present. This theme is repeated in the Epilogue of the book, where Vives summarized his argument.

> The mind is immortal and capable of divine blessedness, toward attaining which it ought to stretch every nerve. However it cannot attain it unless it is so joined to God that in a certain way it becomes God. This conjunction no glue can achieve save only the love of God. But if true religion ought to see all toward a union with God, so that man may through it somehow become as God and enjoy the divine blessedness through all ages, this can be done in no other way than by the true universal religion which directly or obliquely pertains to the love of God.[29]

If this basis in Christian experience is given, all of Christian faith is involved, and the love of God becomes the bond of our common life.

Arguments for the Existence of God

Thus Vives, and after him (at least in their resort to instinctive feelings) Campanella and Herbert of Cherbury, stood where Pascal later stood too, upon the fruitfulness and self-validating personal power of the "reasons of the heart," which no human logic alone can reveal, but which logic can nonetheless serve by ordering and rendering more consistent and complete their convincing power of conviction and human worth. Understanding is necessary for the fruits of love and faith, but understanding is itself guaranteed by intuitions grounded in the natural light. Arguments for the existence of God, for example, are of secondary importance in the justification of faith, or for that matter, in the justification of a religiously oriented theory of knowledge. Augustinian Platonism has received a new development. The natural light of reason functions instinctively to reveal the truth of God and his Providence, and this instinctive revelation can be clarified and rendered adequate by logic in such a way that Christianity (in the case of Vives, Campanella, and Pascal) or the three European religions (in the case of Herbert) can be known as the "perfect philosophy" (as Augustine regarded the former) or as the perfectly known faith.

It was left to the theologians of the Aristotelian tradition, breaking through to metaphysics once more in the course of the struggles for Reformation, to reformulate the traditional Scholastic arguments for the existence of God. In the German universities, discussions of the relation of metaphysics to theology had become lively, and the problem of God had been assigned to the "special" part of metaphysics, in which the particular species of being were discussed.[30] In general this inclusion of theology in metaphysics was limited to the Reformed universities; Lutheran metaphysicians were inclined rather to follow Zabarella and the Italian Aristotelians in excluding it. It may be said in general that the old Scholastic arguments for the existence of God were revived but arranged in a unified order determined by metaphysical considerations of concreteness and completeness. The influence of Suarez played an important part in this effort to unify the arguments.

Suarez offered a definition of God which differs from the Platonic tradition of the *ens perfectissimum* by avoiding the abstract argument from the notion of being.[31] His own theory rests upon "the vulgar and quasi-primary concept which we all form of God." Thus he appeals to the natural light: "This name (God) signifies a certain most noble being which is superior to all the rest, and from which all the rest depends as from a first author, so that furthermore it is to be worshipped and venerated as supreme numen."[32] Psalm 28, the Wisdom of Solomon 13, and Paul in Romans 1 and 2, all show that God can be known through the natural light,[33] and hence no one can be excused from knowing, and therefore worshipping, him. But Suarez rejects the ontological argument at once, save insofar as it serves to derive the existence of the attributes and their dependence upon each other. He rejects also the argument from motion to a prime mover.[34] The other arguments are developed in their modern form. Though merely probable and preliminary, the cosmological argument does establish the existence of a maker or makers; together with a consideration of the beauty of the universe and the wonderful connection and order of its parts, it gives a basis for believing that there is one unchanging maker. But the cosmological is thus merely preparatory to the teleological argument, which operates in several different contexts. The argument from the nature of the soul, with its interplay of functions, is balanced by a more general argument: That one must infer, from the priority of essences over existents, and of essential relationships over existential relationships, that there is an individual creator prior to both. Suarez holds that the arguments as a whole establish God as a necessary being, though they themselves have no necessity and no compelling force.[35]

Thus a distinct metaphysical advance was made in Suarez and his successors beyond the medieval formulations of the arguments for the existence of God. First, the basis for the argument in the Aristotelian doctrine of causality was modified and simplified because efficient and final causality have received priority over formal and material causality (although Suarez did include an argument from the existence of material things and their properties, indeed, his entire dualistic metaphysics reappeared in the later formulation by Descartes in the *Meditations*). Furthermore, the argument from the interdependence of things to the interrelatedness of their essences, and thence to God, brought the unity and action of the Numen immanently into nature or the created order. In the third place, then, a distinction became prominent between secondary causality, involved in the interacting unity of the created order, and primary causality, the efficacy of the ever and everywhere present sustaining activity of God, the subject of all essences. As a result, the hierarchical structure of Neoplatonism receded and eventually disappeared, whether this hierarchy was formulated as degrees of finiteness or negation, or levels of created being, or a scale of perfections (that is, values). The immediacy of the divine act in every natural thing or process was increasingly recognized.[36]

This immediacy does not, however, eliminate the Platonic essentialism inherent even in the new Scholasticism of Suarez;

indeed, this essentialism is the heart of his effort to reconcile Thomas Aquinas and Duns Scotus. Essences must not only always be referred to the particulars in which they inhere—this is an indispensable phase of Suarez's argument; essences become also the inseparable attributes of the one God. Thus they unify the problems of being and knowledge (*ens* and *verum*). They are at once the content of our metaphysical understanding and the key to our knowledge of existence. The Ideas mediate between the divine and human thinking. They are the assurance of the truth of our judgments, but also of the identities of quality and form which assure the validity of our perception. This role of essences in assuring the unity of direct perception with the discursive work of the understanding is widely adopted by the metaphysicians of the seventeenth century.

After Suarez, the rapid growth of empirical science brought the teleological argument to the fore as a concrete completion of the argument to an efficient cause. In his *Disputatio metaphysica de Deo continens naturalem Dei cognitionem* (1604), for example, Henning Arnisaeus rejected the ontological argument because it leads only to an abstract axiom of the best or most perfect, but not to God. He then reasoned that although God is not to be mixed with physical things, he is the actual unity in all essences, and that the best argument for his existence should therefore be based on our knowledge of visible creatures, interpreted through the unity of the transcendentals—being, one, the true, and the good. As speculation was built increasingly upon empirical descriptions of natural things, many university disputations were held arguing to the existence of God not merely from the wonders of the human mind—that argument was well formulated, after all, by St. Augustine—but from the marvelous structure and function of the human hand or the eye, and from other evidences of efficiency and beauty in nature. By the time of Robert Boyle, and particularly noticeable in the lectures on natural religion and Christianity which he endowed, the heart of the theistic argument was teleological and, as Hume treated it in his *Dialogues concerning Natural Religion*, "empirical" in this sense. The passage from Psalm 94, which the Electress Sophia, Leibniz's patroness, loved to quote, showed that Revelation supported this argument: "He that made the ear, shall he not hear? He that made the eye shall he not see?" Thus the harmonized conceptual arguments for God's existence by Suarez and others combined with the more pragmatic psychological and moral interpretations of natural reason given by Vives and those influenced by him, and this combination dominated the natural theology of the seventeenth and eighteenth centuries.

Evil and History

One aspect of the gradual abandonment of the Neoplatonic hierarchies of being and order was an increasing awareness of the positive nature of evil—both natural and moral. It is true that the Platonically inspired systems tended to blur the distinction between real and ideal. The Republic of Letters, for example, was described as consisting of worthy, venerable, noble readers; and the kingdom of grace was one in which the divine harmony operated inwardly in all spirits. Yet in spite of the formulas of metaphysics, all recognized that the real Republic of Letters involved ambition, strife, and the pride of intellect, and the real kingdom of grace was torn apart by contentiousness and soiled by the politics of ambitious princes. It did not take an earthquake in Lisbon to open men's eyes to the destructiveness of nature; storms, plagues, misbirths, pains, death, the failure of crops, and famine were all too common. The several Augustinian solutions of the problems—the privation involved in all natural things and events, the aesthetic value of contrasts, and the fall of man—explained, but they did not satisfy. New intellectual developments combined with the evils of the age to show the inadequacy of these traditional explanations.

There were at least three grounds for abandoning the theory that all evil could be explained by privation or by a recognition of negativity. (1) Viewed from a logical standpoint, the negative now appeared to have no ontological status, but to be merely the mental denial of a definite positive, and therefore logically on the level of second intentions. Leibniz's generalizations about the ontological bearing of propositions, for example, could be applied only to true affirmative propositions, not to negations. (2) The intrusion of the concept of the *infinite* and its difference from the *finite*, into the scale of being, and the identification of the *infinite* with the "indefinite" (or indefinable) of Neoplatonism rendered absurd any idea of a fixed totality of conceivable qualities and beings within which privation could be specified. Thus Leibniz still retained the theory of evil as privation in his *Theodicy*, and, more generally, used the concept of privation in his account of the creation of finite monads out of the simple perfections of God himself, but he subordinated the abstract hierarchical order which this theory implied to the concrete, existential level of communities of finite beings—the "Realms of Nature and of Grace"—made up of distinct orders of monads. (3) Closely related to this dislocation of hierarchies of being was the difficulty of finding any ontological principle for determining the boundaries of finite beings, in a world in which all existents receive their natures immediately from the nature of God's own being (as discussed above). This, again, was explained by Leibniz as the result of God's willing the best possible, in this case, the greatest possible number of variations of his essence, in his creation. But suggestive though this may be, it does not overcome the paradox that limitations of the very essence of God himself, upon entering into finite beings, should become evil. Moreover, the theory of a scale of beings and a hierarchical order of creation appeared increasingly irrelevant to an understanding of natural evil, which had now to be confronted empirically, at face value, as men like Pierre Bayle did in fact meet it. Infinity, too, became a matter of various interpretations, but the general tendency was to regard it operationally, as an interminable process of analysis within the finite limits of the situation or event under examination. As Leibniz wrote in a note intended for Bartholomew Des Bosses: "There is a syncategorematic infinite . . . namely the possibility of progression in dividing, multiplying, adding, and subtracting. There is also a hypercategorematic infinite . . . this infinite is God himself. But there is no categorematic infinite, or one actually having infinite parts."[37]

A problem also arose in justifying evil which is due to the fall of man. As mathematical and mechanistic accounts of natural phenomena grew more successful, it became increasingly difficult to cling to the Old Testament conviction, present even in Augustine, that natural evil is the consequence of man's original sin. A scientifically effective notion of causality could hardly be distorted sufficiently to sustain such a view.[38] It was easy, as it is today, to recognize a source of evil and corruption in man's essential nature. But Reformed theology was particularly emphatic about the goodness of nature apart from man, justifying this not scripturally but by the Platonic doctrine of harmony. Man himself is the source of disharmony. Hence the theological doctrine that nature is good (which supported an empirical argument for the existence of God, as was shown above) was threatened by a scientific approach which implied that nature is neutral to good and evil.

There were other points, however, at which theological speculation about the evil in man affected the development of new
scientific lines of investigation. An example of this is found in
the disputations about the origin of the soul. The strongest
argument for the traducian theory (that each soul is inherited
from that of its parents) was the empirical judgment that original sin is passed from parents to children, and this theological
position, in turn, opened the door eventually to the beginnings
of the science of genetics. Moral evil, on the other hand, kept
alive the importance of man's moral responsibility, and therefore the problem of man's freedom.

The question of the nature of history arose in large part from
the concern with evil, since all solutions seemed to demand
explanations of historical permanence and change. It is not
surprising that the anticipation of a greater good is one of the
deepest motives in the consciousness of history, second only,
perhaps, to the importance of memory in preserving the order
upon which group well-being depends. It is appropriate, therefore, to point out that the emergence, in this period, of the
study of history from its special role of establishing the legitimacy of princely authority by tracing family lineages to the
great families of Rome into a more general concern for the
well-being of peoples and the human significance of events took
place in this religious context of man's moral need and destiny.

Late in the sixteenth century, Reformed theological circles in
Herborn, Heidelberg, Cambridge, and the Dutch universities
gradually formalized St. Augustine's Christian theory of history,
which concerned the struggle between good and evil and God's
redemptive plan, into a historical theory of divine revelation and
redemption—the Covenant, or the federal, theology. The religions which Europe knew were in essence historical, with historically located and recorded revelations. Implicit in all
theories of a natural religion was the conviction that a single
order of divine providence has been revealed in different measure to all people, but that this has been obscured and mythol-
ogized in various ways by the unclear and indistinct perceptions
of fallen men. At this point the myth of Babel reinforced the
myth of Eden. On this basis the great French preacher and
theologian Jacques Bénigne Bossuet modernized St. Augustine's
City of God by viewing successive ages of history as a conflict
between the transient and imperfect cities of man and the eternal city of God.[39] The Covenant theology, on the other hand,
interpreted history on Biblical grounds as a sequence of divine

compacts with men, aimed at redeeming them from their sinful state following their rejection of the original rational convenant with Adam, that is, with all humanity. As Paul and the others pointed out, this natural light was not completely obliterated by Adam's sin, but it was certainly obscured; in philosophical terms, man was condemned to unclear and confused perceptions and ideas.

History since the fall is a record of God's sovereign will and redemptive grace at work to save men. The first historical convenant was one with a chosen people, and took the form of a Covenant of Works (though the Covenant of Grace is already foretold to Abraham and to the prophets). The Ten Commandments stand for all times as a reduction to simplest moral terms of this Covenant of Works. But the Covenant of Grace, anticipated in the Old Testament, is fully revealed for all men through the death and resurrection of Christ. Similarly, Moses anticipated the Greeks in grasping philosophical truth, both practical and theoretical.[40] The Covenant of Grace is to be fulfilled, as Christ himself promises, through his Second Coming, in which the powers of evil will be overthrown and a reign of peace will begin—whether on earth or in heaven, and for how long, was a matter of further dispute. Thus history is a record of the struggle of God against evil, which is due in part to man but also to supernatural powers of evil; in this struggle, ultimate victory is assured when history, or its present age, comes to an end. It is in this historical hope that one of the beginnings of the modern theory of progress is to be found.

Eschatology and the Limit of History

Eschatology is inevitable in the mentality, if not in the philosophies, of any age which is caught up in historical conflict and the destruction of human values. It is the mark of the limits of historical relativism, the effort to answer two complementary questions: What will be our state when revolution is achieved and the good we sought is ours, with nothing more to strive for? Or what will be our state when historical forces have plunged us into depths beyond which we can sink no further, so that the very historical processes involved must end? Facing these questions, men of thought have resorted not so much to other-worldliness as to a new-worldliness. This new state of being in which history as we know it has ceased, apocalyptic thinkers, whether Christian, Jewish, Marxist, or National Socialist, have sought to make convincing by the most attractive symbols available to Scripture and imagination.

The chiliastic hope which characterized both Christian and Jewish apocalypticism spread with a particular sense of urgency in the late sixteenth and early seventeenth centuries. Contrary to the impression given by some recent interpreters, it was not limited to such radical religious groups as the Levellers, Anabaptists, Familialists, and Fifth Monarchy men in England.[41] The general doctrine had been an ingredient of Christianity from earliest times, and belief was fairly continuous from the Middle Ages on, as the names of Joachim of Flora, Nicholas of Cusa,[42] and Martin Luther will suggest. Paracelsus had proclaimed the early return of Christ with the fervor of a social revolutionist; Christ was to overthrow the rich and exalt the poor.[43] Bacon's *Advancement of Learning* and *New Atlantis* reflect the Puritan teaching concerning it, as does Hobbes's discussion of the limits of the secular commonwealth, and his distinction between the Commonwealth of Grace and the Kingdom of God, discussed above.[44] In the middle of the century, Henry More undertook to interpret the visions of the Book of Revelation for Lady Conway; he later discussed the conditions of the Second Coming at length in his *Divine Dialogues.*[45] When Isaac Newton turned from his scientific studies to theology, he devoted a book to the study of the prophecies of Daniel and Revelations.[46] Even the learned Anglican bishop Thomas Sprat, first historian of the Royal Society, who had expressed the hope in his history that the Society's work would help to silence the fervor and excitement of eschatological agitation (stimulated by the Great Plague and the Fire of London) urging, as did Newton and other moderates, that "no man can know the time of his Coming," nevertheless also found in that same Society a ground for hope that one sign, at least, of the Second Coming would soon be achieved: "We may well ghess that the absolute perfection of the true Philosophy is not now far off."[47]

More significant for our understanding of the impact of millenarianism, however, are the predictions of those who, scanning the signs of the times and checking them with scriptural prophecies, proclaimed the imminence of Christ's return and judgment. These proclamations differed from many earlier ones in their Pelagian impact—people were urged to activities which should more quickly bring about the Biblical signs, so that Christ's return might thus be hastened. There was a paradox in the optimism and spirit of activism with which the end was proclaimed, which must be explained by the fact that those who proclaimed the early return of the Lord were also those who had the assurance that they would reign with him as saints for a thousand years. Many of the signs had already been abundantly witnessed: the riding of the four horsemen spreading war, famine, pestilence, and death; the Great Fire of London; other signs and portents such as the comets of 1664, 1665, and 1680; and the finding of fish in the North Sea with markings prophetic of the Second Coming;[48] and even the apparent disintegration of nature itself. Among the social signs were political unrest, the falling away from the faith by atheists, the threat of the Moslems, and the conversion of Jews. All the more important, then, to hasten the end, which to the believer could not be fearful but a matter for rejoicing, by accelerating the predicted signs of His Coming. Thus once more, as so frequently in the history of Christianity, a predetermined and predictable event stimulated a vigorous, freely chosen, voluntaristic program to bring it about. In spite of a predestinarian theology, to believe in Christ's Coming was to strive with one's whole energy to help bring about the conditions, and so to prove oneself worthy of citizenship with the saints in His reign of a thousand years.

Thus believers were impressed both with the degeneracy of the times (millenarian convictions explain much of the literature of decay in this period) and with the promises which the age contained for a glorious future. Among the signs were the return of Elias (and sometimes Moses) to prepare His way: Joachim of Flora had considered St. Francis to be Elias, and in the sixteenth century various candidates were suggested, depending upon the particular religious loyalty involved—Luther, Loyola, and so forth. The conversion of the Jews and the heathen was a factor in the prophecies. One important precondition, of course, was the overthrow of Antichrist—either Luther or the Pope, depending upon the side taken in the religious schisms. Many on both sides hoped for this issue from the Thirty Years' War, and the Duke of the small Protestant enclave of Transylvania sent John Bisterfeld as emissary to London and Paris to encourage diplomatic action in prolonging the war until this end should have been achieved.[49]

Most significant, however, as a sign of the Coming was the prophecy, in Daniel 12:4, of the rapid increase of learning. Tommaso Campanella wrote his theocratic Utopia, The Sun State, under a strong conviction of the imminent end of the world.[50] Francis Bacon, who more than any other man inspired Europe with the urgency of activating intensive scientific cooperation to close the existing gaps in human knowledge, quoted the passage from Daniel (from the Vulgate) in the *Advancement of Learning* (1604) and repeated it (inaccurately, perhaps from memory) sixteen years later on the handsome title page of the *Nova Instauratio*, along with the fine engraving of the stately ship of learning sailing out through the pillars of Hercules to uncharted seas.[51]

The influence of the millenarian fervor in stimulating the search for truth and the effort to perfect the encyclopedic ideal can be traced clearly in England as well as on the Continent. Samuel Hartlib, one of the propagators and disseminators of the new knowledge, and a friend of most of the founding members of the Royal Society, labored under the influence of such fervent millenarians as John Henry Alsted and Amos Comenius, to construct Protestant "colleges" as "engines of faith," interpreting the Second Coming "rather in the lightsome beams of his gospel than in the burning flames of his wrath."[52] Hartlib's urgency was conveyed to many others, as for example to Robert Boyle and his sister, Lady Ranelagh, who intensified efforts to expand the gospel in foreign lands and to persuade nonbelievers at home, as well as to increase the knowledge upon which the coming Kingdom was to be used.

In his *Diatribe de mille annis apocalypticis*, which first appeared in 1627, Alsted argued from the number symbolism of the Book of Revelations and from other sources that the year 2694 must bring the thousand years of Christ's reign on earth to an end, and that therefore it must begin in 1694 or sooner. A German translation of Alsted's work by Sebastian Francke was published in 1630, and at least two English translations appeared during the Civil War years, one in 1643 by William Burton, entitled *The Beloved City or the Saints Reign on Earth a Thousand Years*.[53] In his foreword to the reader, Burton admitted that he "stands close to" Alsted's opinion though he is not dogmatic about it, and urges the value of the work for a number of ends, including "comfort and consolation to the Church of God" and a mode of solving the Jewish problem through the conversion of the Jews. To Alsted's argument Burton added the testimony of other men, based on a variety of scriptural, astronomical, and historical grounds; among them are Tycho Brahe, Andreas Osiander (the editor of Copernicus), Johannes Kepler, and the three English Puritans William Twisse, George Hakewell, and Joseph Mede.

Comenius based his *Pansophia*, upon which he labored so long (and so ineffectually)[54] upon millenarian presuppositions which he derived from the prophecies of Christopher Kotter and Nicholas Drabick. When invited by Parliament to come to England in 1641 to complete the *Pansophia* and to "overhaul the college of the nation," he formulated principles which include apocalyptic assumptions.[55] The Utopian work of Samuel Hartlib, *A Description of the Famous Kingdom of Macaria . . . in a Dialogue between a Schollar and a Traveller* (London, 1641), was less apocalyptic in undertone than was Bacon's account of Bensalem; it sought Utopia through economic reform rather than through the scientific pursuit of truth.

The zeal that "knowledge be increased" and used for the improvement of life, though evoked by the millenarian spirit, outlived that conviction itself. Thomas Burnet, whose apocalyptic account of the geological changes of the earth from a perfect beginning, through a universal flood, to its present imperfect physical and astronomical state, and thence (in the future) to a restored perfection brought about through a universal conflagration, when the Millenium is to begin, thus impelled apocalypticism toward catastrophism in nature rather than toward social and intellectual progress. Indeed, Burnet warned against confusing "a melioration of the world" with the millenarian hope.[56] Leibniz in his youth wrote notes on the Book of Revelation,[57] in which he formulated the principle that the prophecies of these men must be understood in terms of their own times, not of ours; yet no one assimilated more fully than did he, Bacon's ideal of a cooperative effort to push forward scientific knowledge and the mastery of nature. This sense of urgency was carried over into the next century, along with the scientific academies, journals, programs of research to which it gave rise, where it accompanied the hope that man was at last approaching his maturity—the "emergence (as Kant put it) of man from the immaturity for which he is himself to blame." But as this quotation itself suggests, this new freedom was accompanied in the Enlightenment with the victory of the libertine.

The eschatological compulsion is still unavoidable in every mode of thought which accepts the contingency and inconclusiveness of temporal events. The effect of the eschatology of the seventeenth century, however, was to eliminate the idea of perfection as a metaphysical force within history but to stimulate Utopianism as an ideal to be aimed at as an end; the result was, therefore, that it was transformed into the modern conception of progress, with its own complex mixture of inevitability and moral responsibility. This very mixture, in the ideal of progress, of Calvinistic determinism and Semi-Pelagian voluntarism attests its theological origin in the eschatology of the Covenant theology. The concept of progress was thus an expression of the imperfect effort to absolutize the moral and human achievements of an age in time. The modern dynamic theory of history was freed from theology and theological absolutes, and turned over to libertine reason.

Practical Efforts for Reunion
in the Kingdom of Grace

It was compatible with the dynamic, projecting nature of the century that, beyond the discussion of the ideal of a kingdom of grace and the principles upon which it was made to rest, great practical efforts should be made to apply these ideals by bringing the divided churches back together. In contrast to attempts of reunification in the twentieth century, which are based directly on issues of church organization and cooperative programs of action, the plans for union in the seventeenth century were made on the basis of assent to the common intellectual articles of faith and reason.

In spite of the bitterness of the schisms between Rome and the Protestant churches, and within each separately, there were many issues about which all were agreed. Though the Council of Trent failed (through the recalcitrance of human nature) to facilitate a return to the Church, and its conclusions were in many ways further divisive, even within the Roman church itself, it also served to clarify the theological issues involved in the break and to develop some grounds for assent. The metaphysical, political, and ethical works of the Jesuits and Dominicans which reflected the new spirit of inquiry were used in Protestant as well as Catholic centers of learning and their ethical casuistry was appropriated directly by Reformed moralists in the Netherlands, England, and the German states. Suarez's *Metaphysical Disputations* and Juan Azor's *Moral Institutes* were the outstanding examples of such synthesizing and harmonizing works which provided a common ground of discussion. Azor's casuistic ethics was appropriated directly by William Ames and by John Henry Alsted in his *Encyclopaedia.*

But though agreement was fairly easy on these highest levels of thought, certain articles of faith and of church order caused greater difficulties. It was in this field, and the theological commitments which they entailed, that the chief efforts toward the healing of the schisms were aimed. Most prominent were the issues of Church authority as between sacred Scripture and the postapostolic tradition, and between pope and councils. The nature of the Eucharist, the nature of sin and penitence, and the relation of the divine providence and grace to human freedom were also serious theological problems at stake.

Efforts toward peace in the Church were intensified by the seemingly endless destructiveness of the Thirty Years' War, and were first effective where that destructiveness had been greatest.[58] The efforts of Hugo Grotius to find a theological basis for unity drew abuse from all sides. The record of John Dury's extensive travels and discussions has been preserved through his close association with Samuel Hartlib and other religious thinkers in England as well as the memories of his visits to Amsterdam, Hamburg, Mainz, the Swedish court, and his associations with Comenius and other innovators.[59] Partly through his influence, the theologians of Lutheran Helmstedt, the university of the Guelph princes of Brunswick-Wolfenbüttel-Hanover, developed a mediating position of considerable influence, not only at these courts, at which Leibniz later spent forty years, but in cities and at courts where the students of the founder of the mediating theology, George Calixtus, were active.[60] Among his students who labored for reunion were the Baron von Boineburg, who returned to the Catholic Church, Count Ernest of Hesse Rheinfels, another convert to Rome who later mediated the correspondence between Leibniz and Antoine Arnauld and other prominent French Catholics, Gerard Molanus, Abbot of the Lutheran convent at Loccum, who supported Leibniz in his discussions, and Herman Conring, brilliant jurist, historian of the Empire, universal savant, and anti-Cartesian at Helmstedt, in correspondence with whom Leibniz formulated his first mature theories of method. Much of the correspondence between Conring and his erstwhile pupil Boineburg in the 1650's was published from the Hanover archives by Johann Gruber.[61] In this very interesting correspondence Boineburg sought to win Conring to the Catholic side, while the latter strove to draw his old pupil back "to the altars" which he had deserted. In the long political and military struggles between the declining Empire and the rising power of France, Conring supported the Empire while Boineburg, along with the court at Mainz, favored France. In 1656 the two engaged in a discussion of the prevalence of atheism, the Protestant Conring finding it to predominate in Italy, while the Catholic Boineburg considered it strongest in England, Holland, and "even our Germany." Finally, in a letter of November 14, 1660, Conring stated the terms, in eighteen propositions on which he considered union possible; they were obviously unacceptable to the Roman church.

Thus by mid-century there were certain centers at which the possibility of church unity was being discussed—among them the liberal court at Mainz, where Leibniz was captivated by the idea and formulated his first plan for enlisting men of honnêteté for engaging in carrying it out, and Hanover, where he met and discussed his ideas with the papal legates, the newly converted Swedish biologist Nicolaus Steno and Ambrozio di Spinola. The long efforts of Leibniz to put his plan into operation and his long correspondence with both Catholic and Protestant leaders have been extensively discussed;[62] like his other great projects, this too remained unsuccessful.

Meanwhile, the Roman church had in part reversed the old principle of *cuius regio, eius religio*, reaffirmed by treaties ending the long war, by its vigorous effort, through legates to the various courts, to bring back to the fold the rulers of the Protestant states.

Conclusion

In the seventeenth century, Christian thought, facing divided authority in the face of individual nonconformity and disbelief, in the face of the new learning and interest in nature and the self-sufficiency of the order of nature, and in the face of the recognition of other religions, saw itself as having primarily an apologetic task. In this task it continued its appropriation of the humanistic tradition, which it interpreted as primarily an intellectual and rational one resting upon the doctrine of the universal natural light. It succeeded in enlarging the scope of humanism into an ideal of universal harmony which included many individual variations and differences, and understood this increasingly in an empirical, immanentist sense.

In reaction to the individualistic and manneristic forms of dissent, Christian apologetics took the form of a metaphysics of the infinite, striving toward a more inclusive, intuited, but less clearly conceived unity, within which the variety and plurality of Scripture, nature, and history were interpreted symbolically. The eschatological vision itself provided a world view in which the relativity of changing things was accepted and an effort was made to correct it.

4 The New Science:
Its Intellectual Foundations
and Humanistic Claims

Pondere, mensura, numero Deus omnia facit.

[Vulgate, Ecclesiasticus 11:21.]

There are two books from whence I collect my Divinity; beside that written one of God, another of his servant Nature, that universal and publick manuscript, that lies expansed into the eyes of all; those that never saw him in the one, have discover'd him in the other.

[Sir Thomas Browne, *Religio Medici.*]

The world is an epistle written by God to mankind (as I believe Plato has said); he could have added, written in mathematical characters.

[Robert Boyle, *The Excellency of Theology* (London, 1674), pp. 36-37.]

The New Cultural Grounds for Science

Essential to the development of the sciences in the seventeenth century and to a definition of their method was the close combination of an empirical interest in nature with the pursuit of mathematics. Both of these were stimulated by the revival of classical learning—the one through renewed interest in the problems raised in Aristotle's physical writings, the other from the restudy of the Greek mathematicians. A third factor, the importance of which has more recently been recognized, was the steady advance, through the late Middle Ages and Renaissance, of technological achievements in mining and mineralogy, agriculture, alchemy, medicine, and applied mechanics. With these three factors, the material conditions for the success of the physical sciences were given.

A more general question, however, concerns the wider cultural patterns which permitted the new sciences to develop in relative harmony and agreement (excepting a few instances of Inquisitorial interference by narrow ecclesiastical powers)[1] with the religious interest in reform and reunion, and with the humanistic ideal of freedom and creativity in the arts. To understand this unity, one must consider the pattern of beliefs and attitudes which emerged from the great social transformation in the late Middle Ages and Renaissance, from a feudal, agrarian, peasant culture in which men depended upon the magic of occult forces in nature and in human life to an urban culture in which power was expressed socially in civic, eventually state, authority, and social life was regulated by guilds, which encouraged the ideal of craftsmanship, and other customary orders which freed the individual to achieve socially approved ends.

The ideal of an overarching, transcendental unity of the three cultural determinants—religion, the arts and letters, and the concern for an understanding of nature based on experience—was an eventual result of this great cultural shift. The revival of Christian Platonism provided the conceptual frame for this new unity, and the conviction of Telesio, Campanella, and others at the turn of the century, that revelation, reason, and experience all converge upon the same truth, was the faith which closed the old Ockhamist breaches between knowledge and belief and provided a common bond, wider than each special interest, for the kingdom of grace, the Republic of Letters, and the sodality of those who searched out the secrets of nature—alchemists, physicians, engineers, physicists, astrologers—in fact, the *virtuosi* and *curiosi* in all fields. The model of creativity, moreover, as Will-Erich Peuckert suggested, which united the three areas was the figure of the workshop.[2]

God, the *opifex mundi*, was once again seen as Plato saw him, the potter at the wheel, but his greatness was enhanced by the newly discovered magnitude and orderliness of his creation—even though the manner of his work seemed less that of aesthetic intuition than of mathematical calculation. Man, the artist and poet, created in God's image and reflecting his glory, became less the servant of faith and more the craftsman, each man a microcosm giving forth its unique reflection of the macrocosm. And finally, the *laboratorium* with its new instruments and techniques for wrestling with nature for her secrets emerged as the ideal seat of knowledge and power. It is noteworthy that these focal concerns of man, so closely related at their modern inception, have by the end of the twentieth century drawn so far apart that their "alienation" from each other and from our social life is a conspicuous mark of our chaos.

The purpose of this chapter is to explore certain aspects of this bond which tied science, in the century of its first greatness, to religion on the one hand, and to the arts and letters on the other, and then to point out some of the internal factors which were already operative to bring about their separation.[3]

Some greatly oversimplified explanations commonly held about the emergence of modern science have been corrected by the scholarship of recent decades. To explain it as the mind freeing itself from the authority of Aristotle is doubly misleading, for even if it were true, such freedom would be purely negative, whereas the new science rested upon positive commitments about goal and method. But it has been well shown by Pierre Duhem, Anneliese Maier, Herbert Butterfield, John Herman Randall and others, that these issues of aim and method were first raised by the Aristotelians themselves, of Ockhamist and so-called Averroistic inclinations, as early as the late fourteenth and the fifteenth centuries. Aristotle was himself, after all, a proponent of empiricism and of a theory of how mathematical knowledge is related to experience—the two important axes of the new scientific position. Certainly the reactions of humanists, among them the left-wing Aristotelians, against the Scholastic distortions of Aristotle were a factor in the rise of exact sciences, as was also a purging of Platonism, both of its rhetorical versions by Plutarch and Cicero and later by Nizolius and Peter Ramus, and of its animistic, Cabalistic, theosophical tendency to multiply souls and other occult explanations. These corrections within the humanist traditions all provided for the emergence of a theory of objective, mathematical harmony of meaning, immanent in the world and available to our observation.

With respect to the dependence of the new science upon the Christian tradition, the effect of the millenial hope in making urgent the effort of believers, operating collectively, to exhaust the possibilities of human knowledge, has been discussed in Chapter 3. More deeply rooted than this, however, were two Christian convictions of long standing: the idea that Christian devotion involves the intellectual life (the *Logos* concept) and the idea that Creation is an act of divine revelation. These convictions were carried into the seventeenth century in two forms: the view that science is a glorification of God, and conversely, the interpretation of nature as a second book of divine revelation.

The Glorification of God and the Book of Nature

Plato's teaching, in the *Republic* (Book VII), that each mathematical discipline included in the education of the rulers of the state serves a twofold function—a baser one of serving military and civil ends, and a nobler one of leading the soul further on the way from mere opinion to the Ideal of the Good—was widely repeated, in Christianized form, by the founders of modern science. It is found in Nicholas of Cusa and in his modern interpreter, Giordano Bruno. Before the practical consideration of Francis Bacon that *scientia est potentia*, came his argument that it serves the glory of God; both the *Advancement of Learning* and *The New Atlantis* of Bacon contain frequent reaffirmations of this;[4] Galileo made the point in his letter to the Grand Duchess Cristina.[5] Robert Boyle frequently cited Galen as urging that the study of nature is "a hymn to the Creator," and Leibniz appropriated this figure from Boyle, distinguishing the practical uses of science from its higher purpose—the glorification of God. "The greatest usefulness of theoretical natural science, which deals with the causes and purposes of things, is for the perfection of the mind and the worship of God . . . What more beautiful hymn can we sing to (God the author of the universe) than one in which the witness of things themselves expresses his praise?"[6]

Essential to this higher divine vocation for the new study of nature was the very old doctrine that nature is a second Book of Revelation, derivative, as is the historical revelation, from the eternal Logos, not as complete for the purpose of redemption as is the New Testament, but more universal in its persuasive force impelling a rational acceptance of the existence and the perfection of God. Whether contained in Plato (as Boyle thought) or not, the metaphor of the book of nature requires a symbolic reference from the order of sensible things to the spiritual reality which they represent. The figure was continued in the Latin tradition and thus transmitted to the Middle Ages and Renaissance, as E. R. Curtius has shown.[7] The two books of the divine revelation were held to supplement each other perfectly—the *liber scripturae*, available to faith, and the *liber naturae*, available to reason based on sense but capable of revealing the spiritual significance of the sensible order.

The figure is thus suggestive of many epistemological problems—the relation between what is immediately given and what is indirectly known through it; the nature of the forms which symbolic reference from *representans* to *representatum* can take; a reasonable criterion for divine revelation. Plato and Aristotle and their medieval commentators provided the categories with which these relations were examined—causality, purpose, activity and passivity, potentiality and actuality, and later and most difficult, the relation of finite to infinite. But in the course of modern thought, the metaphysical reference of this relationship was shifted from the Platonic distinction between changeless reality and changing appearance, through the Aristotelian realism of particulars, to the Christian distinction between Creator and a created world, and then back, by way of a modern renewal of Augustine's subjectivism (in Leibniz, Kant, and their followers), to the restored notion of a phenomenal as related to an intelligible order.

At first it seemed easy, through the use of prophecy and parable, aided by the Platonic tradition, to read the spiritual significance directly in the "book" of natural events. The immanent teleology which the Greeks found within nature readily seemed to justify the goodness of God, the purposiveness of his creative order, and his righteous love in determining man's destiny. In the medieval use of the figure of the book of nature, for instance in Alan of Lisle and Hugo of St. Victor, the Idea of the Good was readily transposed by reflection (that is, mirroring) upon the images of sense. Even in the early seventeenth century, the book of nature was so understood; Sir Thomas Browne could still call it "that universal and publick manuscript, that lies expans'd unto the eyes of all." This was true also of Galileo's use of the metaphor in his letter to the Grand Duchess (although it needs to be remembered that in the tradition in which Galileo was trained, the clarity and adequacy of the book of nature had been rediscovered in the conviction that it was, as he put it, written in mathematical characters and therefore clearly legible only to those schooled in that language).[8]

Indeed, as late as Amos Comenius and the encyclopedic movement within which he operated, the openness and universal legibility of the book of nature was still assumed, even as men, inspired by St. Augustine's Platonic version of Christianity, were rediscovering that man's inward perception of his own nature added a depth and subtlety to God's plan for creation and redemption, which nature as presented to the senses could not hope to fathom. It is significant that in his *Prodromus Pansophiae*, in which Comenius formulated the principles upon which his never-completed encyclopedic project was to be based, he added to the two books of divine revelation a third, in which this profound Augustinian insight into the importance of man's inner experience served to deepen the older fusion of sense, reason, and revelation which Campanella and others had taught. Comenius proposed not two, but three books of divine revelation—the *liber scripturae*, the *liber naturae*, and the *liber conscientiae*—since, he said, God is revealed in Christ, in the visible creation, but also in the human spirit.[9] Descartes undertook a new metaphysical application of this old discovery of the revelatory role of man's self-consciousness as distinct from the natural objects of his awareness, and it was to complicate the reading of nature as revelation from his time on.

The Secrets of Nature

Comenius's addition of the book of man was but one indication of a much greater shift that had taken place in the Renaissance concerning the openness of nature as divine revelation. It was proving much more difficult to read the book of nature than earlier ages had found. New and bewildering characters were found in it, and man showed himself increasingly illiterate in mastering not merely its message, but even its language and style. The obscurities in the text first appeared in natural events which were obviously portentous but whose spiritual meaning could not be discerned through the classically recognized evidences of purpose. A popular Platonism was therefore forced to invent a multiplicity of conservative, regenerative, and creative powers as explanations, all of which seemed, for the intelligent, merely to accentuate the growing sense of mystery and secrecy which natural events carried with them. The book of nature gradually assumed less clarity as revelation, and more character as a message in code, a cryptogram in need of deciphering.

This growing sense of the esoteric in the book of nature was but a part of a wider feeling of mystery and hidden meaning which characterized much of Renaissance humanism. Edgar Wind has examined the use of pagan myths, not only in art but in poetry and other writings, to represent to the initiated basic Christian doctrines, particularly in the ethical field.[10] Wind refers the intellectual sources of this cult of the enigmatic to Nicholas of Cusa and the Florentine Platonists. Critical attacks were made against the new fashion by Aretino and others on the grounds of the impropriety of its secretive manner and its inconsistency with a didactic purpose. Similarly Francis Bacon criticized crypticism in the *Advancement of Learning* (II, xvii, 5; p. 163). The attempt made later in the seventeenth century to make membership in the Republic of Letters open even to tyros and the unlearned was also a reaction against this esoteric tradition.

The secrecy of nature became more convincing as its investigation advanced. That nature had secrets was itself a very old tradition; Heraclitus had said that nature loves to hide. And though Thomas Browne in 1635 could still speak of it as a "publick manuscript," not only his fellow physicians but all who were seeking answers to the questions of human value and worth involved in the observed facts which evoked them were discovering that some key was needed to reveal the sense of the "manuscript."

Modern sensitivity to the complexity and variety of experience obviously intensified this sense of its mystery. The new empiricists themselves, who never divorced sense qualities as such from the total perceptual situation, recognized this persistent evasiveness in nature. Psychologically-oriented thinkers like Vives and later materialists like Telesio agreed that while sound knowledge must be based on sense, the senses are to be treated as themselves the passive, inert aspects of the active operation of perceiving the world and thinking about it. When Francis Bacon argued that nature could be conquered by obeying her, and Campanella proclaimed the harmony of sense with reason and revelation, both were recognizing the need for a perceptual knowledge more concrete and active than mere sense data if men were to wrest from nature its secret meanings.

It was the physicians who seem first to have stripped away from the secrets of nature the false psychic and spiritualistic interpretations of popular Platonism and occultism; and it was they who limited the solution of these mysteries to perceptions and the operations "causally" related to perceptions. Thus began the modern groping for empirically confirmable causes or desirable effects. Paracelsus, for example, held "Erfahrung" to be the *"Grunt"* for all practice, and proposed an empirical pragmatism which would penetrate the *mysteria naturae*, in particular, the hidden conditions sustaining or destroying life and health.[11] This was true also of the great medical opponent of Paracelsus, Jean Fernel, whose dialogues on the hidden causes of nature[12] involved this same realistic and operational theory of experience (based on Aristotelianism) and assigned to it the task of penetrating analytically into the hidden causes of conception, birth, death, and the healing of wounds and illnesses, and then of moving by synthesis from these causes to the desired ends.[13] The medics were in fact moved further by their attempts to understand these mysteries of life, to distinguish three classes of causes—those *secundum naturam* (health itself, for instance), those *praeter naturam* (illness and its causes), and those *super naturam* (knowable only by revelation; incurred by divine infusion); thus their search for causes removed a part of nature, at least, from the immediate jurisdiction of God.

In other fields, too, experience fed the sense of mystery in nature. The awesome new star of 1572 in Cassiopeia belied Aristotle and the medieval doctrine of the fixed heavens; the comets, those irregular and portentous events in a ruled universe, impelled new chartings of the sky and enlarged models of its cycles; and few were the professors of physics who did not dispute or write on the mysterious powers of the magnet, which called for an extension of old classifications of elements, motions, and potencies.[14]

Though the recognition of this secret quality in nature arose from the failure to understand certain phenomena which did not readily fall under the explanations current at the time, the essential nature of this hiddenness lies deeper. In 1600 the force causing bodies to fall was no secret for most scholars, for they fell in accordance with Aristotle's definition of nature as an internal power of motion or rest. But in a few decades, Galileo had shown the mystery by refuting Aristotle's opinion (as had other critics before him), and had then proceeded by refined tools of observation and analysis to unravel the relations contained in this mystery by using an operational mode of thought, based on the principle that acceleration must be constant. By the end of the same century, Aristotle's definition had thus been rejected as mere verbalism, a precise quantitative relation between rate of fall and time was established, and a generalized mathematical "law of gravity" had been adduced to explain the motions of all systems of two moving bodies. But the mystery remained. There was still something unexplained which led Newton himself to refer the explanation of the motion to a power beyond the law itself in his reply to the charge of the Cartesians that his theory of gravity was a return to Girolamo Frascatoro's old theory of sympathism. The scientific solution remained entangled in issues about the nature of force and motion, and the validity and locus of the concept of cause.

There were old mysteries besides those connected with local motion, however: the terrible flash of lightning, the mysterious processes of crystallization and the properties of crystals (intensified in the seventeenth century by Huygens's discovery of the polarization of light through Iceland spar), the supposed mysterious properties of gems, the nature of life, and in general the persistent old question of how simpler entities in composition acquire new qualities and powers. Surprising new mysteries were now added—properties such as the light-bearing powers of phosphorus or (as Boyle named it) lucifer, other new chemicals with strange powers, the existence of microorganisms revealed by the microscope, and the rings of Saturn revealed by the telescope, sympathetic vibrations and overtones in music, the increase of mass in a process of combustion, the expansion of mathematical processes, the measurement of rates of change of physical processes, and many others, so that the range of meaningful experience was enormously increased, far beyond the available rational explanations.

The recognition of the subtlety of nature, as shown in the mystery of so many of its manifestations, led to a revival in revised form of the old issue of the relation of nature to art, a distinction at least as old as Aristotle. To Jerome Cardan's challenging thesis that the so-called subtlety of nature is inferior to the subtlety of human art since nature is one, and its subtlety is due to the mind of its creator, and all subtlety originates in mind, Julius Caesar Scaliger replied that although there is a subtlety in art which is due to the *ingenium* of the artist, there is a greater subtlety in nature which renders the scientist unable to discover the proximate causes of things.[15] Nature is like a prestidigitator, the quickness of whose motions causes us to see appearances which conceal the underlying, far more subtle reality. Nature's secrets thus rest upon the intricacy of her arrangements as well as on the inadequacy of method and technique on the part of those who pry into them.

The concern about the hiddenness of nature thus gave a strong impetus to the new scientific effort to discover her secrets, for it suggested anew the importance of distinguishing between nature as it appears to the senses and to precritical intelligence, and the far more subtle nature-as-it-really-is. Then it went a step further by suggesting that this difference, which is nominally one between *apparent* causes and *real* causes, is really one between *remote* and *proximate* causes. This latter distinction was not merely important in shifting the application of the

Aristotelian causes in physics from the perceptual objects of common sense to the micro-objects of conceptual analysis; it was also important in preparing for the modern shift from a causal theory to the new mathematical explanation which is satisfied with a functional account of the observed quantitative dependence between variable qualities and relations in natural events. The change undergone by the principle of causality in the rise of science will be discussed from another perspective in Chapter 9 on "What Is Nature?"

Arguments concerning the relation between nature and art continued through the seventeenth century, when they became an essential aspect of the teleological argument for the existence of a Creator. By Leibniz, for example, two distinct views were offered. In his defense of the new scientific mechanism against the skepticism of Pierre Bayle and others, for example, he defended the infinite subtlety of nature as an ideal beyond human comprehension, yet serving as directive for human craftsmanship. Men, for example, can create a mechanical man with built-in feed-backs and telic servomechanisms which simulate life. On the other hand, when it comes to man himself and his moral perfection, Leibniz held that "art can give us powers which nature has denied us . . . (for) art reunifies and renders useful, powers which nature has scattered and misdirected."[16] The subtlety of nature is evidence for the infinite intelligence of God and a regulative ideal for the art or *techné* of man, but it is always inadequate for the perfection of man. Only in the eighteenth century, with the victory of the nominalist and libertine, is the entire question of subtlety reduced to the limitations of human intelligence, and the issue of nature versus art thus vacated.

Mathematical Explanation and the Problem
of the Origin of Forms

The development of a disciplined empirical method for deciphering the secrets of the book of nature required, as I have already suggested, the rejection, as misleading and irrelevant, of a naive Platonic tradition of explanation in terms of souls or other magical powers. This rejection included the logically defendable "substantial forms" of the Scholastics. Dark though it was, Aristotle's definition of nature (as opposed to art), as "that which is the ground of motion and rest, in that in which these states inhere by principle and not merely derivatively"[17] had provided an approved foundation, not merely for orthodox Aristotelian physics, but for a vast multiplication of Neoplatonic souls or animate principles which were invoked to explain natural events. The aim of Pico della Mirandola and others to synthesize Plato and Aristotle encouraged a fusion of Aristotle's internal source of motion with the Platonic world soul and the lesser souls derivative from it; common to both was a theory of animation as the basis of natural (as opposed to violent) motion and a causality efficient in the production of a varied array of natural effects. Some of the resulting theories were monistic, others were pluralistic. Included were theories of the World Soul, angelic spirits, Paracelsus's Archaeus and his hypostatic principles, Scaliger's plastic powers and seeds, the sympathetic and antipathetic forces of Frascatoro and his followers, More's "spissitude," and a rapidly multiplying host of lesser seeds, viruncules, cabalos, and similar occult powers—a new power often being specified for every new mystery. An extreme instance was Kenelm Digby's notorious "sympathetic powder," which healed wounds when applied to the weapons which had inflicted them.[18]

The investigation of nature had obviously to be purged of this easy resort to explanations which did not explain, before a more sober approach to scientific explanation could be made. This more sober approach was compounded of three distinct traditions—a nominalistic, empirical spirit of economy of explanation arising in the Ockhamists' interpretation of Aristotle; the revival of atomism with its effort to explain qualities in terms of quantities; and a purified Platonism and Pythagoreanism which found the explanation of things to lie in numbers and their relations.

1. It was no doubt a nominalistic spirit which uncovered these various internal animistic powers for what they were— appeals to ignorance, mere verbalized redundancies, interpretations of the unknown through the more unknown, and so forth. So rapid a multiplication of forces rested entirely upon the idols of human nature, and the exposure of these idols by Francis Bacon was but one of many exorcisms which eventually swept aside this entire mode of thought.[19]

Yet the trend was more than a mere error. It was an essentially imaginative anticedent of the dynamic conception of force which developed in seventeenth century science. Ernst Cassirer was right, long ago, in remarking that "the preparation and leverage for the modern reformation of the concept of nature" is to be found in a "basic conception of dynamism" (*dynamische Grundauffassung*).[20] But before this dynamism could become scientifically fruitful, the unempirical and speculative multiplication of invented spiritual powers to correspond to all newly isolated and not previously explained natural events had to be subjected to Ockham's razor, which served to eliminate such ad hoc animistic assumptions in the interest of logical generalization and mathematical reduction.

To this task Bacon, the atomists, the astronomical studies of Copernicus, Kepler, and Galileo, and Descartes, Boyle, Huygens, Newton, and Leibniz all contributed. But without the earlier logical and conceptual analyses of sober thinkers like Zabarella, who restricted method to simple, empirically available causal relations, the possibility of referring all motions (in the inclusive Aristotelian sense of *kinesis*) to a quantitatively definable force (*vis*) contained in all bodies and arising from their organization, could not have developed.

The thinkers in this new tradition agreed in rejecting the Scholastic doctrine of substantial forms as principles of *scientific* explanation. Robert Boyle's only clear thesis in his *Origine of Formes and Qualities* (1666) is his argument that such forms are sterile and therefore irrelevant to useful knowledge, an argument which he and others learned from Francis Bacon, and which Leibniz repeated after him.[21] Bacon, however, retained the Platonic forms in metaphysics (in contrast to physics) and his exposition of the role of the forms, though confused, suggests what had already become explicit in Kepler and Galileo— the notion of universal laws of nature by which (as Bacon says) "knowledge may abridge the infinity of individual experience."[22] Bacon's unclear insight at this point was no doubt one of the factors which led Leibniz, many decades later, to propose the restoration of substantial forms to metaphysics, after they had been replaced in science by merely descriptive laws.

2. The effort to quantify the order of nature, and in particular, to reduce qualities to quantitative relations, had its origins in the human tendency to count and to measure. This tendency was common, though with different ontological presuppositions, to both the new atomism and the new revival of a mathematically disciplined Pythagoreanism. Both were supported in this metaphysical turn to mathematics, however, by an old passage in Scripture which had become a widespread folk saying in the Middle Ages. Ecclesiasticus 11:21 had expressed the classical ideal of balance and moderation in the conduct of life, and

had justified it by quantifying creation: "God makes all things by weight, measure, and number."

This bit of Pythagoreanism from the Apocrypha had been cited by church fathers, Scholastics, and thinkers of the Renaissance. How widespread and proverbial it had become is shown in Lady Jane Gray's account of her childhood:

> When I am in the presence of either father or mother, whether I speak, keep silence, sit, stand, or go, eat, drink, be merry or sad, be sewing, playing, dancing, or doing anything else, I must do it, as it were, in such weight, measure, and number, even as perfectly as God made the world, or else I am so sharply taunted, so cruelly threatened, yea presently sometimes with pinches, ups, and bobs, and other ways which I will not name them, so without measure misordered that I think myself in Hell.[23]

It is true that Lady Jane's lament for her girlhood still reflects a hierarchical order of measurement, with a Heaven of order at the top and a Hell of disorder at the bottom, and with woman occupying a place in the middle somewhat lower than her mate and master, man. As Sir Thomas Browne put it more succinctly much later, "The whole world was made for man, but the twelfth part of man for woman. Man is the whole world and the breath of God; woman the rib and crooked piece of man." (*Religio Medici*, 99.) This hierarchical universe was now in collapse, yet the old text of Ecclesiastes still demanded an objective order and measure for the world. It furthered the operation of measurement in the practical arts and technology, and if Lady Jane's experience was at all common, it imposed a norm for human action and character. Nicholas of Cusa had used it as a theme in his third book for the Layman (*Idiota*), which had to do with experiments with the balance and weights. In the seventeenth century both Kepler and Galileo used it in justifying their labors before the court of religious authority. Later in the century Leibniz in his system sought to fulfill its metaphysical promise; on the margin of a short dialogue on the problem of knowledge he wrote, "When God calculates and exercises his thought, the world is made."[24]

"Weight, measure, and number" are hardly independent variables, however, and with the revival of the ancient atomists, a triad of measurables was introduced which seemed more plausible in the explanation of physical events; Gassendi, in particular, was influential in the wide acceptance which these received. They were magnitude, figure, and motion (or size, shape, and motion). The atomistic or "corpuscular" philosophy regarded these as adequate primitives for the mathematical reduction of all physical properties and events. They seemed to Robert Boyle sufficient for his theoretical speculations about the new science, although he did little to bridge the gap between such speculation and his own experimental efforts.[25] And in Leibniz's early attempt to reconcile Aristotle with "the moderns," that is, with the corpuscular philosophers, in his letter to his teacher, Jacob Thomasius, in 1669, he undertook to show that Aristotle's effort to explain things in terms of matter, form, and change could be reduced to the modern triad of magnitude, figure, and motion.[26]

The difficulties in this atomistic theory of measurables proved to be many. For the three concepts turned out to be neither simple (since they permit further reduction to space, time, size, continuity, relation, mass, and so forth) nor adequate to probe such basic physical qualities as hardness, elasticity, ductility, and cohesion. One difficulty in particular, recognized by the earlier atomists and one which was becoming a prominent issue by the seventeenth century, is worth discussing. This is the question of the origin out of these merely quantitative properties, of qualities and forms. If atoms differ only in size, shape, and motion, whence come the qualities and powers of the composite bodies arising from this combination—the sensory qualities, first of all, then sensibility or irritability itself, life, consciousness, and mind?

The general problem of the origin of forms and qualities was as old as materialism itself, but had become acute in the Ockhamistic physicists of the Renaissance.[27] The question "Where do the qualities come from?"—when atoms which differ only quantitatively, collectively acquire new qualities, and lose qualities which they previously had in other combinations—became urgent because of the scientific principle that such qualities, like all other events in nature, must have a cause sufficient to explain them. The ready solution of Galileo and Descartes, who stripped the physical order of all qualities not reducible to quantitative measure and relegated to them to a subjective realm, did not help to resolve the real issue, which, as Boyle pointed out, has to do with the real new qualities and forms, not with subjective effects. But in his own classical treatment of the problem Boyle himself could give only a vague answer by speculating about the "textures" which a large numbers of atoms, acting in concert, form, and which support new qualities.[28] What he said was obviously unsupported by empirical evidence, and led Locke directly to the denial that we can know the real (as opposed to the nominal) essences of bodies. But this was the road to positivism or Berkeleyan idealism—a nullification of the realistic temper of seventeenth century science.

The theological issue of the origin of the soul was a special case of the problem of the origin of forms, which was particularly acute as a result of the theological altercations of the sixteenth century. Atomists like Gassendi avoided this problem by exempting the human soul from their theory. But the principle of sufficient reason demanded a cause either in natural events or in God. Granted that the soul is the form of the body, or even, with the Scotists, something itself possessed of form and matter, and qualitatively distinct from the body—whence comes it? From God by creative act, or from the parents by traduction?

The issue between creationists and traducianists was not merely a theological and a moral one involving the problem of original sin and its origin. It is also a psychological and social one, which continues the endless arguments about the role of God in creation, about the relative strength of heredity and environmental influence, of innate determinism and self-adaptation to the world. Philosophical disputations at the turn of the century abound in theses on the question—Reformed theologians usually urging traducianism to explain original sin; more liberal theologians, impressed by the Godlike powers of man, stressing creationism. In 1590 Rudolph Goclenius, the compiler of a widely used philosophical dictionary, collected the arguments of many men, pro and con, on this "spinosam et scrupulosam questionem" under a new title, *Psychologia*.[29] John Sperling, pupil of the early atomist Daniel Sennert and a quarrelsome "modern" influenced by Zabarella and Keckermann, wrote a defense of traducianism entitled *Antiparasceve pro Traduce* (1648) in which he reasoned that creationism is impossible because, by the principle of sufficient reason, soul can be derived only from soul, as body only from body. This position, an application of a general scientific principle that qualities and forms must naturally be educed from previous ones, was presupposed in the genetic theory of preformation, which Leibniz held in a more sophisticated form, and which remained the prevailing theory of genetics until Darwin.

3. The new ideal of physical knowledge thus demanded a basis in experience rather than tradition, and an exactness which implied counting and measurement. But the problem of developing mathematical tools adequate for determining "laws" or rules (*regulae*) adequate to explain and control the empirical facts still remained. It is remarkable that these were developing almost simultaneously with the ideals of empirical economy and of precision. Johannes Kepler, who could not accept a deviation of eight minutes of arc between theory and observation, may well be considered as the thinker who established scientific exactitude as the condition for truth.[30] But it was in the revival of Greek mathematics, both in its Platonic direction toward astronomy and pure forms, and in its Aristotelian direction toward the abstraction of quantity from experience, that the remarkable union of empiricism with mathematics which characterizes modern physical science must be sought. The works of Archimedes and of the Alexandrian mathematicians provided the tools which made possible the great developments in the sixteenth and seventeenth century applications of mathematics to science.

The rapid succession of mathematical discoveries by which these tools were perfected can only be suggested here. From the study of the ancients there developed four successive advances:

(1) Primarily through the efforts of Italians like Cardan and Franciscus Vieta, arithmetic was generalized into algebra, the "specious analysis" of the seventeenth century, and with it a new method arose of solving problems by formulating them in equations in which the value of the unknown could be discovered from its determining conditions through axiomatic mathematical operations. The equation was a generalization from Archimedes's balance.

(2) Descartes (anticipated by the efforts of others) succeeded in working out a point-by-point correlation between mathematical equations and the relations of geometry, and this correlation between mathematical and spatial relations provided analytic exactness to the previously intuitive study of space. (The idea of portraying the relationship between two variables through a graph, which was a necessary presupposition of Descartes's achievement, was as old as the late Ockhamist Nicholas of Oresme, who died in 1382).[31]

(3) The theory of equations as balance between two sets of conditions of a problem was in a few decades developed into a general theory of functions and the conception of a functional

(in contrast with a simple causal) natural law. The prototypes of functional laws of planetary motion were at hand early in the century in Kepler's laws of planetary motion and were much more clearly demonstrated in Galileo's law of falling bodies. But the theory of functions required an extension of Euclid's analysis of ratios and proportions (in the *Elements*, Book VIII) through a sharper distinction between variable and constant terms in the entities symbolized in the equation, and the application of the concept of a continuum in the treatment of the variables.

(4) Finally, this new mathematical tool had to be generalized beyond its correlation both with space (through conic sections by Descartes and Pascal), and with simple accelerated motion (in Galileo), to cover higher, transcendental mathematical relations, and to serve in determining mathematically definable rates and momentary states of change, as well as in formulating the rules for the generation of more complex functions and calculating summations for series, areas enclosed by curves, and other composites of events and quantities. With the invention of the infinitesimal and integral calculus later in the century, this degree of development in the mathematical tools of science had been achieved. Aristotle's old problems of change, generation, and corruption had received a modern, mathematical resolution.

Nothing is more suggestive in confirming the analogy, developed in Chapter 1 of this work, between styles in the arts and the intelligible forms of culture in the seventeenth century than this extension of the mathematical tools of science to the dimensions of the dynamic and changing, to the totality of aggregates, and to the possible infinite series within actual finites. The extension of mathematical analysis and synthesis to make possible the solution of problems of motion, acceleration, and growth; the formulation of summary laws of infinite series; and the understanding of new dimensions, not merely of space but of force, correspond remarkably with the expansion of art forms, spurred on by mannerist deviations, from the classical into the ampler, less clearly bounded, dynamic forms of the baroque. But the new mathematical devices also provided new and convincing theoretical support for a Neoplatonic metaphysics, now enlarged in its cosmology and theology by Bruno and the later metaphysicians of the century. And this metaphysics, in turn, aimed at supplying a theoretical support for both the enlarged scientific insights and the enlarged aesthetic visions of the time.

This mathematical achievement also strengthened a recognition of the importance of a priori principles in scientific knowledge. Whatever may be the philosophical interpretation of scientific method and its results—whether realistic or positivistic, whether Platonic, conceptualistic, or nominalistic—it must be admitted that ever since Francis Bacon saw (however unclearly and indistinctly) that the middle axioms sought in nature implied the adjustment of raw empirical data to a priori forms, and ever since Kepler and Galileo, understanding these forms as mathematical, made their great discoveries of the first functional laws, it was clear that the method of science consists not merely (1) of induction from observed uniformities in nature, but also (2) of a conceptual analysis of these observations in terms of preconceived principles which impose order upon them a priori (including the functional orders between constants and variables which can be formulated mathematically, and further, (3) that the conclusions arrived at in this combination of a posteriori and a priori reasoning must themselves be justified as far as possible by further observation under as great experimental control as the problem allows.

This can be shown in detail in the case of both Kepler and Galileo. Both men found it necessary to free themselves from false a priori considerations which blocked the way to discovery. To mention only two instances, Kepler had to free himself from the assumption that perfect motion is circular, and from the Platonic ideal that the solid regular figures offer a scheme for the dimensions of the solar system; Galileo had first of all to refute the Aristotelian notion that the rate at which bodies fall is a function of their weight. Studying the measurements which his master, Tycho Brahe, had made of the positions of Mars, and accepting Copernicus's heliocentric theory as a priori sound, Kepler, after many false attempts, was driven to the hypothesis that the motions of the planets must follow elliptical paths. This opened up a new area of priori knowledge, the properties of conic sections other than the circle and straight line, which, when he applied them to the observations of planetary motions, enabled him also to develop the famous law of areas. The three laws of planetary motion contained no reference to cause or effect (though causes and effects were still regarded, a priori, as involved), and only two of them involved measurements, which, when corrected by the new a priori of heliocentric theory, could be formulated in equations, as prescribed by Archimedes's principle. Moreover, they involved a host of further a priori assumptions, some of them well known in Kepler's day, some of them first explicated by Newton—among them an adaption of the Scholastic theory of impetus, and the principle of uniform motion (later Newton's first law). They involved presuppositions about what motion must be like (the composition and resolution of motions, and so forth) and of what scientific generalization should be like. But the final verification of the fitness of the mathematical formulations for the observed facts was pragmatic; it involved predictions of future observations based on these generalizations which could be confirmed, at the right time, by further observations.

In the case of Galileo's law of falling bodies, the a priori components were much stronger; the mathematical and physical reasoning involved in relating motion along an inclined plane and in the pendulum to the problem of a freely falling body entailed assumptions such as the principles of the composition and resolution of motions, the conservation of forces and of momentum, and many more, some of them drawn from pre-critical common sense. Galileo's deduction of the principle of constant acceleration was a case of brilliant a priori reasoning which required both common sense principles and mathematical knowledge. That he chose to develop his entire reasoning in the form of a three-cornered Platonic dialogue between a dogmatic Aristotelian traditionalist, a representative of common sense open to reason, and himself, the scientist, reveals the Platonic foundation of his teaching method but not of his analytic scientific method.

Options Inhering in Scientific Explanation

Although the success of the mathematical explanation of physical events established the usefulness of artificial languages in deciphering the secrets of nature and led to a rapid expansion of mathematical symbols and models, it served also to revive, with some urgency, several old ambiguities connected with the use of logic in attaining empirical knowledge. The decisions reached about these ambiguities mark the division between the honestas of the first scientists and the libertinage of later centuries, and the issues calling for these decisions still divide the field in the philosophy of science. Three of these have already been suggested. They are (1) the relevance of universals in relation to existence; (2) the meaning of causality and of law as applied to existence; and (3) the problem of the nature and existential reference of scientific truth. Implicit in all three is the more ultimate ambiguity between order and method (to be discussed in Chapter 7): Is objective order presupposed by method, or is order imposed by method?

1. The ambiguity about the nature of universals had been a matter of controversy between Platonists and Aristotelians for centuries. As Christian (that is, Augustinian) Platonists, both Kepler and Galileo could argue for the reality of mathematical laws as ideas or forms of creation in the mind of God; in Galileo's use of Plato's *Meno* in describing his dialectic method, he assumed an intuitive dimension in all analysis which assures that through logical rigor and the necessities of mathematical order one may penetrate more and more deeply and soundly into nature and into the mind of its creator.[32]

Yet as Ernst Cassirer pointed out in his criticism of the Cambridge Platonists, Platonism was a weak foundation for science itself because it divorces mathematical order from becoming; on this point the Aristotelian view that number and numerical relations are abstractions from experience seems to be more fruitful. "The mathematical mastery of becoming," which reached a triumphant peak in the development of the differential calculus, seems to confirm this Aristotelian position, which would limit the role of mathematics to the degree of effectiveness with which its principles provide predictability in the fields from which its elements are abstracted.

In the seventeenth century there was an accommodation of the two viewpoints, which derived indirectly from the Scotist doctrine of the univocity, ultimately the identity, of the divine attributes with the essential qualities of created things. This accommodation, which amounted to an immanence of the divine order, or at least of abstractions from it, in creation, could therefore render in fixed concepts the conditions of change and even of individuality itself. This immanence theory, which abandoned the two-world theory of older Platonism, was itself dropped in the deistic and nominalistic developments of eighteenth century thought and virtually disappeared from the philosophy of science in the more positivistic nineteenth century.

The closely related problem of the adequacy of a priori reasoning to account for scientific knowledge, on the other hand, was essentially settled in the seventeenth century itself, on the basis of a distinction between the knowledge of possibilities and knowledge of the actual. The rationalists maintained the theoretical adequacy of reason to determine possibilities, but added many qualifications about man's capacity to carry out such reasoning with regard to knowledge about facts. The fourth book of Leibniz's *Nouveaux Essais* develops a theory of scientific knowledge which supplements Locke's inclination to stop with mere empirical induction, by systematizing Kepler's and Galileo's discovery of the importance of a priori principles in giving form to our generalizations from experience. Like them, Leibniz recognized that experience achieves a higher degree of certainty and generality through this organization, but must always face the test of verification by the future confirmation of predictions based upon it. The unifying bonds between Platonism and Aristotelianism in the seventeenth century were found in a complex of principles—the immanence of forms in particulars, the completion of analysis in intuition, a conceptualistic theory of mathematical forms existing as "exemplary" or "archetypal" in the mind of God, and a dynamic theory of the potency of these forms; ideas are active or, as Leibniz put it, have an exigency to actualize themselves, and are therefore discoverable in things by scientific analysis.

2. This conceptualistic synthesis of the problem of law and other universals also showed the way to resolve the ambiguities involved in the understanding of causality in nature. The same issues of the relation of knower to known, and of eternity to time, to which the conceptualistic theory proposed an answer, also arise in considering the nature of causality.

Of these ambiguities, the first concerns the gradual emergence into preeminence of efficient causality from Aristotle's fourfold theory of causality, which still served as a basis for most discussions in the seventeenth century. This process will be discussed in Chapter 9.

A second ambiguity led to considerable confusion among rationalistic defenders of the new sciences such as Descartes and Spinoza. The predominance of geometric modes of thought kept these thinkers from distinguishing sharply between logical and causal connections, or between reasons and efficient causes. The strong modern sense of dynamism in nature implied an emphasis upon efficient causality, but the method of logical inference from sufficient reasons suggested a static panlogistic metaphysics. The argument has not yet been resolved between those who, like Hume, hold to a logical theory of scientific causality, and those who demand a real efficacy in it. But for the seventeenth century, Leibniz resolved the problem by pointing out that both Spinoza and Descartes were convinced that possibility and existence are coextensive, or in other words, that every logical possibility must exist, but that once this is seen to be false, it will also be seen that logical reasons alone can establish only possibilities, never facts, and that actuality requires some principle beyond mere logic for its determination.

A further ambivalence is that between causal and functional laws of nature. It has been shown above that the concept of mathematical functionality was seen to have values of exactness and utility in prediction superior to those of causal laws. But functional laws make no claim to discover causes; they merely *describe* the relations between variable qualities and relations abstracted from experience itself. This fact did much to encourage an upsurge of positivistic thinking about science. But as the discussion of the problem of the origin of forms and qualities has shown, an a priori principle of sufficient causality was also still essential for scientific order. Galileo, for example, retained a belief in causes, even though his own greatest discoveries consisted of merely descriptive functional laws. This is true also of Newton, who was unwilling to speculate about *why* bodies move, but offered laws only to explain *how* they move.

By the end of the century, Locke and Leibniz had offered two alternative solutions of these ambiguities, both of which point to the limitations of a scientific knowledge of reality. According to both, mathematical laws are desirable in science because of their clarity and precision in prediction, and such laws are essentially descriptive, not explanatory in any causal sense. They agreed also that there is involved in all natural order a deeper relationship of causes and effects, which mathematical laws alone do not reveal but which are needed to ensure the necessity of natural events. According to Locke, however, the *real* causes lie beyond our comprehension, concealed in the unknowable "real essences" of things, even though we do have a fairly distinct conception of power in general, derived chiefly from impressions of reflection. Leibniz, on the other hand, found real efficient causality where Locke searched for the idea of power, internal to the real individuals (the monads) and known to us through our self-awareness or internal perception. Thus all efficient causality is for Leibniz metaphysical in nature and takes the form of the actualization of possibilities within each created individual entity according to the law of its nature, while the scientific discovery of "causes" and "effects" in external nature is merely descriptive and preliminary to further analysis leading to the discovery of the mathematical relations between the variables in the problem being explored.

Both thinkers rendered the conception of efficient causality irrelevant to science itself, thus drawing a sharp line between metaphysics and science and removing from the scientific study of nature the causal relation as it had been formulated by such writers on method as Zabarella, Hobbes, and Descartes, and particularly by the atomists who had sought to reduce physical causes to motion.

3. The third ambiguity in the new method of science, the problem of the *adaequatio intellectūs ad rem* through the mathematical method, has already been touched on in the preceding section. The view suggested there, that the descriptive nature of mathematical law tended to confirm a positivistic position which limited science to things as they *appear* rather than as they *"really" are*, is supported by many considerations in the development of science and of mathematics.

Descartes, it is true, thought to exhaust knowledge of real space by his new analytic geometry; similarly the new dynamics and phoronomy were intended to exhaust knowledge of time and motion. But such mathematical notions as that of an infinite continuum were no longer applicable merely to God as in the Scholastics, nor to space as in Bruno, but to mathematical processes of analysis which were carried out within finite empirical bounds. Along with this the introduction of modal categories into metaphysics—the recognition that discrete actualities are selections from a wider range of possibilities and therefore require some further principle of selectivity—and the recognition of the a priori nature of mathematical functionality were developments which suggested a restriction of scientific understanding, not only to description instead of explanation, but to processes with numbers and relations detached from reality. And this internal ground for a positivistic view of science was aided by an adventitious historical circumstance which made it expedient for scientists to abandon their claim to know *reality* and to profess only to be "saving the phenomena."

Before discussing this further external inducement towards positivism, it may be pointed out that mathematics itself, in the early seventeenth century, was involved in the same process of purging itself from the popular Platonic conceptions of occult and unempirical powers which other more empirical scientific fields were shedding. The remarkable anticipations of modern conceptions in applied mathematics made by Aristotelian thinkers in the fourteenth century, and developed in our own century, had been forgotten,[33] and popular Platonism and Pythagoreanism still haunted the efforts to develop scientifically useful mathematical tools. This can be illustrated from an examination of the mathematics which interested Leibniz in his youth, before his contacts with the Royal Society and his reading of Buonaventura Cavalieri and Pascal. The three works which influenced him most in his early period at the culturally isolated University of Leipzig were the revived commentaries on the *Ars Magna* of Raymundus Lullus, brought out by John Henry Alsted in 1609 (from which he learned the ideal of a "combinatorial art" by which the possibilities of human knowledge could be explored through the combinations of all possible categories or primitive notions); the *Commentary on the Sphere of Joannes of Sacro Bosco* by Christopher Clavius (from which Leibniz learned the simplest rules for the calculations of combinations and permutations); and the teaching and writings of Erhard Weigel (whose phantasies about the uses of mathematics gave Leibniz the ideal of a *Mathesis Universalis* and inspired him in an attempt to apply mathematical relations to moral problems).[34]

Each in his own way, Alsted, Clavius, and Weigel might be designated as mannerists in the field of mathematics, for each sought in very individualistic ways to advance new uses and powers in mathematical reasoning, although all lacked the discipline involved in the classical mathematical tradition. In Clavius's work, for example, the theory of combinations is mixed with a large number of other remarkable mathematical interpretations—he proves that astronomical and theological considerations require a total of eleven heavenly spheres; he defends the existence of the antipodes on earth (against Augustine); he digresses on the new star of 1572 in Cassiopeia; he offers considerations on the composition of motion, and on the problem of the greatest of all isoperimetric figures, and so forth. Clavius was a fair geometer with a wide-ranging fancy. Yet the inventiveness of these men was suggestive of the more purposively free discoveries of new mathematical forms and processes by the geniuses of the seventeenth century.

The collision with ecclesiastical authority, on the other hand, which was alluded to above, operated in the reverse direction to reduce these refined new philosophical systems to the role of ideologies, and to reinforce a positivistic position in the new sciences themselves. This collision took place after the Council of Trent brought about a new rigor in the definition of religious authority. Although Copernicus himself died before this effect was felt, the publication of his work on the *Revolution of Celestial Orbs* (1543), a work whose conclusions Copernicus himself intended to be understood as having direct realistic reference, contained a preface by the theologian Andreas Osiander which suggested another interpretation. "It is not necessary [he wrote] that these hypotheses be true, or indeed, that they be even probable; this alone will suffice, that they show the calculation to be congruent with observations." This repudiation, in behalf of science, of truth in the sense of an *adaequatio ad rem* was a revival, on grounds of theological expediency, of the old theory originating with Eudoxus, that it is the function of philosophy "to save the phenomena".[35] This device was also used by Galileo in securing the approval of the Inquisition for the *Discourse on the Great World Systems;* it had been made clear that his work could be accepted as an empirically satisfying hypothesis, provided no explicit claim was made for its objective truth.

Stated thus, the scientific quest could not, it was assumed, in any way conflict with revealed truth, and the onus of a twofold truth could be lightened. To use more recent terminology, the phenomenal and functional truth of science, and the existential truth of salvation, far from entering into conflict or nullifying each other, became mutually irrelevant. The dualism of reasons which Pascal later recognized—that of the understanding and that of the heart—were no longer bound together, not even by the terror evoked in finite sinful man by the two new infinites of the sciences. What remained for ensuing centuries as a satisfactory adjustment of two orders of knowledge and truth, the phenomenal and either the noumenal or the more inwardly personal, has become in the twentieth century a radical divorce between the intellectual perspectives of two opposing cultural ideals—the scientific-technological and the existential-personal.

In Chapter 9 other evidences in the seventeenth century of the rise of a positivistic and nominalistic interpretation of science will be discussed. Although "saving the phenomena" could still be interpreted in its original Platonic sense of subsuming particular events under Platonic forms, its use to escape the realistic reference of scientific discoveries had the effect of founding science upon a basis of merely empirical verification and of generalized hypotheses without a realistic reference—a position impossible in such sciences as astronomy, geology, and biology, and one which should in the end destroy both the theoretical and the practical motives of science itself—both the drive of curiosity to know the world and the concern to apply this knowledge technically in improving the circumstances of human life.

As confirmation of this realistic claim, it may be pointed out that hypotheses were themselves considered in the seventeenth century as merely preliminary and uncertain approaches to verisimilitude, needed in the attack of certain difficult problems too complex to be analyzed categorically, but to be superseded when possible by more certain and adequate methods. Prior to his study of Locke, for example, Leibniz regarded the state of science in which hypotheses are set up and verified merely through the relevant phenomena as a preliminary and unsatisfactory one.[36] Behind this use of hypothesis there still remained the ideal of a completely derived mathematical law, based on sufficient reasons, which was the aim of distinct and adequate knowledge. It was the essence of rationalism to regard such complete reduction possible, even though rarely attained in truths of fact. The recognition that there are unavoidable degrees of uncertainty in science marked the beginning of the break toward the more empirical and indeterministic viewpoints of the future.

The Break-away of Science

In the seventeenth century the device of "saving the phenomena" did serve, along with other considerations, to develop in the sciences a sense of self-sufficiency and independence from more general metaphysical considerations. Other considerations, however, demanded some reliance upon a revised metaphysics and a more inclusive conception of knowledge. Primary among these was a realistic theory which supported a conception of truth as the gradual, never completed approach of analysis to a real order of things (the ad-*aequatio* of understanding to the "thing"). The conception of *force*, which both Leibniz and Newton found indispensable in their dynamics, required a metaphysical foundation beyond science; Keckermann had called it the *vis dei*. The problems of causality, of law, of time and space all could be justified logically only with reference to extrascientific interpretations. Thus, in various ways, the seventeenth century was able to retain a bond between science and its mother, philosophy. But a victory of

the libertine-nominalistic trend was foreshadowed in the limitations which science imposed upon its central concerns, and
positivism grew into a dominant spirit, encouraged both from
within science and from without.

The growing self-sufficiency of science was shown in several
ways.

1. It gradually found itself excluded from the Republic of
Letters, and more generally, from the humanistic tradition, with
a subsequent loss both to itself and to them. The humanities
gradually surrendered the disciplinary function of clarity and
distinctness, becoming belles-lettristic, subjective, and emotive
in their appeal, while science surrendered its close connection
with problems of value to extraneous political and economic
influences.

2. Science also affirmed its independence from the Christian
theological framework within which its modern beginnings are
to be found. This involved a diminished view of nature, as the
conception of creation was dropped, and thus encouraged what
the seventeenth century called atheism, and what in our own
age is labeled secularism. Secularism is not without great values,
and it was the fault of religious thought that, confronted by the
new sciences, it became predominately theoretical in its own
defense, neglecting the human values of both religion and
science—for example, placing too much weight upon the metaphysical arguments for the existence of God.

On the other hand, the realistic scientific tradition in which
we have been interested opened the way also to wider and more
firmly grounded realistic interpretations of a theory of natural
law and a theory of analytic meanings which are completed by a
natural intuitive light. Both of these might have served to place
human values within a context of reason and critical analysis.

3. As a result of its internal successes, science found itself
operating in ways which encouraged it to neglect its own history, and therefore its philosophical antecedents and implications. Since scientists are human, this exposed it to the sin of
self-sufficiency and intellectual pride (as its separation from the
humanities induced in them the obverse sin of pride in irrational
emotivism and historicism). Inevitably, each eventually encouraged the intuitive sense that what it was doing was all that
needed to be done.

The seventeenth century went further than any later century
in showing that the dualism of fact and value, of science and
art, which emerged could have been resolved in a unifying

harmony. For the century enlarged the classical conception of the importance of man and his experience of the world, through an emphasis upon self-knowledge as a source of insight about possible order, and upon freedom as requiring obedience to a universal order revealed by reason. Thus it enveloped the two libertine-mannerist ideals of individual self-determinism and freedom in a more inclusive ideal of reasonable order.

Part II.
Metaphysical Issues
in the Struggle

5 The Ideas:
The Old and the New Way

I reply that there is here concealed an equivocation in the word idea. For it can be taken either materially, for the operation of the understanding, in which sense it cannot be said to be more perfect than me (*quo sensu me perfectior dici nequit*); or objectively, for the thing represented through this operation, and this thing, even if it is not assumed to exist beyond the intellect, can yet be more perfect by reason of its essence.

[Descartes, *Meditations on First Philosophy*, Preface to the Reader.]

My new way of knowing by means of ideas may in the full latitude comprehend my whole *Essay*; because, treating of the understanding, which is nothing but the faculty of thinking, I could not well treat of that faculty without considering the immediate objects of the mind in thinking, which I call *ideas* . . . And this in short is my new way by ideas; which, my Lord, if it be new, is but a history of an old thing.

[John Locke, Second Letter to Stillingfleet (London, 1968), p. 72.]

As a figure is in space, so an idea is in our mind . . . Ideas are in our mind as differentials of thoughts. Ideas are in God in so far as the most perfect being consists of the conjunction of all possible perfections in one subject.

[Leibniz, *Elementa philosophiae arcanae.* Edited by Ivan Jagodinski (Kasan, 1912), p. 126.]

The idea of things in us is nothing but the fact that God, the author alike of things and of mind, has impressed this power of thinking upon the mind, so that it can by its own operations produce what corresponds perfectly to the events which follow from things.

[Leibniz, 1678 (Gerhardt, VII, p. 264.)]

117

One intellectual key to the cultural crisis of the seventeenth century may be located in its division of opinions about the nature of ideas. The order of being and value to which the *homo honestatis* was bound in obedience was an objective order of ideas or forms, in the Neoplatonic-Stoic tradition. Indeed, Leibniz sometimes described the divine mind as "the region of ideas."[1] These forms were universals often stated as laws: the laws of logic, of scientific order, of moral conduct. In the libertine ideal, on the other hand, ideas originated in the human mind out of composites of impressions, and were therefore subject to significant expansion by the human understanding, imagination, and will. This difference comprised the issue between "the old and the new way of ideas." The old was primarily metaphysical, the new primarily psychological.

This tension between old and new ways of ideas was a sharpened version of the late Scholastic disagreement between the *via antiqua* and the *via moderna*—the issue drawn between Scotists and the late Thomists on the one hand, and Ockhamists on the other. But by the late Renaissance the complexities of that earlier controversy had been reordered and simplified, and its effects upon both humanism and the early beginnings of modern science[2] had been generalized and intellectualized to serve a new reemergence of metaphysics and a growing ethical-political concern for European order. Renaissance Platonism and the renewed Aristotelianism in Italy had combined in support of the old, while the left-wing Ockhamists and the new Democritians, or atomists, provided a foundation for the new.

Julius Caesar Scaliger may be cited for the new Aristotelian view which considered ideas or forms actualized in re by a real process of eduction from the seeds inhering in matter as potencies. A vigorous defender of the notion of a world soul unifying the animate forces in nature, he urged a corresponding immanence for the ideas. In opposition to all who seek admiration for the "veils of Platonism" by placing ideas in the divine mind, and also the "recentiores" who identify ideas with "notions" (that is, concepts) as accidents in the mind, Scaliger agreed that concepts are signs of things which occur in the understanding when it knows these things through "species," but argued further that by contrast the ideas are forms present in matter, first *in potentia* as seeds, but educed *in actu* from the seeds. Using this interpretation, he made Aristotle the founder of the preformation theory of generation.[3]

At the turn of the century most thinkers held that ideas are forms inhering in things as their essential nature, and that they are also forms of the understanding (whether man's or God's) in thinking rightly about things. In Scaliger's thought another dimension was added to these ideas—their role in the generation and actualization of forms through the seeds. In the new century, God's perfections were widely considered as the originals of the ideas, and his will, the assurance that ideas will be actualized in things and minds in an orderly way, and inclusive of the true and the good.[4]

New Tasks for the Ideas

The intellectual burdens placed upon this metaphysical doctrine of ideas by the idealizing and ordering thinkers of the age increased greatly in the face of growing diversity of interests and social patterns in the seventeenth century. Ideas not only served to bring together God and creation and the knower and the known, they also provided a synthesis of fact and value, an assurance that there are good reasons for all facts, including a reason why existence is narrower than possibility. They reconciled plurality with unity, individuality and community, the real and the ideal, in areas as diverse as individual tastes, the controversies about revelation and reason, disagreements among political and religious faiths, and the relation of natural to moral laws.

One of the great teachers of modern Europe, Francisco Suarez, introduced the discussion of ideas in this enlarged context. In the twenty-fifth of his *Metaphysical Disputations*, Suarez identified ideas with exemplary forms, the "first or original forms," ascribing to them a force or power to actualize themselves in particulars. He quoted St. Augustine: "Tantum vim in ideis posuisse, ut nisi eis intellectis sapiens nemo esse posset." To deny the ideas would be to say that what God made he made irrationally; they are "the sempiternal reason by which God made the sensible world." The office of an idea or exemplar is "to determine the external action of an intellectual agent." An exemplar "is in the intellect not objectively but formally"; it is objectively in the created order.[5]

Thus the metaphysical preceptor of the new century, whose *Metaphysical Disputations* Descartes studied at LaFleche and the boy Leibniz "read as if it were a novel" (Spinoza too shows signs of his influence), assigned to ideas more explicitly the role which St. Augustine had given them. As archetypes of created things they contain the essences of things according to which the various orders of being can be established, and they are the grounds in the divine mind and in things for men's knowledge of these orders. For as Suarez says, they "are internal to mind properly *ex prima impositione*; they are external only *per accidens.*"

Suarez's Neoscholastic account, obviously influenced by the Scotistic theory of univocity (although his theory of individuation was Ockhamistic), was reinforced by a Neoplatonic strain which emphasized the degrees of clarity and adequacy which differentiated the human perception of the ideas from their original in God. The metaphysics of light and shadow which Giordano Bruno developed, and which he spread more widely in his travels through Europe than is generally recognized, involved a gradation of creatures and of ideas as growing shadows cast by the One, the Sun of the universe, into the outermost darkness of the negation of being.[6] Thus several paths lead from late Scholasticism and Renaissance Platonism to the position that ideas are the metaphysical ground of degrees of being, degrees of truth and falsehood, degrees of goodness and badness, but that they are in fact (or "materially") mental, and only derivatively and externally ("accidentally") in things as their essences. They are the measure of the order of things, which is in varying degrees mixed with finite limitedness, disorder, meaninglessness, as reason is mixed with mere feeling, action with passion.

Platonism in Descartes and Spinoza

It is with this heavy metaphysical, cognitive, and ethical burden of functions that the "old way of ideas" served the systematizers of the age. Ideas are *formally* the nature of things, *materially* components of mind or intelligence, but *objectively* principles of order in the world. The doctrine, as was noted in Chapter 4, was a fortunate one for the development of the modern physical sciences, as well as for an ethics of obedience, for it provided the ground for a conception of *laws*, both physical and moral.

There is still controversy about when and by whom the discovered orderliness of the physical world was designated as "law." Descartes seems still to have used the terms *regula* and *lex* interchangeably in this context. The inclination to interpret Platonic forms as laws is noticeable in Francis Bacon, whose contributions to the new sciences consisted almost entirely in his exhortations to the erudite of his day to pursue knowledge based on observation rather than on books and on speculation, and to pursue such knowledge collectively. But in the *Advancement of Learning*, Part Two, in his well-known revision of Aristotle's division of the philosophical disciplines, Bacon limited physics to the detection of material and efficient causes, and assigned formal and final causes to metaphysics. Though he condemned the consideration of final causes in physics, he did not explicitly discuss formal causes. The context of his discussion shows, however, that what occurred to him under this rubric was a generalization or universalization of the particular efficient and material causes observed in physics. Thus he seems to have had in mind a conception of forms as universalized "formulas" or rules of efficient and material causal connections. The Platonism of the men who first actually formulated such laws, Kepler and Galileo, is well known. A juristic frame of thought was thus implicit in early science as well as in the realm of Christian morality in the seventeenth century; God's creation and providence were conceived as jurisprudential acts.[7] The ideas are given to the natural and moral reason as laws.

Descartes has been understood by many interpreters to have initiated "the new way of ideas" by defining them as "whatsoever is the object of the mind when it thinks," and by introducing a dualistic concept of representation according to which idea re-presents object, thus breaking apart the bond of essence or form which ties the knower (if not the doer) to the world known. It is true that Descartes can be read in this way. The order of his argument from skepticism to self-knowledge and then to the ideas as given in self-knowledge, his skeptical denial of the objective reality of secondary qualities, his conviction that men's knowledge of God is intellectually prior to, and a necessary condition for, the knowledge of physical things, place him with Locke on the side of the "new way." If he was the founder of modern subjectivism and its failures, however, he was promptly corrected by Spinoza and by Leibniz, each in his own way.

Yet a close examination of Descartes's admittedly ambiguous theory of ideas and their relation to essences justifies another interpretation which makes clearer the transition from the theistic arguments in Meditation III (from the nature of my ideas and of myself to God as the eminent cause of both), to the argument from the essence of God to his existence in Meditation V. In the Preface to the Reader which precedes the *Medi-*

tations on First Philosophy, and again in Meditation III, Descartes gave a complex and inadequately short account of the role of ideas in the knowing relation, essentially derived from the Scholastics and Suarez. In it he ascribed a double role to an idea by distinguishing its matter and form: materially, the idea is mental, that is, as a *res*, or ontological entity, it is constitutive of mind. But "formally" or "objectively" it "expresses" or "represents" or simply *is* the form of the known object. According to this interpretation, which runs contrary to the traditional one by interpreting the "re" in "representer" to indicate intensification rather than duplication (as in *recherche* and similar words), there is in the idea (as its "objective" form) an identity of essence with that of the object, substantiated in space and time.[8]

If this interpretation is accepted, ideas function in the mental context of *essences* which are identical in the mind and the object, and are further partial identities in God's nature and our own, serving as the rational content in both. But essences as ideas manifest themselves in different degrees of clearness and distinctness. The essence of the thing known is as God sustains it by his own perfections through his constant creative understanding; the essence as present materially in the knower's idea is subject to finite limitations of spatiotemporal perspective, memory, passion, and sensory qualities which are due, if we take Descartes's psychology seriously, to the action of the knower's body, particularly his nervous system and pineal gland. The essence as *ideated* in God has been particularized and limited by mixture with "matter" in becoming my idea, but has been realized less incompletely, without the befogging effect of affective and sensory qualities, in nature as the essence of extended things. This interpretation has the virtue of showing how plausible were the occasionalistic interpretations, and particularly Malebranche's simplification, of Descartes's dualistic metaphysics and theory of knowledge.

According to Descartes, therefore, we perceive the essence of the object (the natural light of reason justifies an inferred knowledge of its substantial nature as well) when we perceive our idea of the object, and this is possible because the essence of the object is also in God as an entirely adequate idea. Descartes's conception is further explicated and developed by both Spinoza and Leibniz, both of whom more carefully define the logical nature of clearness, distinctness, and adequacy, but retain the identity of essences of things with ideas (as forms) in the minds of God and of men, but who differ in their conception of the relation of the ideas to perception.

It may be added that this interpretation has the additional virtue of explaining why self-awareness or internal perception is the necessary precondition of thought according to all three of these thinkers.

Spinoza's accounts, like Descartes's, are incomplete and ambiguous, being incidental to his wider aim of developing a rational ethics. Yet his entire metaphysics can be developed from the central notion of ideas and their *ideata*; in this as in many basic notions he remains a Cartesian. Ideas are the essences of things (*res*) in their mental context; indeed, the mind is constituted by ideas—"the object of the idea constituting the human mind is the body."[9] Yet there is no idea without its *ideatum*. Essences are doubly present as ideas constituting minds—primarily God's, as intellect, actualizing itself, and secondarily in created beings as *natura naturata*—as well as in the physical order of space, time, and motion, as the qualities of things and their relations.

Spinoza was able to sharpen Descartes's doctrine of ideas by abandoning the old Scholastic terminology for a fresher one, and even to clarify and extend the functional role of the ideas by a new interpretation of their internal ("material," for Descartes) and their external ("formal" or "representative") roles. Externally thought moves from the unclear and indistinctly perceived essences to things and their motion, causal relations, and spatiotemporal orderings. Internally the essences carry thought, through self-awareness and "reflection," ("ideas of the ideas of the body")[10] to the primary One or Substance itself—the one *causa sui* upon which all other orders depend. Not only is the bridge from creation (*naturata*) to creator (*naturans*) provided by the ideas, but with it also the dependence of time upon the eternal and the particular upon the universal. The distinction between ideas viewed inwardly and ideas viewed outwardly also offers an explanation for the degrees of clarity, distinctness, and adequacy of knowledge, and with this, for the two moral states—that of bondage to plurality and externality, and that of freedom through the internal path of reason.

Spinoza's revision of Descartes's doctrine of ideas thus restored the unity of the inner vision of truth by subordinating to it the order of intellect based on the external senses and their explanation. It replaced the Cartesian dualism with a two-level view of the universe in which the alternatives of truth against opinion, and value against disvalue (or better, nonvalue), are offered to man for his understanding and for wisdom in conduct.

This framework, however, needs to be supplemented with Spinoza's theory of the affections, which make it possible to pass not merely to the intuitive vision, but to the intellectual love, of God. I have already discussed (in Chapter 1) the new insight into the nature and power of affections which appeared in the high Renaissance (especially in Luis Vives's *De Anima et Vita Libri Tres*), and, together with a revival of the Augustinian concern for inwardness, gave richness and a certain humane profundity to the enlarged conception of the reasonableness of the world. This new recognition of the emotions added personal richness to the absolutes of reason in the later century, but also opened one way to subjectivity and to the collapse of the rationalist goal. For feelings seem to lack the public nature which clings to external sense qualities and to the logical ordering of concepts.

Being inclined toward a Stoic ethics, Descartes distrusted the affections, or "passions," of the soul, which he attributed, like the sensory impressions, to the activities of the body. Yet he found the affections closely mixed with the inclinations and therefore with the will, on the one hand, encouraging it to function beyond its reasonable bonds (particularly the passions of desire and anger), but also with the intellect, preventing it from the clear and distinct perception of ideas.[11] Thus the affections undisciplined by the virtue of *generosité* lead the will to intrude beyond the clarity and distinctness of intellect, and cause the mind to fall into error. Error rests upon the freedom of the will to advance beyond the limits of clear and distinct understanding.

This conception of the affections was a dangerous concession to the libertine spirit, and Spinoza drastically altered it. His system involved a vigorous challenge to the old Stoic attack upon emotions. All ideas, however adequately or inadequately grasped, are (he held) accompanied by affections and, indeed, determine them. Moreover, like Vives before him, Spinoza held that affections are greatly varied by their corresponding objects; thus they not only accompany the ideas but are modified by them. There is therefore a gradation of affections from the passive affects, in which we are in bondage to the external plurality of things and events, to the most active affections, which rest on adequate ideas, and give complete freedom from the transient and external, in order to achieve the abiding highest good. This scale of growing freedom applies to the whole series of the affections, from the simplest—joy, sorrow, and desire—to the most unifying and abiding—love. Thus the clearest, mose adequate intellectual insight—that I am one with God—involves also the highest affection, the intellectual love of God, and therefore also our highest good. For values do not determine our affections, our desires determine our values.[12]

In Spinoza, therefore, the division between the plural world of things, minds, and their relations, and the one world of being actualizing its essence, is not merely bridged by the ideas; it is also transformed, through the feelings which are given "objective" content by the ideas, into a moral duality of personal distractions versus personal unity, a duality of the commonplace versus an all-unifying personal fulfillment through love of the Eternal, a duality of transient joys versus mystical bliss—and a final mystical union of insight and love. But in this scale of being and of value, the individual himself, the person of honor and good will, tends to be lost, for in his escape from the chain of natural, externally caused relations, he may escape also, by transcending them, the everyday problems of social order, peace, and social well-being which largely depend upon them. The real loses itself, so to speak, in the ideal, the facts in the norm.[13]

The Old Way of Ideas in Leibniz

Against this tendency in the *Ethics* of Spinoza, Leibniz undertook an alternative view of the good. Although the grounds of Leibniz's thought (apart from a common root in the Platonic tradition) are quite distinct from those of Spinoza, he did in fact learn much in the process of criticizing him. Four shifts of emphasis are particularly significant in relation to his doctrine of ideas. First, his conception of the relation of perception to the idea differs. We do not merely perceive the *ideas*, we perceive the *world* from a point of view (or individual nature) which determines the degrees of adequacy of the forms in which we perceive it. The ideas constitute the determining principle of each individual nature. The ideas, in short, determine the limiting forms or possibilities within which we perceive the details of the world, but also provide the assurance that we perceive it truly. "The idea of things in us is nothing but the fact that God, the author alike of things and of mind, has impressed the power of thinking upon the mind, so that it can by its own operations produce what corresponds perfectly to events which follow from things."

A second trait of the ideas, which is more explicit in Leibniz than in his predecessors, is their dynamic character. The conviction that ideas are active is as old as Plato, and is explicit in Neoplatonism and St. Augustine, becoming an important factor in idealistic thought. In Leibniz it becomes the justification for the extensional as well as the intensional explication of logical meanings. It is the mental character of the ideas which imparts to them their striving toward specific actualization. In Leibniz this specific actuality is, metaphysically speaking, the complex interacting process of many temporal series of perceptions; on the secondary level of science, it is force and the doing of work.

In the third place, the affections are not merely accompaniments of the ideas and are not merely modified by them; the affections, like sensations, are the passive, limiting aspects (the *materia prima*, or content) of unclear and indistinct perceptions, and are therefore imperfections in our perception not merely of the world but, secondarily, of the ideas themselves.[14] This insight of Leibniz had a direct influence, not merely on his own aesthetic theory, but on that of the early Romantics in the eighteenth century.[15]

Finally, the individual person is not lost in the logical structure of total meaning, nor in the quest for the abiding and absolute value; his individuality is intensified in both. The ideas must realize themselves in individual beings. The analysis of ideas which leads Spinoza to the one true Substance, leads Leibniz (though he never succeeded completely in showing how) to the essence of my being, the "law of my individual series" of actions and passions, and by analogy to the nature of other individuals as well.

Like most of his contemporaries—Descartes, Spinoza, and the British empiricists—Leibniz accepted from St. Augustine and the Scholastics an empirical distinction between internal and external experience—the *via interna* and the *via externa*. In his judgment, internal perception is of the acts and passivities of the mind itself, and given "reflection," also of the ideas which constitute its nature, in distinction from an environing world of being which is perceived externally. Thus my ideas present the forms of outer perceptions, but may themselves be the objects of internal perceptions; indeed, all conceptual thought rests upon this character of inward perception, or "apperception."

Since thought itself involves memory, (it was an early insight of Leibniz that memory distinguished the human mind from other linearly ordered events),[16] and since thought consists in part of the perception of ideas, ideas are the basis of the nature of man, and in their total unity provide his dispositional constancy or character. Thus, again, ideas serve as the binding ingredient both of individuality and of universal order—one being given through the cognition and cogitation of inward natures, the other through the perception and interpretation of outer order.

It is beyond the scope of this study to trace the development of Leibniz's system from these distinctions. It can be said, however, that out of the diverse relationships implicit in his doctrine of ideas he developed a modern teleological dynamism according to which the universe unfolds by a principle of value (the principle of the "Best Possible," or of the "Plenum"). Parallel to this unfolding of a dynamic world order, there is also, in each thinking subject, an order of increasingly clear, distinct, and therefore adequate perceptions of the ideas. This process includes not only scientific knowledge but also the moral governance of the individual's own nature; it moves from mere logical possibilities to a metaphysics of individuals in universal harmony, and to a scientific knowledge of the world as it is imperfectly perceived, that is, as "well-founded phenomena." But the entire world, thus known from without and within, consists of a unified order of similar dynamic series of dynamic states acting according to laws of their natures. Leibniz's metaphysics, which he hoped would be adopted and made a blueprint, so to speak, by men of good will (*honestas*) for the restoration of European order, may thus be regarded as the intellectual high point of the century's efforts toward a renovation of Europe through the ideal of loyalty and obedience to a universal natural and moral order.

The New Way of Ideas: Locke

Yet in these same thinkers who undertook to provide intellectual grounds for this ideal order, the intrusion can be seen of points of view which support an alternative interpretation of human nature, human thought, and the good. As has been suggested, this is the ideal of the *libertine*, the ideal of free, inventive creativity unbound by any superior authority commanding loyalty, however reasonable, save that created by men themselves. The intellectual basis for this is another theory of ideas—that of nominalism and positivism.

The historical grounds for this position as well can be found in the events of the age—bad and conflicting laws, regicide and other disavowals of authority, uncertainties about the historical bases of legitimacy, the strengthening and multiplication of conflicting political and religious powers, the knowledge of new and radically different cultural orders which exploration and the expansion of trade introduced to Europe. Coupled with the new emphases upon individualism and freedom arising in the Renaissance, these new trends presented a threat to all efforts to establish a metaphysical support for principles of universal order, such as the old doctrine of ideas offered.

The "new way of ideas" had been long in formation. Its modern ancestry is traceable to late Scholasticism, especially thought in the fourteenth and fifteenth centuries which undertook to free Aristotelianism from its overload of Christian Platonism, discarding the role of "intelligible species" in knowledge, of intentional meanings in logic, and of the help of the "natural light of reason" in theology and in ethics. With these aids to certainty removed, some thinkers sought a support for religious faith in religious experience or, going even further, sought to ground knowledge not only upon experience alone, but upon a narrow limitation of experience to disparate qualities of sense and of feeling (the old "sensible species"). In extreme cases this restriction was carried further by regarding all terms not just as abstractions but as arbitrary names.[17] This movement had the effect of restricting qualities and forms, in short, meanings, to a realm of the mind, derivative from sense data, arbitrary in its symbolic expressions, and incapable of adequation to things (*res*) by human reason except through the goodness of God, which is given only in revelation. The same tradition, pushed further, had the effect of freeing man's will from the necessity of obeying any objective order of law or of reason. Moral reason must be based, practically and empirically, upon feeling.

Evidences of this view were by no means rare in the Renaissance and the early seventeenth century, even though Neoplatonic and Stoic patterns of thought remained dominant. Montaigne, for example, could assume an ultimate cultural relativism in spite of the strong Stoic tenor of his writing, although the skeptics whom he defended were more thorough in their nominalism. The revival of Sextus Empiricus and other skeptics was indicative of the trend. Bacon's emphasis on knowledge through the examination of things, and his warning against beginning with the highest maxims, still suggest a more functional conception of experience analogous to that of Telesio in Italy and Paracelsus in Germany. But his criticism of the idols strengthened the tendency toward skepticism. Thomas Hobbes repudiated Bacon's Platonism to develop a Supernominalism (as Leibniz called it) and a materialism derived from it by a sensationalistic theory of knowledge. Hobbes did not, of course, abandon his conviction that absolute authority is needed, but he restricted such authority to the individual state, and based it on a kind of conventionalism arising of necessity out of the irrational impulses of human nature. Nearer the end of the century, John Locke, caught between the old and the new and seeking a commonsense middle, formulated the modern epistemology of empiricism by his theory that ideas, both theoretical and moral, have their origin in impressions of sense and reflection, and can be verified only by resolution into these.

Yet Locke himself could not fully dispense with principles self-evident to all men, and therefore with the old way of ideas. Indeed, it can be argued plausibly that "the new way for ideas" refers less to a change in the definition of ideas than to the method of philosophy in establishing them clearly and distinctly, and testing their distinctness and adequacy in the human mind. It remained for thinkers of the eighteenth century to develop a purer empirical and nominalistic philosophy in support of libertinism.

Trends toward Subjectivism and Relativism

Meanwhile the great defenders of universal order and *honnête* obedience did not themselves escape certain internal concessions to the "new way." Descartes's methodological doubting made him more liable to this than were his successors, for the hypothesis of an isolated subjectivism was an essential ingredient of this method, which he was able to overcome only by affirming and using certain rules of thought left free from doubt, such as the principle of sufficient reason, the definition of substance, and the general rule "that everything I apprehend in a genuinely clear and distinct manner is true."[18] Descartes also brought into common use that bête noire of the epistemologists which was introduced by Galileo and which threatened the theory of knowledge for the rest of the century—the distinction between the primary and secondary qualities of objects. The mathematical and physiological considerations which led thinkers of the century to treat the primary qualities as real because they could be quantified, but the secondary as subjective and private, yet somehow dependent upon the real object, knowledge of which was to be explained, led surely to the skepticism of men like George Berkeley and Hume. Descartes's theory of the will, furthermore, freed it from the intellect and made it decisive, in connection with unclear or indistinct ideas, in his definition of error. To this extent, at least, truth depended, for him, upon the will; it is the role of the will to regulate itself by clear and distinct ideas. Thus subjectivism and a nonintellectual voluntarism were explicit in Descartes's thought.

Descartes's theory of the will was promptly corrected by both Spinoza and Leibniz in the interest of the older tradition; both of them affirmed that "will is nothing but (or "does not differ from") the intellect."[19] Both also undertook to correct the conceptions which led Descartes to his ultimate dualistic division of the world into two orders—a subjective and an objective—which must interact, yet cannot interact since they have no common nature which could make this possible. This correction was achieved, as we have seen, by restoring a two-level order of being—creator and creation, or in Spinoza, *natura naturans* and *naturata*—with man finding his true freedom, and all plurality finding its true unity, only through participation in the higher level. Yet there was in both, if read in the context of their views of nature, that which would encourage the nominalist and the libertine. For Spinoza the ordinary values of life were not merely vain, they were purely subjective—a matter of feeling or passive affections. "We do not desire things because they are good; they are good because we desire them." God is completely remote from the everyday evaluations of man which are modes within modes; he is accessible only to the mind which is completely disciplined by intellect, and which dwells in its own internal self-sufficiency. Life in society, on the other hand, is recommended on the commonsense ground of utility and conservation, and such active affections which contribute to them. There is no great overarching order of commands whereby the social order is to be regulated.

This trend away from the Platonic ideal was not so distinctive in Leibniz, who learned from Malebranche in the matter of the ideas. In his confrontation with Locke's *Essay*, Leibniz was clearly aware of the difference between their conceptions of ideas, and of the theoretical and practical consequences entailed by this difference. Like Spinoza, Leibniz rejected an indeterministic basis for man's life, though he did make more of man's spontaneity and of the role of self-awareness and decision in his conduct. Locke changed his mind several times on the problem of freedom. But there is a degree of convergence between him and Leibniz in the treatment of truths of fact; although Leibniz retained a rationalistic, a priori component in the analysis of such truths, the two men agreed that the final verification of which man is capable is a pragmatic test by prediction and confirmation by future experience. Leibniz did, however, object vigorously against Locke's inclination to define moral principles by social consent.[20]

In all of these thinkers, therefore, there is a subjective and relativistic trend which undermines, a little, the eternal verity, rationality, and imperativeness of general ideals. Thus they themselves foreshadowed the new conceptions of freedom and self-determining creativity which were to come. In 1711 Leibniz could read with full approval and satisfaction the third Earl of Shaftesbury's reduction of moral Platonism to the moral affections,[21] as Lord Herbert of Cherbury had reduced Platonic principles to instincts many decades earlier. And in Leibniz himself, as in Locke, the long struggle for reunion and agreement in politics and religion gave way to the new ideal of toleration of differences.

6 The Transcendentals

Being, the true, the one, and the good have unity by
their very own essence. Hence wherever they are
found, they are really one, although the unity of the
reality whereby they are united in God is more perfect
than that whereby they are united in creatures.

[St. Thomas, *De Veritate*, I, i.]

The word good, then, expresses the conformity (that is,
the agreement in form or idea) of being to appetite, as
stated in the beginning of the Ethics: "the good is what
all desire." The word true, however, expresses the
conformity of being to intellect.

[*Summa Theologia*, I, 16, 3.[1]]

In our method something unique is encountered—indeed, something wonderful, namely (the insight) that all
the more important classifications of things take place
through triads. I protest that I did not seek this out by
artifice, from some superstition, but that it presented
itself so unexpectedly in all outstanding matters of
highest importance from the first attributes of things
on—the *one*, the *true*, and the *good*—that I stopped
transfixed in awe for a while, struck by the novelty of
the thing.

[Comenius, *Prodromus Pansophiae*, section 107, pp.
144-145.]

New Significance of an Old Doctrine

The ecstatic discovery of Comenius that the Scholastic
doctrine of the transcendentals could serve the Baconian ideal
of a new attack upon nature to discover and organize its secrets,
by assuring an underlying *unity* of being in the many aspects of
experience, expressed a conviction also held by the later
systematizers and systematic activists of the seventeenth century. It is the purpose of this chapter to examine some of these
applications of an old doctrine to the new concerns of the age,
as well as to uncover some of the intellectual issues raised by

the new sciences and the pluralistic forces in thought and life which induced a gradual disintegration of the doctrine. In short, the doctrine of the transcendentals became, in the Platonism of the early century, the guarantee that thought and things, truth and goodness, reality and ideal, understanding and practice, subject and object, indeed, man and his world and God, all cohere in a single, unitary, and humanly relevant order. Yet this total intellectual burden proved too great, too varied for such a doctrine to bear, and it fell apart under a more empirical and discriminating examination of its discrete components and their relations. This was a precondition for the triumph of a more empirical and pragmatic temper in the ensuing Enlightenment.

Although the doctrine of the transcendental notions was clearly stated and generally discussed by the Scholastics and their followers, a cloud of ambiguity as to its meaning, scope, and metaphysical role has clung to it throughout its history. The following components of the doctrine may be distinguished. (1) Basic to it is the recognition that there are certain concepts, or terms, whose relevance extends beyond (or "transcends") our experience of the world of particulars, and therefore beyond Aristotle's categories, but which demand metaphysical consideration; the oldest examples are Plato's One, good, true, beautiful. (2) Yet since these concepts are as general as being itself, they apply to all particular beings as well as the unified whole, or, as the Scholastics held, they are problems in both parts of metaphysics—the general and the specific. (3) Furthermore, since they are as general as being itself, they are logically convertible with it, though not without limitation or qualification; that is, they apply to all being and beings, but in different relationships—being is true with respect to the intellect, good with respect to the will or active principle, and so forth. (4) Since God is the primary individual to be discussed in special metaphysics, he must be describable by the transcendentals, and this description will differ from that in general metaphysics because the first transcendental, unity, will now be personal, and the others will be attributes of God—none will have metaphysical independence; they will not be *really* distinct, but they will be more than merely logically distinct; that is, they will (as Duns Scotus put it) be "formally" distinct. (5) But in their application in special metaphysics, the transcendentals must apply to all particulars—individuals, qualities, and relations, as well, and therefore, in the theological context, to all created finite beings. Here it becomes clear that, in contrast to categories, they have opposites: unity is opposed by plurality, goodness by evil, infinity by finiteness. This in turn suggests transcendentals on another level, such as number, relation, infinity, and so forth. It also demands the recognition of subclasses of transcendentals (as in Duns Scotus). The line between transcendentals and categories tends to disappear, and the role of the transcendentals in metaphysics changes from their early classificatory function. This was the case in the seventeenth century. Specifically, the role of the transcendentals became more than a covering classification for the value dimensions of being; it became one of providing logical props to faith in the perfections and the completeness of God and of creation as the unfolding of this perfection in limited forms.

Scholastic Conceptions of the Transcendentals

As formulated in repeated writings by Thomas Aquinas, the transcendentals were the most general attributes of being, "transcending" the categories, which apply only to finite beings. From Aristotle was derived the common criterion of transcendentals—they are all convertible with being itself since they are coextensive with it. Aristotle, however, criticized the Platonists for placing being, one, the true, and the good in the realm of the Platonic ideas as first principles; as such they would contradict each other. They were for Aristotle most general attributes which cannot themselves be used as predicates of particulars.[2] It was the intrusion of Augustinian Platonism into medieval thought which made possible the identification of the transcendentals with the most general attributes of God[3] and their opposites or limitations with the essential notions requisite to every assertion about created beings.

The enumeration and interpretation of these most inclusive but indefinable essences had involved considerable discussion. Thomas's discussion distinguished transcendental from accidental qualities of being, transcendental predicates (the *unum* is always central in his discussion) differing from accidents in adding no new and distinct reality to being. But this fact did not, for Thomas or for that matter for Duns Scotus or William of Ockham, make them merely nominal distinctions. It is true that Ockham sometimes seems to treat them as nominal, but not in an extreme sense which denies them any reality. They are distinctions *a ratione* rather than *in re*, for as real they would threaten the unity of God. Scotus's attempt to find a middle ground for them as "formal distinctions" explained very little, while Ockham's efforts to restore Aristotle's intent by assigning them to reason did not prevent him from discussing their metaphysical relevance.[4]

From the perspective of modern uses for the doctrine, the expansion by Duns Scotus of the transcendentals from Thomas's three or four is very significant. Scotus divided all transcendentals into four classes: (i) *being* itself ("the first of the transcendentals"); (ii) those coextensive and convertible with being (*passiones entis simpliciter convertibiles*)—unity, truth, and goodness; (iii) disjunctives such as infinite-finite, substance-accident, actual-potential, necessary-contingent; and (iv) "pure perfections," which include all of the convertibles but only the more perfect member of each disjunction.[5] Concentrating upon *unum*, William of Ockham noted that the distinction between the convertible and the disjunctive trans-cendentals is not sharp, that unity has its opposite in diversity, and in number as well, and that furthermore unity implies, not as its opposite but as a consequent, *order*. Moreover Ockham saw that the distinction between transcendental and accidental attributes is not firm. Thus number, relation, order were added to the list; indeed Ockham's reform of logic involved the restriction of the "categories" to substance-accident; all other universal terms are transcendental in the sense that they apply to all objective reasoning whatever.[6]

The trend among later Scholastics was thus to apply the transcendentals to the being of God as his perfections, but also, through the diversifications, limitations, and specializations of creation, to the being of his creatures. The result was to expand these universals to apply to all order, and thus to destroy the Aristotelian distinction between them and the categories of nature. The transcendentals became dimensions of a universe which God has made by number, measure, and weight, and in a corresponding degree, became detached from the discussion of *being*, as the most universal concept, itself. Or, to state the obverse view, *being* itself, as the most general concept, tended to become absorbed into the copulas of a great diversity of propositions, based upon experience, about the complex exist-ing world.

A trend toward polarization thus appeared in the doctrine of transcendentals by the end of the sixteenth century. With the growth of empirical and nominalistic convictions, on the one hand, they appeared as the formal rules of order and value in truths of fact—including both mathematical and moral judgments in this class of truths—and as such became a part of the logical analysis of judgments. But on the other hand, they also remained attributes of the supreme being whose perfections are the source of created order.

It is in this latter sense that the theory of transcendentals is by its essential nature apologetic; its abstract metaphysical status serves to establish the universal perfections of being in the divine providence, and therefore the ultimate identity of what is with what ought to be. As Scotus said, "Being is the subject, God is the end of metaphysics." What was still needed for the purposes of the *homo honestatis* of the seventeenth century was the appropriation of the notions of power and of law as the basis of order—law that is natural, yet normative and teleologically directed at unity in diversity. But the unity of the diverse is essentially an aesthetic concept; it is the definition of harmony, and this, too, became a unifying ingredient in the doctrine of transcendentals.

It is thus clear that the doctrine of the transcendentals as developed in the Scholastic tradition confirmed the univocity of ideas or essences, yet also moved implicitly toward regarding them not only as convertible with being, but also as principles of reason in judgments about all being. Using later terms, they are therefore truths of fact of highest generality, but whether analytic or synthetic is not clear, for they add a relation not explicitly contained in their subject—a relation to intellect, will, or affections; yet, by the doctrine, these are parts, themselves subsumed under the whole of being. An epistemological or metaphysical dualism is not permitted, and the way is already open for Kant's analysis and Hegel's later synthesis.

Renaissance Expansions of the Doctrine

In discussing the meaning of the transcendental *unum*, Gottfried Martin has said that "the question of the Greeks is aimed at the unity of the living, the question of the Scholastics is aimed at the unity of God, the modern question is aimed at the unity of the world as a mechanical system. But precisely this question about the unity of the world as a mechanical system leads to the point where its peak was reached in Leibniz and Kant, in the old question about the relation between being and unity in general."[7] Thus, as I have tried to show, the thinkers of the seventeenth century must be viewed as in transition between the Scholastic and the modern view; they strengthen the Scholastic synthesis by Neoplatonist motifs, but are also moved by empirical considerations toward the modern view. As Comenius said, "Art borrows its ideas from nature, nature from God, God from himself."[8] Among these Neoplatonic themes are the microcosm-macrocosm relationship, a hierarchical order of being and perfection, the univocity of the attributes of uncreated being and created beings, the continuity of infinite with finite, a logical principle of individuation in terms of essences, a universal basis for interpersonal synthesis (*symbiosis*) and a resolution of the antithesis of potency and act through a concept of power.

This extension of the doctrine of the transcendentals can be illustrated in the thought of several men belonging to distinctly different philosophical and theological traditions, but all influential in different ways in the formation of the great systems of the century.

The Dominican priest Tommaso Campanella, whose extensive writings were directed at the reformulation of Christian theology and the defense of papal authority, but who was nonetheless widely read and followed in Reformed church circles, focused the transcendentals concretely on an Augustinian doctrine of the trinity—the three "primalities" of God, which are reflected in all creatures, are power, wisdom, and love.[9] Thus the abstract Platonic eternals (being, the true, and the good) now appear in the concrete form of divine virtues or powers, perfections which are manifested through the finite orders of creation, yet are normative for these orders. As a student Leibniz seems to have read Campanella, from whom he derived two important convictions—the ultimate harmony of truth based on experience, reason, and revelation, and the doctrine of the primalities: God or ultimate being is power manifesting itself in wisdom and in love—and (the combination of the three) in justice.

The same transcendental trinity appeared in the *Prodromus Pansophiae* of Amos Comenius, who discovered the triads in all things, demanded by the microcosmic mirroring of the greater macrocosm and its Creator. The possibility of knowing truth and acting for the good requires that power be distributed in proportion to wisdom (truth) and goodness. To later thinkers it seemed that Descartes's voluntarism and Hobbes's conventionalism both raised again the old issue of the Euthyphro concerning man's duty to God and the relation of reason to authority, but in the enlarged context of new political forces, of religious dissent, and of the new science. Is duty good, true, unified because God decrees it, or does God decree it because it is good, true, and so forth? In opposition to Descartes's voluntarism, constructive thinkers chose the answer of the Platonic Socrates: it is always the principle of reason, never the personal will, which determines order.[10] But in the case of God the two are identical since God is, first of all, power actualizing itself reasonably and wisely. Thus power and order become the unifying, concretizing transcendentals.

In Francis Suarez, the schoolmaster in metaphysics of all Europe, power and pure act stand out as closest to the nature of being, and other transcendentals are related through them. In the third of his *Disputationes Metaphysicae*, Suarez emphasized the absolute simplicity of God and recognized only the Thomistic transcendentals as defining his nature. But he further assigned to his essence the inseparable attributes of perfection, infinity, pure act, immensity, eternity, unity, and power, all of which can be treated *transcendentaliter* as well as *accidentaliter*. In subsequent disputations, potency and act stand out as the principles which unify the rest; potency and act are in God and (secondarily) in created nature as "principles of operation." In *Disputation 43* potency and act are again discussed *transcendentaliter* as related, neither being prior to the other, in a way which suggests Leibniz's later expansion of the concept of potency into active and passive force.[11]

The traditional doctrine of the transcendentals was also related by Suarez, in *Disputation 8*, to the primary concept of power. For here *unitas*, *veritas*, and *bonitas* are described as *passiones entis*, but add nothing to the *actuality* of being. Since intellect is a power prior to will, *veritas* is a *passio entis* prior to *bonitas*. Veritas can be contemplated in two forms—in *actu exercito* (in our knowledge of things and their properties) and in *actu signato* (in formal truth)—this is obviously a forerunner to Leibniz's truths of fact and of reason, respectively. Consequently truth, in its human derivative, falls into a threefold order: *in significando* (in words, concepts, writings); *in cognoscendo* (in the knowing intellect, or in conception); and *in essendo* (in the things themselves which are designated as true)—an analysis of great influence upon the theories of knowledge and of ideas which followed Suarez. This ordering of human truth corresponds to the fields of logic, epistemology, physics, and metaphysics. Thus the unity of the world is the unity of God's power manifesting itself in the orders of being and, passively, primarily in the orders of truth, derivatively (as actions follow knowledge) in the orders of goodness.

This interpretation of the transcendental order as an intimate dependence of truth and goodness as passive aspects, upon the unitary active powers of the divine nature (all mirrored, however, in nature and in lesser spirits) was given concrete expression in Suarez's theory of ideas as exemplary or formal causes (discussed in Chapter 5). In *Disputation 1*, "On the Nature of Metaphysics," Section V, part. 38-40, Suarez had reasoned that although all four causes of Aristotle are meaningful in metaphysics (material cause being interpreted more broadly than merely "sensate matter"), nevertheless, since creatures are not beings *per essentiam* but merely *per participationem*, their existence can be understood only through efficient causality. "The first and noblest of causes," on the other hand, are final causes, because they, more than other causes, bestow the properties of existence. God, as the simply necessary being, cannot be known through efficient causes but only through their negation. Final causes, which involve the divine exemplars "which are called ideas, cannot be known in themselves unless God is seen in himself." Instead of using efficient causes, as in physics, we are thus driven to ideas, exemplary causes, or forms, in our contemplation of the divine and its purposes. "By whatever reason the exemplary cause is known . . . the best medium is by demonstration, and is proper to metaphysics."

Disputation 25 contains a further discussion of these exemplary causes or ideas, making extensive use of St. Augustine and other church fathers. As Clement of Alexandria has said, mind is the *locus idearum*. Ideas or exemplary causes are found properly in intellectual agents, and are external to these only *per accidens*. Formally in the intellect, they provide the objective content whereby the intelligent acts of an agent attain their ends or final causes. And since the idea is a universal form or potentiality it is applicable to all similar actions and ends. An idea is thus a transcendent form, which imposes order upon the power of the intellect to give direction to the will; it provides the universal in the particular, unites truth and goodness, determines internal essential being and external objective being by participation in this essence, and establishes the knowability, and indirectly, the potential goodness of things for all intelligent creatures.

This transcendental unity of being in an idea supplied a basis for the criteria of truth which were widely held after Suarez. In the understanding of God all ideas are clear, distinct, and intuitively adequate (to use terminology older than Suarez but perfected in Leibniz).[12] But just as no one can intuit God's being completely, even so human knowledge exists in varying degrees of unclear, confused, inadequate symbolic "formulations"—imperfectly perceived ideas with symbolic content. The measure of truth is the degree of clarity, distinctness, and adequacy of form or order achieved by the human intellect in spite of its inescapable sensory content. The Scholastic conception of truth as the *adequatio intellectus ad rem* is thus still relevant, but is transformed into an internal logical criterion applied to thought to bring the idea into distinctness—a conception of truth which rests upon the metaphysical principle of conformity or isomorphism of imperfectly perceived idea-in-mind with Idea-in-the-created-order. The transcendental order of being is thus the ground for human criteria of truth (although Leibniz in his later years, when his phenomenalism grew in importance, suggested that this transcendental ground has little significance in the actual search for truth.)

The role of *perfection* as a transcendental, with its differentiation into various degrees of finite perfections, also received further qualifications in relation to the new cultural concerns of the modern era. Perfection is related logically to the transcendental *bonum*, and is generally interpreted as the indefinable and unqualified ultimate source of hierarchical orders of created beings and therefore also of the finite, specified perceptions of which each such being is capable. But with a new emphasis upon individualism, and the corresponding interpretation of forms as laws to be obeyed by either a metaphysical or a moral necessity, the hierarchy of values implied in the idea of perfection lost much of its meaning. For although individual substances, whether physical or spiritual, may possess certain degrees of perfection within a hierarchical order, the individuals themselves constitute horizontal classes and societies, such as the kingdoms of nature and of grace discussed by Malebranche and Leibniz. The vertical hierarchical scale of perfections tended to disintegrate before the conception of natural and of human groups, and was replaced by a more direct, positive, quasi-judicial approach to the problems of finiteness—error, evil, matter and its organization (all of which were merely negative privations of form in the hierarchical distributions of perfection) now emerged as the positive facts about which the solutions of human problems must turn. The *immanence* of the transcendentals (and their opposites) within man and nature assumed greater importance than their *being* the perfect grounds for universal hierarchical orders.

The Immanence of the Transcendentals: The Herborn Group

The process of enlarging and modifying the role of the transcendentals which we have noted can be observed in the doctrine as it is presented by the encyclopedist John Henry Alsted and more vividly, by his pupils John Bisterfeld and Amos Comenius, both of whom undertook simplifications in the eclecticism of their teacher.

Though Alsted, unlike Suarez, retained the distinction between general and special metaphysics, he did, like Suarez, base the transcendentals upon the prior conception of God as most perfect being. But he attributed our knowledge of these transcendentals not to a rational process of inference as did Suarez, but to a universal natural intuition, in the tradition which also included Luis Vives and Lord Herbert of Cherbury. "The theoretical principles implanted in the active intellect, and the practical ones implanted in the *synteresis*, are those which man understands without a teacher. They are of this kind: God is; there exists something highest and first which is supremely one, true, good, beautiful, etc. (*unum, verum, bonum, pulchrum,* etc.); God is to be worshipped; God is supremely lovable, honorable, etc."[13]

I have observed in an earlier chapter that Alsted solved his problems by the Ramistic method of classifying them. Thus he organized his thoughts on the theory of transcendentals in the following way.[14] He asked first, "Is it rightly said that God made all things by weight, measure, and number?" and answered affirmatively, since (he said) number is neither a substance nor a mode of substance, and must therefore be something transcendental; it applies to angels and souls as well as to bodies. The first modes of all being are unity, verity, and bonity, but from them there are derived such secondary or "ortive" modes (*modi ortus*) as order, number, perfection, pulchritude. He gives an extensive explication of these ortive modes in the Ramist manner of subclassification. Order, for example, is defined as "a mode of being in which it is understood that being is unconfused (*in-confusa*)." Order is further subdivided into absolute and relative order: order is absolute when being is unconfused within itself, relative when it is unconfused with other beings. (For "unconfused with" one may substitute the more common "distinct from.") Order is also either subordinate or coordinate; either archetypal (in the divine mind) or ectypal (in nature, science, and the art of logic). Relative, formal order consists in the relation of prior to posterior. Thus order unfolds being to logical development by the understanding, by transforming the mixture of disorder and order into the more logical separation of confusion from distinctness. This implies process and intelligent action, rather than a static hierarchical relation.

Other ortive transcendentals are treated similarly. "Perfection is a mode of being through which nothing is understood to be lacking (*deesse*) from it, and furthermore it is the measure of other (modes)." Perfection is thus the absence of nothing from the context to which it belongs. It too is subdivided into three kinds. Transcendental perfection is that by which anything is absolutely perfect *"in suo genere"* or "has its own essence." (Thus all absolute perfection implies a plenum.) Natural perfection is "that by which a thing has the good which is ascribed and fitting (*convenient*) to it." Moral perfection is ethical virtue. Alsted says that some add a fourth and a fifth meaning to perfection, namely, spiritual and artificial.

Noteworthy in the distinction between absolute and natural perfection is the principle of convenience or "fittingness." Convenience marks the first suggestion of a unique aspect of order which Alsted here does not treat as a part of its transcendental nature, but which becomes a mode of all being later in the century, sometimes as symbiosis, more generally as the old Platonic-Pythagorean principle of harmony. Alsted's next ortive mode, that of beauty, approaches this more closely.

Pulchritude is subdivided somewhat differently from the preceeding modes. It is "a mode of being through which being is understood to give pleasure (*delectare*)." Although he argues that the Platonists have erred in confusing goodness and beauty, Alsted nevertheless shows that he himself considers it a derivative of goodness: "Beauty is a circle of the divine light, flowing forth (*manans*) from the good, residing in the good, always flowing back through the good to the good." Beauty in its turn "excites and draws to itself admiration, love, and desire"; it is the "affection whose escort (*comes*) so to speak, is *grace*, in terms of which being is called gracious and lovable."

Finally Alsted discusses an ortive mode of being which appears to be disjunctive, though Suarez, as has been shown, had regarded the pair rather as complementary—*act* and *potency*. Act is prior to potency and is "that which is directed at perfecting potency." Its priority is threefold: by definition, in time, and in essence. The primary act of existence is itself to be distinguished from the secondary act, or "the operation which goes forth from the form." Potency again is either active or passive, and so forth, as it was in Suarez.

It will be clear that in spite of his prolixity and his resort to divisions which neither explain nor relate the terms, Alsted has introduced a new feeling into the transcendentals and their finite externalizations. Though Suarez's selection of power and dynamism as central is not rejected, neither is it emphasized. Instead, there is a tendency to find the transcendentals to be a rational order determined by a process of thought in which attributes fan out (*mano*) into plurality and distinctiveness, transforming disorder into order. Though still treated objectively and realistically as modes of being, moreover, the transcendentals are brought into close relationship, not merely to the intellect, but to the affections of men. The transcendentals are forms of thought whose synthesis, whether in the divine or in created individuals, appears more and more personal. With the recognition of beauty as a type of goodness[15] characteristic of both primary and derivative being, moreover, the transcendental notions of order, number, and measure are combined and completed in harmony. This metaphysical concept of harmony is thus supported by mathematical and empirical interests.

In the works of John Bisterfeld, whose writings breathe a fresher and freer air than his teacher's, this enlarged order of transcendentals provides the immanent structure for a still Platonic, yet empirically oriented metaphysical system. His *Philosophiae Primae Seminarium* (1641) drew from the young student Leibniz an enthusiastic marginal exclamation. "A most brilliant (*praeclarissimum*) little work, and one whose equal in this field (that is, in first philosophy) I have not seen."[16] To Bisterfeld's account of being and its "notions" (that is its modes), which are directly "given to the mind" and include the mutually convertible conjugates of the theoretical *est*, the practical *debet* and the poetical *potest* (or "is," "ought," and "can") Leibniz wrote a note pointing to the corresponding fields of human experience: *scientia, prudentia,* and *ars.* Later in his notes he also correlated them with the modal categories—actuality, necessity, and possibility. In a new and suggestive way, Bisterfeld, stimulated perhaps by Francis Bacon, whom he had read and may have met in London, proceeded to set up the "rules of being." Among these rules, two are particularly suggestive of the movement toward a concrete plurality of beings in a harmonious unity: "No being is absolute," and "No being is solitary; all being is symbiotic." From a later rule, that "the notion of being united with being is reciprocal," he derived a further principle, that "all things are essentially related to other things." To the rule "No being is so small and abject that it has no proportional operation," Leibniz added a marginal note, "and would be a useful member of the Republic of Beings." Elsewhere Bisterfeld analyzed the symbiotic relations between individuals in terms of *perception* and *appetite* (Bacon had assigned this role to perception alone),[17] and interpretation which Leibniz was to recall and appropriate many years later in developing a theory of interrelatedness of the monads in his mature system.

Bisterfeld's work was remarkable, not merely for its apparent influence upon the thought of Leibniz, but intrinsically for its subordination of the hierarchical conception of being to a more direct approach to the interrelationship of finite but substantial beings. This further suggested an abandonment of a logical theory of the convertibility of transcendental concepts, for one emphasizing their systematic, coherent interrelationship, a theory sustained by the intellectual, moral, and aesthetic requirements of thought. He swept aside Alsted's serial derivation of subforms from the transcendental essences, in the interest of an immanent but dynamic order of interdependent beings and binding values—a significant breakthrough into modernity in metaphysics, of which the great rationalizers of the latter half of the century were the heirs.

The rapid multiplication of the number of transcendental attributes of being of which I have given some evidence, and the confusion of questions which arose about their mutual relations, are well reflected in one of Leibniz's maturer summaries of his ethical position. In the well-known essay "on Wisdom" he named two prime determinants of being—*power* and *harmony*. From these, however, he educed a list of derivative attributes which are obviously not in any direct sense convertible, but which are closely dependent upon each other, and together provide a great part of the structure of his philosophy. "From this one can see (he wrote) how happiness, pleasure, love, perfection, being, power, freedom, harmony, order, and beauty are all interbound, something which very few have rightly seen."[18] Here such ethical notions as happiness, pleasure, and love, and aesthetic conceptions such as beauty and harmony, are mixed indiscriminately with more abstract metaphysical attributes such as power and order, and it is more appropriate to speak of the relations among them all in terms of logical implication rather than of simple convertibility. Judged by the standards of later thought, Leibniz's comment appears as an uncritical mixture of subjective and objective, of descriptive and normative concepts. Yet before we discuss the process of decay which the doctrine of transcendentals underwent through subjectivization and the descriptive reduction of norms, a brief examination of the role of the transcendentals in the so-called rationalistic systems of the later century is necessary.

Transcendentals in the Great Systems

In the thought of men like Descartes, Spinoza, Pascal, Malebranche, and Leibniz, a great victory had been won in metaphysics in favor of concreteness and an empirical approach to rational order. Modern metaphysics had developed from its beginning in the service of theological controversy in the sixteenth century,[19] to a fresh effort to comprehend and unify the categories involved in all being in the seventeenth. In this development the transcendentals were expanded to include much which Aristotle had relegated to the categories, and were thus relativized through an intellectual clarification of the diverse fields of human experience. Essential prerequisites for this merging and differentiation of orders and principles were: (1) the elimination by Suarez and others of the Scholastic distinction between general and special metaphysics; (2) the resulting resolution, in the affirmative, of the old issue of whether theology has a place within metaphysics; (3) the widespread adoption throughout Europe of the related epistemological theory intiated by Telesio, Campanella, and others in the late Renaissance, that reason, revelation, and experience are three compatible and mutually supplementary approaches to one truth; and (4) Ramus's expansion of Aristotle's doctrine of the scope of predication in propositions, as stated in the *Posterior Analytics* (I, iv, 73b), to apply to all being, and therefore to the transcendentals as well.

Aristotle's original intent in formulating this doctrine (*kata pantos, kath'autò, kath'olou*) is far from clear, and Ramus's contemporaries found his appropriation of it generally opaque and unintelligible as well; his Aristotelian opponent Jacob Schegk called it Ramus's "incessant and nauseating little song." But Bacon, who distrusted the Ramistic "canker of epitomies," nevertheless gave him credit for "reviving the good rules of propositions" and actually appropriated part of them (the *kath'autò*) as a general principle of "how far one knowledge ought to intermeddle with the province of another."[20] In spite of Ramus's opposition to metaphysics, therefore, his adaptation of Aristotle's principles of predication to his own method was accepted by the encyclopedists and became a part of their theory of knowledge. Comenius, for example, introduced the rule *de omni, per se, universaliter* as a precept necessary for his rational pansophistic program of revealing the secrets of nature, as promised by scriptural revelation (Deuteronomy 29:29; Colossians 2:3). All principles in the *Pansophia* must be clear and distinct (*perspicua*), must be affirmed only for a specified application (*non nisi certi usūs*), and must be *per se*, always and everywhere true (*omnia vera per se, semper et ubique*).[21]

Thus these precepts correspond in general to a methodological application of the transcendentals *unum, verum, bonum* (taken operationally and teleologically). Their meaning is shifted beyond the structure of metaphysics itself to the consideration of reason, method, and logical implication, in all sciences and arts. Yet the transcendentals are still, though largely implicitly, the bonds between being and our ways of knowing it and acting and reacting upon it, between being and its particular actualizations, and between being and values. Method, following the advice of Bacon, still follows order, and order includes within itself the method needed to perceive it.

In the great metaphysical triad of Descartes, Spinoza, and Leibniz, in which each member is less a disciple than a critic of the preceding ones, system and method, truth and value, are similarly convergent upon being in all of its differentiations. It is in this sense, rather than in the sense of direct convertibility, that we may find the transcendentals, in their expanded and somewhat confused variety, still operative in their systems.

The metaphysicians of the late century were all influenced by the rise of nominalism (in its moderate, Continental form) and by skepticism. Yet in one way or another, all avoided subjectivism and its skeptical consequences. As we have seen, their construction of metaphysics about the doctrine of ideas enabled them to achieve a theory of being as a subjective-objective unity. The nature of independent things on the one hand, and the relevance of sense perceptions, acts of will, and the emotions on the other, can be understood only in relation to the unifying ideas or essences.

Of the philosophers under consideration, Descartes and Pascal, whom Léon Brunschvicg grouped together as "students of Montaigne," felt the seriousness of the skeptical challenge most strongly, and sought ways of accepting and overcoming it. Both were, in different ways, mannerist in temperament and style;[22] the libertine thread in their thinking was manifested in the new imaginative approaches which they made to man and his nature, though they met the problems in different ways. Influenced by modern atomism and mathematical determinism, Descartes removed the physical world from many transcendental concepts; nature is a mathematical order determined by the laws of geometry and of physical motion. Bodies are entirely passive, depending completely upon spirit as a source of motion and of change of direction. Unity, number, and measure were still held to have a universal application to being, but the Aristotelian categories of substance and mode dominate the metaphysics. Perfection, power, action, and wisdom apply only to spirit, primarily to the supreme spirit and indirectly to finite spirits as the divine providence is required for their continued existence. Yet these spirits are free and have a relative degree of self-determination, so that human goods are made relative to man's choices and are to that extent detached from the absolute attributes of God.

Pascal also regarded the universe as a duality, but the cut was more sharply made, not only between nature and man and between man and God, but, underlying both of these separations, also between man in need of redemption and man in a state of grace. God the *Immensum*—infinite force and inexorable order, and their manifestations in infinite space—are the transcendentals which unsaved men confront without themselves having a share in them. (Save for their intelligence, men are the weakest of reeds). Infinite goodness, as mercy, is added for the redeemed, on condition that they manifest faith. The dualism is thus shown to lie in man himself, divided between the spirit of geometry and the spirit of finesse, but even more deeply, between the two levels of human experience—the fear and trembling of doubt and the peace of assurance. Not only has the divine transcendence lost the quality of *unity*, at least in relation to human experience, but there is a strong tendency, as there is in Descartes, toward subjectivism, not merely with regard to sensory and affective experiences, but also with regard to the *verum* and the *bonum*.

This subjectivity with regard to values was considered notorious in Spinoza, with some ground, as is shown by the Appendix to Book I of the *Ethics* and by his repeated assertion that we do not desire things because they are good, but they are good because we desire them. Yet the earlier *Essay on the Emendation of the Intellect* had placed his entire metaphysical and ethical system within the context of the human quest for escape from transient goods and the discovery and appropriation of an abiding good. As the *Ethics* shows, this abiding good turns out to be not merely the discovery of God, but active participation, through the life of reason, in the very essence of God as *intellectual love*. The dualism in the universe—*natura naturata* vs. *natura naturans*—which separates the transcendentals in Descartes and Pascal is overcome in man through the subordination of passive to active affections. And the transcendental essence of God is discovered to be, on the *abstract* level, infinitude, perfection, power (self-causality), and *concretely* power, wisdom, and love.[23] Perfection is actualized throughout the universe of modes, either actively or passively. There are no more degrees of being, but only gradations of difference in the limitation or freedom of the activity of the modes—their power, affections, and intelligence, and therefore their capacity for intellectual love.

Spinoza's system may be understood as an attempt to restore the unity of the transcendentals as originally held in the Platonic tradition, by subordinating the many, the diverse, and the changing to the one, the whole, the eternal, and by making the metaphysical attributes of unitary being the abstract supports for its moral (and aesthetic) attributes. Unity, perfection, power, and love are convertible with being, but (as in Plato himself) only reason and wisdom, governing the affections of men, can assure their elevation from the level of passivity and divisiveness to full participation in the concreteness of being.

In this endeavor to restore the full meaning of the transcendentals in their new and enlarged formulation, Leibniz agreed with Spinoza; what separated them was his emphasis that the transcendentals must be explicated in each individual *as* individual, according to his limitations, not in each individual merely as a mode of the infinite. For Leibniz power is a transcendental which is convertible with all being, as is also perfection. But both, together with their moral accompaniments—wisdom, love, justice—are allotted to finite beings in proportion to their essential limitations, that is, the laws of their individual natures. "Just so, perfection shows itself in great freedom and power of action, since all being consists in a kind of power, and the greater the power the higher and freer the being . . . The greater any power is, moreover, the more there is found in it the many revealed through the one and in the one, in that the one rules many outside of itself and represents them in itself. Now unity in plurality is nothing but harmony."[24]

Thus the old Platonic conception of a microcosm-macrocosm relationship was restored but developed into a pluralistic system of individuals, each with power and each acting in such a way as to include others in its unique perspective in a community of interacting events and correspondingly passive internal states. The assurance of individual power rests in the identity of the qualities making up each individual's nature with the simple perfections (or Ideas) of God which were used in his creation. Power is not the mere potentiality of Aristotle; it is not merely the possibility of action, but a positive striving into actuality.[25] According to the differences of degree of power among monads, they fall into two great societies or groups of interacting actions and passions—the simpler ones constitute a kingdom of nature whose goodness is not intrinsic but extrinsic, in part as service to God, in part to the other kingdom, that of grace, which consists of spirit monads capable of self-awareness and therefore of memory, thought, moral judgment, and decision. The monads in this kingdom, furthermore, have as their purpose, each his own perfection in love, and together, the perfection of the divine harmony and love of the whole. Thus Leibniz attempts a systematic completion of the ideal of a perfect society of finite beings as envisioned earlier in the century by Bisterfeld and Comenius.

Nevertheless, in spite of its logical clarity, its remarkably modern insights, and its inclusiveness, there are factors in Leibniz's system which tend again to undermine this restored unity and universality of the immanent transcendental qualities. And this tendency was strengthened in the later decades of his life, when his logical studies gave way to more empirical and temporal considerations.

To avoid Spinoza's conclusion that every possibility is or

will be actualized—which Leibniz considered an invitation to atheism, since it implies that all evils as well as all goods must sometime exist—he restricted the quality of perfection, as it applies to creation, to "the best order of compossibles." Not all logical possibilities can exist together in a good universe, and the transcendental nature of goodness and wisdom differ from that of knowledge and power in that they involve the elimination of some possibilities and a creation only of the best. Thus the three are not directly convertible.

Leibniz's ethics, moreover, requires a further restriction of the good beyond the limitation of possibilities. All existence is good, but morality turns less about the good than about the right (*jus*) and the dependence of the right upon wisdom and love. "Justice is the love of the wise." "Love is finding one's joy in the happiness (or the perfection) of another." Goodness therefore becomes the power of perfection, of whatever degree, to evoke joy or happiness.

Leibniz in this way arrives at a synthesis of the transcendentals within a social order in which persons and things mix in two interrelated kingdoms. He still retains the realistic interpretation of the objects of perception and knowledge which Descartes is in danger of losing. But the transcendentals do not simply imply each other as component notions in the abstract concept of being or as perfections of God; they comprise the positive qualities of a society of individuals, to whose unique relations to each other they impart the norms of wisdom, justice, and love. Leibniz has carried the problem of being and the transcendentals close to Hegel, though without adopting Hegel's logic or the intervening analysis carried through by Kant, of interpreting transcendental concepts as logically required mental acts.

Leibniz's shift was made explicit in his comments on Locke's discussion of the nature of *truth*. In Book IV of the *Nouveaux Essais* he rejected Locke's tendency to reduce essences to names and therefore to find philosophical distinctions based on language rather than things. In contrast, he defined truth in terms of his own theory of the proposition as "the relation between the objects of ideas which causes the one to be or not to be included in the other."

> This does not depend upon languages, and is common to us with God and the angels; and when God manifests a truth to us we shall acquire that which is in his understanding, for

although there is an infinite difference between his ideas and ours as regards perfection and extent, it is always true that they agree in the same relation.

Thus far Leibniz goes in affirming the transcendental character of the *verum*. Yet at this point he draws back.

Metaphysical truth is commonly taken by metaphysicians as an attribute of being, but it is an attribute very useless and almost devoid of meaning. Let us content ourselves with seeking truth in the correspondence of the propositions in the mind with the things in question. It is true that I have also attributed truth to ideas in saying that ideas are true or false, but then I mean, in reality, the truth of propositions affirming the possibility of the object of the idea.[26]

Thus truth is put into its human, interpersonal context, without, however, forgetting its real reference to things.

The Unresolved Status of the Transcendentals

The enlarged, but considerably more complicated, doctrine of transcendentals in the seventeenth century was proposed (as I have suggested) as a metaphysical support for the duty of the man of honor to live justly, wisely, and in sympathy with his fellows, and to further European unity by his active pursuit of unity, truth, and goodness in the diverse fields of science, law, morality, and religion. The systems embodying this doctrine were proposed in a century which was fully conscious of the problem of evil; the succession of European wars, recurrent plagues, the quarrels of religious and intellectual divisiveness, the injustice of absolute political power were commonplaces in the experience of the period. The philosophic solutions offered were apologetic systems which defended the reality of completely coherent ideals of being, truth, goodness, and beauty, all sustained by a trinity of power, wisdom, and love, and intended to prove the inevitability of a culmination of life in a real universal harmony and unity.

Yet in the critical process of examining these most general properties of being, their relativity to the human order in its efforts to achieve harmony becomes apparent, and their immanence in this order more explicit. Certain weaknesses which developed in the effort to render a more dynamic, comprehensive, and detailed theory of the transcendentals have been pointed out. It remains to comment briefly on three such immanent defects which threatened the collapse of the doctrine as the century approached its end.

1. The identification of the real and the ideal (and normative) involved an inadequate conception of personal freedom and self-determination, and a confusion and lack of clarity in programs of action.

2. The subjective aspect of experience tended to break loose from its objective bond, with the result that the isolation of the individual in knowledge and appreciation of the world became a threat. The cultural components built about the new sciences were divorced from the humanistic interests resting upon man's inwardness. In short, the split into "the two cultures" about which we have been warned in our own age, had begun. This isolation of disciplines and individuals did not, however, develop until the Enlightenment of the following century.

3. The fact of contingency in the universe and in man's actions in particular was recognized as the condition of morality and social order. If this contingency is authentic, it introduces a hazard for the human quest for any values which transcend the relative. Empirically the agent and the power for achieving the existence of goodness, truth, and beauty is man, though man may not himself reveal the norm, the universal, which such achievement presupposes.

A recent critic of the effort to restore the significance of transcendence in contemporary thought has urged that the new ontologists must decide, finally, whether "ontological structures are things having being in themselves (*an sich*) or are mere products of thought."[27] He concludes that the grounds for the objectivity of principles and norms have been eroded away in the thought of the seventeenth and eighteenth century, and that no viable way of restoring them has been found.

This is particularly true of the metaphysical effort to find in a nobler conception of the most perfect being, and of the order of finite beings which mirror his nature, a basis for the unity of what is and what ought to be. In Martin Heidegger's early study of Duns Scotus, which foreshadowed the shift in his thought from Scholastic rationalism to existential relativism, his restriction of the transcendentals to their personal ground was anticipated with respect to the disjunctive transcendental *unum et diversum:*

From this mode of characterizing categorially the real world of objects, sensible and supersensible, there results a very unique insight into the sphere of existence in which perspectives of value have achieved the power of determining existence. The purely logical, which is in the medieval sense [and we may add, in the seventeenth century sense as well] also metaphysical . . . seems now to have been brought . . . into a unity—although admittedly a unity of a unique kind. If one brings the transcendental philosophical perspective to bear, it comes to be seen that medieval realism, whether naive or critical, which clings to the firm character of natural existence (*Naturwirklichkeit*) is anything but naturalism. It is spiritualism, and it is precisely the hierarchical character of real existence, grounded in analogy, which is intended to overcome the problems which arise in every dualism without bringing back an impossible monism.[28]

To reduce the doctrine of transcendentals to the dimensions of the human spirit in a divided world is certainly to do violence to the intent of Duns Scotus and those who succeeded him. It is certainly not compatible with the intent of the seventeenth century thinkers whom I have briefly called to witness. Yet I have tried to show that the dissolution of a transcendental unity began in that century and has continued until our times. It was Immanuel Kant who resisted the critical rationalism and the growing subjectivism of the Age of Reason by finding the seat of the transcendentals to lie in the potency and action not of an infinite mind, but of man himself—man whose thought involves the universal, whose imagination bridges the gaps between what he understands and the reasoning he must do about the good, the right, the beautiful, the divine, man whose reasoning can be effective only when he is seen as a member of a social unity, a kingdom of ends. Heidegger represents the mood of our century so well because he has further devalued the transcendentals from the character which the Kantian idealists gave them, of emerging in power in human history. Although he has retained the term to describe man's inner independence of nature, the transcendentals become restricted to an essentially subjective realm. The metaphysics of being becomes a phenomenology of the "*Sein des Daseins.*"

Nevertheless, Heidegger's astute interpretation does uncover the duplicity of the systems which attempted a unity of being (in the most universal sense) beyond the dualisms of *is* and *ought, self* and *others, truth* and *goodness, conflict* and *harmony*, and were therefore caught in the absurdity of treating the end of their apologetic task as already in essence achieved in the nature of being—the kingdom of grace a present reality as much as the kingdom of nature; God's absolute sovereignty binding man in a kind of freedom which consists solely in an obedience to superior law; natural and moral evil alike justified as contributing to a higher good. Leo Spitzer has described this "telescoping of reality with speculation," which he regards as characteristic of the Greek tradition and essential to the Renaissance, as "synaesthesis,"[29] or the "feeling-together" of the real and ideal opposites. These opposites have provided the substructure of the thesis of this work—the diverse and the united, the dissonant and consonant, darkness and light, the controversial real and the rhetorical ideal of the Republic of Letters, the inclusion of all men, even sinners, in the kingdom of grace, the coalescence of the duty of the *homme honnête* with the already existing universe. According to Spitzer, synaesthesia is conceptual in the Renaissance, but is given a new sensual depth in the baroque (as in the baroque ceilings which bring intuitions of infinity into the finite as its limit). This intuitive fusion of actuality with the norm or ideal inherent in it rests intellectually upon the Platonic doctrine of the ideas and Plato's and Aristotle's attribution to things of a potency for actualization of their ideas.

It may be added that a clearer recognition of the ultimacy of the temporal dimension of existence is needed to conserve the power of the ideal in the face of man's actual situation. But when the temporal is thus pushed to the fore, the golden chain of existence is broken and a new relativism and indeterminism threaten to destroy even the ideal of the systematic wholeness.

We have already noted small inroads of subjectivism into the thought of Descartes. It may be said that in Leibniz's doctrine of justice as the love of the powerful and wise, but even more, in his theory of the complete internal self-determinism of each individual, he has made concrete and personal the subjectivism which Descartes introduced in his theory of sense data and subjective values. Unfortunately the Age of Reason overlooked the "symbiotic," interpersonal dimensions of experience which the great systematizers built into their thought, so that the great introversion of metaphysics became irresistible; henceforth it would be written either from the centrality of nature or from the centrality of man, his knowledge and his needs, rather than from the centrality of being and its attributes.

A third factor in this breaking of the chain of identity of the real and the ideal was the fact of contingency. Its recognition was Aristotelian in origin, but it became widely accepted only slowly in the seventeenth century, as men came to see that the scope of the existent is not as great as the scope of the possible, and that all existence (save only God's) could have been different than it is. For a long time this insight would continue to be resisted by the new determinism of science. It was to achieve its widest interpretations only in the nineteenth century, when the pragmatists and their associates in personalist and spiritualist circles pressed the scientific and ethical case for indeterminism. But the growing emphasis of Leibniz upon the temporal dimension of being in the last decades of his life, presaged a new era in the interpretation of history and of philosophy.

These trends—subjectivism, the recognition of the contingent, the empirical separation of existence from the normative, and the distrust of universals—supported the coming libertine revolution. Arising within the tradition of the transcendentalist metaphysics, as well as in criticisms from without, they were reflections of the sobering influence of the new science and the new individualism. It is true that the first atomists—Gassendi, for example, and after him Boyle, whose commitment to the corpuscular philosophy did not keep him from claiming superiority for a higher knowledge based on revelation, explicitly exempted the human spirit and God from their effort to explain all things in terms of weight, measure, motion, and the internal interrelation of parts. In both cases, the effect of this was to restrict the application of the transcendentals—particularly the *verum, bonum, pulchrum,* and *justum*—first to the bonds between God and men, and then, after the failure of both analogy and univocity to sustain this relation, to men themselves. This is still clearer in Locke and Newton at the end of the century. It was the real ground for Leibniz's charge (in his First Letter to Clarke) that the new mathematical philosophy was contributing to "the decay of natural religion in England"[30] and encouraging the atheism and libertinism which Boyle's lecture foundation was designed to check. In contrast to the efforts of men like Malebranche and Leibniz to show that human love and justice themselves required as necessary conditions the grace of God (and even the work of Christ), efforts now were made to find an adequate ground for such good and needed human orders even in atheistic societies. The way to libertine interpretations of human life and social order was opened through nominalism, skepticism, mechanistic science and its technological uses, and more democratic ideals of freedom.

Within the traditional microcosm-macrocosm idea, the analytic emphasis was increasingly placed upon the microcosm and its reflection within finite limits, of the infinite perfection (or ideas) of the macrocosm and its creator. Corresponding to this, the permanent residue of the changes undergone by the doctrine of the transcendentals, when emphasis was focused on human intelligence and action, was the insight that the transcendentals must, on empirical grounds, be considered as immanent within the finite boundaries of our experience of the world. The immanence of the transcendent within human reason is that aspect of the immanence of the infinite within the finite (Jean Buridan called it the syncategoric infinite) which limits the transcendental ideas, whether primalities or disjunctives, to the role of regulative ideas giving to man's finite thoughts and actions their direction and their moral motivation—never completely attainable but constantly drawing them on.

7 Order and Method

Just as the order of beings follows the order of intelligence, so our intellect follows the order of beings.

[J. C. Scaliger, *Exercitatio* II, in *Exotericarum exercitationum* (Hanau, 1634), p. 6.]

Order, in so far as it is order, does not have the force of drawing together (*colligendi*, i.e. drawing conclusions), but only of arranging (*disponendi*); method, however, has an inferential force (*vim illatricem*), and gathers (again *colligo*) one thing from another . . . From what has been said about the difference between method and order, this definition of method seems to follow: method is an intellectual instrument bringing about out of the known a knowledge of the unknown; "intellectual instrument," which is the genus of "method," also includes order; but to bring about a knowledge of the unknown from the known is the differentia which separates method from order.

[Giacomo Zabarella, *De Methodis*, Book III, chaps. i and ii.]

Knowledge that is delivered as a thread to be spun on, ought to be delivered and intimated, if it were possible, in the same method wherein it was invented.

[Francis Bacon, *The Advancement of Learning*, II, xvii,4 (The World's Classics, p. 162).]

Order and Method in Zabarella

Much ambiguity and unclarity has marked discussions of the transcendental property of order and its relation to problems of method, ever since Aristotle discussed them in his scientific treatises. In this chapter I propose to examine some of these ambiguities as they appeared in seventeenth century thought, and the role which they played in reversing his concept of the relationship of the two.

Three questions are particularly involved in this shift: (1) Is order the presupposition of method, or does method itself establish order? (2) What is it which is ordered, and to which

157

method applies: nature, the content of the disciplines, or the ideas? (3) What is the goal of method: to establish an order of what is already known so as to facilitate teaching and learning it most effectively? (This was the accepted view of method in the traditional textbooks on logic.) Or is it the discovery of new knowledge? (This was the tradition of method transmitted from Galen, through the medics, to the new sciences.) Or (somewhat between and overlapping these two views), is it to replace opinion, or what is known unclearly and indistinctly, with knowledge that is certain and adequate?

To begin with the view of Giacomo Zabarella: Zabarella restored a distinction between order and method which both supporters and detractors of Aristotle had already begun to abandon, but which he clarified by explicating Aristotle's doctrine and practice, as it had been restated by Galen and later generalized by Averroës.

Briefly summarized, Zabarella's doctrine is as follows. Both order and method are aspects of disciplines, that is, of fields of learning. As has been shown in earlier chapters, Zabarella denied the possibility of finding an order applying to the totality of all disciplines. Both order and method (the Greek terms "odos" and "methodos," that is, "meta-odos" suggest the closeness of their relation) imply a progression from the known to the unknown, and both have two aspects—the resolutive and the compositive, or, more commonly, analysis and synthesis. The resolutive order involves an arrangement from the composite to its more simple (prior) ingredients; the compositive proceeds in action from known simples to the composite ends which they imply, or from means to sought ends which are seen to follow from them. Like Bacon after him, Zabarella divided all disciplines into the contemplative sciences and the applied arts. Thus the resolutive order applies to contemplative disciplines, the compositive to arts or practical disciplines. (As an example, Zabarella used the medical distinction between anatomy and the order and method of medical diagnosis and prescription.) But in both instances, whether in theoretical or in practical disciplines, order is merely the *arrangement* of related structures from simpler and independent to more complex and dependent, or the arrangement of knowledge as causally related to the attainment of desired ends. Method, on the other hand, is the actual reasoning, on the basis of order, from a known composite (whether a theorem, a material compound, a legal case, or any other known complex truth) to its sufficient causes, reasons, or components; or it is specific action to achieve a desired end through the use of causes which are known (by previous ordering) to be sufficient to achieve that end.

Thus Zabarella agreed with Aristotle that order precedes method, or that method presupposes order.[1] From Aristotle's position he concluded that only order, not method, is proper to the discipline of logic; method must be left to the individual disciplines.[2] Zabarella's account of the relation of logic to disciplines with an empirical content anticipated the recent distinction between the syntactic and the semantic dimensions of meaning.

His interpretation differed in general from Aristotle's, however, in that he applied both order and method to the content of disciplines; both apply to knowledge and its organization. Aristotle, on the other hand, treated order, as distinct from method, as also applying directly to things. By Zabarella's time, the discussion had swung from the *pars rerum* to the *pars rationis*. Logic and discipline are discussed as mental *habitus* or faculties.

There are, therefore, two reasons why Zabarella's discussion of order and method are important for the argument of this chapter.

1. I shall try to show that by the end of the seventeenth century the priority of order to method will have been reversed, and that there is an increasing tendency to make order the result of method—order is imposed on nature by the scientific mind. Zabarella was still on the side of those who hold that method selects from order according to its aims; the mentalizing of order had not yet begun.

2. However, Zabarella's shift of the context of order from nature to disciplines revealed a tendency, arising from Renaissance nominalism, to limit logic and method to reason, leaving the reference of knowledge of things to the symbolic role of language. This, Hobbes, with a nominalistic theory of logic, borrowed from him, though Hobbes carried the trend further toward the emergence of a skepticism in which thought is separated from its object.

Zabarella already stood midway between a realistic theory of knowledge and a mentalistic one. On one side, Aristotle applied both order and method directly to experienced things and objective ends, natural or human. On the other side, later empiricists offered a theory of ideas according to which method is determined by the content of man's inquiries and purposes, and is completed in a reasonable order of understanding. Between the two positions, Zabarella retained the priority of order to method but restricted both to the area of human knowledge and its disciplinary aim and worth.

Yet it is significant that both Zabarella and his more realistically oriented follower, Bartholomew Keckermann of Danzig, have already introduced, though without explicitly acknowledging it, a secondary order which *results* from the synthetic method rather than providing the precondition for it. When the teacher, medic, or empirical logician proceeds to arrange his knowledge of causes, gained through analysis, into a pattern which is a sufficient cause for his desired end (one might modernize this by labeling it technological or experimental design), he is not only bringing into being an order derived from the analytic method and possible only after its application, but introducing a new component—the end sought. This is an instance, therefore, of an order which is not rooted in first principles and prior concepts alone, but one in part determined by human thought for man's own purposes.

Ambiguities in the Aim of Method

According to Zabarella, and to the logicians who preceded him, the aim of method, as distinct from the order on which it is based, is the arrangement and presentation of knowledge in the way most appropriate for learning and teaching it. Whether analytic or synthetic, method implied a reasoning from effects to causes or from causes to desired effects, but its end was the presentation of such knowledge in a way proper for learning it and demonstrating its truth. This is shown in the logic books of Aristotelians and anti-Aristotelians alike, in which method is treated only after invention and judgment have been discussed. Francis Bacon was essentially Platonic in his modes of thought; this can be seen, among many other ways, by his search for an order which shall not only contain all knowledge, but shall be logically exhaustive enough to aid in the discovery of the gaps in human knowledge; in contrast to this, the Aristotelian Zabarella had denied any order more inclusive than that of separate disciplines. The unifying order was thus less closely related to method in Bacon than were the disparate orders of the disciplines in Zabarella (or in Aristotle); for Bacon the question of order was settled when he had outlined the plan of his several great digests of learning by deriving its subdivisions from the basic potentialities of man. Nevertheless, method was treated in *The Advancement of Learning* and its enlarged Latin version, the *De dignitate et augmentiis scientiarum* (1623), in its traditional place within the third part of logic or dialectic—that given to the effective organization and teaching of what is known, whether through disputation (which Bacon abhorred), lecture, or other forms of study. Bacon's discussion of logic followed the tripartite division of Invention, Judgment, and Didactics or Canonics, which conformed to the late Scholastics' rearrangement of the Organon and which Ramus and the later Port Royal logic also retained.

What was fresh and new in Bacon is his recommendation that the method of teaching (the "delivery" of knowledge) insofar as it aims at practice and utility ("a thread to be spun on") ought to be the same as the method by which it was "invented," that is, discovered.[3] Thus, while adhering to the tradition of learning, Bacon did recognize another use of method—a method for discovering new knowledge rather than one for ordering knowledge already given for teaching and learning. He proposed that the traditional methods of learning through disputation, abstract classification, or logical ordering be replaced by a genetic order reproducing that of discovery. Bacon therefore brought together again two applications of method which had grown apart—the method of teaching or learning what is known, and the method of discovering what is not known—erudition and scientific-technological advance.

Method as arranging knowledge had, as I have said, dominated the later sections of the traditional works in logic, after the earlier discussion of "invention" and judgment. This older tradition continued well into the seventeenth century—the discussion of method was at most a guide to purposive operational procedure (directed at ends) within the context of a given order or structure of meaning. For example, Peter Ramus's *Institutiones Dialecticae* (first ed. 1552; widely reprinted and used for a century) had stressed the rhetorical role of method in its final section on Canonics or Didactics. Not only did Descartes's *Regulae* and their reduction to the four rules of method in the *Discourse* point to the arrangement of knowledge to attain clearness and distinctness rather than to discovering new knowledge, his entire metaphysics, as discussed analytically in the *Meditations* and then ordered by the "synthetic method" in his *Response to the Second Objections*, aimed at persuasion and clarification rather than at discovery. It was intended to elevate the understanding of those who already possessed *bon sens* to the level of right reasoning (*recta ratio*).[4] In the logic of the Hamburg scholar Joachim Jung, whom Leibniz regarded as a creative innovator in the field, method was still discussed as the way of teaching or the order of learning (*via doctrinae* or *ordo didascalia*), only after the first parts of his logic had been treated—the first covering the principles common to necessary and probable reasoning (apodictic and dialectic), the second covering each of these separately.[5] In his work on *A New Method of Teaching and Learning Jurisprudence* (1667), the young Leibniz retained this plan, criticizing Descartes's rules of method early in the book for their inadequacy in making knowledge certain.[6] Even the influential Port Royal logic, *La logique ou l'art de penser* (1662), composed on Cartesian principles by Arnauld and Nicole, placed method in Part IV (*De la méthode*), though their definition made clear that while method consists of analysis and synthesis, the former aims at the discovery of knowledge while the latter provides the proper arrangement of what is already known. "Thus there are two sorts of method; the one for the discovery of truth, which is called *analysis*, or *the method* of resolution, and which can also be called *the method of invention;* and the other to make others understand the truth one has found; this is called *synthesis* or the *method of composition*, or could also be called the method of doctrine."[7] The authors then proceed to present Descartes's rules of method in the *Discours de la méthode* as rules for discovery, and other selections from the earlier *Regulae ad directionem ingenii* rules for the arrangment of doctrine.

Scientific Method: Unity of the A priori and A posteriori Approaches

The success of the new sciences, of course, stimulated and accelerated the shift of method from the aim of reordering what is already known to increase its clarity and certainty, to that of discovering the new. The method of discovery had had a prescientific history, particularly in the medical tradition, which inherited Galen's application of method. Both Paracelsus and his Aristotelian contemporary, Jean Fernel, regarded the physician's method as a personal habit of thought applied directly to a real order of causal and teleological relations—the end being the recovery of health or the prolongation of life. In his book on *The Hidden Causes of Nature*, Fernel described the physician as proceeding from the common observation of a disease to an analysis of its hidden causes by means of the accepted symptoms, and then, from an understanding of these causes and the natural effects resulting from them, to a synthesis of causes sufficient to achieve a desired cure.[8]

This is obviously a realistic application of the same analysis of resolving and compounding which Zabarella later put forth, being applied directly *ad rem* instead of *ad rationes disciplinae* as in Zabarella, whose methods, as we have seen, were copied in Bacon and in Hobbes.[9] Like Bacon, however, Hobbes failed to understand the further selective and discriminatory step which is involved, after the mechanistic analysis of causes, in the synthesis of those causal conditions which will suffice for the desired effect. Hobbes seems to have assumed that causal connections and telic applications are directly convertible, as the old theory of transcendentals suggested. It required nicer tools of logical analysis, especially those revealed in the new mathematical discoveries, to show that a teleological synthesis requires a determining factor beyond the mechanical causes, namely the limits imposed by the defined purpose, and is therefore not directly convertible with the causes or reasons discovered by analysis of the phenomenon concerned. Purpose thus requires, within the possibilities of action implicit in the analysis of efficient causes, a further selective choice, based upon synthetic reasoning, of those particular causes which will serve as sufficient means to the desired end. This was to be seen later in the century by Leibniz, and to be made central to his metaphysics and philosophy of science.

Among methods for discovering new knowledge, the a priori applications to experience of mathematical forms of reasoning proved to be most instructive. In addition to leading to the discovery of the first precise insights into the order of nature—insights of which Bacon had no clear conception—they successfully related the two essential components of method in establishing truth: a posteriori, precise observation under controlled conditions, and a priori, the principles and definitions determining the form of the hypotheses which guide the observations and impart universality and a higher degree of certainty to the observed relations. The analytic-synthetic method of Euclid, enriched by the new algebraic method of discovering the values of unknown variables in a defined situation by analysis, provided the guiding principles and forms used in theorizing about physical problems, and then, when experiments—controlled observations—designed with these principles as premises brought success, also provided the order in which the new discoveries were shown to be logically convincing. Thus after Kepler, balked for years by the problem of the distances and periods of the planetary orbits, failed to determine them by the geometry of the concentric regular geometric solids and their circumscribed spheres, he turned to the harmonic series based on the first integers—those whose harmonic inversions were known as the basis of musical harmony—as clues to the distances of the planets from the sun, and remarkably succeeded in "explaining" (that is, in fitting into this a priori scheme) the measurements of planetary positions by Tycho Brahe and others.[10]

Galileo's even more complex and systematic success in solving general problems in mechanics, particularly his brilliant synthesis of the principles of pendular motion with motion on an inclined plane and with a general theory about falling bodies, gave a new meaning to the method of analysis and synthesis as applied to physical problems.[11]

After the work of Kepler and Galileo, the mutual dependence and interaction between Aristotle's two orders, a priori and a posteriori, were established in the investigation of nature. The subsequent history of the century shows that this combination was recognized in metaphysics as well, in spite of the distinction made between rationalists and empiricists in the textbooks. Spinoza, for example, used the geometric a priori method in his *Ethics* to carry conviction (expanding Descartes's own "synthetic" demonstration at the end of his Response to the Second Objections), but his theorems were based on definitions, many of which are derived from experience, and were usually proved by the indirect method, that is, by showing that their denial must conflict with earlier established truth. Insofar as they are synthetic propositions, making some concrete advance in knowledge, he does not provide sufficient reasons, synthetically, for their truth. Scholia provide a further rich empirical texture of insights, illustrative of the theorems but not proved from them.

Leibniz frequently suggested that his entire system could be derived synthetically from first principles and primitive terms, and did in fact provide many suggestions about how particular axioms, for example in various geometries and in dynamics, could be derived from the primary laws of identity, contradiction, and sufficient reason through the additional use of fitting definitions. Yet his one attempt to derive the general principles of his philosophy from the laws of identity, contradiction, and sufficient reason, was done entirely by the indirect method, which cannot provide positive grounds for understanding the principles proved.[12]

Both Spinoza and Leibniz thus recognized the value of the geometric method for imparting certainty and conviction to knowledge, but also its insufficiency as a basis for demonstrating truths of fact. Before the end of the century Leibniz clearly restricted a priori reasoning from axioms and primitive concepts alone to truths of reason, that is, truths whose structure is empty of any facts not given in the definitions used in the reasoning, and which are therefore "tautological."

In the empirical tradition, on the other hand, while Locke still professed to discuss the "original" and "truth" of ideas by deriving them, through another nonlogical type of synthesis later identified as the association of ideas, from impressions of sense and reflection, it became clear in Hume's writings that the empirical analysis gave no account of origins, but served chiefly to identify the empirical content of perceptions and propositions, and thus to determine their validity by this empirical criterion. The result was that, by the early eighteenth century, it was clear that reasoning a priori and a posteriori were both ways of certifying the validity of knowledge, but that the one, taken alone, could only do this for truths of reason, the other, only for truths of fact without any determination of necessity or order. But since truths of reason can be built into the ordering of facts, it was also clear that success in science, and also in a metaphysics of existence (in contrast to a metaphysics restricted to mere possibility or logical necessity) depended on a proper use of the two, experience to give content and reason to give form or necessary order to the content—in establishing valid truths of fact. In his examination of Locke's *Essay*, Leibniz went further to conclude that since a priori reasoning from first principles and definitions was alone insufficient to establish the truth of such mixed propositions, the degree of certainty of which they were capable must be achieved through future verification of predictions made from them through observation, preferably under experimental control.[13]

It must be added that in their pure forms neither a priorism nor a posteriorism recognized the importance of hypotheses in the methods of either science or philosophy. In both methods, hypotheses were to be considered temporary generalizations, essentially uncertain, and to be abandoned when better evidence is made available through observation or reason. Yet in 1699, Leibniz, writing to Burcher de Volder, called his philosophy a hypothesis, "but one which is clear and beautifully consistent with itself and with phenomena."[14] The pragmatic dimension of prediction and future verification in Leibniz's discussion of Locke's *Essay* seems a step in the direction of recognizing once more the role of the venturesome design of experiments, conjecture in the realm of possibilities—in short, imagination, however disciplined, in the search for truth. Bacon had put it there, however unclearly, in his remark that "sense sendeth over to imagination before reason have judged, and reason sendeth over to imagination before the decree can be acted."[15] But the creative, imaginative role of the intellect was, for a while, lost in the quest for rigor and certainty. Léon Brunschvicg was right in noting that "the passage from childlike imagination to a proper human intelligence is achieved in history with the seventeenth century,"[16] but in achieving this, the century's ablest minds seem to have lost sight, for a time, of the importance, for new knowledge, of the free play of an imagination schooled by reason.

The Loss of Certainty

Between the conception of method as the most effective way of ordering what is known to improve understanding, and the conception of method as a way of discovering the unknown, there was a third conception which has something in common with both. This conception was related to the rise of skepticism, and aimed at the elimination of uncertainty. Its most distinguished exponent early in the century was Descartes, who urged his rules of method for use in establishing an order of knowledge that was certain and beyond challenge. This was meant as a return to the Platonic and Aristotelian ideal of knowledge as distinct from opinion. The method of certainty has in common with the pedagogical aim the fact that necessary knowledge would be more convincing to the learner than uncertain; it has in common with the aim of discovery the fact that to replace uncertainty with certainty a new order must be attained. And since mathematics is the ideal of certain knowledge, this new order must necessarily be mathematical.

At the well-known meeting of the Oratory in Paris in 1628, Descartes discovered his vocation by challenging the Sieur de Chandoux's proposal that probabilism was the proper approach to the intellectual problems of the times, and by urging a new method of certainty. Descartes's method of certainty presupposed a point-to-point correspondence between an algebraic order of thoughts, and a geometric order of space—thought being the order of ideas given to mind, space being the one attribute of things fundamental to our knowledge of the outer world. Thus the question of the relevance of thought to the physical order was answered through an equation of *ratio* with *res*, the logical structure of thought with that of things, which Descartes assumed he had established in his analytic geometry. The method of algebra, or "specious analysis," seemed to be the perfect method, being a device for discovering any quantifiable unknown by a rigorous mathematical manipulation of the symbolic formulation in an equation (or continuous proportion) of the circumstances which determine it. It seemed the ultimate device for unlocking the secrets of space by ordering them in a necessary way and operating mathematically with this order. The order of mental symbols of algebra was one with the order of spatial symbols of geometry.

Descartes's identification of the forms of thought and things, or of methods and objective order, however, was itself soon seen to occupy an unstable middle position between two opposing views: the Aristotelian realistic tradition supported by Descartes himself, according to which both series, the algebraic and the geometric, are abstractions from the order of things, and a modern mentalistic adaptation of the Augustinian view according to which the order of things is imposed by mind, a view which Malebranche furthered by his conviction that God is the seat not only of the ideas and therefore of the mathematical order, but also of intelligible space. This polarization of mental and objective orders in knowledge brought to an end the easy assumption which led thinkers of the century, such as Hobbes and Spinoza, to confuse the order of reasons with the order of physical causes. The scientific investigation of necessary and sufficient causality could no longer be treated as coextensive or "convertible" with the logical use of the principle of sufficient reason, but at most only as a particular application of this principle to the area of experience given through sense perception, that is, the physical world.

This sharpened distinction between the mental pole, conceived as the method of achieving certainty, and the objective pole, the order known, also encouraged skepticism. In the course of the century the conviction that, given an adequate method, certainty could be achieved, not merely in the new sciences where the use of mathematics seemed to assure it, but also in ethics and in a metaphysical reinforcement of theological doctrine, gradually gave way to a recognition that such apodictic certainty was impossible and that one could hope for only that degree of certainty in each discipline which the clarity and adequacy of its data and first principles allowed.

As late as 1680, Leibniz had still claimed ultimate conclusiveness for the demonstrations in his proposed apologetic work, the *Catholic Demonstrations*, and professed to have mastered mathematics during the years spent in Paris (1672-1676) chiefly for the higher purpose of applying the method learned in this study, where it was clear and conclusive, to problems of the Christian faith, where such application was more important but also far more difficult.[17] Much later, however, although Leibniz still agreed with Locke that the knowledge of God is the most certain knowledge of all,[18] his investigation of the conditions of knowledge had convinced him that one cannot and need not always push the search for primary notions and first principles in a science back to true primitives, but may stop with those which will serve as sufficiently stable and useful in that discipline. The consequence of this was that each science is entitled only to that degree of certainty of which it is capable.[19] This position was supported by Leibniz's criticism of Descartes's method of universal doubt, as expressed in his considerations on Descartes's *Principles of Philosophy*,[20] where he maintained that Descartes, rather than beginning his method with universal doubt, should merely have recognized the various degrees of uncertainty in the various fields of our experience, and therefore have discussed ways of establishing degrees of probability in these fields. Thus the recognition that truths of fact are incapable of being established with absoluteness, since they are incapable of complete analysis, was well established by the end of the century.

A number of considerations therefore forced a distinction between the order of method and the order of the known. Basic, of course, was the obvious fact that method depends upon prior order for the definitions and principles which it uses, but also, when successful, brings into being new order or, more commonly, additions to the old. Method is thus a means to the end of new or better knowledge of objective order, but since the order which it uses includes sensory and imaginative content, the order that it knows must be phenomenal in nature, even though the a priori components (resting on the ideas) assure its real structure. For several reasons, therefore, complete certainty is impossible in empirical knowledge, even though it has inhering in it an a priori structure.

The Variety of Orders in Leibniz

It has been shown that whether method is aimed at the proper order of knowledge for teaching, at the discovery of new knowledge, or at establishing the certainty of knowledge, it brings into being new order, but also rests upon prior order, and that this order is in part logical (concerned with norms of reason) and in part factual (consisting in definitions of content). A variety of orders is therefore involved in the world which we know, and in the way in which we know it. We must limit our discussion here to the interrelationship between orders of knowing and orders of the known universe.

Descartes's attempts to relate these two orders by the polar correlations of algebraic and geometric analysis were, as the criticisms of Descartes's physical theories soon showed, oversimplified and unfruitful in physics. But the conception of ideas which he reaffirmed was, as I have shown in Chapter 5, one which served to give assurance that the order of thought was adapted to give knowledge of an order of things, since the ideas are the metaphysical source of both.

At one point, however, both Descartes and Spinoza failed in their efforts to build metaphysics upon a priori principles. They failed to recognize the contingency of things, indeed, of the entire world. This is revealed in Descartes's underlying principle, which he based upon the light of reason, that whatever is the object of a clear and distinct notion must exist. In the Port Royal logic this was put in the form of an enthymeme consisting of two axioms.

Axiom I: Everything which is contained in the clear and distinct idea of a thing can be affirmed of it with truth.

Axiom II: Existence, at least possible, is contained in everything which we conceive clearly and distinctly.[21]

The conclusion is obviously that "existence, at least possible," can be affirmed of everything which we conceive clearly and distinctly. But neither Descartes nor Spinoza accepted this qualification; for them it was implicit in the logical necessity of the a priori principles, that everything conceived clearly and distinctly, and therefore, logically necessary, must exist.

It was Leibniz whose system, though incomplete, achieved the peak of refinement of the rationalist ideal by providing the fullest account of the various orders involved in all being. But by reuniting method and order, not through an identity, but by showing how the orders of the world have the principles of method imbedded in them, this account was also intended to be used by every inquiring mind in finite abstraction from the logical structure of being.

In developing this new account of order (and method) Leibniz used four new insights which his rationalistic predecessors had failed fully to apply.

1. Man is a microcosm reflecting the macrocosm (and therefore a unified substance, not merely a mode of substance as in Spinoza). As such he reflects the logical order of the universe in the order of his thinking. But being finite, he can think clearly, distinctly, and adequately only within limits, and with symbols, but not intuitively as God does. If man were able to think intuitively and adequately, his thinking, like God's, could create the universe which he thought.

2. Everything in the world, indeed, the world itself, is contingent; it might have been other than it is. Thus the clarity, distinctness, and logical adequacy of thought does not determine existence; logical necessities are merely metaphysical possibilities. Another principle, not merely logical, is needed to explain why this world is as it is, and is not another of the infinitely many possible worlds. This new principle for the determination of this particular world is the principle of the best possible (or the optimum). It applies to God's creation of this world, and it applies to every thoughtful choice of the best possible decision out of the many possible decisions in a particular situation.

3. The empirical content of knowledge has two sources— sense perception for the external world, and internal perception, or reflection for man's knowledge of his own mental processes. But external perception is not intuitive; it is part symbolic and limited by the *materia prima* of sense, while internal perception is not thus limited and gives reality immediately. Therefore man's knowledge of the external world is phenomenal; science deals not with reality but with "well-founded" appearances. Man's knowledge of himself, on the other hand, is the basis of metaphysics, for reality consists of many series of appetitive-perceptive events such as he finds himself to be.

4. The ontological formula which is required by man's immediate perception of himself as an appetitive-perceptive series

of events must be enlarged to include a factor explaining the order of the series. Every individual existent, then, consists of a "complete individual notion," compounded out of finite determinations of the ideas or perfections of God, and of the series of appetitive and perceptual events which follow from this notion or law, as the members of a class follow extensionally from the intensional definition of the class, or as the particular values in a mathematical series follow from the functional law of the series. This is Leibniz's definition of substance—a series of active-passive events determined by its individual law and participating perceptually in the universal harmony of beings. God, being the source of order and power in the whole, is himself not a monad, though he is universal intellect (the "region of Ideas" and their force) and universal will as the determination of the best possible in existence; in both of these functions he is reflected within widely different ranges of imperfection, in every derivative substance.[22]

With these insights Leibniz set up a system in which orders and classes of being, from the highest to the lowest, are distinguished, and to each order of which there corresponds a definite human discipline. On every level of being (and of knowledge) the primitive principles reappear in a specialized form determined by the definitions fitting for that level. Primitive terms or concepts in every level of being or thought are also compounded of the ideas or the perfections of God. The interdependent system of orders in his design of a synthesis falls into the following classification:

I. *Orders of reason or of the Ideas* (Perfections) (*The Realm of Possibility*).
   A. *Theoretical*
      1. The logical order of constancy and mutual consistency of the simple essences (infinite or indefinite), conforming to the first principles of logic: Identity, Noncontradiction, Sufficient Reason.
      2. The order of possible combinations of these simple essences, and of all possible deductive or synthetic systems which can be constructed from them.
      3. An ordering of various sets of compossible "complete notions" of individuals into possible worlds with varying degrees of harmony.

Together these orders constitute all possibilities, or the truths which are valid for all possible worlds. It is in this context that Leibniz called God the "region of ideas." The most general principles of being apply here: identity, noncontradiction, excluded middle, and sufficient reason.

Their analogous disciplines for human minds are the fields of formal logic, mathematics, and the metaphysics of possible being. Truths in this realm are "truths of reason" only.

B. *Practical*

1. Imposition upon this infinite set of possible order systems, of an intelligent choice (or a maximal-minimal calculation) of the best possible order—a many-valued set of logical individuals, all compossible with each other, and each within itself capable of actualizing the best possible series of events involved in its own logical nature and in the whole.

   The new principle involved is teleological: the Principle of the Optimum or Best-Possible; or in logical terms, the requirement of maximal consequences with minimal assumptions.

   The human analogue consists of the serial pattern of appetites directed at best-possible ends, and the moral principles governing them, which concern the moral determination of the best possible act out of a wider range of possibilities.

II. *Orders of created reality* established by a priori principles informing empirical data of two kinds: internal and external perception. These orders are all spatial and temporal, since space and time are necessary forms for a plurality of individual beings. The basic principle is that of limitation through finiteness. (The Realm of Actuality). This is the realm of truths of fact: (a) in metaphysics; (b) in science.

A. *Internal perception:* an order of monads and their perceptual interrelations, each giving expression to the others and each striving for fulfillment in the best possible way. This again takes place in two orders:

1. The moral order of self-conscious monads (the kingdom of grace). The realm of freedom in obedience to the laws of the individuals and of the social order. Monads are the source of all efficient causality in the created world, and all efficient causality is internal to monads. (The Moral Order.)

2. The order of unconscious monads (the kingdom of nature). A natural order serving the kingdom of

grace as best possible means to its ends. (The Natural Order.)

The analogous human discipline is the metaphysics of existence.

B. *External perception:* An order of *phenomena bene fundata,* that is, an order of sensory perceptions interpreted by principles derived, by physical definitions, from those of all possible worlds and those of this space-time monadic world.

1. The commonsense physical order; observations of monadic complexes (bodies) interpreted in terms of substance-accident categories, and in terms of causality of a descriptive kind, based on the relative activity or passivity of motions and forces observed. (The Order of Causal Laws.)

2. The physical order, based on refir.ed observations interpreted or ordered according to such laws as conservation of force, equivalence of force and motion, equivalence of force with work done, and so forth. A world of functional interdependence according to mathematical laws. (Order of functional Dependence.)

3. Intermediary orders of chemism (qualitative modes) and vitalism (organic order in the combination of monads with a dominant monadic unity).

The laws of the order of this scientific world are each a best possible instance of an infinite number of possible solutions of the phenomenon involved. This world is the world of well-founded appearances. The analogous human discipline is natural science.

III. A disorder of mere phenomena: dreams, illusions, delusions, and so forth, incapable of being ordered through a priori principles except in a fragmentary or misplaced way.

Leibniz's ideal projects of a universal science and encyclopedia would require that all of the a priori principles, definitions, and terms required in this descending specification of orders should be themselves capable of being ordered in a single axiomatic-deductive system. The difficulty of proving this to be possible has been shown by R. M. Yost,[23] though Leibniz himself showed how the principle of identity for example, and the principle of the best possible, operate in different forms in distinct orders of his system. Several aspects of his thought, however, also suggest the impossibility of such a deductive unity.

The first to be considered is his distinction between truths of reason, which apply to all possible worlds, and truths of fact, which are analytic in God's thought but require empirical synthesis for human knowledge since their analytic reduction would require an infinity of steps. Truths of fact were therefore finally admitted by Leibniz to be only incompletely verifiable, and only through a logical deduction of their possible consequences and the confirmation of these consequences through further observations.[24] In short, the recognition of contingency conflicts with the conception of a total deductive system.

In the second place, the introduction of the principle of the "best possible" involves the intrusion of orders of purposiveness and of value not reducible to the deductive order. For although Leibniz treated the principle of the best possible after the analogy of the analytic calculus of minima and maxima, this analogy does not fit into the total deductive scheme, nor does it square with the logical determinism involved in the complex complete notion of the individual monad. In short, a teleological means-end judgment cannot be the simple converse, without limitation, of a cause-effect or ground-consequent judgment; the antecedent is never a *sufficient* reason for the consequent without additional determining considerations.

The freedom and responsibility which Leibniz ascribed to spirit monads is a further consequence of this moral conception which is incompatible with the logical necessity of his system.

To fit his conception of an analytic-synthetic method, moreover, and of the propositional structure of his thought, Leibniz found it necessary to hold that all relations must be reducible to the relation of *inclusion* of the predicate in the subject, or of the *containment* by the subject of the predicate, in any proposition. This limitation made it impossible for him to prove the varied derivative principles necessary to extend the deductive system into diverse subordinate fields of knowledge.

Leibniz's further teaching that all relations are additions by the mind to the external order showed the weakness of his systematizing tendency, for although he made it clear that this mental reduction of relations applied to God's mind, not to ours, his system required a further distinction between those relations which were implicit in his choice of this best of possible worlds and are of direct empirical concern in making theoretical and moral judgments, and those relations, like space, time, and action or force which are necessarily implied in the creation of a plural order and are therefore compulsory to us. This subjectivization of relations made a real order increasingly doubtful, since it reduced the orders of things in large part to the order of thought.

These considerations show that Leibniz's great effort to establish a reasonable order of being and value, which should be derivable from the simple perfections of God and thus show that all real orders are subordinate to a single ideal order, itself involved a trend toward destroying the condition upon which the apologetic role of the philosophers was based, namely the view that reality itself entailed the validity of the ideal. Not only the historical realities of the century but the empirical demands upon thought itself resisted this intellectual reduction.

Summary

The following sources of tension and instability are found in the discussion of order and its relation to method by the close of the seventeenth century.

1. The shift from an emphasis upon the priority of order to the priority of method, and an emphasis upon method as creative of new or more desirable forms of order.

2. The recognition that certainty in knowledge and therefore in action is impossible in truths of fact, and that uncertainties can be dealt with only through a logic of probabilities.

3. The separation of subject from object in knowledge; in particular the tendency to subjectivize method as the old way of ideas gave way to the new, and thus to separate it from objective order.

4. The intrusion of experience into rational order, and the resulting recognition of the synthetic nature of truths of fact.

5. The emergence of pragmatic conceptions of verification which result from a reliance on experience and on the recognition that purposes, values, and ends require that possibilities outreach actualities and thus involve uncertainty.

In these considerations the thought of the century seems to anticipate, in its difficulties and its complexities, a shift from a cosmic, God-made order to an order made by human thought and determined by human ends. This shift to a humanistic, historically relative, technologically progressive conception of order was already implicit in Zabarella, and intruded into the Platonic unities of Descartes and Leibniz (though not so clearly in mystically committed thinkers like Spinoza and Male-branche).

In the subsequent century, this second, immanent meaning of order was to eclipse or to absorb the transcendental one. It received application in the Enlightenment in both its skeptical and its utilitarian moods and was explicated philosophically by Kant, in whose thought the logical role of the transcendental order, immanent in mind, in giving unity, necessity, and universality to thought gave rise to new attempts at a synthesis. The break between right and left in the followers of Hegel exemplified in a particularly clear way the effects of emphasizing the transcendental source and the human source, respectively, of this order.

8 On Universal Harmony

Musicians call a pleasant consonance of many voices harmony. Of this nature is the consenting concord throughout all things—that of the eternal virtues [or powers] in God, of created virtues in nature, and of the virtues expressed in art. For just as each one of these is a harmony within itself, even so they are to each other. For nature is the image of divine harmony, and art is the image of the harmony of nature.

He who knows the reasons for tones and modes in music knows enough not merely to play but even to compose any melody whatever; indeed, a theory has been thought out by which musicians can, by merely observing the so-called general bass, sing entire melodies in such a way that no disharmony can result, even though the concert should consist of a hundred voices. Even so, he who knows the general principles of artificial, natural and supernatural matters will be able to understand and to create innumerable things.

[Comenius, *Prodromus Pansophiae*. Sections 75, 79.]

Harmony is diversity compensated by identity; or the harmonious is the uniformly difform.

Praise is a kind of echo and duplication of harmony. If God had no rational creatures in the world, he would still have the same harmony, but alone and devoid of echo; he would still have the same beauty, but devoid of reflection and refraction and multiplication. Hence the Wisdom of God demanded rational creatures in which things may multiply themselves. Thus each mind may be a kind of world in a mirror, or as it were, in a lens or in a kind of point collecting visual rays. Therefore we will try, if we are prudent, to give satisfaction to those whom we believe to be in a position to judge our actions as good and evil. Thus I hold that he is the most powerful and inviolable being of all, who seeks as much of the highest good as possible.

[Leibniz, *Opera omnia*, Academy ed., VI, i, 484, 438 (1671).]

Harmony is a particular subclass within the general conception of order, and was considered a transcendental property of being. The vigorous expansion of the classical ideal of harmony in the arts, in the sixteenth and seventeenth centuries, whether in music or in architecture and the visual arts, may be regarded (as Comenius affirms) as an "artificial image" of the enlarged intellectual vision of a complex unity binding together the great variety of differences and oppositions in the new world view. The disparity between the seventeenth century faith in this expanded ideal of harmony, dynamic and intensified by the resolution of internal disharmonies, and the almost universal acceptance and retreat into unresolved disharmony, in the twentieth century, which is only momentarily and passingly relieved by bits of consonance, is a measure of the extent to which the rational ideal of order has collapsed and libertinism has triumphed—and failed. It seems obvious, too, that the collapse of accepted harmonious forms in art and music today arises from the same mood as does the collapse of confidence in objective order, whether in nature, society, law, or morality.

Linguistic and Musical Analogies to Harmony

In the long history of the intellectual concept of harmony from its beginnings in the Pythagoreans and in Plato, the forms of harmony in the sensible world, whether of music or the visual arts, have been held to be images or copies which depend for their being upon participation in a cosmic harmony. This universal harmony is grounded in the nature of the ideas, and particularly in *number*. The Western religious tradition had found confirmation for Pythagoras's dictum that "All things are number" in the *Book of the Wisdom of Ben Sirach*: "Thou hast made all things in measure, weight, and number." The universal harmony sought in metaphysics, including the cosmic, must be found in the unity of the ideas themselves.

This dependence of the visible and sensible upon the invisible and spiritual can be shown in many traditional forms.

One basis has been shown to lie in the nature of language, particularly in the origins of the conception of poetic rhyming. In the English tradition, the words *rhyme* and *rhythm* still give evidence of their common etymological reference to regular repetitions or identities of form in *sound*, but the English language no longer gives evidence of a more general moral or aesthetic meaning. In German, on the other hand, the root *reim* still contains this more general meaning, particularly in its negative form of *Ungereimtheit*, which is a term of opprobrium, applied to unfitting, incongruous, inept words or acts. Rhyme and rhythm seem thus to be special artistic applications of a more general principle of mutuality, fittingness, or consonance.[1]

More generally, the grammatical structure of any language reveals an order of mutuality among words and their relations which reflects or echoes—more or less perfectly—the objective physical, social, and cultural order in which the language occurs and to which it refers. And when the rhetorical dimensions of metaphor, logical reference, and emotive color are added to this objective reference, the scope of this inclusive mutual fittingness is greatly enhanced. Language itself is thus to be understood as possessing its own harmony, reflecting the general cultural order, and in a limited way, the unity of all order. It has been pointed out that Leibniz's remarkable studies in comparative linguistics were inspired by his conviction that the universal harmony demands that there be a continuous evolution of forms and structures among all of the languages of the earth.[2]

This Platonic doctrine of the dependence of the particular upon the more general receives a more detailed exemplification, however, in the application to music of general mathematical principles of harmony, which are themselves rooted in reality as experienced aesthetically. The view that musical theory was based on a selection of harmonizing numbers, and was therefore a miniature model of the creation of the world in number and measure, was well established by Plato, and was given an expanded formulation by St. Augustine and his later interpreter Boethius.[3] It dominated musical order well into modern times, when Marin Mersenne supplied its classic statement for the seventeenth century.[4] As early as the Renaissance, however, this mathematical theory was challenged by more empirically minded students who held simply that music must be judged only by what is pleasing to the listener.

It lies beyond the scope of this study to attempt a historical account of the complex development of greater freedom in music through the expansion of the classical scale based upon the Platonic series of harmonic ratios—1/1, 1/2, 1/3, 1/4 (or better, 1, 1/2, 2/3, 3/4) to which additional intervals were gradually added through the use of added ratios of 1/5, 1/6, and so forth, and of subordinate ratios (such as 8/9). For centures this a priori mathematical approach to music stopped with the harmonic fractions based on the Pythagorean tetrad—the first four integers, whose sum equals 10 and was therefore associated early with another numerical harmony, the Golden Section, or the mean and extreme ratio,[5] a classic appearance of which is found in the divided line of Plato's *Republic*.

An early seventeenth century example of the philosophic use of this traditional approach to musical harmony, written in criticism of the expanded conceptions of Johannes Kepler's *Harmonice Mundi* (1591) is available in its strange treatment by the English physician, alchemist, and hermeticist Robert Fludd.[6] The "symphonic" dimension of Fludd's treatment of harmony does not rest upon musical polyphony; rather, it applies to the parallelism with diverse theological, cosmological, and psychological relations which he finds in the basic intervals of the major musical scale. Ignoring the musical development of polyphonic and contrapuntal effects in the Renaissance, Fludd based his confused analogies upon the monochord and its divisions, and primarily those of the octave (or *diapason* with the ratio 1/2), the *diapente* or fifth (the ratio of 2/3) and the *diatessaron* or fourth (with a ratio of 3/4), with further subdivisions in the ratio of 8/9 which approximated the modern diatonic scale with its two more irregular halftones. In Fludd's analogies this monochord is adjusted to a Neoplatonic scale of being from *Deus seu Aleph parvum* (the God revealed in the creation of the world) at the low end, corresponding to C with a vibration rate of 384/sec. to *Deus seu Aleph Magnum* (God emerging from the obscure earth, or created shadows, revealing Himself to men for the salvation of the world) at the high end, corresponding to the maximum of infinity to which a C, six octaves higher, with a vibration rate of 10,368/sec. is the highest approximation. But the divisions of the intervals on this monochord apply (1) not only to the scale of the divine Being itself, but to the cosmic hierarchy of beings ranging from God, through the spheres of angels and saints, to the fixed stars, the planets in order from Saturn to Mercury (with the sun between Mars and Venus at the point of the first octave, C = 768/sec.), and on to earth and the four elements of the sublunary world; (2) to the world of spirits, from the three orders of angels to man; (3) to the parts of man, from reason and the *anima lucida* to the humors of the body and the lower vital forms, animal and vegetable; and finally (4) to that visible architectural symbol of the monochordal harmony, the tabernacle of Moses from its outer courts to the Holy of Holies.[7]

Such analogical constructions belong, of course, to the occult theosophical thinking of the Northern Renaissance, and are of little significance here except as an instance of the opposition of the old against the new. (The harmonic generalizations of Kepler, many of which were also fantastic but were kept largely within the astronomical sphere, were remarkably successful.)

Expansion of the Ideal of Musical Harmony

Though Kepler's hypotheses about the third law of planetary motion were themselves far from meeting the rising empirical and philosophical standards of science, he was informed about the harmonic speculations of his contemporaries, and considered his analogical reasoning in applying harmonic series accepted in music to the accurately observed Rudolphian tables of Tycho Brahe as scientific, in contrast to Fludd's crude analogies.[8]

The theory of musical harmony was confronted in Kepler's time with pressing problems which demanded adjustment and compromise in any rigid mathematical theory. Though some of the issues raised were not resolved satisfactorily until Johann Sebastian Bach's work in a later century, three of them possess a more general significance for this study.

An old argument about the bearing of the mathematical "science" of music upon the more personal and empirical question of musical taste had been revived. The issue of whether music is to be judged by its conformity to preestablished numerical ratios or by the pleasantness of its combinations and sequences was given new sharpness by the discovery, attributed to Giovanni Benedetto, of a physical explanation of pleasant consonances, not through mathematical ratios but by the consciousness of coincidences in the termination of different cycles of musical vibrations. The result was twofold. Vicenzo Galileo, father of the great founder of modern dynamics, became a staunch defender of the empirical grounds for judgments of musical consonance. But there was also a growing recognition (explicit, for example, in Kepler) that harmony and disharmony are not matters to be determined atomically in terms of single combinations of sounds in separation from the musical sequence, but that the same combination may become pleasing or displeasing in different contexts.[9] An empirical theory of musical harmony thus resulted which freed itself from mathematical apriorism, but also introduced consideration of the organic and dynamic development of the musical theme in determining the pleasantness of its parts.

A consequence of these developments was the acceptance of

tonal combinations which had previously been considered as dissonant, as conforming to the test of consonance. The popularity of madrigals in the late Renaissance contributed to the acceptance of dissonances as components of a more inclusive harmony which was actually intensified by the momentary discord. The extension of the musical ratios beyond the tetrad to include all ratios up to 1/9 was a theoretical expression of this tendency to include what was previously considered disharmony in the context of a greater and more pleasing harmony.

The third factor was the increasing recognition of the need of further compromising theory in order to make possible a greater scope of expressiveness in music. The necessity of "tempering" the mathematically ordered scale to resolve difficulties in adapting the diatonic to the chromatic scale, and further, in adapting the scales in different modes and keys to each other, particularly in instruments with fixed tuning, was not fully achieved until Bach produced his "well-tempered clavichord"; indeed it is still the source of innovations in musical theory and practice. But it was a process begun in the seventeenth century, in the very beginnings of what is now regarded as baroque in music.

These shifts in the musical ideal become noticeable when the quotations from Comenius and Leibniz at the head of this chapter are compared. The two men agreed in regarding music as a particular aspect of universal harmony, and in regarding this harmony as mathematically determined. Indeed, Leibniz's aesthetic theory, which rests upon the assumption that sensory qualities are indistinct perceptions of objective mathematical combinations, and that the enjoyment of music consists of the unconscious perception of such harmonies, was influential not merely in the Enlightenment but with the early German Romantics.[10]

Yet there is a change in the musical ideal of the two men. Comenius's conception was still one of static consonance, and one which excluded dissonance as unpleasant. Although it was freed from the restricted single-voiced melodic interest of the Middle Ages and the Renaissance, it remained within the established ratios for consonance which the Renaissance regarded as received from the ancients—the octave, fifth, fourth, and diminished seventh. In Leibniz's passage, in contrast, the dynamism of reflection, inversion, refraction, echoing, and multiplication were involved. Dissonances become important for enhancing the pleasure of the listener through their resolution. The type of Comenius's music is a four-part hymn based on the simple major and minor chords, each of which can be given a harmonious construction from the prefigured bass. On the other hand, Leibniz, without yet recognizing the complexities of counterpoint and the well-tempered clavichord, found harmony unfolding itself in the interweaving of diverse but similar melodic themes (like monadic individuals), with different temporal extensions and variations of thematic elaboration. His view reflected the baroque acceptance and reconciliation of mannerist diversities and discords through a dynamic expansion of the classical ideal of total and balanced pleasure.[11]

It may be noted in passing that the theory of musical order entailed many of the same logical qualifications which were proving useful in science and illuminating as analogies in metaphysics. Chief of these was the growing recognition that although the mathematical a priori is indispensable in providing form and pattern in music (including quantitative physical determinations such as the length of strings or pipes, the tension of strings, the intensity of wind, the structural relations of the vibrating materials, the measure of rhythms, and the balance of voices), the criterion of musical effectiveness, and therefore also of validity, though grounded in these quantitative forms, is definable only by the pleasantness or unpleasantness of the resulting experiences. Moreover, tonality, as opposed to noise, was seen as a particular selection from the larger and more continuous experience of pitch. Actual aesthetic value is thus the result of a selective determination and choice of particular sounds and their relations from the larger continuity of possible sounds which could be produced; this is an apt illustration of the principle that actuality is a teleologically determined selection from a broader continuum of possibility, made according to some principle of the best possible or optimum. Harmony was considered as a functional dependence of the pleasure in hearing (as one variable series), upon another, telically specified, series of musical vibrations, simultaneous and in succession, which is itself but one of many possible orders—the one selected by the composer as most pleasing to the educated ear. The nature of music seemed to justify Leibniz's final judgment about the justification of truths of fact: musical compositions are generalizations of form made in accordance with an a priori theory of harmony, but must ultimately be justified by the emotional responses of the hearers.

Other Derivative Applications of Harmony

In addition to the linguistic and the musical, several other applications of the conception of harmony to particular contexts were significant during this period. Like music, they too had been understood in the Platonic tradition as particular echoes or reflections of a universal cosmic harmony.

Architectural harmony underwent changes analogous to those in music. The conception of architecture as "frozen music" was certainly as old as Christian Platonism, which idealized Solomon's Temple as a visual symbol of the Christian church or Kingdom of God. Von Simson has traced a brief history of this symbol as an introduction to his theory that the Gothic style is not so much a further development of the Romanesque, as a positive reaction against the darkness, mystery, and excessive variety of forms of the Romanesque, in the interest of an architecture of luminosity and measure. Chartres Cathedral was designed by its architect to be a visible embodiment of the mathematical emphases of the School of Chartres, and as Von Simson has demonstrated by the study of actual measurements, the architect built into the stonework of the west front, the proportions of the sections of the nave, and the several levels of elevation in the interior, the ratios of the Golden Section and the harmonic series.

This architectural expression of mathematical Platonism was kept alive in the classicism of the Renaissance, and later extended in the baroque to the use of curves far more complex than circle and straight line—all of the conic sections (now restudied by Descartes and Pascal), as well as spirals and other transcendental curves whose properties were now becoming known. The engraving of Solomon's Temple which Alsted included in his *Encyclopaedia* illustrates this enlarged vision; the temple is a baroque structure whose upper story and roof are supported by spiral involutes. Architecture may be said to reflect the preoccupation of the time with "the labyrinth" of infinity and the continuum.

The architectural effects of openness in the treatment of walls and ceilings now becomes a visible analogue to intellectual interpretations of the infinity of the universe found in Bruno, Spinoza, and others. In its spatial forms the baroque style marked the limits of ambiguity within which the ideals of proportionality and harmony could still be expressed within the striving for the unbounded. After ensuing centuries of lapse into

a variety of ornamental details, renewed mannerisms, and experimental revivals of old traditions, Western architecture in the
twentieth century is once more showing a striving for openness
and freedom, and is still seeking new forms adequate to express
it.

A fourth application of the principle of harmony approached
more nearly the greater conception of universal harmony. This
was the ideal of harmony applied to human nature and human
relations,[12] particularly in the relations involved in symbiosis.
War is discord, peace is concord; hate is the dominant affection
of conflict; love, the feeling of unification of the diverse. In his
De Concordia et Discordia in humane genere (1587), Luis Vives
gave an account of the fall of man and his regeneration. In
contrast to the harmony of nature in animal life, as illustrated
even by sheep, storks, and other species which live in "crowds
rather than societies" but especially by bees, whose society
(*civitas*) men find admirable, human societies are torn apart by
wars and dissensions. The cause of these is perturbed affections;
only through reason and thought, and the virtues based upon
these, can peace and tranquillity be established.

In Vives the Renaissance ideal of human solidarity based on
noble virtues becomes explicit. But the harmony of the whole is
not merely the product but also the precondition of the proper
harmony of attitudes and powers in each member of it. To the
long influence of Vives's doctrine of the affections upon European thought must be added the influence of his conviction that
all mankind constitutes a corporate unity which has been disrupted by the fall—a fall from grace which is at once a fall from
reason to feeling. It remained for Jean Jacques Rousseau in a
later century to attribute this fall to the rise of civilization and
its corruption of nature. For Vives the harmony of the affections induced in each individual by reason corresponds to and
interacts with the universal harmony of mankind.

Determinist though he was, Leibniz echoed this conviction,
and placed a responsibility upon the individual person to develop, out of the chaos of impulses which nature has produced
in him, a harmony of talents striving together toward the highest good. This transformation is a matter of art, Leibniz holds,
not of nature.[13] The shift between Vives and Leibniz, from the
goodness of nature to its incomplete and neutral character, is
remarkable as a sign of a rising tide of pessimism concerning the
natural human condition.

Further evidence of the importance of the conception of

social and political harmony is to be found in Johannes Kepler's great work, the *Harmonice Mundi*, which he dedicated to James I of England, misled by the hope that this royal patron of letters was in an effective position to overcome the "dissonance" prevailing among the three branches of Christianity—Roman Catholicism, Lutheranism, and Calvinism. There is a strange "Political Excursus" in Book III of Kepler's work, in which he applies his theory of harmonic series to various aspects of social order and of law, an exercise in confused ingenuity which he offered in correction of Bodin's proposal that democracy, autocracy, and monarchy are analogous respectively to arithmetical, geometrical, and what Bodin considered harmonic number series. Bodin's theory, in turn, had been an extravagant amplification of Aristotle's remark that commutative justice is arithmetical while distributive justice is geometrical.[14] In spite of their opaqueness, these speculations were frequently repeated in the seventeenth century in support of universal harmony. As in other bits of alleged a priori insight inherited from the past, their meaning is lost for the modern reader.

What the young Leibniz drew from these considerations about the nature of justice as harmony becomes apparent in his early attempts to base law upon the self-interest of each man as well as his sympathy for others—an indispensable ingredient of his conviction that the various orders of the law must be derived from the basic definition of justice as the love of the wise—love itself being one's joy in the perfection or well-being of others (and obversely, one's grief in their imperfection and failure).[15]

Universal Harmony: Its Metaphysical Basis

The applications of the concept of harmony to the different fields of culture and art—the rhetorical-grammatical, the musical and architectural, the astronomical, and the social-juristic—leave still unanswered the metaphysical question of a theory of universal world harmony which may subsume all lesser harmonies and assure the ultimate dissolution of all existing disharmonies. The further question also arises, of whether this universal harmony too can be understood as having an a priori basis in the Pythagorean theory that all things are numbers. Both questions received an affirmative answer in the seventeenth century, particulary by Leibniz, who had, however, to develop a new dimension of mathematics in support of his answer.

Musical harmony had been regarded by the Greeks as a partic-

ular image or "reflection" of a more inclusive universal harmony. The general inclination of the Scholastics and Renaissance thinkers to include beauty among the transcendentals,
even though on a more derivative level than goodness, supported this view, which reinforced the metaphysical emphasis
upon teleology. By the end of the sixteenth century, the mixture of rationalistic and empirical considerations in the discussion of musical theory made it clear that in this field harmony
requires a selective teleological choice, based on numerical considerations of a determinate nature, of the best possible (that is,
the most pleasing and in this sense the most perfect) tones and
combinations out of a great many possible combinations. In
generalized form, then, the thought lay near that all harmony,
whether universal or particular, is a selective determination of
one possible order, resting upon principles more restricted than
those governing the greater continuum or series of possible
orders, a selection made on quasi-mathematical rules and achieving the highest possible degree of perfection. This was the
theory of the nature of harmony which Leibniz developed.[16]

Prior efforts to define harmony in metaphysical and epistemological terms, had proceeded by means of analogies rather than
through this direct insight. This is shown in an advanced stage in
the works of Giordano Bruno. This man, who dared to fracture
the crystalline sphere and to spread the stars through an indefinite space, and who developed a renewed Neoplatonic cosmology designed to make such an all-inclusive harmony of harmonies possible, also must be credited with stimulating a widespread effort to introduce into the concept of harmony the new
dynamic dimension which it was acquiring in music, and to
describe the nature of harmony in an unbounded universe. In
his Latin work on the *Shadows of Ideas*, the degrees of finite
being are interpreted through the varying intensities of shadows
gathering as umbra and penumbra about the individuals at various metaphysical distances between light and utter darkness.
These degrees of darkness he called "intrusions" of shadows.[17]

We live in Plato's shadow world; Bruno opens his work with
the scriptural word, "I sat under the shadow of him whom I
would have desired." But shadows must be considered as relative, in distinction from darkness, which is absolute. Shadows
are the vestige of light in darkness, or of darkness in light.[18]
Everyone sits in shadow, but the shadows of the mind, in contrast to those of the body, are shadows of the good and the
true. All shadows are the objects of appetite and of the "cognos-

citive faculty."[19] The shadows are multiplied into infinity (as in mirrors), by the senses, receding further from the truth as they recede from the "supersubstantial unity" to which they owe their origin; yet they remain always vestiges, images, simulacra of truth and goodness.

Upon an analogy to this assurance that the shadows of our world depend for their being upon the very light which they serve to dissipate, Bruno built not only a theory of the dynamic interconnectedness of unity and plurality, or of ideas and their sensible simulacra, but also, within the details of the changing, shadow world, an order of vital interdependence which receives its dynamism and its harmony from its striving toward the light. The relations involved are quasi-psychological: the desire for union requires a conceptual grasp of the unity which fulfills it. From this Bruno drew his definition of beauty as harmony: "In ipsa varietate totius pulchritudo consistit."

> Since there is indeed an order and connection in all things such that lower bodies enter into the middle ones, and the middle into the higher ones, composites are united with simples and simples with composites; material things adhere to spiritual, spiritual to material things. So that there is one body of universal being, one order, one government, one principle, one end, one first, one last. And as the princes of the Platonists were not unaware, there is a continuous migration from the light to shadows (since certain minds submit to nature and fate through their turning to matter and their avoidance of action). There is nothing to prevent the lower from being recalled step by step to the sound of the universal cythara of Apollo—to the higher level.[20]

Thus the "indissoluble concord," the "golden chain which is cast from heaven to earth" can be descended to the depths of darkness or remounted through ordered ascent to a higher level of understanding and action.[21]

Metaphysical Harmony in Its Psychological
and Epistemological Bearing

The cognitive aspect of this ascent—for the desire to ascend and the perception of the light must be guided by intellect—involved Bruno in a discussion of the relations of thought by which the harmonious order can be known.[22] Knowledge is by propositions. But at this point Bruno broke with the Aristotelian tradition by denying that these propositions must refer adjects to their subjects "as the comprehended is referred to the comprehending, or proper clothing to the clothed, what is taught to the teachers, etc." As for relations, "Things are related according to all their parts, to all parts as relevant or irrelevant, as ordered or disordered, as resisting or agreeing (*conveniens*); and this is done so that the concept of one is connected to the concept of another. Who would conceive the adject 'royal dignity' cut off from all subjects. Adjects are to be understood simultaneously with their subjects." Relations are thus intrinsic to substances, but they are animated by the upward and downward way. Thus Bruno anticipated a logical analysis in which properties, along with the substances in which they inhere, cannot be understood in isolation but are dependent upon each other for their meaning. Concretely, this requires that individuals be understood only in terms of the relations which determine them, so that ultimately the meaning of the whole is involved in each particular individual in which it is expressed. Bruno thus explicated (at least partially) the logic implicit in the macrocosm-microcosm relationship.

Bruno seems also to have derived the notion of innate ideas and the natural light from this pattern of thought. The duality and parallelism of thing and thought everywhere converge upon the same shadows. "Nature can make all things out of all things, and the intellect can know all things out of all things."[23] Even on the sensible level, the principles of order by which the data are made meaningful are innate. Thus he shared with Marsilius Ficinus, Vives, and Pico della Mirandola before him, and was at least partly responsible for passing on to such readers as Alsted, Comenius, and Bisterfeld of the Herborn school (not to speak of Descartes, Spinoza, and Leibniz), the view that the basis of certainty in knowledge, and of right action and just social order in human relations, is to be found in the same normative principles built into the nature of the mind itself.

The natural light is therefore a primary intellectual factor in existence which assures the operation of universal harmony uniting the structures of human knowledge and action with that of the world order. Bruno's theory of this unity reinforced the educational role of philosophy in the sixteenth and seventeenth centuries, which was discussed in Chapter 2. In his *Encyclopaedia*, Alsted continued this educational application of harmony through the natural light, conceiving the constellation of the new all-knowledge as a great sphere revolving about the double center of the Sun of metaphysics and the Moon of logic, which together preserve the parallelism between the world of being and the world of knowledge. The four fields into which Alsted divided the practical sciences or the sciences of action—ethics, economics, politics, and scholastics (or as he elsewhere calls it, didactics)—he described as "a tetrachord which, rightly plucked, brings forth the most agreeable harmony." (*Tetrachordium quod recte pulsatum suavissimam edit harmoniam*).[24]

Thus it was recognized that although harmony rests upon the desire of the soul for participation in a higher order of being, such harmony will not appear without a common basis for intellectual agreement in the natural light. The docility of the emotions and will is therefore required; it is necessary to be assured of a "consent" of the lower levels of man's activity to what becomes known as truth. The a priori intellectual order is completely confirmed and conformed with by the a posteriori of emotion and act. Plato's old insight into the harmony of the three levels of the soul is given a new interpretation. This harmony is not merely moral possibility, it is fact; appetite, will, and understanding are brought into operational unity.

The scriptural teaching that understanding is fulfilled in love was of service to both Alsted and Bisterfeld, who gave particular emphasis to the quality of love as a harmonizing power. In his *Philosophiae Primae Seminarium*, a work which Leibniz read in his youth and annotated with marks of enthusiasm, Bisterfeld described his notion of harmony in a correlation of the three transcendentals (or "attributes of being") with the three immaterial causes of Aristotle. This correlation he repeated in tabular form in his *Alphabetum Philosophicum:*[25]

Unitas)		(efficientiae)	
Veritas (	est pancharmonia omnis)	exemplaris (	Tres istae causae
Bonitas)		(finis)	concurrent in
			omni
			affectu.

The table presents the three transcendentals as direct, immanent forces corresponding to the Aristotelian causes, and constituting a total harmony.

Within this general plan, Bisterfeld developed the psychological and epistemological as well as the political bearing of his *panharmonistic* theory. The docility of the will, as well as the understanding, he achieved by identifying the two: "Will is nothing but intellect"—that is, practical intellect. This doctrine both Spinoza and Leibniz adopted as well. It confirms the convertibility of truth and goodness.

Bisterfeld's doctrine also offered the assurance that men can think, and therefore live, in harmony with each other. The Reformed philosophers, Alsted and Bisterfeld, clearly were addressing themselves to men in a state of grace, not, as did Pascal, to the unredeemed. The logical outcome of their view was to support the Puritan contention, implicit in the Covenant theology, that only saved men could live together in peace in a republic. For the Herborn philosophers, understanding was an abstract aspect of divine grace, and love was the concrete interpersonal fulfillment of such understanding.

Bisterfeld held that this personal and interpersonal harmony must be achieved through discipline or learning, for it is only through learning that will, which combines the affection or appetite for the good with the practical understanding of it, can be developed. Logical order is therefore essential to harmony. In his *Alphabeticum Philosophicum* (Chapter 1)[26] he presented the ideal of an encyclopedia as "the most ordered structure (*compages*) of all disciplines"—a view directly opposed to the Aristotelian conviction, reaffirmed by Zabarella, that it is impossible to place all disciplines in such a single order, but that orders are restricted to individual disciplines. The presupposition (*praecognitum*) of an encyclopedia is the *convenientia disciplinarum* and the mutual harmony of the disciplines consists of the effectiveness with which they "conspire together for one effect." "The efficacy of principles is their congruent power (*congrua vis*) by which, when congruently joined, all disciplines procreate, conserve, and amplify." Without the terms "convenientia," "congruentia," "consensus," and "conspirare," the explication of harmony would have been difficult.[27] And without these concepts, which separate Platonists from Aristotelians, even the present issue as to whether we can have authentic universities or only pluriversities could not be discussed.

"Veritas, claritas, harmonia" are therefore the "Lydian stone" of the disciplines and the "axioms"[28] on which they rest; for "the congruence of the knowable" is the "magnet" of the will or executive faculty of man, which is stimulated both to thought and to action by the affection which it arouses.[29] All human comprehension of truth depends upon this objective logical "convenience" (although Bisterfeld recognizes that there may be higher unattainable truths; "not all things are comprehensible by the human mind.") Like Campanella and others, Bisterfeld found this knowledge of "convening" principles available in three distinct but related sources: experience, right reason (*recta ratio*), and Sacred Scripture.

In his catalogue of the disciplines, furthermore, Bisterfeld made the virtue of *honestas* depend upon the harmony of things. "*Actio honesta* is that action which is produced with convenience, or which fits congruously into the excellence, nature, and state of things."[30]

The doctrine of harmony, thus given a psychological and ethical grounding, supplies not merely a theory of learning and knowledge, but also a societal theory of reality. "Out of the goodness of being flows its convenience, by which one being is congruent, or unitable, with another . . . From this flows all *society* . . . This congruence is between all consentient beings." It will be obvious that Bisterfeld, following Bacon, used the term "society" and other anthropocentrisms such as appetite and perception, in a generalized metaphysical sense which applies to all beings in their plurality. Thus his social theory developed into a cosmology. "From the convenience of a being flows its communicativity and appetability. Communicativeness is the unitivity, so to speak, of a being; appetability is its communicativity . . . Appetite, taken metaphysically, is the habituation of being to being, or its disposition."[31] In common speech, appetite is either love or nonlove (or hate), taking these terms in their widest extension. In the different classes of being, appetite may be either vital or nonvital. Nonvital appetite is that by which nonliving or inanimate substances receive order, not so much by force of their own perceptions as by inflowing perceptions. Vital appetite is that by which living substances order themselves through their own power around the perceived thing.

On the basis of the distinction between vital and nonvital perceptions, Bisterfeld offered an "accurate disposition" of the appetites. Nonvital appetite belongs to celestial bodies, the elements, meteors, minerals—in short, in the fields accurately observed in physics. Vital appetite is somewhat obscure in plants, but clearer in beasts, where it is called instinct. Will is the appetite of spiritual, that is, of vital and intelligent beings. Finally, "sympathy is the convenience of appetites."[32]

Bisterfeld thus developed his Platonism into a universal vitalism, with the vital force (perception plus appetite) scaled from passivity to activity and from the physical to the self-conscious and intelligent. Nature or the physical world was still included in the universal harmony, but was reduced to a passive, receptive role—at the opposite extreme from the sympathism of some of Girolamo Frascatoro's followers.[33] Bisterfeld rewrote the doctrine of sympathy into a metaphysical conception which served as a basis for a social theory of personality. The light of nature assured a harmony which achieves its fullness in man who can order himself through his appetites and perceptions according to other socially ordered beings, whether through unreasoned instinct or through the clarity of reasoned perceptions.

This social application of harmony therefore finds its completion in Bisterfeld's definition of a person as a symbiotic being possessing intelligence. (*Subjectum vel objectum symbioticae generalis est persona quatenus consociari potest et debet. Persona est subsistens intelligens.*)[34] For Bisterfeld, the physical world lacked efficent causality. Though not excluded from the total harmony, it was reduced to a lower, passive, and therefore incomplete level of that harmony. Reality is essentially social, reaching its highest created form in the order of human persons related by mutual "immeation" with each other and with the rest of the universe—but supremely in the nature of God, the trinity of persons.

It was many decades after reading Bisterfeld that Leibniz succeeded in fully adapting these insights, along with others of Hobbes, Bacon, and Galileo, into his own mature monadology, where perception and appetite are the two dimensions in which the individual, within the limits of his nature, actualizes the harmony of universal order. Although the mature Leibniz would shrink in aesthetic horror from Bisterfeld's tendency to reify abstractions, it is clear that Bisterfeld's metaphysics anticipated his at least in this: he was an empiricist in affirming that there is nothing in the intellect which was not earlier in the senses—save the intellect itself; he was a nominalist in the (Ramistic?) assertion that *terminus est vox*; he was a Platonist in holding that principles are real and harmonious, *ex Deo;* and he was modern in formulating a panpsychist metaphysics in support of a socialized theory of the person. Leibniz did, however, add a clarification of the concept of power and its role in metaphysics, physics, and society.

The Exclusion of Nature from Harmony

The gradual exclusion of the physical order from the conception of universal harmony, a suggestion of which has been seen in Bisterfeld's reduction of the physical world to a merely passive role, was an important aspect of the collapse of the ideal of a total metaphysical harmony, to which I must return. The process in which the merely external mechanical relations of physical causality emerged can be examined by contrasting the views of Kepler and Galileo with those of the atomists and "corpuscular" philosophers of the century. Both of these men were instrumental in applying the mathematical ideal of harmony in their use of the new mathematical order of functional dependence between variables. The laws which both discovered thus presupposed the ideal of physical harmony in a form purified of animistic and occult forces, and justified this harmony through a Platonic realism of principles which seems somewhat at odds with the Aristotelian sources of the problems with which they dealt. Both assumed that the discovery of scientific laws was a penetration into the harmony of nature. Both held that God geometricized, writing the book of nature in mathematical symbols. And through their reliance upon mathematical laws, both largely avoided the problem of efficacy in nature, along with the scientific challenge to the Aristotelian doctrine of causality.

The atomists, on the other hand, intent upon explaining all things in terms of magnitude, figure, and motion, undertook to pull the realm of science out of the context of such an aesthetic ideal as harmony; machines operating by the directly applied motion of their parts rendered unnecessary the anthropomorphisms suggested by the ideal of harmony.

As Book IV of his work on *The Harmony of the World* shows, Kepler still supported the principle of harmony by his notion of a world spirit which embodies God's mathematical order in matter through its own independent action. Kepler's laws are geometrical in pattern, even though the second and third do require time as a variable. As a consequence he was not driven into further efforts to establish the independence of the mathematical order of nature; his conception of harmony was, like Bruno's, entirely within the Neoplatonic tradition of late humanism. There was in both a clearly aesthetic approach to the harmony of the world which anticipated Leibniz's later, more rationalistic view that in the experience of beauty the individual indistinctly perceives what his intellect could grasp mathematically with clarity and distinctness. This "fog of indistinct knowing," this "love without reason"[35] is the emotional response to perfection as it appears in creation. Thus Kepler still held that harmony involves a teleology of perfection which operates not merely intellectually but as feeling or appetite in imperfect individuals. Harmony is teleological in its essence, and science abstracts from this teleological whole when it makes its descriptive generalizations in mathematical order.

From the perspective of logic, the laws of Kepler supported Bruno's vague remarks, mentioned above, on the nature of relations. Both men required a logical theory of relations which could support analysis beyond the relation of containment or inclusion expressed in "S is P". Leibniz later also recognized this need, but undertook in his logical studies to avoid the necessity of it by reducing all relations to mental additions resting upon "intrinsic denominations" or on "relational predicates" included in the substantive descriptions of the things related. Thus there was a tendency, not merely in Bruno and Kepler, but in such earlier thinkers as Raymundus Lullus and Ramus (their influence must have been felt by both Bruno and Kepler) to exclude the order of knowing, and the relations essential to it, from the harmonious order of nature to which it refers.

This tendency was increased in Galileo by the very nature of his problems and their analysis. Galileo's goal was still the discovery of mathematical harmony in nature, but both method and form were no longer primarily geometrical. His subject matter was motions, forces, strengths, stresses, and their composition and resolution in an order modeled after Archimedes's balance. The rules or laws which he discovered were descriptive and functional; they implied efficacy and dynamism, but did not express it. Dynamism entered into Galileo's analyses in the form of *impetus* or *moment of motion*; but it was Leibniz who later discovered that this impetus is really a moment of force. The concept of force, which Galileo needed and which appropriated the old Aristotelian definition of nature as a principle of internal motion, lay beyond the new conceptions of physics and could not be introduced into Galileo's laws except as a component of motion. Thus Galileo went far beyond Kepler in providing support for the view that science is merely descriptive of appearances, and uses a method of analysis and generalization which serves to "save" these appearances. It is true that Hobbes, who admired the achievements of Galileo and hoped to further them, thought that the same analysis and synthesis could be satisfied by efficacious material motions and the reasons we discover for them. But the tendency of science was (a) to mechanize nature in a way which eliminated the telic reference of harmony; (b) to disengage the order of knowing from the order of being; and (c) to find its accounts restricted more and more to nature as appearance or phenomena, failing to uncover by its methods the "really real" causes of the appearances.

Harmony remained as an ideal, a "regulative principle," of science, the selection of the best possible of an infinity of possible orders. But the new science, whether based on mathematical dependence or transeunt efficacy, actually moved toward an abstract, mechanistic and instrumental order separable from the more inclusive order of ends which contained purposes and the striving or will of individuals to achieve them.

Harmony as the Best of All Possibilities: Leibniz

In the great metaphysical constructions of the later century, the role of universal harmony was buttressed by the ideal of a rational method which was to unify scientific and philosophical methods, psychological and logical insights, theoretical and practical demands, through value arguments for the most reasonable, and therefore the best, of all possible worlds.

It is true that Descartes's concern for the advancement of the new sciences encouraged a separation of the physical-mechanical from the spiritual-valuational which not even the sovereignty of God, the perfect mechanic and the lawgiver and redeemer of spirits, could bridge to the entire satisfaction of philosophers, as the occasionalist followers of Descartes showed. Descartes had little to say about harmony aside from his discussions with Mersenne on music, though he did appeal to its great synonyms: "fitness," "consent," and "congruence." Both his dualism and his methodological doubt—a method which played into the hands of the very libertines and doubters whom he sought to convince with its aid—were hardly compatible with the appeal to the natural light which he had to assume to establish his positive case for God and immortality.

In Spinoza's thought the break between systematic unity and the pedagogical order was shifted. As the *Essay on the Emendation of the Intellect* shows, his apologetic purpose was to convince the doubters that there is a "true and abiding good," and that the way to it must be gained through distinct and adequate thinking. The division between the truly good and merely transient goods corresponded to that between the eternal and its temporal spatial modes. The two realms of the eternal and the temporal were bound together, however, in his conviction that all goods—the transient and the eternal—depend for their being upon the affections, the eternal upon the highest affection man is capable of—the intellectual love of God. Spinoza's subjectivism was no impediment to the harmony of his system, for it was firmly tied into his revived Neoplatonism. Though he rejected human teleological judgments about the harmony of the world, along with its beauty and goodness, in the Appendix to Book I of the *Ethics*, he restored the potential harmony of the world in the climax of Book V. However, his *mos geometricus* was inadequate to the degrees of pluralization, temporalization, diversification, and imperfection in his system. To put it in Leibnizian terms, the total of his reasons—primitive notions, first principles, and definitions—did not prove sufficient for his conclusions. Antecedent cause did not equal consequent effect. It remained for the German idealists to discover that the *Ethics* is in reality a dialectic process of reasoning from abstract being to its full concreteness as Idea.

These were the matters which pulled apart the Platonic ideal of world harmony in the seventeenth century—the lack of unity among various categorial analyses of harmony: the geometrical, the aesthetic-mathematical, the homocentric, the cosmic, the sociojuristic, the pedagogical, the linguistic. The concept of harmony, which demanded (as it always had), the unity of the diverse, the mutual conformity of the many, proved to be sufficiently elastic to move from the static to include the dynamic and the powerful; to introduce discord or evil as instrumental to an intensified resultant harmony; to absorb the infinite in extending the ideal of harmony to levels within levels, without specific limits; and finally, to recognize that in a world of finite beings whose natures must exclude many possible perfections, a total harmony cannot be a fact, but only a regulative ideal. As the thinker most committed to the Platonic ideal of harmony in this fuller dynamic, temporalized, limit-absorbing sense, Leibniz achieved great clarity among the diverse regions in which harmony was held to prevail. Yet in spite of the logical advance in adequacy of his system, it encountered the same difficulties which inhered in the other attempts to achieve harmonic unity. In the last decades of his life his philosophy began to show trends suggesting the recognition of an ultimate temporalism and of a harmony which comes into being in the interacting perceptions and inclinations (appetites) of individuals in history—even if not in the history of nature.

Harmony had been a guiding principle in Leibniz's thought

even before his sojourn in Mainz revealed to him the enlarged intellectual horizons of modernity, and many decades before he attached the adjective "preestablished" to the term—a qualification of limited scope which has unfortunately suggested a deistic interpretation which his thought does not support.[36] This "preexistent harmony" (preexisting not in time but as eternal cause) is but an abstract aspect of the harmony of mutual consent and congruence which the sequences of action in the many existing individuals show by virtue of their natures having been (and continuing to be) determined by the Ideas or the perfections of God. The harmony of existence is never complete, and never will be until each individual and the whole total of individuals in their various limited perspectives and qualities, achieve the greatest perfection of which they are capable—when the total symphony of existence (to use the musical analogy) has been performed and the dissonances have been resolved in the final sustained chord by many voices but in the dominant major mode. Then the Composer's design will have been executed and will stand complete for all to grasp.

Though never completed, however, the united harmony of existence is more complete than any other harmony in the universe, even that of God in his primordial being, of whom the young jurist wrote: "If God had no rational creatures in the world he would still have the same harmony, but alone and without echo; he would still have the same beauty but without reflection, refraction, and multiplication. Hence the wisdom of God thrust forth (exigo) rational creatures in which things may be multiplied."[37] No other possible world could exceed it, and all existent harmonies, whether of speech, or thought, or knowledge, or law, or science, or civil order are parts of it.

After some years of thought, Leibniz saw what was needed to establish this optimal harmony of a created order in which God's power is distributed over many varieties of beings and over the undefinable reaches of time and space which such a great plurality would demand to achieve the best. It was what was lacking in Descartes and Spinoza: a distinction between the power of God as expressed in his intellect, a quasi-mathematical power of dividing and multiplying, and the power expressed in his moral will—the affirmation of a teleology of the highest possible in each finite individual and act.

With the limitation of existence to a selection of many individuals, each striving for the best possible of all ends—goodness, love, justice, joy in perfection, and so forth, Leibniz's conception of harmony thus absolutized the musical ideal of his day. But with the distinction between the possible and the actual, which it demanded so as to enhance the harmony, other qualifications become necessary. A basic one was the recognition that truths of fact differ in the same way from truths of reason as the created world differs from the totality of all possible worlds. Truths of fact cannot be verified by analysis alone, as can truths of reason; their verification would involve an infinity of analysis, but they can be justified through experience, though never with the complete certainty of logical truth demonstrated a priori. Humans cannot reconstruct the rational fitness of the whole by reasoning from the present state of affairs, or from remembrance of the succession of events of the past. Conceptual generalizations from such events may receive some validity from being formed by a priori principles, but, short of first principles, these too share in the uncertainties of the past through the definitions used in forming them. And this applies to moral as well as to scientific judgments; in both, to use other terms, man is bound to the consideration of well-founded phenomena. The general principles by which these are ordered must themselves be brought to interplay with new experiences which serve to confirm or refute them.

Thus there are various levels of harmony in the order of the universe, according to Leibniz. But as the intensity and concreteness of harmony increases, the degree of certainty and ever present finality decreases, as does also the adequacy of our grasp of an ultimate reality without phenomenal distortion. These levels may be summarized as follows:

I.   The harmony of God's thought in creating the best possible universe. This consists of three levels:

    a. The harmony of God's perfections. These are not distinct *in re* but only *a parte rationis.* Therefore God is *unity* in its power or potentiality for plurality.

    b. God's thoughts of all possible individuals in all possible worlds. This is mere logical consistency, not true harmony. It corresponds (in the musical analogy) to a mastery of the possibilities of tonalities and their combinations in all major and minor scales.

    c. God's determination of the compossible individuals and their relations in the best possible world.

       The musical analogy would be the comprehension, by a Mozart, for example (if musical historians are right), of the complete essential structure of his best possible symphony, in dimensions melodic and symphonic, and with each note, properly evaluated, in its place. There would be dissonances, inferior melodic sequences, and so forth, to intensify the ultimate and total perfection.

II.   Harmony as the consonance or consent of monadic events in the created world; here the melodic sequences of each independent voice involve a mutual fitness—whether dissonant or consonant—which conforms to the rules of the composer and work up, gradually, with many regressions to the final and total perfection.

This is the most concrete harmony. It consists of two inseparable parts, the order of best possible laws of each individual monad or actual series, and the order of events which actualize these laws. The harmony of the laws is complete, but a logical abstraction from existence. The harmony of the monads, on the other hand, is not yet complete, but continually a process toward completion in time.

In his late years Leibniz liked to explain the historical catastrophes of the past and of his own time by the figure of an athletic technique: *reculer pour mieux sauter* (to step back in order better to leap forward).

III.   Harmony in the perceptions and generalizations of individual self-conscious monads, confirmed by communication with their peers. This, as Leibniz saw, consisted of discovering the common proportionalities involved in our different perspectives of the world, and thus discovering the "subordinate regulations" of divine Providence, both physical and moral—the laws of nature and of spirits. This again has two subdivisions:

a. In the physical sciences a high degree of distinctness and adequacy is possible. But the order of science does not well satisfy Leibniz's definition of harmony; as we have seen, a push or pull mechanism is not adequately harmonious.

However, two phases of harmony are suggested in the scientific study of nature. One is the unification of diversity in theories of the highest generality in the various sciences, particularly when these are mathematical generalizations in the form of functional laws. The harmony suggested by such generalizations is still largely regulative and repetitive.

The other aspect of harmony appears when it is seen

that each law, each subordinate regulation, is the solution of a problem of maximum and minimum, or the result of a decision as to the best possible. Leibniz was convinced that he had proved this, and the attractiveness of the idea in the eighteenth century and for many scientists since, including Max Planck and Albert Einstein, indicates a residue of aesthetic evaluation in the natural sciences of our day. In short, nature can be seen as harmonious only in the mathematical perfection of its laws and its instrumental meaning for spirits.

b. In the realm of spirits (or of grace), laws are completely individualized. As a result, our knowledge of social relations and history cannot be pushed to complete distinctness and adequacy. Here not intelligence but rather the affections and appetites are final arbiters, and these, Leibniz holds, themselves involve indistinct perceptions. True, the ground of harmony is expressed in the creation of self-conscious individuals who share a finite but high degree of the perfections of God, including power, wisdom, and love. But under human conditions the love of the wise man (Leibniz's definition of justice) itself must be manifested on lower levels—that of retributive justice for the criminal, and that of equity, which rests on such motives as security, pride, and self-esteem. Thus Leibniz's argument, on its empirical side, introduces serious qualifications of the theory of harmonious existence.

It is clear from this that the great seventeenth century justifier of the ways of God and of universal harmony fell short of the goal and himself recognized the weak points in his great construction.

At the end of the century there were still few thinkers who were inclined to argue that the amount of dissonance, of evil, of ugliness is too great to be resolved in, or at least to contribute to, a greater harmony. Not even the founders of the libertinism of the eighteenth century were willing to do this; Leibniz's *Theodicy* won wide approval in liberal circles abroad. It took Voltaire's reaction to the Lisbon earthquake to shake this half-empirical optimism. The principle of the best possible (sometimes in the scientific form of "least action") continued in force in the Age of Reason, even Hume's telling blows not forcing skepticism concerning it.

But the emergence of historical studies into an objective level, to which Leibniz himself made distinctive contributions, forced a realism about human evil which Leibniz in his old age seemed partly to share. In the last book of the *Nouveaux Essais* he expressed his anxiety about a coming revolution, and his hope that the discovery of printing and the growth of libraries would lessen its evils. He also continued his forlorn hope that a great Monarch might still be found who would forestall Europe's collapse. The Sun King of France, the Emperor, and Peter the Great, all of whom he had tried to challenge, had failed him. In letters he expressed himself satirically about new projects for European peace.

It remained for future centuries, preeminently the twentieth, to find the weight of evil and discord so great that all ideas of harmony were abandoned, even in music, that most abstract and pure image of being and becoming, where dissonance has replaced consonance and become the token of aesthetic normlessness. Pierre Luis Moreau de Maupertuis and Hume had suggested pessimism on hedonistic grounds in the Age of Reason. Experience intruded increasingly upon the ideal of harmony, not only in music but in other fields as well, as theory continued to break down before experience, and ideal types surrendered to social and individual realities. In the rising nominalism of thought, *variety* replaced rules, old laws were refuted and new ones were not discovered.

The order of retreat, even in the century itself, was marked in all of the special fields of harmony. In language and logic, Leibniz himself introduced the search for a perfect ideal language, but founded only the beginnings of comparative linguistics. In music the technique of tempering was begun (that is, of compromising the mathematical ratios of the tonal scales for the sake of greater universality). In architecture, the intractability of materials proved a limit to human aspirations and experiments. And in society and law, not to mention morals and religion, the human imperfections of forms (that is, ideas) inevitably manifested themselves. Philosophically, the separation of feeling and sensation from understanding and from its objects further heightened the dualism of knowledge which made objective harmonies seemingly unattainable. The subordination of the eternal to the temporal in history and to the experience of the individual has continued until today.

9 What Is Nature?

(Men) have seen that the divine benediction has accompanied the business (*negotium*) of nature, so that neither nature may act without God, nor God, without nature.

[John Sperling, *Antiparasceve pro traduce* (Wittenberg, 1648), p. 194, Preface.]

I have often wondered, that in so inquisitive an age as this, that among those many learned men, that have with much freedom as well as acuteness, written of the works of nature (as they call them) and some of them of the principles too, I have not met with any, that has made it his business to write of nature herself . . . And because many atheists ascribe so much to nature, that they think it needless to have recourse to a deity for the giving an account of the phenomena of the universe; and, on the other side, very many theists seem to think the commonly received notion of nature little less than necessary to the proof of the existence of God: I, who differ from both of these parties, and yet think every true theist, and much more every true Christian, ought to be much concerned for truths, that have so powerful an influence on religion, thought myself, for its sake, obliged to consider this matter, both with the more attention and with regard to religion.

[Robert Boyle, *A Free Inquiry into the Vulgarly Received Notion of Nature* (1685), *Works*, ed. Thomas Birch, v, p. 158.]

Nature forms us, but art perfects us. Those who urge that in the education of children everything be done according to nature have not sufficiently observed nature. Let them study horsemen and sportsmen who trained horses, dogs, and birds.

It is true that it is not in our power to increase the forces of nature. But art can give us power which nature has denied us . . . Art unifies and makes useful the forces which nature has scattered and distracted . . . By nature our spirits are distracted through the trifles which have conmmanded our attention from childhood. Only art can reunify our thoughts and give them a right direction . . . Most men are children. They take delight in pursuing trifles. We ought to have only a single magnet (*aimant*) to attract us and fix our direction. This magnet is the true blessedness (Glückseligkeit).

[Leibniz, *Discours sur les beaux sentiments*, in J. Baruzi, *Leibniz* (Paris, Bloud, 1909), p. 368.]

Nature, Its Reference and Its Reality

Taken together, these passages suggest three somewhat diverse conclusions: that the advance of science as well as the practical issues of life require that we regard "nature" in the realistic sense of an environing realm of being which is dependable in its order, seems never to be entirely free from man's experience of it, yet also provides the conditions, and the materials, which make it possible for man, individually and in cooperation with his fellows, to control his environment and create an order of values. However, that "nature" is also a concept which the new methods of science encourage us to abandon because of its emptiness and ambiguity, or at least to reduce to the minimum of what science knows; but that in still another sense, though nature is an order which brings men's action into a determining context of causality, it must be transcended by human art in order that human harmony may be attained.

In his *Free Inquiry into the Vulgarly Received Notion of Nature*, Robert Boyle criticized the term for its inescapable and misleading ambiguity, and urged that it be dropped. Boyle was not the first, nor the last, to lament this obscurity and to recommend the adoption of more specific and adequate substitutes. Ambiguities in the use of the term *physis* appear in Aristotle's writings, where the term is applied both to the quality of individual things which contain their own source of motion, and also more generally to the collective quality of events which have this property: they occur "according to nature."[1] The Stoics had another meaning: *physis* is the power of world reason acting in all things according to law and determining their essences or essential, unchanging properties. Translated into Latin as *natura*, the term became in Lucretius a synonym for the physical universe, as the *rerum natura*. Through the influence of Neoplatonism, the Scholastics regarded nature as a manifestation of God (as in Thomas Aquinas's *natural law*), the universality of which provides rational norms for all classes of created beings. Thus there arose a distinction between *natura naturans,* or God himself and *natura naturata,* or created things, insofar as they manifest God's creative power.[2]

By the seventeenth century these ambiguities had been intensified and augmented not only by new meanings arising from the sciences but from metaphysical combinations of parts of the classical meanings. In one sense or another, nature was opposed to the supernatural, the "unnatural" as irregular or miraculous, the merely apparent or conventional, art or what is man-made. Interrelations ranged from one extreme of applying the term to the essences of all things, divine or created, to the opposite extreme of denying the term completely because the new science recognized no internal action or source of motion within physical things at all.

In Spinoza's thought, nature was the inclusive unity of self-causing being within which all individualization and change takes place, but which contains purpose and efficacy only insofar as the subjective dimension of being—affections harnessed to thoughts—strives for self-preservation and for perfection. Nature is both one naturans, and the many naturata. At the other end were those who anticipated the skeptics of the eighteenth century by maintaining that since external perception gives no evidence of efficacy or independent substantiality in the physical world, and therefore no independent being can be ascribed to a realm of nature, science must content itself with mere appearances and find its task completed when it has "saved these phenomena" by analyzing the mathematical relations which serve to "explain" them, or by revealing the abstract but changeless relations discoverable among selected aspects— qualities and forms—which they present. There were also occasionalistic followers of Descartes who found nature absorbed almost completely in God. For these extremes, then nature was either all or nothing.

There was a third way, however, which mediated between these extremes. Though it did not succeed in removing the ambiguities in the term, it did offer an interpretation of nature as substantially and efficaciously real, yet not completely independent from other real parts of the universe. In this group belong the atomists or corpuscularists and the Cartesians, for whom nature was a mechanical order of material particles combining and moving according to laws. To it belongs also the tradition of Christian Platonism, which found a twofold meaning for the term, one metaphysical and one physical. Identifying the Christian doctrine of creation with the Platonic realm of appearance, it found nature to be a realm of phenomena, yet not "mere" phenomena but rather appearances well-founded in being.

According to this view, nature as studied in the empirical sciences remains a realm of appearances. But by penetrating more and more deeply into the causal-mathematical order of relations involved in these appearances, science approaches more and more adequately, yet never completely, a real order of intelligible forms and forces; science can partly reveal this intelligible order, but must always presuppose the yet unattained order and the force which is manifested in the phenomenal processes. But nature as this underlying being can also be understood coherently after the analogy with man's inner experience of himself as a dynamic, yet ordered being, responsive to the environing order of the whole. Man, therefore, is the scientist who discovers the orderly phenomena of nature by using forms which he finds most fitting and successful in predicting and controlling these phenomena; but man is himself, through his self-experience, also the source of a coherent understanding of the metaphysical foundation of these phenomena. This is the resolution of the extremes in the general formulation given it by Leibniz.

Polarities in the Interpretation of Nature

Among the several antitheses which arise from the ambiguities of the term, are the following:

1. The contrast between nature and the supernatural, corresponding to that between reason and revelation. This is the issue involved in the discussion of natural law and natural religion, in contrast to "positive" law and revealed religion. In the case of both law and religion, "nature" here expresses a claim for the universality of reason as against the particularity of experience and revelation. This universality provided an assurance of reasonable agreement in thought and action in the fields of religion and social order.

2. A second contrast between nature and the supernatural, somewhat different from the first, parallels the distinction between creation and Creator. In the earlier instance the supernatural is to the natural as special is to general or example to rule; in this instance nature is subordinate and dependent upon the supernatural in being, even though the supernatural event (in the former sense) is manifested within nature. For the seventeenth century, committed to the predictability of natural

events, the crucial problem based on this distinction was that of the possibility and nature of miracle. This was only one aspect, however, of a deep sense of that mystery of nature which constantly challenged the scientist.[3]

3. In both of the above distinctions, nature is understood to include man and the human order as well as the independent physical world. In the third sense, however, although man may still be included in nature, his works are not. This is Aristotle's distinction between nature and art, or between natural and the artificial. Man in this sense transcends nature as a self-conscious, self-directing being, though he is "thrown into nature," to adapt a Heideggerian expression. It must be noted, however, that the distinction between nature and art had been reversed since Aristotle. Nature no longer consisted of the sum of all self-moving beings; both the new descriptive view of science and the new atomism deprived it of independent internal efficacy. And though art in its broadest meaning was considered as the external imposition of a desired, ideal form upon nature, man, the human technologist, was himself the prototype, in the created world, of self-aware and self-determining activity. Man in this sense is a part of nature only to the extent of his biological existence; as self-controlling and creative mind he is beyond it.

4. Dependent upon the distinction between *nature* and *art*, yet involving problems different from it, is the distinction between *nature* and *history*. Although this was to assume independent importance only in the next century, and particularly in the beginnings of the Romantic reaction, there were strong intimations of the distinction in the seventeenth, noticeably in the late thought of Leibniz and in Giovanni Battista Vico. The difference was found in the distinction of the natural and the human, and this depended again upon the externality of conscious purpose to nature, and its essential presence in history. Though the categories used to analyze this difference may vary—for instance, mechanism vs. purpose, fact vs. values, external vs. internal or organic relatedness, determinism vs. creativity, the essential distinction was man's transcendence of nature and his immanence in history.

Thus there is a human *nature*, if nature be understood in terms of distinction (1) and (2), but in terms of (3) and (4) man has no *essential* nature, save that which he himself brings into being through his intentions. Man is what he does. This is the underlying truth in the libertine tradition, which libertinism may, however, push too far.

5. Closely related to the distinction between nature and art

and nature and history (yet involving a new concept) is that between the natural and the civil. This rests upon a distinction in law between the *jus naturalis* and the *jus civilis*, but has an even deeper philosophical ground in Protagoras's Sophistic distinction between *physis* and *nomos*, or between nature and convention. There is a direct affinity between this and the broader distinction between nature and history, but also, more specifically, between laws as describing a real order of nature and laws as merely verified conventions of the scientist. This distinction, obviously, brings the meaning of nature into direct connection with the logical problem of nominalism vs. realism, a fundamental issue between the libertine ideal and that of honestas. In a legal note *On Possession*, which Gaston Grua dates tentatively in 1696, Leibniz set up the essential connection between the two poles of the law in the principle *Nulla est possessio tam naturalis quae non habeat effectum civilem.*[4] More generally, nature, whether understood as a logical order of essences, or as something physical or biological but more basic than art, always demands empirically based completion in an enlarged human context.

Robert Boyle's Misgivings about Nature

Robert Boyle's criticism of the term "nature," and the controversy to which it led, began with a study of its ambiguity, but developed into a charge of its emptiness and lack of a real reference.

By Boyle's time the restriction of nature to an external order of events observable through sense perception and capable of being explained in forms determined by the human intellect had become widely accepted, though other usages were not excluded. Boyle, like Gassendi and Descartes before him, whom he classified with himself as corpuscular philosophers and with whom he shared an antipathy for Aristotle's conception of nature, explicitly excluded from their conception "the rational soul or mind of man."[5] As a devout theist he found meaning not merely for the nonnatural but for the supernatural.[6] Although the conceptions of nature which he examined critically and for which he proposed more definite substitutes have been largely superseded in the later naturalistic tradition, they forced certain abiding issues; among these are the problem of the unity of nature, its substantial basis and the relation of this basis to change, the relation of its phenomenal aspects to what is real (or that upon which these aspects depend), the status and origin of qualities and forms (particularly the generation and corruption of qualities and forms), the place of teleology in a mechanical order, and the relation of nature to the realm of value—moral, aesthetic, political, and religious.

All of these issues, when analyzed, cast some doubt upon the independent ontological status of nature, and all were implicitly involved in the various conceptions of nature which Boyle found prevalent in his time. The two charges which he brought against these notions may be inferred from his leading query: "Whether the vulgar notion of nature has not been both injurious to the glory of God, and a great impediment to the solid and useful discovery of his works."[7]

Of the nine meanings of nature which Boyle found in current usage, all of which he found guilty as charged, all but the last two derive from Aristotle or (as in 1 and 7) from Christian thinkers who are recognized as Aristotelian, but with seventeenth century turnings.

1. Nature as being, and therefore as God: *Natura naturans.*

2. Nature as the essence or quiddity of a thing.

3. Nature as signifying qualities not acquired accidentally or artificially.

4. Nature as internal principle of motion, or as spontaneous motion.

5. Nature as the established order or course of corporeal things.

6. Nature as the aggregate of powers of a body.

7. Nature as the system of the world or universe.

8. Nature as divine, as a goddess.

9. (A view attributed to Franciscus Mercurius Van Helmont): Nature as the law of things received from the Creator.[8]

The controversies to which Boyle's work gave rise show, however, that in spite of this complex of meanings, the force of his discussion came to bear on the single issue of whether nature, as discussed in science or in theology, may be regarded as in any sense having independently real status, or whether it must rather be considered phenomenal and without substance.

Perhaps the best-known controversy which followed the appearance of the work took place between John Christopher Sturm of Altdorf, a Cartesian eclectic who proposed that a philosophy of nature be dispensed with, and Gunther Christopher Schelhammer of Kiel, an able physician who insisted upon the reality of the bodies upon which he labored. The former, following Boyle, regarded the reification of nature as idolatry and sacrilege; the latter found it to be a glorification of the Creator. The works involved were Sturm's *De Naturae agentis idolo* (1692) and *Physica electiva sive hypothetica* (1697), Schelhammer's *Natura sibi et medicis vindicata* (1697), and Sturm's reply, *De natura sibi incassum vindicata* (1698). An allusion by Sturm brought Leibniz into the controversy, and he gave an illuminating account of his mediating view in *De ipsa natura* (1698).[9] This paper was written a few years after Leibniz's criticism of Descartes's principle of the conservation of momentum and his laws of motion impelled him to the conclusion that a force or power must reside in nature as a source of activity and motion as well as inertia. Thus he showed the significance of his own monadology for the argument about nature. The existing created order, comprising both the kingdom of nature and that of grace, consists, according to this, of monads or metaphysical individuals, each of which has a life history expressing the complete law of its individual nature— this law being an expression of the perfections of God, and therefore the source of both the power or force involved in this history and its determining order as well—both its dynamism and its purposeful meaning.

Another controversy at the close of the century which also arose out of Boyle's challenge to define nature more precisely led Leibniz to write on the obverse side of his conception of the ontological status of nature. This was the argument between Friedrich Hofmann, who urged a mechanistic, atomistic interpretation of nature, and the phlogiston theorist Georg Ernst Stahl, who urged a vitalistic and organic interpretation. In this exchange Leibniz sided with Hofmann against Stahl, restricting science to the discovery of functional mechanisms in the qualified sense which he had learned from Boyle several decades earlier.[10]

Leibniz's reaction to these two controversies reveals the essential ambivalence in the understanding of nature which the scientific approach evoked by the end of the century. On the one hand, since the scientist's quest is for certainty and predictive value, he must eschew teleological considerations, as Bacon had urged, and restrict himself to the causal or mathematical categories which were successful in the understanding of observed events through the universalized qualities and relations abstracted from them.[11] Thus the scientist is restricted to phenomena. But he is not, for that reason, restricted to a subjective temporal ordering of sensory qualities and their associated composites. Without the assurance of an independent order of investigation and the conviction that method when adequate approaches this real order, science would be without motive and without dependable rational content.

The scientist therefore operates with a "well-founded" order of phenomena which must be understood mechanistically, but which needs completion in a dynamic ontological order within which the scientist achieves his purposes. It is from this more substantial order that the phenomenal order draws its presuppositions, and by it, its merely descriptive and functional findings are further explained. This ontological order will not at all be phenomenal in the scientific sense, but can be understood by analogies with experiences of another kind, namely, the internal experience which the scientist and other men have in the awareness of their own nature. Thus nature in its ontological being is the self-determination of dynamic processes within the context of a greater harmony, while nature as the physical scientist examines it is a mechanism of events occurring according to the descriptive laws, causal and functional—Leibniz early called them "subordinate regulations"—which the scientist abstracts from his observations and experiments, however complex.

Both natures rest on reasons, but physical theory is driven by empirical discoveries to alter its formative a priori principles to attain greater adequacy (the Scholastic *ad-aequatio*) to the new facts and to a closer approximation of a cohesive theory. In this adequation (Leibniz and Kant would say) the metaphysical theory of a cosmos serves as a regulative ideal, never achieved (since truths of fact can be verified only through an infinite analysis), but somewhat unsteadily approached as scientific theories advance. Thus recent physics, with its changing theories of energy-particles active within dynamic fields, is an analogue to the metaphysical conception; its still rather insecure combination of minute individual self-moving force centers acting within larger "symbiotic" or societal structures, from atoms through larger field units, to molecules and beyond, already has great similarities to the outlines of Leibniz's monadology. Both natures have their internal patterns of dependencies, but nature in the metaphysical sense has the greater harmony. In the nature of metaphysics these dependencies are social and organic—each monad perceives the universe from its point of view or its individual notion; this Leibniz had learned from Bisterfeld and others. Both orders of nature have their eternal and their temporal aspects. The same space and time are in both, but in both, space and time, whether interpreted metaphysically or in relation to physical phenomena, are merely relational and without content apart from the particulars which they relate.

In another, greater controversy about the "nature of nature," Leibniz himself, shortly before his death in 1716, was one of the controversialists. This was the clash between Leibnizian and Newtonian principles as it was carried out in the correspondence between Leibniz and Samuel Clarke in 1715 and 1716.[12] In contrast to Leibniz's duality of a metaphysical order and a phenomenal nature, Newton had proposed to follow the earlier atomists and corpuscularists in absolutizing the categories of science and thus recognizing only one order of nature, metaphysical and scientific. This proposal was largely incidental to the great achievements of Newton's work on the *Mathematical Principles of Natural Philosophy*, but it fixed the thought of the Age of Reason and much of the nineteenth century in the path of deism, God, the perfect Machinist, having created a machine universe operating, with perfect precision, yet leaving room within it for the free man of the libertine.[13] It may be said that Newton's physical absolutes were scientifically acceptable and regulatively fruitful in the great centuries in which classical mechanics achieved its successes, but that Leibnizian "well-grounded" phenomenalism and relativism have come once again into ascendancy with the new physics.

Nature Beyond Mechanism

As the categories of physics became rigidified and absolutized, philosophical interpretations lost sight of much in nature that remained unexplained by them, yet were empirically either inescapable or claims made by the religious consciousness. The efforts of the Cartesian school and Leibniz to explain the law of inverse squares (long known in the dissemination of wave motions in light and other phenomena but newly validated for gravity by Newton) through the impact of particles moving in a vortex was a futile effort to protect empirical explanations. Both Aristotle's explanation of the fall of bodies through an internal telic force, and all forms of sympathetic external action at a distance, had been banished from the new mechanistic theory; the charge of reviving the mysterious principle of sympathism was aimed at Newton by the Cartesians for his account of gravity as action at a distance. Physical relations other than gravity were also readily seen to be unexplained in the new mechanics. Although the Cartesians, following the lead of Giovanni Borelli and other biologists, had undertaken to translate biological behavior into mechanistic terms, the hypothesis of the "beast machine" seemed to most thinkers inadequate to that end. For such phenomena as inertial resistance, the cohesion of bodies, and the recoil of springs, Leibniz rejected all atomistic explanations, commenting:

> Concerning these properties, if someone could explain them to me in terms of size, figure, and motion, I should not quarrel about calling him a great philosopher.[14]

These apparently nonmechanistic properties of nature, along with others which have been discussed in Chapter 4, kept alive the efforts to explain them through nonmechanistic principles or powers—not only the substantial forms of the Scholastics but the fanciful spiritual powers postulated in the Renaissance to explain such long-recognized events as the healing of wounds and recovery from illness, and such newly recognized ones as electrical and magnetic phenomena, and amazing new chemical reactions as well. The light of the new science was not yet bright enough to illumine the dark mysteries of singular events in nature. The immanence of the magical and supernatural within nature had not been dispelled, as Boyle's eighth definition—nature as divine, as goddess—shows.

No doubt Boyle introduced this conception, which flourished as a literary figure in the Renaissance, to justify his opposition to all theories of nature which use it to supplant God. In this sense the eighth definition permeated his entire discussion. Naturalism is idolatry, for it involves the deification of nature.

The popular tradition which treated *Natura* (sometimes named *Physis* or *Venus*) as a goddess had its beginnings in the Roman inclination to deify anything, whether concrete or abstract, which had a bearing on human good or ill. This habit was probably abetted by Lucretius's invocation of Venus at the beginning of his poem on nature. Through the Middle Ages it persisted as a popular and poetic tradition with affinities to libertinism, and in spite of the opposition of Christian theologians.[15] The deification of nature was generally found compatible with a Neoplatonic hierarchy of souls subordinate to the One, especially with the theory of a world soul. It was supported by the Renaissance tradition of mystery, which found a deeper Christian significance, available only to the initiated, in the pagan nature myths.[16] That such syncretism of pagan and Christian thought could survive the mystery tradition of the Renaissance and still be a living issue early in the seventeenth century, the fate of Julius Caesar Vanini clearly shows, for of his two surviving main works, the first was devoted to proving the existence and the providence of God, but the second (the notorious dialogues which scandalized orthodox Europe and led to his death at the stake), was dedicated to the glorification of Venus, the goddess of nature.[17] Though Vanini was burned and quartered for impiety, there is little evidence in either work of irreverence, although there is typical Renaissance scurrility in the second work. The men of the Renaissance would have understood. But in this later period, when Aristotelian science had been debased by a multiplication of deified subordinate orders claiming empirical efficacy, Christian thought had awakened to the sacrilege involved. Boyle, and following him, Sturm and others, regarded the reification of nature as itself the basic impiety. "Not only the Gentiles made it a goddess (*Nos te facimus, fortuna, deam, coeloque locamus* . . . writes Boyle) but eminent writers in verse and in prose, ancient and modern . . . do seriously talk of it as if it were a kind of Antichrist, that usurped a great share in the government of the world."[18]

Nothing in the created order, according to Boyle, may be glorified at the expense of its Creator. Van Helmont's suggestion that nature be defined as the law of things received from the Creator, Boyle regarded as improper and defective, since a law is but "a notional rule of acting according to the declared will of a superior."[19] God impresses powers or determinate motions upon insensible bodies, but not laws. The laws are men's formulations of these powers for the sake of action. A primary purpose in most of Boyle's writings was to maintain in the scientist the spirit of Christian humility, and to protect the Christian virtuoso from every temptation to excessive intellectual pride.

Miracle and Order

A more lively problem involved in the question of the limitations of the new mechanism, however, and one which orthodoxy could not avoid, was the problem of miracles and their role in the divine providence. As mechanical science advanced, miraculous portents and answers to human needs, even the most urgently sought or most awesome in effect—miraculous cures, comets and other unusual heavenly manifestations, violent storms and other abrupt natural violations of established order—were regularized and absorbed into the causal chains of observed events. This effort to naturalize miracles rested upon the resolution of two general antitheses: the subordination of revelation to reason, and the accommodation of primary causality (that is, divine causality) to secondary causes, sometimes to human causality operating within the realm of created nature.

The first of these antitheses has been treated above in Chapter 3. It may be added here that insofar as the seventeenth century libertine was motivated by the conviction that revelation lies beyond reason,[20] he tended also to defend unlimited possibilities of miracles; this is clearly implicit in Descartes's exemption of the divine will from the principles of human reason—even the principle of sufficient reason itself, even though Descartes himself, in contrast to Pascal, seems distrustful of miracles. Among other refutations of this libertine view, Grua has published a dialogue of Leibniz's in which he argued that since revelation itself rests upon a previous miracle, it cannot be appealed to in justification of miracles; miracles must be justified by tradition, and this implies the authority of reason.[21] To the further objection that if revelation must be tested by human reason, all future revelation would be human, not divine, Leibniz replied with a distinction between the human analysis of faith with respect to its credibility, which rests upon the context of history and the reasonable examination of history, and the divine analysis of faith, which involves the efficient operation of the Holy Spirit in our hearts. This latter appeal to religious experience was further justified by the Leibnizian claim that there are principles of reason which must be common to God and man. Once the spiritual ground for the justification of faith was dropped, as it was by Hume in the eighteenth century, the skeptical demand that miracles must be subject to standard criteria of historical truth at once follows.

A further philosophical issue bearing on the problem of the existence and the nature of miracles was that of the compatibility of primary divine causality with secondary causality, and particularly with human freedom of action. The complicated discussion of Francis Suarez in the twenty-first and twenty-second of his *Metaphysical Disputations* set the pattern for much thought in both France and the Protestant countries. Beginning with an argument for a genuine indeterminism in both divine and human freedom, with real alternatives for action based upon the reason of the agent, Suarez proceeded to expound a theory of divine providence as the permanent, continuous foundation for human choices.

In spite of some resulting paradoxes, particularly related to prevailing theories of substance and of efficient causality, the Cartesians generally followed Descartes's lead in developing Suarez's theory into an explicit voluntarism (which Suarez's inclinations toward Scotism abetted), until the occasionalists settled the question of efficacy by attributing it solely to God, leaving only the determination of the occasion to secondary causes. That this was done in a Platonic spirit (suggested by Descartes himself), according to which providence operates through the eternal ideas actualizing themselves in secondary, empirical situations, was overlooked in much of the discussion of occasionalist writings. Malebranche, however, offered another solution in his theory that God's foreknowledge is restricted to the knowledge of general rules, which enable Him to foretell man's actions without determining them.[22] Though this view seemed to contradict the Cartesian conception of freedom, it did suggest to Leibniz his theory of miracles, as affirmed in the *Discourse on Metaphysics* in 1686, a few years later. Miracles, he there asserted, are not extraordinary and anomalous events breaking into the natural order of nature, but merely particular volitions of God which may themselves be instances of order higher than the "subordinate regulations" of which we have knowledge. "Since nothing can happen which is not according to order, it can be said that miracles are as much subject to order as are natural operations and that the latter are called natural because they conform to certain subordinate maxims which we call the nature of things, for we may say that this nature is merely a custom of God's with which he can dispense for any reason stronger than that which moved him to use these maxims." God "has particular volitions which are exceptions of these subordinate maxims." But "the most general of God's laws which rule the whole sequence of the universe, is without exceptions."[23]

One may generalize by saying that the Platonist thinkers of the seventeenth century agree in recognizing that miracles lie beyond nature as determined by the methods of science, but do not lie beyond the scope of ordered existence itself, or of its rational determination. The successive stages in which the libertine tradition rejected this view consisted, first, of excluding miracle from the realm of reason and of order completely and relegating it to a nonrational experienced revelation, and then, of denying, on the grounds of a narrower, more critical interpretation of experience, the possibility of miracle entirely. This did not, however, reduce the element of mystery which remained within the realm of science itself as tools and methods of investigation were perfected and the scope of experience was widened and deepened. The novel, the unexpected, and the paradoxical were to challenge the scientific intellect increasingly and to force it into new perspectives and horizons of rationality.

Causality as Principle and Problem

Two problematic factors involved in the rise of modern science which have already been discussed in Chapter 4, effectively hastened the positivistic tendency to deny the significance of the concept of nature. At the same time, both also intensified the sense of mystery involved in the task of science. They were, first, the deflation of the notion of causality as a principle of scientific method; and second, the difficulty made by the problem of the origin of forms and qualities for the principle of sufficient reason.

In the first book of his *Physics*, Aristotle defined nature (in contrast to art) as the principle of motion in that in which it is; in art, on the other hand, the cause of motion is external to the thing moved or changed. This was an accepted definition of nature throughout the Scholastic period and the Renaissance. Fernel, for example, wrote, "Things which proceed spontaneously from their own interior impetus are called nature."[24] As we have seen, these interior powers were often given a magical animistic interpretation, and the concept of force, which later proved so important in physics, was a scientifically disciplined result of them. But Aristotle recognized the importance of external, transeunt causes as well, and in the modern development of science, the conception of a method of analysis and synthesis in terms of causality required an emphasis upon these inter-substantial causes.

The transition to this preference for transeunt causality is notable in Zabarella. Asking the same questions which Boyle asked later, *Quid sit Natura?* and *Quaenam sit?* (or in terms of Scholastic logic, what is the intensional meaning of nature, and has it any extensional import?), he replied with Aristotle's "trite and popular (*vulgata*)" definition: "Nature is *per se* the principle of motion in that in which it is; and furthermore, that is understood to be natural which has this principle in it, i.e. an internal propensity to motion." But external causality is implicit in this definition. "I most strongly hold that this [definition] is to be interpreted as follows: nature is the cause of motion in natural things, not only in the body itself in which it is [immanent motion] but also on another external body [transeunt motion]."[25] This emphasis on the transeunt character of causality was associated by Zabarella with the position that causality as applied to motion involves both activity and passivity. Avicenna had been wrong, he argued, in restricting nature to the active power of motion, while Simplicius had erred equally in restricting it to passivity. Zabarella concluded that according to Aristotle (and later, to Duns Scotus), form is the principle of all motion, active *per se* but *passive* in the matter whose motion it affects. Form without matter can have no passive principle, and therefore no existence. But causality can transport form from one body to another.

A similar shift of emphasis from immanent to transeunt causality can be discovered in other intellectual traditions late in the sixteenth century; indeed, it seems to be a correlate of the rising consciousness of a need for a unity of scientific methods and principles. In his *Metaphysical Disputations*, Suarez gave extensive discussions of all of the four causes of Aristotle, but distinct priority to transeunt efficacy as a duality of process involving a duality of action and passion; his unfortunate use of the figurative term *in-fluence* to describe the essence of this causality was taken over by Descartes and by others. Thus in arguing some theses on "the kinds of causes insofar as they fall within Physics," under the direction of Caspar Posner in Jena in 1656, a student proposed the following rather appalling definition: "A cause is the beginning (*principium*) of another thing into which its being flows (*influit*), or, if it does not flow in, it nevertheless intends this by its action, or indeed by its conferring or failing to confer this action upon it. To this definition we shall reduce all causes with which the physicist is concerned." And Otto Casmann's definition of nature in 1605 fixes the definition of nature in terms of this new emphasis upon externally effective causality: "Nature shall signify (as in Aristotle) these two: an active and a passive faculty. The active faculty or power is that by which a body is itself active and efficacious in moving and putting forth actions entrusted to it by God. Its passive power or faculty is that native ability of a body by which it is capable of receiving some motion from without."[26]

The greatest force, however, in the simplification of the concept of causality came from the revival of ancient atomism in Sennert, Gassendi, and others. Their attempted reduction of the universe to figure, shape, and motion in a void reduced natural causality to the transmission of motion from body to body by impact. It is this conception, according to which even action at a distance would become supernatural, which encouraged the further empirical reduction of scientific causality to the description of events concurring in spatial and temporal immediacy, and with some frequency.

In the preceding chapter the role of a mechanistic interpretation of nature in causing a collapse of the idea of universal harmony was discussed. We may now proceed further to point out that in this reduced form, causality does not even offer a ground for considering nature a unity. As Zabarella's definition of method and his denial of an order uniting the various disciplines implicitly require, no aspect of the method of the new sciences offers a ground for the unity of nature. In fact, the very conception of a realm of being to be designated as nature disappears in the positivistic and reductionist doctrine of "saving the phenomena."

The Problem of the Origin of Forms and Qualities

A second problem operating to destroy the status of nature as a mechanistic order of being was that of explaining the origin of forms and qualities.[27] This problem is as old as ancient materialism, which required that composite groups of atoms have qualities and properties which the simple atoms of which they are composed do not have. The persistence of the problem attests the depth and endurance of the conviction that the principle of sufficient reason is essential to all scientific understanding, and that there can be no new form, property, or event without an antecedent cause sufficient to produce it. The problem is also a continuing challenge to the Platonic theory of the eternity of ideas or forms, for the question involved is, What happens to the forms and qualities of simple components in a compound when they disappear, and whence come the new forms and qualities of the composite thing of which the simples are ingredients? (After all, the whole must be equal to the sum of its parts; and everything, old and new, must have a sufficient reason.)

For nearly a century the problem seemed solved (at least for science) when Galileo, Descartes, and others before them distinguished within nature the primary forms or qualities, which are quantifiable and therefore objective, and the secondary qualities, which are in causal connection with the primary, and therefore natural, but are not quantifiable and are therefore subjective.[28] The philosophical effect of this was to tie man to nature, at least so far as the qualitative content of his experience is concerned, yet to require that nature contain in its causal order a subjective as well as an objective realm of meaning. Thus this distinction was of little use in explaining the new properties of composite bodies and events, for subjective qualities must themselves have a sufficient cause in the real essences of things. Nor did Boyle's classic discussion of the problem in his *On the Origine of Formes and Qualities* (1666) contribute to clarity on the issues; as we have seen, he got no further than to assume that the new qualities and forms (he was concerned with what for Descartes were "objective qualities," such as freezing and melting, electrical fluidity, cohesion, and the new qualities of chemical compounds) resulted from a new "texture" which composites acquire; this conjecture seems to have set the scene for Locke's later theory of the unknowability of real essences. There was also a third effort to arrive at some general interpretation of the origin of the properties of composites. This was suggested, but not further generalized, by Leibniz's a priori mathematical resolution of the problem of the total force and momentum of a composite system of separate bodies moving at random by equating them to the sum of the forces and momentums (including directions) of its members.[29] Together with his theory that the occurrence of various attitudes and mental structures in a monad depends upon the relative strength of the impetuses involved in the law of its nature, his mathematical ideal of perfect knowledge, and his theory that sense perceptions provide an indistinct and inadequate knowledge of mathematical order, this might have been developed into a general theory of the mathematical basis of the origin of composite properties or forms, analogous to bend points, maxima, minima, and so forth in a curve.

The failure of all three of these suggestions for a solution of the problem points to a positivistic and phenomenalistic position about nature which removes the quality of explanation from causal generalizations, and renders them merely descriptive of the connections between appearances and their verifiable concomitants. The question of the origin of a form is reduced to the question, "Under what circumstances does it appear?" This is the general form which the positivistic formulation of the aim of science as "saving the phenomena" has taken in more recent science.

The Ambiguous Status of Nature

If conclusions can be drawn from the very complex set of issues raised in this chapter on the meaning and justification of the term nature, they must be of a tentative, loosely overlapping, and incoherent character.

1. The thinkers of the seventeenth century did not succeed in removing the ambiguities of the term nature. Their solutions to the problems of theology, law, education, and the new sciences required uses of the term which overlapped but resisted unified definition. The acceptability of various definitions depended upon questions of the relationship of God to the order of creation, of the place of man within creation, and of man's work in relation to natural order.

This variety of meanings attached to the term can be understood as a stage in the development of modern thought from which several distinct philosophical interpretations of the new science were to emerge. Among them, the alternatives of a metaphysical dynamism or a skeptical positivism are particularly significant.

2. In the conflict of opinion between Aristotelian and Scholastic cosmology on the one hand, and the new corpuscular philosophy which provided a temporary support for science on the other, there was a tendency toward synthesis which treated nature as consisting of a force (*vis*) functioning according to principles of order. This force was widely understood as the *vis dei*, or the exigency of the Platonic ideas. These ideas also provided metaphysical support for the principles of order.

3. This effort to provide a real order of nature adequate for the development of science involved a revision of the concept of causality in three directions: (i) the elimination of final and internal efficient causes and a central emphasis upon external transeunt efficacy, which preserved the logical principle of sufficient reason in its causal form; (ii) the replacement, whenever

possible, of the concept of efficient causality itself by an empirically grounded descriptive theory establishing continuous mathematical dependences (functions) among abstract variable qualities or meanings in the observed events; and (iii) the further restriction of scientific meaning by a dualistic division of nature, in which its phenomenal aspect is explained through underlying mathematical or real "causes" or "reasons." As this dualistic distinction was gradually freed from notions of a divine providence and revelation and from the explanatory references to subordinate powers, it encouraged the development of a positivistic theory of science, in which the concept of nature was itself dispensable. The reduction of mathematics to subjective thought processes, and of matter to form or idea, strengthened this positivistic trend.

4. The recognition of a real order of nature in seventeenth century syncretistic philosophies not only proved adequate to assure the development of the new science, it also provided an account of the role of man as scientist, and a foundation for man's quest for values, following Bacon's conviction that nature, properly studied, would be the servant of man in this quest. Toward the former end, this realistic account of nature was proposed as the basis of a theory of knowledge in which a priori forms of reason, used to penetrate more and more deeply into the analysis of observations, could be justified as a steadily more "adaequated" approach to the order of nature. For the latter purposes, nature was interpreted as presenting itself as neutral to human values when analyzed scientifically, but also as itself determined by a more inclusive context of purpose and value. Both of these external roles, however—the epistemological and the teleological—tended when overemphasized to dissolve the unitary reality of nature and to render it an unnecessary abstraction from experience.

5. In this realistic interpretation of nature, man was included insofar as he could be studied in terms of the categories which apply to nature; however, he transcended nature as the scientist who studies it by imposing his universals upon it, and as the humanist and moralist who use it, directly or symbolically, to achieve human ends. The view that man is both a part of nature and also transcends it illustrates the instability of the ideal of *honnêteté*. For it implies that man's own nature (the theory requires a human nature) is both determined by the order of which he is a part, but also insofar as he transcends this order, by himself as a rational being. Thus stated, this antithesis is the

very heart of the issue between the *homo honestatis* and the libertine. Does rational man express his nature in obedience to inclusive order, or does he create his nature as he creates this order? To postulate an order higher than that of nature—a kingdom of grace above a kingdom of nature—resolves the ambiguity on the scientific level, but may compound it on another level. This was the accepted solution as the century came to a close. The kingdom of grace, being a realm of values, could be, and was, relativized into psychology or history even more easily in the ensuing centuries than the kingdom of nature.

6. The doctrine of creation, coupled with a Scotistic theory of the univocity of human and divine attributes, served to assure the continuity of man with both natures—the *physical* and the *inclusively essential*—and to impart a strong immanentistic emphasis to its doctrine of God's relation to man. In transcending nature, man thus finds his own nature defined by laws, and by ends; in both cases the continuity of man and nature is determined by God—in the case of laws, by the continuity of natural and civil laws; in the case of teleology, by the principle of the optimum or best possible, which must be applied not merely to the human world but to the physical—as the debate about the principle of least action showed in the eighteenth century.

7. Finally, however realistically the conception of nature was developed in science and cosmology in the seventeenth century, and however completely the mysteries of the book of nature were converted into commonplaces as sciences advanced, the total mystery of things—their "real essences" as Locke designated them—not only remained unsolved but increased; the growing complexity of explanations resulted only in growing mystery. This Leibniz sensed when he saw that an infinity of analyses is needed to establish with absoluteness the verity of truths of fact. It was this ultimate insight about the scientific enterprise, continually assuring the indeterminateness of the future of science but in continual doubt about the certainty of the present, which undermined the theory of a block nature, or a "block universe." By 1715, structure and space itself were suborned to time, physics to history. The limits of nature remained unfixed, and the very uses of the term still confused and variable.

10 Man and His Nature: From Microcosm to Mind-Body

He [God] therefore took man as a creature of indeterminate nature and, assigning him a place in the middle of the world, addressed him thus: "Neither a fixed abode nor a form that is thine own nor any function peculiar to thyself have we given thee, Adam, to the end that according to thy longing and according to thy judgment thou mayest have and possess what abode, what form, and what functions thou thyself shalt desire . . . We have set thee at the world's center that thou mayest from thence more easily observe whatever is in the world. We have made thee neither of heaven nor of earth, neither mortal nor immortal, so that with freedom of choice and honor, as though the maker and molder of thyself, thou mayest fashion thyself in whatever shape thou shalt prefer. Thou shalt have the power to degenerate into the lower forms of life, which are brutish. Thou shalt have the power, out of thy soul's judgment, to be reborn into the higher forms, which are divine."

[Pico della Mirandola, "Oration on the Dignity of Man." trans. Elizabeth Forbes, in *The Renaissance Philosophy of Man* (Chicago, University of Chicago Press, 1948), sec. 4, pp. 224-225. Used by permission.]

Poor intricated Soul! Riddling, perplexed, labyrinthical Soul!

[John Donne, *Sermons*, 48 (Vol. I, p. 486).]

The grandeur of man is grand in that he knows himself to be wretched. Man is but a reed, the weakest in nature—but he is a reed that thinks. It does not require the entire world to arm itself to kill him; a vapor, a drop of water, suffices to kill him. But when the universe shall have destroyed him, man will still be nobler than what has killed him, because he knows that he dies, and the universe knows nothing of the advantage which it has over him. Our entire dignity therefore consists in thought; it is in this that we must lift ourselves, not in

224

space and time, which we cannot fill. Let us labor, therefore, to think well; this is the principle of morality.

[Blaise Pascal, *Pensees*, ed. (Paris, 1865), pp. 210, 212.]

Now that we are conquerors of the world, there assuredly remains an enemy within us; everything is clear to man but man, the body to the mind, and the mind to itself. To drop the tragic style and speak more naturally, we are ignorant of the medicine of bodies and of minds. We treat the former as does an agent something for the sake of gain; we treat the latter as a boy does his lesson—as nothing, for he learns it in the hope of forgetting it. It is not surprising, therefore, that until now we have established no science of the pleasant, the useful, or the just. The science of the pleasant is medicine, that of the useful is politics, and that of the just is ethics.

[Leibniz, Notes for the *Elements of Natural Law* (1670-1671) Academy ed., VI, i, 459-460. Loemker, rev. ed., p. 132.]

"What is Man?" asked the ancient Psalmist. His answer, as rendered by King James's translators, is entirely in the spirit of *honestas*, for it gives man his proper place in the hierarchy of beings and recognizes his virtues:

Thou hast made him a little lower than the angels,
And hast crowned him with *glory* and *honor*.

Yet the answer to the question was not at all clear. Pico della Mirandola had denied that man had any nature which he did not freely choose for himself, yet by the seventeenth century he was the microcosm whose nature and powers were both directed and limited by the degree of distinctness with which he mirrored the macrocosm. He was the crown of creation, assigned a unique governing place (under law) over the lower orders of creation, and in his knowledge of himself was the clearest clue to the understanding of the universe and its Creator, yet he was ridden with fears and a sense of his own imperfection, and aware of deep urges, not merely toward order and the good but toward evil and chaos. He was aware of himself as an individual, yet largely dependent upon the world, especially the world of his fellows, around him. Suspended midway between the One and nothing, between the unified perfection which was the source of his being and the norm of his rationality and goodness, and the chaos of negation in matter without form, man found himself dependent in three directions—through external perception and action upon the world he lived in and depended upon, through his passive affectional nature upon lower levels of imperfection and evil, and through his internal sense and reason, upon the divine source of his unity and moral being. Self-consciousness or the internal sense was the essential ground for his rational intuition of God; along with the external sense it provided the rational basis for his just relations to his fellows and the physical world (the indirect revelation of deity). But insensitivity, the surrender to the unclear and indistinct passivity of felt feelings and impressions, doomed him to the lower darknesses of impoverished being.

In this dilemma, several intellectual convictions emerged in the minds of the thoughtful, which, if not themselves new, introduced new elements in man's understanding of himself. Man was inclined to think of himself, less as a unitary microcosm and more as a duality of mind and body. The principle of sufficient reason required the recognition of an unconscious level of mind, not accessible to self-awareness, and the old need for redemption was expressed, consonant with the doctrine of the light of nature, in secular forms. Men became aware of an abyss, hidden even to reason, which nonetheless threatened him and his world.

In Pascal this thought of the fragility and frustration of man was still put theologically, and addressed to man in a state of sin. But even before he had read Pascal, Leibniz, the great projector of universal order, diagnosed man's condition in more secular terms, recognizing the need for intensified efforts in the field of medicine for the body, but calling for a medicine of the mind as well. However the two men may have disagreed about the grounds for man's weakness and failure, they agreed that human understanding was essential for man to escape from his moral illness. Life and power were important categories for both, but in Leibniz the medicine of the mind—a concept which Walther von Tschirnhaus, Leibniz's associate in his last fruitful winter in Paris, later adopted and made the title of his philosophical treatise[1] —was to be the use of understanding by men of *honestas*, in establishing the sciences of ethics and politics, and using the true concept of justice (as the love of the wise) to restore personal integrity and social order.

The doctrine of two medical sciences, one for the body and

one for the mind, clearly encouraged a dualistic notion of man, and both theories together with the new notion of an unconscious mind, presuppose a common human nature which can support such ideals. Thus the old question of how the uniqueness of each individual can be possible in the face of a common human nature once more became crucial.

Human Nature and the Uniqueness of the Individual:
The Principle of Individuation

It followed from the microcosm-macrocosm idea that every man, reflecting all the levels of the cosmic harmony within finite limits, is uniquely endowed, but that all men together also constitute a distinct class of individuals differing from all lesser ones by their possession of common attributes and powers, notably that of inwardness or self-awareness. It was this which made possible memory and imagination, and therefore reason itself. It was also this which enabled men to rule over the lower orders of nature and to form those bonds of association, through language and law, which constituted their social nature.

To the recurrent question: Is there a human nature?, the answer was thus affirmative, but with the further qualification that no two human beings have identical natures. Each differs from all others even though all have determining characteristics in common. The indefinitely many properties which human nature contains (by reflection of the infinite nature of God) vary also in the degree of perfection in which individuals possess each property. It is this variation in kind and degree, all of which involves varying degrees of activity and passivity, which makes possible the distinction of classes and, bridging these, the causal interaction and cooperation which sustain human society.[2]

How then does the *homo honestatis* assess his own nature as an individual? The microcosm-macrocosm formula was too general to provide specific guidance, and was also too ennobling, fraught with too much "honor and glory," to appropriate old metaphysical theories which explained individuality in terms of primary substance and sought some *principium individuationis* to supply further insight into man's particularity.

Two notions of substance, both of which stem from Aristotle, were applied in seventeenth century efforts to understand the individual. The first was derived from Aristotle's logical analysis of the proposition: a substance is the real subject of a proposition whose predicate consists of the attributes and properties of this subject; it cannot itself be the attribute of any further subject. This formula was used and further restricted by Descartes and his followers, who concluded that each substance must be definable by a single attribute—a restriction which obviously conflicts with the microcosm-macrocosm formula, and which both Spinoza and Leibniz at once rejected.[3]

The second notion is more dynamic and comes nearer to the modern conception; it is the daring interpretation of Aristotle's theory of substance as form actualizing matter, as it was expressed in the Latin formula *causa sui*. The very concept of a self-cause, though old, appeared paradoxical to an age in which external transeunt causality had become established in science. How can a being be the cause of itself? The answer was, through idea becoming actual, or essence becoming existence. The effect was to force a distinction between the external determinations of a thing, as examined in science, and the internal determination of a thing by its nature or idea, a concern for metaphysics. The concept forced Spinoza to the conclusion that God alone can be a substance, man being relegated to the status of modes. But Leibniz, operating with a different theory of the relation of knowledge to being, applied the same formula, idea actualizing itself, to man. Wherever a completely individualized idea actualizes itself in a temporal series of active and passive states, there is an individual substance.[4]

Leibniz's conception of monads thus combined the two meanings of substance and adapted both to the new dynamic microcosm-macrocosm conception; the individual is a subject—a complete notion—actualizing itself in a real temporal series; the complete notion, being uniquely compounded of God's attributes in finite ways, assures that the individual's experiences and acts reflect or express the universe from a unique point of view, and this expression is the way substances actualize themselves. Since a substance now assumes the Platonic pattern of a complete composite idea acting in a series of events, Leibniz's conception fulfills the demand that a theory of man include an account not only of the discrete experiences which give content to the successive states of his existence, but also of his more permanent dispositional nature—the habits, attitudes, and sentiments which constitute his character.

As a criterion, however, by which the honorable man of the century was to determine his station and its duties, Leibniz's doctrine had its limitations and difficulties. The Socratic maxim "Know thyself" became the law: "Discover the complete notion of your individual being, the law of your individual series of actions and passions." This law is after all a very complex truth of *fact* rather than of *reason*, and therefore cannot be arrived at short of an infinite analysis—and man is incapable of such an analysis. Thus the concept of a complete, determining notion of each individual could serve no purpose beyond that of a regulative ideal which man's understanding of himself might be said to approach as his analysis of the variables included in his nature becomes more detailed and his judgments increase in clarity and distinctness. Being a truth of fact, this functional and dynamic notion of substance, which also defines a principle of individuation, draws the thinker away from metaphysical speculation to a reliance upon knowledge based on a reasoning interpretation of self-experience.

The quest for a principle of individuation had been revived because of the empirical awareness of change and of the coming into being of composites with new properties, which once again raised the metaphysical problem of the one and the many. With few exceptions, the discussion of individuation in the seventeenth century proceeded under the spell of Suarez's solution,[5] which itself followed Ockham's avoidance of abstractions. A metaphysical individual is determined neither by signate matter as the Thomists had held, nor by a unique individuating formal principle like the 'thisness' or *haecceitas* of the Scotists. Individuation results from the entire nature of the individual whole. Any complete being is its own individuating principle—the unity of form and matter, of property and function, action and passion, constitutes the individual.

This is obviously compatible with the microcosm notion, according to which every particular being is a relative whole reflecting or expressing the universal whole. But it is also empty, offering no explanation or sufficient reason, but merely the fact itself—an individual is wherever one experiences a functioning whole. Thus Suarez's principle, to which Leibniz also adhered in his first Leipzig dissertation, *De Principio Individui* (1663), leaves the philosopher only a recourse to experience. Individuals are where you find them.

The related but opposite views of Hobbes and Spinoza give interesting examples of the variety of interpretations to which this surrender of an a priori principle led. As a nominalist, Hobbes held that the continuing identity of any individual thing is relative to the continuation of that property (whether matter, form, or both) in consideration of which it has been named.[6]

The answer to "Is Socrates the same man?" differs from the answer to "Is Socrates the same body?." That Spinoza held a similar relativistic and pragmatic theory is shown in the casual remarks in the *Ethics* (Book II, Lemmas 4, 5, and 26 to Proposition 13, Axiom 2), where he assigns individuality to any composite of bodies which operate toward a unified end. Though this conception, like Hobbes's, applies only to corporeal individuals, one needs only to be reminded of Spinoza's definition of mind as the idea of the body along with the idea of the idea of the body, and so ad infinitum,[7] to be able to infer that Spinoza recognizes only corporeal individuality: the way of ideas leads to an intensification of the active affections until the mind becomes one with the intellectual love of God.

As I have shown, Leibniz was indebted to Spinoza for his conception of substance as *causa sui*, applying it, however, to finite individuals rather than God, and interpreting it as a law, that is, an essence, of the individual whole actualizing its possibilities in a series of acts or states. This sophisticated effort to explain the microcosm-macrocosm idea in the spirit of the mathematical and logical thought of the age presents a metaphysical resolution of the problem of the determinant of human individuality which transcends the scientific effort to place man in a network of causal relations which determine his place in nature. Thus Leibniz avoided Descartes's dualism of mind and body by opening the way for another dualism: on the one hand, metaphysical beings, each of which internally determines its life history; and on the other, scientific relations between phenomenal things which are arrived at by abstraction from the way in which the metaphysical individuals, acting in harmony, *appear* to a scientific observer. Some of the Cartesians, however, also disturbed by their master's dualism, in which man's spirit reflects the unity of the Creator but his body is a part of the mechanism of nature, reduced the concept of the individual to a minimum; according to Malebranche, for instance, only man's will is significant for his individuality while his body inheres in God the Immensum, as the locus of spatial motions, and his intellect has its abode in God's Ideas.

By the end of the century, therefore, the general trend is to find man's individuality in experience, not in a logical criterion. Although this empiricism was already implicit in the microcosm-macrocosm conception, it was pushed further, by the popular appeal of the new mechanistic ideal, to attempt to absorb human life into the nexus of natural processes. The way was opened for science to neglect the whole of man for the sake of the component causal connections required in understanding him.

This growing empiricism about human individualism and identity is shown in Locke's *Essay*. Retaining a mind-body dualism like that of Descartes, Locke found the basis of individual identity in bodies as obscure as the problem of substance, but he found the identity of spirits assured through self-consciousness along with memory of the past. With this view Leibniz in his commentary on Locke was in essential agreement. The two men agreed that self-knowledge is rare and never complete; on this they stood with Socrates. They agreed also that there is an empirical source in knowledge sufficient to establish self-identity, and therefore moral responsibility. Though limited largely to a grasp of mental states and actions, self-experience or reflection does support (though not completely) this moral end. But Leibniz differed from Locke in two respects: he found in self-consciousness more than merely combinations of atomic sensations, feelings, and discrete mental acts detached from external (or internal) objects; and furthermore, he recognized the continuity of this self-awareness with reason and its a priori principles. He agreed with Locke that *moral* identity is established through self-awareness or reflection, but held that *metaphysical* identity and, as a result, true self-knowledge require a law of the individual nature and are therefore the object of an endless but also, with limits, successful and fruitful quest.[8]

The reasonableness but also the instability of the seventeenth century quest for the individual is thus shown in its contention that self-knowledge is possible through self-experience, that the two are distinct, but that self-knowledge itself is never complete.

The Internal View and Man's Growing Isolation

Insight into man's nature through self-consciousness is a renewed emphasis in the individualism of the late Renaissance. The empirical approach through inward-directed experience was not new. The internal sense had been a commonplace for Aristotelians, with no general agreement about what it revealed. It was St. Augustine who emphasized its revelatory power, not only with respect to man himself but with respect to God as well. It is important that even in the seventeenth century, self-awareness was seldom divorced from the objective pole about which the acts and attitudes of the mind revolved. The *pars rationis* and the *pars rei* were not treated in complete separation, not even by Descartes, in spite of the blame bestowed upon him generally for having introduced into modern philosophy a falsely isolated subjectivism.[9] Like the ideas, reason was held to have a foundation in internal processes of thought, as the moral decisions of man have a subjective basis in his feelings of well-being and sorrow. But both draw their content from the perception of, and the affective or willed response to, what is without. It was only when this internal relation of subject with object was broken that the great age of synthesis ended, leaving individual man in solitude and isolation from his peers. When this took place, the bond between social order and the inwardly felt needs and efforts of individuals themselves was broken.

The beginnings of this isolation of the individual are to be found in the Augustinian tradition itself, as St. Augustine's tendency to restrict his concern to "God and the human soul" suggests. Ockhamism strengthened individualism through its emphasis upon the subjective nature of rational order, though it did not, as did the "supernominalism" of Hobbes and his predecessors,[10] tend to reduce meanings to words and condemn the mental operations of man to an isolation from the world about him. In spite of the Ockhamist's denial of intelligible species, reason did not lose its content *a parte rei*, for man's reason rested upon the inwardness of his mind precisely because his internal processes of memory, thought, and will are expressions not merely of the world incompletely represented by the sensible species, but of a logical order inherent in man through his divine origin. Yet this inwardness nevertheless assumed a stronger separative role as the dualism of mind and object was defined in terms of unrelated attributes, such as activity versus local motion, or as thought versus extension. It was this rather than his conception of ideas which led to the threat to the unity of experience in Descartes and some of his followers.

In a direct way which his critics attributed to St. Augustine, Descartes sought in self-awareness the basis for a certainty which no outward form of knowledge could attain; it was the gateway to answers for all doubt, and the knowledge of God and of bodies could be established with certainty only by beginning with it. Yet what Descartes himself found through this self-certainty of insight into himself was rather thin and unhelpful. It revealed "thoughts," that is, mental qualities and acts, and then, with the aid of reason, two attributes, an inner (thought) and an outer (extension). But spiritual substance must be inferred, as "the thing that thinks." And since motion was not included in the attribute of bodies, it must be assigned to spirit. There is no consciousness of self or of personal identity.

Descartes's effort to establish certainty through inwardness was of course aimed at refuting the skeptics on their own terms. Skepticism had always been invited by the fact of subjective privacy and by disagreements in the judgments of individuals and groups about observed fact, matters of taste, and moral convictions. Petrarch's essay on *His Own Ignorance and That of Others* was an example, at the beginning of the Renaissance, which had many followers. The sixteenth century had its share of such protests against easy acceptance; for example, the *Essays* of Montaigne, and the skeptics and relativists whom he defended—Raimond de Sebonde, Peter Scarron, and the rest. In the seventeenth century Pascal faced the awful mystery of the infinities revealed in mathematics and the new optical inventions, and portrayed natural man as terrified by his lonesomeness, for the very reason that in contrast to lesser creatures, he thinks—"a reed, the weakest in nature, but a reed that thinks." Pascal's *fideism*, fed on the one hand by the mystical strain in him, and on the other, by his close association with libertines such as the Chevalier de la Méré and Saint Evremond, converted Ockhamistic nominalism and Augustinian individualism into an intense pragmatic apologetic for Christian faith. Mannerism, in one of its phases, corresponds to the individual's protest against the obvious weakness of conventional appeals to natural law as a ground for knowledge, taste, and morals, and thus merges with the individualism of the libertine.

A supplementary cause, moveover, of the growing isolation of man through his inwardness and his subjectivistic preoccupations, was the exclusion of human values from nature as the new science progressed and strengthened the bond between reason and sense observation, thus leaving the emotional, appetitive side of man undisciplined by scientific order. To this stimulus to irrationality there was added the recognition, which grew as the acquaintance with other cultures expanded, that human evaluations are relative to the varying cultural traditions of men. The growth of toleration thus actually undermined the doctrine of a natural light of reason on which human unity and order could be based.

Feeling and the Trend toward Subjectivism

One of the results of the split between inward and outward aspects of experience (with the outward becoming increasingly neutral with respect to human desires and ends) was to encourage thinkers to seek the grounds and tests of meaning and truth in subjective experiences alone. Involved in this separation from objective authentication were not merely the so-called data of sense, Hobbes's phantasms, but also the primary feelings or affections, usually taken to be joy and sorrow, or pleasure and pain. Not that these were the only emotional states given in internal perception; but as the empirical temper grew, they became the ones which analysis pointed to as primary and therefore the basis for the validity of all the rest—sense qualities for the validity of theoretical knowledge, and the feelings in the validation of moral judgments and, ultimately, the virtues. The rejection of objectivity included not only existence but universal a priori principles. Finally, after Locke added a chapter on the association of ideas to Book II of his *Essays* in its fourth edition, the empirical fallacy was encouraged, which confused the association of perceived impressions with the rational ordering of knowledge based on them—a confusion which has played into the hands of agencies of mass mental coercion to the present.

The last hope of a realistic account of knowledge now seemed to lie in the close but mysterious connection of sensory qualities with the physiological and physical processes involved in perception. But all of the paradoxes involved in efforts to bridge the gap between subject and object in knowledge now recurred in this reduced context—the causal sequence was an obvious part of the process, but the relationship of knowing an object which was so closely dependent upon it remained unillumined by causal connections, and called for explanation of an intra-mental, psychological kind. The several theories formulated in the seventeenth century to resolve the mystery of this relation of the physiological order to the mind all still have defenders, though the identity theory of Spinoza, or its more explicitly materialistic version by Hobbes, appears to have a favored position, not entirely unjustified empirically or on grounds of fruitfulness.

The seventeenth century exaggerated the amiability of man's emotions and impulses, as well as their amenability to the discipline of the Ideas and of reason. The complexity and power of

the emotions was discovered anew as a result of the preoccupation of earlier thinkers with the understanding of human moti-
vations. The contribution of Juan Luis Vives to this study, and
his influence in correcting the Stoic view that all affections are
passions which enslave the soul, have been discussed in Chapter
3.[11] Applied to the affections, the method of analysis and
synthesis undertook to classify them, to derive the more complex from the primary feelings of joy and sorrow, and sometimes to trace them to their causes. Descartes's treatise on the
Passions of the Soul was a classical derivation of this kind,
though Descartes still clung to a Stoic conception of virtue,
holding that the passions must be suppressed by *generosité*, or
great-minded self-esteem. Spinoza, in contrast, delineated the
affective nature of the free man—that is, the man who has reordered his thought to attain distinct and adequate ideas—
through a scale of complexity and adequacy culminating in the
highest, most active, and enduring affection of all, the intellectual love of God. At the same time, however, Spinoza reduced to subjectivity all ends and values (less than the supreme
end) by finding their causes in desire, desire itself being a complex emotion based upon an inadequate idea.

The new doctrine of the affections thus served to throw light
upon the conception of man from several directions. It repudiated the Stoic doctrine of stern detachment from all affection
for the sake of the only ground of virtue, reason. It introduced
a psychology of motivation which was diversified, radically
pluralistic, and responsive to the new richness of life which
scientific discovery and humanistic creativity made available.
The role of reason was retained, however, as arbiter and orderer of
this diversity into a harmony of appetites depending upon the
rational harmony of their causes or ends. In a real sense, therefore, the new analysis of the affections served to support and
amplify the idea of man as microcosm who, from his unique
perspective and in accordance with his innate powers, not only
expresses the entire variety and fullness of meaning in the universe, but can also be moved by this unity to achieve his true
goals and values.

On the other hand, however, the doctrine of the affections
also tended to undermine the rationalistic conception of order
upon which the classical and baroque conceptions of man
rested. This it did in two ways: first, by developing a theory of
human motivation which could easily be divorced from reason
by detaching both motives and acts from their rational ends and

fitting them rather into the new mechanistic order of the sciences; and secondly, by providing a new theory of the human will, stressing its derivation from feeling and impulse rather than from the intellect as the older traditions had done.[12] The new doctrine of the affections, which analytic empiricists took to be detachable from their objects and transferable from one object to another, also had the effect, like their sensory counterparts, of making the subjective order normative for the objective—this time in the fields of morality, the arts, and ultimately of religion as well. Thus the new doctrine encouraged an attempt at a psychology neutral to values, a part of a mechanistic world view, on the one hand, but also an irrationalistic libertinism on the other. The case of Descartes, who encouraged both points of view,[13] shows the difficulty of establishing a relationship between these incompatible positions.

Even before Descartes, physiological speculation had moved toward mechanism by affirming a relation between the circulation of the blood which centered in the heart, and that of the animal spirits centering in the brain, since human action after all involved interaction between brain and heart. Hobbes had presented a theory of nervous traces, suggesting an explanation of sensory experiences as caused by the resistance of motions in the nervous system. But it was Descartes's effort which set the problem for modern thought. He brought the mechanisms of animal action, which man shares with the "beasts," into causal connection with a higher order of conscious choice through the pineal gland, and adopted Suarez's "influence" theory, to explain the causal relations involved.

In addition to encouraging this effort at a physiological explanation, the theory of an emotive ground of action also served to support a voluntarism of which libertinism was a possible consequence. The will was made to rest, not upon reason, but upon inclinations or impulsions to action in which feeling or emotion is the subjective motive. This view the seventeenth century quest for rational absolutes found as unacceptable as that of a universal mechanism. Between the causal determinism of Hobbes, who limited philosophy to what could be resolved and compounded, and therefore to bodies and their motions, and the indeterministic theory of freedom held by the libertine, which rejected an objective order of law available to human reason and urged a "liberty of indifference," Leibniz, and in spite of some wavering, also Locke, found nothing to choose. Both argued, as had Robert Boyle, that the rational knowledge of God through His revelation was the most certain of all knowledge, and that the higher freedom of self-determination in obedience to the requirements of this reason was the only valid interpretation of freedom.

Libertinism, on the other hand, rested from its beginnings upon a rejection of the reasonableness (at least the human reasonableness) of the divine revelation. Fideist and nonbeliever joined their attacks upon the adequacy of the human intellect to understand a way of salvation. Practical life must be grounded on inclination or feeling. Although the libertinism of the next century, particularly in France, abandoned an irrational fideism for unbelief, the vestiges of the old roots are still discernible in Rousseau's appeal for the goodness and adequacy of feeling as this is shown in natural man, in contrast to "fallen" civilized man, and the failure of reason which civilization brought with it. The Pascalian dualism of man the sinner and man standing in divine grace was now freed from revelation; corrupt man because man with his reason corrupted by civilization; man saved was man freed from civilization to obey his own nature. Natural man superseded both the religion of nature and the fall of man. Rousseau's faith in feeling thus launched the modern revolt against reason and against sin alike.

The Unconscious and Disharmony

If the new recognition of the role of the affections could be used both for and against the ideal of the *homme honnête*, the same must be said for another extension of man's understanding of himself—the recognition of levels or depths of the mind to which self-consciousness cannot penetrate, but which must nevertheless be recognized as existent, both on empirical grounds such as the study of sleep and dreams, and on rational grounds derived from the nature of the mind itself. For mind is a microcosm, continuous in its expression or perception of the world, yet discrete and selective in the content of its actual awareness. There must therefore be a process of perception of which man is not himself aware.

In theory the conception of unconscious mind is very old. It may be said to have had its origins in Aristotle's doctrine of the soul, which recognizes lower levels of functioning which the internal sense cannot reach but which are responsive to the order of the whole. To this was added the effect of the Stoic *logos* doctrine: through the *logos* all souls contain as seeds representations of the universe as a whole, but they are unconscious of most of the minute responses involved in this wide fecundity; only unclear and indistinct qualities and relations arise in consciousness itself, even in the most reasonable soul. Thus man, responding in his internal nature to the entire macrocosm, must surely have depths in his soul of which he is unaware, and the lower levels of distinctness must shade off into total unawareness. As Leibniz put it while catching up with the new philosophy and the new mathematics in Paris, "Every mind is omniscient but confused."[14]

Leibniz's conception of the unconscious was supported by astute observations of his own marginal states of consciousness and those of others.[15] Dreams, after-images and reflexes, the recovery of a sense of self-identity upon waking, the operation of an unconscious censor, the solution of problems during sleep or in a dream—these and many other unusual mental phenomena supported his conviction that the conscious aspect of life (that of which we can actually be aware in self-consciousness) is but the higher level of a complex spiritual process of responsive perceptions, appetitive acts, and reasonings, most of which are too minute and pass too quickly for our self-observation. But there are other levels of the unconscious too—all of those dispositional patterns of thought and action included in habits, inclinations, sentiments, talents, virtues, and vices (Leibniz uses all of these terms) are realities of which we are unconscious save when we conceptualize them. And beneath these, unattainable even to our complete conceptual knowledge, is the law of our nature, that is to say, the share each of us has in the perfections of God—the innate ideas of which our life is a partial realization.

Such a mixture of the empirically grounded and the rationally necessary was needed, according to Leibniz, to close the gap between discrete experiences and the continuum of dispositional patterns which express both our individual nature and our interconnectedness with the physical and social world about us. In Leibniz's thought the theory of the unconscious is fruitful in explaining experience, but its primary role is the rational one of maintaining the fullness and reasonableness of a harmonious universe and the individuals it includes.

Yet the ultimate effect of the theory was to destroy the metaphysics of harmony within which it had arisen. For its effect was to withdraw large regions of man's nature and his spiritual potentialities from the reach and control of his understanding.

As long as the metaphysical foundations held, it did not withdraw these potentialities from *all* reason, for God's wise providence was still held to control all. But it did withdraw them from man's own rational direction and control, and so inevitably helped to bring the era of rationalism to an end. The later history of the concept confirms this opinion. It is notable that little use was made of the theory of the unconscious until the Romantic movement plunged into pessimism in the nineteenth century. Earlier pessimism based itself still upon a calculus of conscious states of pleasure and pain. In the century of the Enlightenment, whose thinkers found little significance in a doctrine of the unconscious, human knowledge and action were treated rather as a type of mechanism in which meanings and purposes are compounded from primary impressions of sense and feelings. Etienne Bonnot de Condillac's statue was the model and ideal, and neutralism the mood, rather than either an optimism of ends or a pessimism based on subconscious forces.

The Social Nature of the Individual

Thus far the discussion has centered in aspects of man's understanding of himself which developed in the enlarged Platonism of the ideal of *honestas*, but which encouraged his isolation as an individual. It is now time to recall that a most important conviction of the seventeenth century about the nature of the individual, and one which distinguishes it most sharply from the prevailing individualism of the following century, whether expressed in the precontractual political individual with rights endangered by his fellows or in Adam Smith's economic man, was the conviction that the individual is essentially social in his obligations and his essential nature as well. This too was not an original insight. The Stoic doctrine of the *logos* was its basis, even though the ground of man's social nature had been, as we have suggested, shifted from universal reason to the feelings or affections. The revival of Augustinian Platonism implicitly encouraged this emphasis upon social interdependence, and the humanists of the Renaissance made the point explicitly and often. The conception was consonant with the idea of harmony, and became clear in Vives's and Erasmus's condemnation of war. It underlay Vives's story of man being taken into the fellowship of the Gods,[16] and was given prophetic utterance in the glowing peroration of John Donne's sermon which portrays man as a promontory of the mainland rather than an island, and the stranger's death as the death of us all. It was generalized from man to include lower orders of living nature. In his work on *Concord and Discord*, Vives began his exposition of concord with the bees, with sheep, and with cranes; all of these are crowds rather than societies, yet give strong witness of interdependence. Bees, however, have a *civitas* which we are advised to contemplate. It was with a touch of satire, on the other hand, that Vives chose examples of human discord from among the savants and the priests, that is, from the Republic of Letters and the kingdom of grace respectively. His long argument against war and discord, whether between states and their princes, between men in communities and families, or within man himself, is always sustained by his conviction that conflict violates both the laws of nature and the Christian revelation, and that violence against man is at once violence against human nature and society. "All wars are civil wars because all are between brothers."[17] As L. S. Gallego writes in the Introduction to his Spanish translation of the *De Concordia*, Suarez's society of peoples and Francesco de Vittoria's international-juridical society followed as logically as corollaries upon Vives's statement.

The thinkers of the Renaissance and the succeeding century may not have discovered the most useful categories for examining and interpreting this social interdependence. Vives himself was still convinced that the basis for it was reason, and that the source of all discord lies in the affections. In the *De Concordia* he quoted Seneca: "*Affectus quidam tam mali ministri quam duces sunt*" (The affections are as often evil counsellors as they are guides) and he listed hatred, distrust, and pride as the most prominent causes of discord, whereas modesty, moderation, temperance, and humanity—"gentle tranquillity, with suavity and benevolence toward others"—were listed as the fruits of reason, which are crowned by the virtues of honor and nobility. "Wars and discords arise from perturbed affections, peace and concord from reason. If counsellors excite discord, if they applaud it, they withdraw from themselves and should be called corrupters more truly than counsellors. If royal affections per se excited by counsellors are also opposed by burning affections, and indeed, with authority and faith, how great will be the conflagration? What ruins? Who could re-erect the tumbling affairs of men? On the other hand, with honor, nobility, moderation, temperance, humanity—that is, gentleness of mind—how great the tranquillity and sweetness, and the benevolence toward others."[18]

With the revival of metaphysics the relations involved in this interpersonal unity and dependence called for closer definition, and the concept of substance required modification to allow for this external dependence upon others[19] and for the surrender of some self-sufficiency. The notion of *sympathy* emphasized by Frascatoro and his followers, vestiges of which are to be found in the ethics of Francis Hutcheson and Hume, was a generalized adaptation of Empedocles's love and strife, relied upon to account for the interdependence of all things. A different tradition, which has already been noted, appeared in Francis Bacon, who suggested that all things are interrelated through perception, that is, through a "grasping through" to others; this, he held, was to be taken literally in conscious beings, analogically in others. To perception Bisterfeld in his encyclopedic studies added appetite, implying not merely a "grasping through" but an effective drive to do so. This appetite he further described as "the desire for union."[20] Leibniz later criticized this desire, which Hobbes used as a definition of love, with the comment, "In this sense the wolf is said to love the lamb."[21] But Bisterfeld's combination must have remained in his memory for decades until he made use of the same two acts—perception and appetite—to express the asymmetrical, internally-externally bound relationship between each monad and the rest.

In both Alsted's and Bisterfeld's encyclopedic writings the terms symbiosis and immeation were applied to this social relationship, which seems to have been widely accepted among Reformed thinkers. What was common to all such attempts to label the relationship involved is the asymmetry but possible mutuality of the bond: A may perceive B (or have an appetite for union with B) without B having the same relational act to A; in each case the relationship is internally determinative for the acting entity, but need not at all be held to determine the nature of the recipient.

In considering these efforts to find a fitting category with which to interpret the social bond between men, one is impressed with their inadequacy. It seems, indeed, that the failure to find an appropriate metaphysical interpretation of the togetherness of men, a fact and a moral ideal which the thinkers all recognized, was the greatest metaphysical failure of all, and one from which the periods following it suffered most.

The Nature of Love

The culminating interpretation of the symbiotic nature of man was a generalized form of the Christian doctrine of love. The argument about the possibility of disinterested love, which became increasingly bitter toward the end of the century, was first of all an argument about the nature of this crowning symbiotic virtue, not one about its existence.[22] Two issues were interwoven in the controversy; the question of whether man is or is not capable of a disinterested act was complicated by the issue of his state of grace. Fénélon and the disciples of Madam Guyon held that disinterested love was the state of the mystic who had achieved the eternal Sabbath, the peace of God, while Bossuet and other opponents rejected this mystical state as quietism and therefore not love at all.

The antimystical answer, which affirmed the necessity of self-interest, even in Christian love, was sustained, first by the French church and then by Rome, and Fénélon was banished to his diocese. It was the answer most encouraging to the libertine movement, since it implied that all altruistic actions expected of Christians must rest on a decision arising from the agent's anticipation of his own satisfaction; no obligation to an absolute moral authority could be involved unless it also commanded this egoistic reference. Insofar as the issue involved was the descriptive psychological question of whether man is capable of a disinterested act, it continued to arise, insolvable yet nonetheless meaningful, among succeeding generations of thinkers. Yet when discussion moved from motives to results, the conception of a love which enriches the lover as well as the beloved seemed to many to provide a sounder bond of unity among people as individuals than one in which service to others involved loss of self.

The argument about the nature and possibility of Christian love must remind us again of the fusion of reality and ideal made by the thinkers of the century. Should the thinker, when concerned for the motivation of the *homme honnête*, write for an existent Kingdom of God or Commonwealth of Grace, or for one which does not, but should, exist? Should he write as if man were saved or a sinner? Is the reign of Christ nonexistent in history, as Hobbes held, and the Commonwealth of Grace restricted to Christ's followers and their common spiritual bond? Or is the kingdom of grace, of which God is King, indeed Father, of all spirits who, unlike other creatures, are responsive not only to the world but to Him, as wide as all human beings, even those who are not themselves in a state of grace, as Leibniz affirmed?[23] Then love, to whatever extent it is motivated by "interest,"[24] must provide the motive for justice of every kind, even that which punishes criminals and prevents intrusions upon rights. Or (what seems to be the sound kernel and perhaps even the true intent) is the kingdom of grace the metaphysically grounded ideal, imperfectly actualized among finite individuals, but always capable of greater finite actualization since its possibility rests upon the measures of his own infinite perfections which God bestowed upon the world in creation? Thus seen (and Malebranche may have seen it more sharply even than Leibniz) the kingdom of grace may be considered a regulative ideal in history—a realm of possibility capable of further actualization.

Leibniz's conception of God as "the region of ideas" and his discussions of progress in history (both in his later years)[25] seem to point to this interpretation, which serves to mediate between the libertine's rejection of all rationality in the divine plan, and the deterministic teleological optimism of an absolute Providence and the foreknowledge of a loving God. Such a God Leibniz in his later years should have called unwise, for, as he had always held, wisdom, whether of God or of men, requires that justice be derivable from the love of the wise, adapted to achieve the best possible at all levels of finite imperfection.

Natural Law and Symbiosis

The view that human nature includes a symbiotic social dependence, whether this is viewed as already the mark of divine redemption, or is to be perfected in love, has its roots in a doctrine of natural law. With it the optimistic view of the potentialities of human nature reached a peak which met with skepticism in later centuries, particularly in the twentieth. It is important to note that the doctrine of a law of nature survived as long as rationalism did, Kant himself giving a fresh interpretation of it at the end of the eighteenth century. The doctrine was shattered by those who, like Jeremy Bentham (on the side of fictionalism and empiricism) and Hegel (on the side of historicism), found it an abstract, functionally inert, uncreative solution incapable of meeting the variety of differences among individual needs and duties in the complexities of modern life. Yet in an age whose problems demand universal solutions and whose ideologies have offered this universalism only at great cost in conflicts and clashing dogmas, no substitute for the doctrine has been found, and leaders in public opinion have no counsel save to return to it.[26] The growing sense of individual differences and of historical relativisms, of which the declining years of the great rationalistic century already showed signs, here too suggests a mediating view which could avoid the opposite extremes of a rigid absolutizing of relative convictions and the modern libertinism of legal pragmatism.

As has already been seen (in Chapter 3), early interpreters of the natural law doctrine showed an interest in affections and instincts as factors in establishing universal rules of conduct. The Stoic-Neoplatonic law of nature was conceived by them as given to men, not in the form of explicit self-evident principles of a Euclidean cast, but in the form of instinctive or inborn drives to certain moral forms of action. The principles or laws were regarded as intellectual abstractions made by jurists to enable their codification and application to dissenters. Moreover, these intuitive patterns of action and conviction provided not merely for rights but for duties commensurate to them, a point largely forgotten in later models of positive law. This was essential to the doctrine of Hugo Grotius, and also to the deep-sighted, minimally instinctive and maximally rational analysis of Thomas Hobbes, who found the natural operators involved in clarifying the rights and duties of man to be the right of self-preservation and self-satisfaction. Cruder but no less effective for his age was Lord Herbert of Cherbury's analysis of the natural principles of religion, particularly as they affirmed that the moral quality of acts must be commensurable with their appropriate punishments or rewards. The assurance that laws are natural was finally sought not in their source in God, the lawgiver, but in the universal human responses to them (even when this universality was sometimes limited to certain classes or groups). Leibniz's enthusiasm at the appearance of the Earl of Shaftesbury's *Characteristics of Men, Manners, Opinions, and Times* in 1711 was largely due to his recognition, in Shaftesbury's doctrine of the moral affections, that the application of moral principles in limited relative situations required a feeling of the universality of these principles.[27]

Such a theory of an instinctive or felt natural law receives its claim of universality, of course, from metaphysical considerations which lie beyond scientific psychology, but the considerations serve as reminders that the intellectualization of natural law which followed had the effect of destroying the "natural" motive power in positive law and leaving it artificial and mechanical through association with an abstract "political man," and detached from concrete personal responsibilities. A deeper root in an order of human values had been expressed in the intuitive, precritical convictions and responses of men. Without this, the abstractions and casuistic processes designed to make the law applicable to all particular cases moved a further long step toward dehumanization and the growth of anxiety and isolation in self-conscious man.

Freedom

What of man's freedom? Leibniz's *Theodiceè*, published ten years after the end of the century but thought out long before, was generally regarded as the height of the seventeenth century effort to adapt the theological doctrine of universal providence and divine foreknowledge to the new ideal of the individual. At its close, Leibniz took up once more, and carried further, Lorenzo Valla's parable in which Tarquin the Proud inquires of Athena why the divine Providence caused, or permitted, him to be so evil. Valla had answered his friend's question about freedom in the vein of the older skeptical and fideistic libertine: We are all free in spite of the divine omniscience; therefore do not doubt but believe. Leibniz's answer went a little beyond Valla's but hardly far enough. In his continuation of the story, Tarquin is taken from Athena to Apollo (which I take to be the movement from discursive reason to a more intuitive, revelatory insight), and Apollo supplements his sister by showing that the contingencies of history would have been worse without Tarquin's sin than with it. Leibniz was in these later years going beyond his own definition of freedom as "spontaneity," that is, the determination of the individual's acts by the law of his own nature. The further step, which he never explicitly made but which he seems in various ethical writings to have implied, was the suggestion that the acts of each man may well be determined by the law of his own nature, but that this law is itself based a priori upon the principle of the best possible, which now becomes a moral principle for each man to apply to the determination of the best of possible solutions in every problem of conduct, even as God's nature includes the requirement that his will should be determined by the principle of the best possible of all possible worlds. According to this interpretation (which Leibniz never himself fully explicated) the law of one's nature is necessary but not sufficient to determine one's acts, without the intervention of a further application of the principle of sufficient reason in the form of man's having to choose, from among the possible specific acts implied by the law of his nature, those particular acts which are best in each particular situation. There is evidence in some of Leibniz's ethical writings that he judged man to have a part in the determination of his own nature—within the general limits which God imposed on him in creation.[28] This would go some distance in recognizing not a "freedom of indifference" (which the honorable man should abominate) but a genuine choice of limited alternatives, and would therefore approach the modified libertinism of Bayle and other critics.

The seventeenth century, however, was widely distrustful of such freedom of choice. The opinion was widespread that the essential freedom of man is an achievement, not a natural capacity, and that man is free only through obedience to a superior order with authority to which he must discover that he has, or must learn to acquire, an internal responsiveness through his affectional, and therefore at least indistinctly rational, nature. This is essentially the freedom of the courtier as *homme honnête*; for when the need of universality is recognized, as it was by the great thinkers of the period, the authoritative order upon which full freedom rests is seen to transcend earthly princes and to be that of creation and its Creator, the monarch whose *éclat* and wisdom make him the most powerful, wisest, and most just of kings and fathers in the kingdom of grace. But as the esteem for science grew and men became increasingly preoccupied with the power of nature manifested in its mechanisms, the shift from the religious meaning of order and power to the natural, anticipated by Bacon's remark that "nature is to be conquered by obeying her," reinforced the secular version of power which grew in the Enlightenment. God was conveniently cared for by pushing him out of nature once he had created it, and the way was opened for a dynamic materialism, in uncomfortable liaison with a libertine view of man.

Power and Goodness

In the modern version of Platonism, power was the ultimate assurance that Ideas will be actualized. Its divine status, together with the other two new "transcendentals," wisdom and love, assured the possibility of all power being just and all existence harmonious. Reasonable power, aiming at the best ends, therefore was available in the created order in three forms—in the individual man as a man of honor (*homo honestatis*), in nature as force operating according to law, revealed by the new science, and in social or political order, as sovereignty and law. The unity of the transcendentals was the assurance that power can and should be reasonable and good. But the key to the achievement of this ideal in the created order was man as individual, bound to other individuals in the kingdom of grace.

It is easy to understand man's frustration with the magnitude of physical power and the values and dangers of its political use, as the seventeenth century conviction of the unity of power, wisdom, and goodness disintegrated through the collapse of its metaphysical base. Though the honorable man was to embody in his own life the trinity of virtues (that is, reasonable powers) which were united with all creation through the triune being of its Creator, power and wisdom soon fell apart when challenged by the empirical, libertine spirit. By the end of the century, the moral ideal of *honnêteté* became externalized into a superficial code of conduct. Private morality and individual power were divorced, and public power throve on private vices as Bernard de Mandeville, an apt learner from Machiavelli of the policy of *raisons d'état*, showed in *The Fable of the Bees* (1714). Physical power, required by Newton's laws of motion and discovered by Huygens and Leibniz to be essential to the theory of dynamics, was no longer regarded (as Leibniz had regarded it) as an anchor of science in metaphysics, but was seen as morally neutral, and capable of destructive effects upon man and his ideals.

Once again it must be admitted that this collapse of the ideal of the unity of power and goodness was made possible, perhaps inevitable, by unresolved ambiguities and antinomies in the Platonic ideal. If the kingdom of grace already exists and includes all spirits, then, given time, the conflicts and horrors of power and "interest" (that is, self-interest) must resolve themselves into greater goods, even though history shows itself always to be a "litany of suffering." If evils result only from the finiteness and privation of creation and the resulting divisiveness of human imperfections, and are required by God for the sake of a better, even more beautiful world in the long run, then this really good order must at some time become recognizable. Yet history soon showed the awful conundrum of a mounting control of physical power by men, along with a growing disagreement about its uses. Leibniz seems finally to have recognized that fulfillment of his ideal was unattainable in history. Though he seems never to have abandoned his faith in progress, he was inclined to hold that progress never achieves its goals, as a curve never intersects its asymtotes. He feared revolution, saw signs of its imminent threat, yet regarded such destructive events as "steps backward in order better to leap forward." The new particularized producers of power, political, economic, techno-logical, which were already demanding men's loyalties but which were to block a more general unity of power and justice, were still unnoticed, but were soon to shatter the Platonic-Christian vision of the commensurateness of wisdom and love with power.

Conclusion

The metaphysical failure of seventeenth century thinkers was due less to the inadequacy in their theories of interindi-vidual dependence in dynamic social groups than to the in-adequacy of their concept of the individual in serving as a basis for the complexity of the human person. Self-conscious aware-ness, isolated and unilateral powers, and the growing subject-ivism of their interpretation of personal values did not suffice to support the rational, orderly development of human under-standing and control. The new insights of the age required a shift in the conception of substance which should meet the demands of community—communication and cooperative action. Leibniz did make such a shift from substance as a per-manent substratum not given in experience but holding together changing properties, to a revised Aristotelian conception of an individual series of events actualizing their law or complete notion and responding to their total surroundings. His approach through the logic of universals and particulars provided for both the changing content of mind (the *materia prima* of the monad) and the permanent habits, attitudes, and temperament of the person. But perception and appetite alone, with their self-con-scious forms of *intellect* and *will*, are insufficient to provide an interpretation of action, not to speak of interpersonal and co-operative actions. Although the whole universe is open to the experience of each individual, Leibniz held also that all indi-viduals, natural and spiritual, act and suffer only on the basis of their own power. They experience the power of others but are not affected by it; by its own law each responds in its own way to every perturbation, every structural change in the world. Only the overarching universal meaning expressed in their separate individual laws is common to them. This is as far as the metaphysics of the period went with the problem.

Clearly the common social life requires further alteration in the concept of individual substance. It implies that a mind can grow in its essence and dispositional nature, and that life is not merely an accumulation and summation of experiences *of* experience (in the mathematical analogy, an integral of the values of a function between two time limits), but an alteration of character and a merging of values and efforts with those of others. The demands of a social universe, or at least a universe in which a society of persons can play an important role, also can be assured only through a flexibility, innovativeness, and exchange or mutual aid which Leibniz acknowledged but which his system did not adequately permit. In contrast to later attempts to define the relation of the individual to his world, however, for example, in terms of the behavioristic formula of stimulus and reaction or response, or in terms of the external legalistic relation of contract, Leibniz's use of perception did have some advantages. Perception and appetite do provide an active bond of direct apprehension which completes the account of knowledge and is essential for the normative relationship of love. It assures that thought can enter all of the decisive human relationships. Love requires a cognitive presence, however inadequate, of the object, and demands critical judgment in the confirmation or correction of the concept of that object. Thus perception, on which reason and knowledge rest, and which they serve to make certain, must be understood as an abstract part of a personal emotive-responsive action toward persons and things which themselves acquire at least for the moment an enriched personal quality through the act.

Love may not be mutual and reciprocated. It must be defined in terms which do not rob either party of his self-determination and individual freedom. Thus Leibniz was justified in criticizing the possessive theory which he found in Hobbes and Alsted, as well as the egoism implicit in Spinoza's definition of love. However short Leibniz's definition falls of the active responsiveness of love, it does in intent preserve the idea that even if unresponded to, love enriches both its subject and its object.

It may be said that the high point of the modern conception of man's potential for individual and social order and value was reached when thinkers of the seventeenth century interpreted the microcosm-macrocosm idea as involving a plurality of individual minds capable of self-awareness and therefore of reason, bound together by love, because they participated in one common ideal order, which each expressed from his own point of view, powerful and wise enough to actualize the best common values. These are made possible by the new scientific mastery of nature and affectively demanded in the best-possible ideal of a kingdom of grace or ideal social harmony.

This pattern of thought, however, contained the seeds of its own failure in its confusion of the real with the ideal. The new trend of separating subject from object and making the norm of intellectual adequacy a subjective one, the dualism of external and internal perceptions and the sharp dualism of body and mind which resulted from it, and a growing perception of the historical relativity of laws and ideals, made way eventually for the libertine acceptance of the neutrality of nature to human values, the separation of the affections from reason and objective order, and the denial or disregard of an objective order attainable by reason, the divine, to which the affective-volitional natures of all men owe a loyalty. Thus the libertine spirit was strengthened and a doctrine of normative providential order was gradually withdrawn. If arguments for God continued, they became empirical and teleological in a narrow restricted sense, the sense in which Hume was to criticize them.

Notes, Bibliography, and Index

Notes

NOTES TO CHAPTER 1

1. According to G. N. Clark, Europe was completely free from wars for only seven calendar years in the century, and the scope of warfare and the strength and size of armies were enormously increased. *The Seventeenth Century.* 2nd ed., pp. 98-102.

2. Hans Baron's detailed argument that "civic humanism" emerged from the revival of classical letters as a result of the successful struggle against tyranny in early fifteenth century Florence has supplied me with a model on a smaller, more specialized scale for my more general application of the process of revolt and synthesis to the seventeenth century. See particularly the Epilogue added to the revised one-volume edition of *The Crisis of the Early Italian Renaissance*, especially pp. 455-462.

3. "The 17th century is a great divide, after which tragedy is doomed by a triple decadence—the decline of the work, the myth, and the audience." George Steiner, *The Death of Tragedy* (New York, 1961) as reviewed in *Time*, July 7, 1961, p. 68. But a part of Steiner's argument applies not merely to tragedy but to literature and art in general. For what is involved in the threefold decline is, after all, a loss of the unified structure of language (and therefore reason), of faith, and of social participation, for all of which the seventeenth century still strove—unsuccessfully.

4. In his "Essay upon Projects," Daniel Defoe wrote, "About the year 1680 began the art and mystery of projecting to creep into the world." But Defoe was over a half-century late in his estimate, for great projectors like Bacon, the Jesuits, Louis XIV and his counselors, not to mention the great experimenters and thinkers who founded modern science and mathematics, had been at work much earlier.

5. Libertinism is here to be understood in its intellectual, not its moral sense. The term seems to be a Renaissance revival derived from the Roman *libertus*, or freed man, and *libertinus*, orginally the son of a *libertus*. In the *accusatio ingrati liberti*, to which Leibniz refers in the *Nouveaux Essais* IV, viii, 12 (Langley's trans., p. 497), Constantine gave to the patron the right to recall a freed man into slavery on grounds of thanklessness or "the violation of his trust or responsibility." See Max Kaser, *Das Römische Privatrecht* (Munich, C. H. Beck, 1955) 2 vols., I, 103; II, 94-95, 252-254; also the dedicatory epistle of John Selden's *Table Talk* (1631): "As if one could be put into the state of libertine without a former servitude."

6. Carl J. Burckhardt, in *Gestalten und Mächte* (Zurich, 1941), pp. 73-96, gives an excellent description of the century's ideal of *honestas*, or *honnêteté*, the virtues it embodied, its linguistic architectural style, and its sudden collapse after the Peace of Nymwegen.

7. In *The Subtle Knot: Creative Scepticism in Seventeenth-Century England* (London, Allen and Unwin, 1952), Margaret L. Wiley has written

a brilliant history and analysis of this "creative" form of skepticism in the wider context of English literature and theology. But her emphasis is upon skepticism as a way of freeing faith, rather than as a method for achieving scientific or philosophical clarity and adequacy. Since even the libertine constructs some beliefs, however subjective and self-centered, there seems to be a series of degrees in the contribution of skepticism to belief and to clear knowledge.

8. Georg Lukács, *Die Zerstörung der Vernunft* (Berlin, 1954), p. 80.

9. John Locke's great chapter on Power in *An Essay concerning Human Understanding*, II, xiii, presents evidence of the importance of the concept and the difficulty of understanding its basis.

10. Nicholas Malebranche, *Reponse de l'auteur de la Recherche de le Vérité au livre de M. Arnauld, des vrayes et des fausses idées*, 2nd. ed., (Rotterdam, 1685), pp. 24-25; also in Antoine Arnauld, *Oeuvres philosophiques*, ed. Jules Simon (Paris, 1843), pp. 279-280; *Oeuvres complètes de Malebranche*, ed. A. Robinet, VI (1966), pp. 23-24.

11. For the libertine tradition, see J. Roger Charbonnel, *La pensée italienne au XVIᵉ siècle et le courant libertin* (Paris, 1919), and René Pintard, *Le libertinage érudit dans la première moitié du XVIIᵉ siècle* (Paris, 1943). The closely related skeptical tradition has been studied carefully by Richard Popkin, *The History of Skepticism from Erasmus to Descartes*, rev. ed., (New York, 1964).

12. Quoted in Ralph Rader, *The Man of the Renaissance* (New York, 1932), p. 351.

13. *Advancement of Learning*, II, chap. xx, especially sec. 7; chap. xxi, especially sec. 6 (The World's Classics, pp. 179-180).

14. *Ethics*, Part IV, Proposition 37, Scholium.

15. All of these men have occasion to discuss *honestas* and the *homo honestatis* in their ethical writings. Examples in Malebranche and Spinoza have been given. Leibniz's descriptions are often related to his analysis of justice; see for instance, Leibniz, *Philosophische Schriften*, ed. C. I. Gerhardt, III, 425; *Deutsche Schriften*, ed. G. E. Guhrauer, II, 18-19; *Mitteilungen aus Leibnizens ungedruckten Schriften*, ed. G. Mollat (Leipzig, 1893), pp. 29, 44. On Leibniz's criticism of Shaftesbury's approval of raillery, see Gerhardt, III, 423.

16. For discussions of the microcosm-macrocosm ideal see Heinz Heimsoeth, *Die sex grosse Themen der neueren Metaphysik*, 4th ed. (Darmstadt, 1958), chap. 5, and Dietrich Mahnke, *Unendliche Sphäre und Allmittelpunkt* (Halle, 1937).

17. For such attempts to apply the baroque to thought systems of the seventeenth century, see Carl Gebhardt, "Rembrandt und Spinoza," *Kantstudien*, 32 (1927), 161-181, and J. O. Fleckenstein, *Gottfried Wilhelm Leibniz: Barock und Universalismus* (Munich, 1958).

18. André Chastel, *L'art italienne* (Paris, 1956). For convenience, I cite the German translation by Herman Buse, 2 vols. (Munich, 1961), II, pp. 40-42, 81-88, 135-140.

19. Heinrich Wölfflin, *Kunstgeschichtliche Grundbegriffe*, 11th ed. (Basel, 1948). English translation by M. D. Hottinger, *The Principles of Art History* (New York, 1932).

20. Georg Simmel, *Rembrandtstudien* (Darmstadt, 1953), pp. 7-47.

21. This is the general theme of the work by Dietrich Mahnke cited in note 16 above.

22. Simmel's essay, referred to in note 20 above, is pertinent at this point too.

23. The literature on mannerism is rapidly growing. John Shearman, *Mannerism* (Harmsworth, 1967); Gustav Hocke, *Der Manierismus*, 2 vols.; I. *Die Welt als Labyrinth*; II. *Manierismus in der Literatur* (Hamburg, 1957, 1959); Franzsepp Würtenberger, *Mannerism: The European Style of the Sixteenth Century*, trans. Michael Heron (London, 1953).

NOTES TO CHAPTER 2

1. Reading *donner* for *damer* in Gerhardt.

2. Gerhardt, I, 26.

3. See H. Merguet, *Lexikon zu den philosophischen Schriften Ciceros*, 3 vols. (1892-1894; Hildesheim, 1961), and *Handlexikon zu Cicero* (1905; Hildesheim, 1962).

4. Leonardo Olschki, *The Genius of Italy* (New York, 1949), pp. 199-212.

5. This is shown by the concern frequently shown for the "rudes" and the "tyro," or the beginner (in contrast to the docti) in the *litterae humaniores* to be discussed later. Alsted addressed one of his books, the *Philosophia digne restituta*, to the zealous reader, the unlearned reader, the little-learned reader (*lector invide, lector indocte, lector nimis docte*).

6. By Robert Boyle's time, however, these terms are applied primarily to experimenters in the new sciences. See his *Christian Virtuoso*.

7. Cf. Voltaire: "Je vois avec plaisir qu'il se forme en Europe une République immense d'esprits cultives"; Similarly, Christian Thomasius demanded a "honnête Gelehrsamkeit, beauté d'esprit, un bon goût und Galanterie." Max Wundt, *Die deutsche Schulphilosophie im Zeitalter der Aufklärung* (Tubingen, 1945), pp. 27-28.

8. Ramus defined logic as the art of disputing well (*ars bene disserandi*). The many editions of his *Dialecticae Institutiones* (1647) have been catalogued and studied by Walter J. Ong, S. J., *Ramus and Talon Inventory* (Cambridge, Mass., 1958).

9. Francis Bacon, in the *Advancement of Learning* (1605), II, address to the King, 8-13 (The World's Classics, pp. 75-79), appealed to the universities to aid in the renovation of learning, but also offers criticisms of their neglect of experimental learning and their pursuit of memory divorced from invention and imagination. He proposes foreign exchange among universities.

The use of student disputations, of which Leibniz still recognized the potential value, seems *in actu* to have perpetuated the doctrines of the professors through the theses of the student respondents who had to argue for them. Costello's description of the procedure in disputations at Cambridge (*The Scholastic Curriculum at Early Seventeenth Century Cambridge*, Cambridge, Mass., 1958) can be applied with few changes to German and Dutch universities as well.

10. Chief among these journals which appeared late in the seventeenth century were the *Journal de Scavans* and the *Memoires de Trevoux* of Paris, the *Nouvelles de la République des Lettres* and *Histoire des Ouvrages des Savans* of Amsterdam, and the *Acta Eruditorium* of Leipzig.

11. *Correspondence de P. Marin Mersenne*, ed. Cornelis de Waard, 10 vols. (Paris, 1945-1967).

12. *Correspondence*, vol. 9 (Paris, 1965), p. 185, note on line 81.

13. John Luis Vives, *De Anima et vita libri tres* (Zurich, n.d.), pp. 92-99.

14. Bruno, *De Umbris Idearum*, *Opera Latina*, ed. Francesco Forentino (Naples, 1879), II, i, 16. See also note 5 above. The distinction between the "rudes litterarum" or "tirones" and the "docti" came from Cicero; cf. Merguet, *Handlexikon*, pp. 384, 641.

15. *Advancement of Learning*, II, xvii, 4 (The World's Classics, London, 1951), p. 162. Hobbes applied the same principle of organization in his *Elementa de corpore*.

16. For Leibniz's enumeration of encyclopedists, see his later revision notes of the early *New Method for Learning and Teaching Jurisprudence* (1667), Academy ed., VI, i, 288, notes to lines 12ff. See also Gerhardt, VII, 67-68e.

17. *Encyclopaedia VII tomis distincta* (Herborn, 1630). The list of encyclopedists is in the (unpaged) Preface to the Reader. Never was the self-coined anagram on his name, *Alstedius-Sedulitas* more appropriately applied than to Alsted's own labors. Though he was charged with plagiarism by Christian Thomasius, an examination of the *Encyclopedia* shows a meticulous effort to credit the sources of his ideas and of the many abridgments of earlier discussions which he included. The term "*encyclopaedia*" was in general use before Alsted appropriated it.

18. Giacomo Zabarella, *De Methodo* and *De doctrinae ordine Apologia* in *Opera Logica*, Editio Tertia, Cologne 1597. On Zabarella's influence see Max Wundt, *Die Deutsche Schulphilosophie*, pp. 213-221, and Peter Peterson, *Geschichte der aristotelischen Philosophie im protestantischen Deutschland* (Leipzig, 1921), pp. 139, 155.

19. The title of the first edition was *Porta Sapientiae reserata sive pansophiae christianae seminarium* (Oxford, 1637), but further editions in 1639 received the title of *Prodromus pansophiae*. A recent bilingual edition (Latin-German), *Vorspiele: Prodromus pansophiae: Vorläufer der Pansophie* (Düsseldorf, 1963), provides a succinct introduction to Comenius's philosophical orientation.

20. According to Cotton Mather in his *Magnalia*, Comenius was also, in 1641 or 1642, invited by John Winthrop, the younger, to become Presi-

dent of Harvard. The evidence for this is discussed by G. H. Turnbull, *Hartlib, Dury, and Comenius* (Liverpool and London, 1947), pp. 368-369.

21. *Prodromus*, secs. 8-13. Sections 30 and 31 deal further with the evils of figurative language and the sects.

22. Francis Bacon criticizes the opinion of Aristotle that the *summum bonum* for man is contemplation, replacing this with action—an important index for the shift of emphasis to utility and projects. *Advancement of Learning*, II, xx, 8.

23. Though Bacon was a strong influence throughout the century, this was not through his ideas on logic or his (unworkable) proposals for the reform of method, but rather for his urgent call for a return to the study of natural causes and forms and a cooperative attack on the unsolved problems of nature.

24. Ramus limited rhetoric to problems of style and delivery, and included under method in the last part of his logic problems of the effective arrangement of material to be disputed or taught.

25. Aristotle, *Posterior Analytics* I, iv, 73b. In an interesting but unfortunately neglected survey of the history of logic, Keckermann showed in some detail the great debt Ramus owed to Juan Luis Vives in his logic. See the *Praecognitorum Logicorum* in Keckermann's *Systema Logicae plenioris, Tractatus primus, Opera Omnia* (Geneva, 1614).

26. For Bacon's criticism of Ramus, see *Advancement of Learning*, II, xvii, 12 (The World's Classics, p. 166) and *De Augmentiis Scientiarum IV*, ii.

27. In a study of *The Gladiators of the Republic of Letters in the 15th, 16th, and 17th Centuries* (Paris, 1860) Charles Nisard has examined the cases of other quarrelers, including Lorenzo Valla.

28. *Prodromus*, sec. 31.

29. Paul Dibon, *La philosophie néerlandaise au siècle d'or*. Vol. 1 (Paris, 1954), p. 259.

30. *De Philosophia et Philosophorum Sectis*, Libri II (The Hague, 1658), II, chap. xxi, sec. 11-13. It is not surprising, however, that John Clauberg, the German Cartesian, condemned eclecticism on the ground that life is too short to complete a thorough eclectic study, and urged that one should rather ignore tradition and begin anew, as Descartes had done. "He that would eclecticize the great philosophers must be greater than they and must have a Lydian stone of truth." *Differentia inter Cartesianiam et aliis in scholis usitatam philosophiam* (1680), pp. 59-60. Descartes had himself criticized eclecticism for its weakness. *Oeuvres*, ed. Adam and Tannery, VI, 11, from 1619.

31. The eclectic spirit in which Leibniz began his philosophizing is well illustrated in his baccalaureate dissertation on the principle of individuation and his letter to Jacob Thomasius in 1669, in which he sought to show that Aristotle's *Physics* was consistent with the modern atomists who sought to reduce all to number, shape, and motion (Gerhardt, IV, 17-26; I, 15-17). Leibniz was always sensitive to the evils of sectarianism and frequently charged Descartes with seeking to found a new sect, insisting that

he read more books than he was willing to admit, as his own writings sometimes show (Gerhardt, IV, 310-312.) Robert Boyle charged Hobbes with reviving the old sect of extreme nominalism.

32. The apex of eclecticism was Brucker's great history of philosophy, published in 1766, which identified it with Neoplatonism; this was in turn attacked, along with the pyrrhonism of the French encyclopedists, in defense of revelation and ecclesiastical authority, in an anonymous *Histoire critique de l'eclecticisme, ou des nouveaux Platoniciens* (1766).

33. Gerhard Ritter, *Via antiqua und Via moderna auf den deutschen Universitäten des XV. Jahrhunderts* (Heidelberg, 1922.)

34. See for example, *Advancement of Learning*, I, v, 1 (The World's Classics, pp. 37-38). Bacon repeats the old argument that it is we who are the ancients since we are the heirs to the past—a point of which Perrault and others in the later century make much.

35. Among Cartesian contributions to the argument between ancients and moderns, the two most influential works (to judge by their reprintings) were John Clauberg, *Differentia inter Cartesianam et aliis in scholis usitatam philosophiam*, which first appeared in 1651, and Jean Baptiste Duhamel, *Philosophia Vetus et Nova ad usum scholae accomodata, in Regia Burgundia olim pertracta* (Paris, 1681; Nuremberg, 1682). See also Clauberg's *Logica Vetus et Nova* (Duisberg, 1656). Both writers were strongly eclectic, Duhamel introducing much Aristotelian physics into Cartesian metaphysics.

The first critical study of the history of the controversy, Hippolyte Rigault, *Histoire de la querelle des anciens et des modernes* (Paris, 1856), treats the debates, from their Greek beginnings, as senseless.

36. Charles Perrault, *Parallèle des anciéns et des moderns en ce qui regarde les arts et les sciences* (Paris, 1688-1690).

37. Louis Dutens, however, writing his *Recherches sur l'origine des découvertes attribuées aux modernes.* (2nd ed. Paris, 1766), after Voltaire's *Letters on the English* and the French encyclopedists had shifted interest, restored science to the center of discussion.

38. Gerhardt, III, 423. Loemker, *Philosophical Papers and Letters of Leibniz* (rev. ed. Dortrecht, 1969), p. 629.

39. Quoted from John Ryan, *The Reputation of Saint Thomas Aquinas among English Protestant Thinkers of the Seventeenth Century* (Washington, 1948).

40. *Respublica Literaria, or the Republick of Letters, being a Vision Wrote in Spanish by Don Diego de Saavedra . . . Translated from the Original* by J. E. A. B. (London, 1727).

41. Leibniz, *Opera Omnia* (Academy ed.), IV, i, 570-571.

42. Steuchus Eugubinus, *De Philosophia perenni sive veterum philosophorum cum theologia Christiana consensu libri X* (Paris, 1577).

43. *Advancement of Learning*, I, vi, 1-6; II, i, 1. Bacon demands harmony as a test of the modern relevance of old philosophy; see II, viii, 5-6. (The World's Classics, 43-45, 81-82, 121-122).

44. *Metaphysica tribus libris tractata* (Herborn, 1613). Preface to the reader.

45. A widely used edition of Lullus's *Ars Magna* with commentaries by Bruno, Alsted, and others appeared in Frankfurt in 1609. Bacon found Lullus's proposal for the completion of the quest for knowledge by means of a theory of combining all the most general concepts in all possible ways barren of fruits and encouraging only to those who engaged in empty talk. But Leibniz cited him in support of his proposal for a combinatorial art, a part of his universal characteristic and encyclopedia.

46. Alsted's instructions to a "peregrinator" on the road of educational progress were striking enough to be included in an anthology on *Erudition* published by Thomas Crenius in 1699. In it Alsted, following the inspiration of Vives and Bacon, brought an empirical emphasis and something of the spirit of the new sciences into the context of literary erudition, by bounding them by moral and political prudence on one side and by eloquence on the other. Alsted defined the four pillars of true science as "the true chemistry," "the true astrology," experientia, and a doctrine of signs. Erhard Weigel's "moral sphere," which Leibniz undertook to revise in his youth, is also significant in the context of this new program of clarifying knowledge by a mathematically arranged use of symbols.

47. *Spanisch-Jesuitische und deutsch-lutherische Metaphysik des 17. Jahrdunderts* (Hamburg, 1935). Both Descartes and Leibniz were concerned to justify a theory of the Eucharist metaphysically; it was commonly argued against Descartes's theory of bodies that it made transubstantiation impossible.

48. This is not to say that the problems of these men did not arise out of the *Physics* of Aristotle and his modern followers, nor that the empirical issues raised by Aristotelians were not effective in determining their methods. The criticisms raised by Strong and Randall against E. A. Burtt's Platonic interpretation of *The Metaphysical Foundations of Modern Physical Science* (New York, 1925) can in part be met by a sharper distinction between the problems and the methods used to solve them on the one hand, and the traditional context in which they were expounded on the other.

49. Gerhardt, III, 222-223.

50. *Ibid.*, 14-15.

51. David Hume, *Treatise on Human Nature* (London, 1739-40), ed. L. E. Selby-Bigge (1896), p. xx.

NOTES TO CHAPTER 3

1. *Leviathan*, ed. Michael Oakeshott (Oxford, Blackwell, n.d.), III, chaps. 41- 42; and IV, chap. 44, especially p. 399.

2. *Ibid.*, III, chap. 41, p. 318.

3. Bacon, *Advancement of Learning*, II, xxv, 9-19. (The World's Classics, pp. 244-251). See also *Works*, ed. William Rawley (1879), II, 399.

4. Gerhardt, vii, 572.

5. *Advancement of Learning*, II, xxv, 3-6 (The World's Classics, p. 241).

6. See the discussion of Herbert of Cherbury below. In the passage referred to in note 5 above, Bacon had limited the light of nature to "a discerning touching the perfection of the world law . . . sufficient to check the vice, but not to inform the duty." Lord Herbert's theory of instinctive grasps of the light of nature goes a step further than this toward the rational clarity of Malebranche's theory.

7. For a further discussion of this expansion of reason to cover revelation and faith, see the section below on "The Natural Light of Reason." For Malebranche's thoughts, see particularly the Eclaircissements to the *Recherche de la vérité*, and the *Traité de la nature et de la grace*; also León Brunschvicg, *Le progrès de la conscience dans la philosophie occidentale.* 2nd ed. (Paris 1953), Vol. II, chap. 8.

8. See the concluding sections (32-37) of the *Discourse on Metaphysics*, Gerhardt, IV, 457-463. Leibniz also distinguished a Kingdom of Wisdom and a Kingdom of Power: *Specimen dynamicum* I (Loemker, 2nd ed. p. 442).

Earlier sources of Leibniz's derivation of justice from love and wisdom have been described by Hans-Peter Schneider, *Justitia Universalis: Quellenstudien zur Geschichte des "christlichen Naturrechts" bei Gottfried Wilhelm Leibniz* (Frankfurt, 1967).

9. The following bibliographical selection may be helpful in addition to the works specified in the text (including that of Casmann at the head of the chapter):

Mornay, Philippe de, Seigneur du Plassis-Marly (Mornaeus), *De la vérité de la religion Chrétiénne contre les athées, Epicuriens, payens, Juifs, Mahumedistes, et autres infideles* (Antwerp, 1581).

Pierre Charron, *Trois vérités contre tous les athées, idolâtres, juifs, mahométans, hérétiques et schismatiques* (Bordeaux, 1583).

Jean Bodin, *Colloquium Heptaplomeres, de rerum sublimium arcanis abditis* (Paris, 1857).

Julius Caesar Vanini, *Amphitheatrum aeternae providentiae divinomagicum, christiano-physicum, necnon astrologo-catholicum, adversum veteres philosophos, atheos, epicureos, peripateticos, et stoicos* (Lyon, 1615).

Marin Mersenne, *Questiones celeberissimae in Genesim* (Paris, 1632).

Marin Mersenne, *L'impiété des déistes, athées, et libertins de ce temps, combattue et renversée* (Paris, 1624).

Joseph Glanvill, *Plus Ultra* (London, 1668).

Henry More, *Antidote against Atheism* (London, 1662), and *Divine Dialogues* (London, 1668).

Robert Boyle, *The Excellency of Theology* (London, 1674).

Gottlieb Spitzel (Theophilus Spizelius), *De atheisimo eradicando* (Augsburg, 1669).

Richard Bentley, *The Folly and Unreasonableness of Atheism* (First Boyle Lecture; London, 1692).

10. Leibniz, *Demonstrationes Catholicae* (Academy ed.), VI, i, 48.

11. Cognatus, Joannes, *Fundamenta religionis, hoc est de naturale dei cognitione, de animi immortalitate, et de justitia dei, adversus politicorum seu atheorum errores* (Douay, 1597).

12. Tommaso Campanella, *Atheismus Triumphatus* (Paris, 1636). Dedication to Louis XIII (unpaged). The political motives which prolonged the Thirty Years' War and determined its outcome strengthened this association of atheism with politics. The account of the war in Carl Friedrich, *The Age of the Baroque* (New York, 1952), especially chapter 6, is particularly informative.

13. Theophilus Spizelius, *De atheismo eradicando* (Augsburg, 1669), p. 13. Dedicated to Antonius Reiser, who had written a *De origine et progressu antitheismi seu atheismi epistolaris dissertatio* (Strassburg, 1669). Spitzel's work also contained Leibniz's early *Confessio naturae contra atheistos*. For the criticism of Campanella, see Spitzel, pp. 42-48.

14. Only one quotation has survived from the work of Geoffroi Vallée, it contains his account of the libertine as a skeptic, but expresses his conviction that "l'homme ne peut jamais être athéiste, et est ainsi crée de Dieu." On him see Bayle's *Dictionary*.

15. Julius Caesar Vanini, *Amphitheatrum aeternae providentiae*, (Lyon, 1615). Leibniz's early attempt, in the *Confessio naturae*, to refute atheism, which Spitzel printed, was also based on motion, making use of Spitzel's principle that in arguing for God, one should look for causes not given in things themselves.

16. Gerhardt, I, 26.

17. Joseph Glanvill, *Plus Ultra* (London, 1668), p. 138.

18. Joseph Glanvill, *Saducismus triumphatus* (London, 1682), Preface, 25-26. See also *A Whip for the Droll, Fidler to the Atheist: being Reflections on Drollery and Atheism, sent upon the Occasion of the Drummer of Tedworth, in a letter to the most learned Dr. Henry More* (London, 1688). Glanvill by no means shared Leibniz's later reservations about the use of raillery.

19. Juan Luis Vives, *De Veritate fidei Christianae libri V* (Cologne, 1568), pp. 181-185.

20. *Ibid.*, p. 273.

21. Campanella, *Atheismus Triumphatus* (Paris, 1636), p. 175.

22. Baron de la Hontan, *New Voyages to North-America. Containing an account of the several nations of that vast continent . . . Also a dialogue between the author and a General of the Savages, giving a full view of the religion and strange opinions of those people.* 2 vols. (London, 1703). The Baron de La Hontan's full name was Louis Armand de Lom D'Arce.

23. Herbert of Cherbury, *De Veritate, prout distinguitur a revelatione, a verisimili, a possibili, et a falso.* 3rd ed. (London, 1656), p. 273.

24. Keckermann's convincing arrangement of the evidence that Ramus owed the principles of his logic to Vives has been generally overlooked. See his impressive history of logic, "*De logicae inventoribus et auctoribus ab initio mundi ad hunc,*" in his *Praecognitorum logicorum tractatus primus, Opera Omnia* (Geneva, 1614), pp. 98-125.

25. Lodewijk Meyer, *Philosophia scripturae interpres: Exercitatio paradoxa* (Amsterdam, 1666).

26. *Atheismus Triumphatus*, Dedication to Louis XIII (unpaged).

27. Vives, *De Anima et vita libri tres* (*Opera Omnia*, Valencia, 1782), III, 421-520.

28. Vives, *De Veritate fidei Christianae* (Cologne, 1568), unpaged preface. Also found in *Opera Omnia* (Valencia, 1790), VIII, 3.

29. *Ibid.*, V, ii, 431. The social effects of such faith and love are further portrayed in pages 576-580 of the Valencia edition.

30. The issues, which have been examined by Emil Weber, Ernst Troeltsch, Peter Peterson, Max Wundt, Karl Eschweiler, are delineated with clarity by Ernst Lewalter, *Spanisch-Jesuitische und deutsch-lutherische Metaphysik des 17. Jahrhunderts* (Hamburg, 1935). See especially chap. iii.

31. Francisco Suarez, *Disputationes Metaphysicae* (Mainz, 1600), Disputatio 29. Influenced by Zabarella, Keckermann rejected all metaphysical arguments except insofar as they established a general essence which, as a whole, is everywhere implicit in being. "But [he adds] all that the intellect perceives, it perceives through the phantasmata or images. But images are finite . . . and an infinite object cannot be perceived through finite images. Moreover, all that the intellect understands, it understands through something else prior to it; but nothing is either prior to or better known than God *per se* . . . since he himself is the *primum ens* and *primum intelligibile.*" (*Systema S.S. Theologiae*, Hanau, 1602), pp. 6, 7. Thus Keckermann too holds God to be given by the natural light of intellect. His dual theory of intellect is significant: it has two distinct functions, perception (or intuition) and understanding (or discursive reasoning).

32. *Disputatio* 29, 2, 5. Herbert of Cherbury seems to have formulated his first two principles after Suarez.

33. *Disputatio* 29, 3, 34: "I will add, however, that although in a rigorous sense God is not known to us as all-evident, this truth is none the less consistent (consentaneous) with natural light and with the consensus of all men, so that it can scarcely be ignored by anyone."

34. Suarez, *Disputatio* 3, 23. The argument from motion had been previously rejected by Scaliger, *Exotericarum Exercitationum libri XV de Subtilitate* (Hanau, 1634), Exer. 6, and later by Vanini. Zabarella, by contrast, had rejected the argument from causality, which he restricted to physical considerations, in favor of an argument from motion. Leibniz revived an argument from motion in his early *Confessio naturae contra atheistos*.

35. See Josef Leiwesmeier, "Die Gotteslehre bei Franz Suarez" (Paderborn, 1938); and Josef Ludwig, *Das akausale Zusammenwirken der Seelenvermögen in der Erkenntnislehre des Suarez* (Munich, 1929).

36. Suarez, *Disputationes* 27-36. It is wrong, however, to label this emphasis upon the immanence of God as pantheistic, for Suarez emphasizes that the relation of created things to the creator cannot be that of modes to substance. The stress on immanence is even more conspicuous in

the tradition of Neoplatonism from Nicholas of Cusa to Bruno. In both traditions, however, the unity of being in God transcends the pluralistic order of experienced (created) beings, whose essences are finite specifications of the divine.

37. Note for a letter to Des Bosses, Gerhardt, II, 314 n.

38. However, a theological theory that physical causality reflected the sin of man did affect prescientific thought in some fields. Thomas Burnet's theory of the stages of the earth's history (*Telluris theoria sacra orbis*, 2 vols. London, 1681), explained these stages as physical correlates to the successive Covenants of God with fallen man.

39. Jacques Bénigne Boussuet, *Discours sur l'histoire universelle* (Paris, 1681).

40. The first histories of philosophy, logic, and science in the seventeenth century therefore begin with Moses or earlier. So Keckermann (chap. 2, note 25; chap. 3, note 24), Vossius (chap. 2, note 30), and Jacob Thomasius.

41. For example, Norman Cohn, *The Pursuit of the Millennium*, 2nd ed. (London, Secker and Warburg, 1957), especially chap. xii and Appendix; and G. P. Gooch, *English Democratic Ideas in the Seventeenth Century*, 2nd ed. (Cambridge, 1927), chap. ix.

42. Nicholas Cusanus, *Conjectura de novissimis diebus*. According to Nicholas the church was to be persecuted until 1700 or 1734, its life paralleling the life of Christ.

43. On Paracelsus's chiliasm see Kurt Goldammer, "Friedensidee und Toleranzgedanke bei Paracelsus und den Spiritualisten," *Archiv fur Reformationsgeschichte*, 46 (1956), 19-46.

44. Hobbes, *Leviathan*, pts. III and IV.

45. *The Conway Letters*, ed. Marjorie Nicholson (New Haven, 1930). *The Divine Dialogues*. 3 vols. (London, 1668), *Preface*, pp. x, xi. The letters of More to Lady Conway interpreting the apocalypticism of the Book of Revelations, not included in the volume edited by Professor Nicholson, have not yet been published.

46. Isaac Newton, *Observations upon the Prophecies of Daniel and the Apocalypse of St. John*, ed. B. Smith (London, 1733). Newton had died in March 1727.

47. Thomas Sprat, *The History of the Royal Society of London* (London, 1667), p. 29.

48. Raphael Eglin, Marburg alchemist, theologian, and summarizer of Bruno, predicted the completion of the first resurrection (i.e., that of the saints) by 1711, on the basis of markings found on three herring in 1587 and 1596 in Denmark, Norway, and Pomerania. *Prophetia halieutica novae et admirandae* (Zurich, 1598 and later editions).

49. John Kvacsala, "Johann Heinrich Bisterfeld," *Ungarische Revue*, 13 (Leipzig, 1893), 171-172, 177.

50. John Kvacsala, "Thomas Campanella, ein Reformer der ausgehenden Renaissance," *Neue Studien zur Geschichte der Theologie und der Kirche*, ed. G. N. Bonwetsch and R. Seeberg, (Berlin, 1909), VI, 5.

51. Bacon was trained in the Puritan tradition by his mother and at Cambridge. Though his writings show no concern about a Second Coming, his views of history conform to the covenant theology, and the eschatological basis for his program of scientific cooperation is suggested both in *The Advancement of Learning* and *The New Atlantis*.

52. For Hartlib's relation to the Royal Society, see G. H. Turnbull, "S. Hartlib's Influences on the Early History of the Royal Society," *Notes and Records of the Royal Society of London*, 10 (April 1952), 101-130.

Also, the letter of Hartlib to Worthington, 1655, in *The Diary and Correspondence of Dr. John Worthington*, ed. James Crossley, *Publications of the Chatham Society*, II (1847), pp. 75-76:

> "The time is most seasonable, whilst war is preparing, and defiance proclaimed to the swordsmen of Rome, to encourage a Society which are to take the the Pen-men to task. I am sure that though we had conquered all the popish Dominions, yet Popery will not be wholly abolished, but by the brightness of His Coming, which I understand rather of the lightsome beams of his gospel than the burning flames of his wrath."

53. *Christlicher und wohlgegründeter Bericht von der Künftigen tausend jährigen Glückseligkeit der Kirchen Gottes Auff dieser Erden . . . treulich verdeutscht* durch Sebastianum Francum (Schleusingen, 1630).

In the Houghton Library there is an anonymous English translation of Alsted's prophecy, earlier than Burton's, with the title: *The Worlds proceeding Woes and succeeding Joyes: in cruell warres and vehement plagues, in happy peace and unity amongst all living creatures, or the triple presage of Henry Alsted . . .* (London, 1642).

54. Hubner expressed his conviction to Bisterfeld in 1638 that Comenius was "incapable of finishing 1/100th of what he proposes." Kvacsala, "Die pädagogische Reform des Comenius" (Berlin, 1903, 1904).

55. Summarized by G. H. Turnbull in *Hartlib, Dury, and Comenius: Gleanings from Hartlib's Papers* (London and Liverpool, 1947), p. 359.

56. See note 38 above. Burnet does argue, however, that "we are almost the last Posterity of the first men; and faln into the dying age of the world" (I, i, 7). He hopes "that knowledge may increase, man's minds be enlarged, and the Christian religion better understood, that the power of Antichrist shall be diminished, persecution cease, and a greater union and harmony establish'd amongst the Reformed. All this may be, and I hope will be, ere long" (*Ibid.*, p. 6).

57. "Explication Sommaire de Apocalypse," *Oeuvres de Leibniz*, ed. Foucher de Careil (Paris, 1864), I, 107-121.

58. John Kvacsala, "Irenische Bestrebungen zur Zeit des dreizigjährigen Krieges," *Acta et Commentationes Imperialis Universitatis Jurievensis* (formerly Dorpat) 19 (1894).

59. For the work of John Dury, see G. H. Turnbull, *Hartlib, Dury, and Comenius* (Liverpool, 1947), and the various papers by Kvacsala in the Bibliography. *The Diary and Correspondence of Dr. John Worthington*, ed. James Crossley, *Publications of the Chatham Society*, II (1847), bears on

his work. See note 52 above. Dury was the father-in-law of Henry Oldenburg, Secretary of the Royal Society.

60. Hermann Schüssler, *Georg Calixt: Theologie und Kirchenpolitik* (Wiesbaden, 1961).

61. Johan Daniel Gruber, ed., *Commercii epistolici Leibnitiani, Tomus prodromus, qui totus est Boineburgicus* (Hanover, 1745).

62. F. X. Kiefl, *Der Friedensplan des Leibniz zur Wiedervereinigung der getrennten christlichen Kirchen* (Paderborn, 1903). G. J. Jordan, *The Reunion of the Churches: a Study of G. W. Leibnitz and His Great Attempt* (London, 1927). For a brief account of Leibniz's plan in a letter to John Frederick of Hanover in 1679, see L. E. Loemker, "The Origin and Problem of Leibniz's Discourse of 1686," *Journal of the History of Ideas*, 8 (October 1947), 449-466.

NOTES TO CHAPTER 4

1. Persecution for scientific views was, after all, rare, and occurred chiefly in those cases in which a literal interpretation of scriptural revelation was challenged. Most executions were for heresy, atheism, and witchcraft. It is true that the development of science was retarded in Italy and Spain and perhaps in France as a result of the case against Galileo.

2. Will-Erich Peuckert, *Die grosse Wende* (Hamburg, 1948). See particularly Vol. 2, iv, pp. 380-389, of the Darmstadt edition, 1966.

3. Two aspects of this separation have already been suggested in Chapter 2: the attainment of a method and aim freed from the occult principles of explanation which involved spiritual or animistic powers, and the related shift from the humanistic context of erudition to simple factuality and its direct exploration through causes.

4. For instance *Advancement of Learning* (The World's Classics) I, vi, on "The Archetype or First Platform of the Dignity of Knowledge": "Two principal duties or services . . . which philosophy and human learning do perform to faith and religion . . . the exaltation of the glory of God . . . (and) a singular help and preservative against unbelief."

5. Galileo quotes Tertullian as saying: "We conclude that God is known first through Nature, and then again, more particularly by doctrine; by nature in His works and by doctrine in His revealed word." Stillman Drake, ed. *Discoveries and Opinions of Galileo*, p. 187.

6. Leibniz, "Elements of Natural Science." Loemker, rev. ed. pp. 280, 290; probably from Robert Boyle, *The Usefulness of Natural Philosophy*, *Works*, II, p. 42. For other references by Leibniz to the Hymn of Galen see Gerhardt, VII, pp. 71, 273.

7. Valuable discussions of the historical development of this theme are found in E. R. Curtius, *European Literature and the Latin Middle Ages* (New York, 1953) pp. 319-347; and Heinz Heimsoeth, *Sechs grosse Themen der abendländischen Metaphysik*. 4th ed. (Darmstadt, 1958), pp. 33-39.

8. See note 5 above.

9. Amos Comenius, *Prodromus Pansophiae* (Dusseldorf, 1963), Secs. 70-71, 92.

10. Edgar Wind, *Pagan Mysteries in the Renaissance* (New Haven, Yale University Press, 1958), especially the Introduction and chap. i, pp. 13-30, and 155-157.

11. Erwin Metzke, "Erfahrung und Natur in der Gedankenwelt des Paracelsus," *Blätter für deutsche Philosophie* 13 (1939), 74-90. Paracelsus's operational interpretation of experience is most explicit in his discussion of the mysterious virtues of medical remedies. "Only a great artist is able to discover them, not one who is only versed in books, but one who has acquired his ability and skill through the experience of his hands . . . These remedies must not be known as physics; they must be termed arcana, occult healing substances." Paracelsus, *Selected Writings*, ed. Jolande Jacobi; trans. Norbert Guterman (Princeton, 1959), p. 86.

12. Jean Fernel, *De abditis rerum causis Libri septem* (Paris, 1548). Note that it is the causes, not the effects (i.e., the symptoms) which are hidden; reasoning proceeds from appearances to the underlying real conditions.

13. It is noteworthy that this interpretation of method conforms with that later described by Zabarella, and found also in Hobbes and others.

14. On this and other occult manifestations, see Otto Casmann, *Nucleus mysteriorum naturae enucleatus* (Hamburg, 1605). A brief examination will show that Casmann, a pupil of Rudolph Goclenius at Marburg, carried out the promise of his title, "to crack the nut of the mysteries of nature," merely by resorting to the Ramistic procedure of classifying the events.

15. For this intra-Aristotelian controversy, see Jerome Cardan, *De subtilitate rerum*, 1550, and Julius Caesar Scaliger, *Exotericarum exercitationum libri XV de subtilitate ad Hieronymum Cardanum*, 1557 and many editions. Exerc. I. is entitled *Quid sit subtilitas*? In his *Physics*, Alsted, devoting a chapter to the role of seeds in inorganic forms (from Scaliger) distinguishes art from nature as follows: art cannot produce substances; only nature can (through seeds). *Encyclopaedia* I, p. 674.

16. On Leibniz compare the reply to Pierre Bayle, Gerhardt, IV, 517-524, with "Sur les beaux Sentiments" in Baruzi, *Leibniz* (Paris, 1909), pp. 365-368, from which the quotation in the text is taken.

17. *Physics*, II, 8, 192b.

18. In the Preface to the *Nouveaux Essais*, Leibniz defends a doctrine of substance, corporeal and mental, on the ground that otherwise we should have to fall back upon the "fanatical philosophy . . . which saves all phenomena by attributing them to God immediately and by miracle" (Fludd's Mosaic philosophy), or upon the "barbaric philosophers . . . who saved appearances by forging occult qualities or faculties which they imagined to be like little demons or goblins capable of producing without ceremony what is demanded." *New Essays*, trans. Langley, p. 63.

19. Francis Bacon, *Cogitationes de Natura rerum* (*Works*, ed. Spedding, Ellis, and Heath, V, p. 433). Bacon condemns men's "supineness and negligence" in the "observation and inquisition of violent motion," which

is "about the commonest of all motions," "of use in infinite ways," and is "the whole business of mechanics." "Most inquirers, when they have pronounced this motion to be violent, and distinguished it from natural motion, think they have done."

20. Ernst Cassirer, *Das Erkenntnisproblem in der Philosophie und Wissenschaft* (Berlin, 1922), Vol I, Book 2, chap. 1.

21. References in Boyle are frequent. For an unusual but anonymous ridicule of substantial forms see "A Brief Account of the New Sect of Latitude-Men, together with some reflections upon the New Philosophy" by SP of Cambridge, dated June 12, 1662, and reprinted in *The Phoenix*, Vol. II, (London, 1708), pp. 508-517. See also Loemker, "Boyle and Leibniz," *Journal of the History of Ideas*, 16 (1955), 22-43.

22. Bacon, *Advancement of Learning*, II, vi, secs. 3-6, especially 6 (The World's Classics), pp. 111-112.

23. Foster Watson, ed., *Vives and the Renaissance Education of Women* (New York, 1912).

24. Gerhardt, VII, 190.

25. It must be pointed out, however, that to size, shape, and motion, Boyle found it necessary to add "the contrivance of parts." *The Origine of Formes and Qualities*, Preface, 12. For the contribution of the earlier atomists, see Annaliese Maier, *Die Vorläufer Galileis im 14. Jahrhundert*, (Rome, 1949), p. 139.

26. Letter to Jacob Thomasius, April 20/30, 1669. Gerhardt, I, 116. In the same year, Leibniz, in criticizing atomism for its failures, said of the physical properties of resistance, cohesion, and reflection (elasticity): "To him who can derive these from the figure, size, and motion of matter, I shall not hesitate to give the name of a great philosopher." Gerhardt, IV, 108.

27. For its history, see A. G. Von Melsen, *From Atomos to Atom*, trans. Henry Koren (Pittsburgh, Duquesne University Press, 1952).

28. *The Origine of Formes and Qualities*, pp. 26, 38. Boyle also resorted to such terms as the "concurrence," "congruence" of parts to explain the qualities or forms of compounds.

29. Rudolph Goclenius, *PSYCHOLOGIA: hoc est de hominis perfectione, animo, et in primis ortu huius . . . commentationes ac disputationes quorundam theologi* (Marburg, 1590). The work contains arguments by Timothy Bright of Cambridge, J. L. Hawenreuther, Herman Vulteius, Francis Junius, J. J. Colerus, Aegidius Hunnius, and Caspar Peucer.

30. Richard Hönigswald, *Geschichte der Erkenntnistheorie*, (Berlin, 1933), p. 87.

31. On Nicholas of Oresme's anticipation of graphical presentations of the functional dependence of physical variables, see Pierre Duhem, *Études sur Léonard de Vinci* (Paris, 1906-1909), III, pp. 375-388, and Anneliese Maier's qualifications in *Die Vorläufer Galileis im 14. Jahrhundert* (Rome, 1949), p. 25.

32. Galileo Galilei, *Dialogue on the Great World Systems*, trans. Salusbury, revised by G. Santillano (Chicago, 1957), pp. 202-203.

33. Particularly the works of John Buridan, Albert of Saxony, and

Nicholas of Oresme, rediscovered by Pierre Duhem, with later corrections and details by Anneliese Maier. Note 31 above.

34. The influence of these men is shown in Leibniz's *Dissertatio de arte combinatoria* (Leipzig, 1666). The books referred to are the following. Alsted's *Clavis artis Lullianae* (Strassburg, 1609, and later editions) contained commentaries on Lullus by Alsted himself, Bruno, Agrippa von Nettesheim, Lavintheta, and others. Christopher Clavius, *In sphaeram Joannis de Sacro Bosco Commentarius* (4th ed. Paris, 1608) is a curious mixture of the speculative arguments and mathematical insights. Erhard Weigel, *Idea mathesis universae, cum speciminibus inventionum mathematicarum* (Jena, 1687) was too late to influence Leibniz, but Weigel's lectures, which he gave twenty years earlier, certainly contained related ideas. The young Leibniz also found his imagination captured by Weigel's proposal that a moral globe be added to the terrestrial and celestial globes, and by his *Euclid et Aristotelis Vindicatus*. His more mature estimate of Weigel is contained in a letter to Christian Philipp, March 11-21, 1681 (Academy ed., II, i, 230, p. 518).

35. Jurgen Mittelstrass, *Die Rettung der Phaenomena*, (Berlin, 1962), gives a careful interpretation and correction of historical judgments on this doctrine, especially those of Paul Natorp and other Neokantians.

36. For Leibniz's conception of hypotheses as *ad interim* devices, see his "Elements of Natural Science" in Loemker, *The Phil. Letters and Papers of Leibniz.* rev. ed. (Dortrecht, Reidel, 1969), p. 283.

NOTES TO CHAPTER 5

1. For example in the *De radicali originatione rerum*, 1697. Gerhardt, VII, p. 305.

2. Gerhard Ritter has provided many clues to these in his *Via antiqua und Via moderna auf den deutschen Universitäten des XV. Jahrhunderts* (Heidelberg, 1922); reprinted by Wissenschaftliche Buchgesellschaft, 1963). For the Ockhamistic influence on the beginnings of modern science consult Pierre Duhem, *Études sur Léonard de Vinci* (Paris, 1906-1909).

3. J. C. Scaliger, *Exotericarum exercitationum*, Exerc. vi, 4-7, expecially sec. 7. (Hanau, 1634), pp. 26-28.

4. This position is fully explicated by J. H. Alsted in his *Encyclopaedia* I, Book xii, *Pneumatica.*

5. Francisco Suarez, *Disputationes Metaphysicae*. Disputatio 25, sec. 1, i (Mainz ed., 1600; p. 616b).

6. Giordano Bruno, *De Umbris idearum*, in *Opera Latine Conscripta.* Vol. 1. (Naples, 1879-1891).

7. How widespread this juristic theology was can be seen in the Puritan casuistic tradition and the pattern of the Puritan sermon, divided into two parts: Doctrine and Use. See also Hans-Peter Schneider, *Justitia Universalis: Quellenstudien zur Geschichte des "christlichen Naturrechts" bei Gottfried Wilhelm Leibniz* (Frankfurt, 1967), which contains detailed studies of the Protestant "Christian jurists."

8. For the intensive use of "re-" see the note by J. Lachelier on "représentation, représenter et les autres mots de ce famille" and his defense of a monism of idea and essence in knowledge, in Lalande, *Vocabulaire de la philosophie*, 9th ed. (Paris, 1962), pp. 921-922.

I find this interpretation of Descartes's doctrine of ideas supported in a qualified way by Norman Kemp Smith, *New Studies in the Philosophy of Descartes* (London, 1952), pp. 147-160, and much more fully in Martial Gueroult, *Descartes selon l'ordre des raisons* (Paris, Aubier, 1953), I, 168-184; II, 291-301.

9. Spinoza, *Ethics*, II, Props. 11, 13, and 15. *The Chief Works*, ed. R. H. M. Elwes, II 90, 92, 97. See also Descartes's letter to Princess Elizabeth, May 31, 1643; quoted in Descartes, *Philosophical Writings*, trans. and ed. Norman Kemp Smith (London, 1952), pp. 271-272.

10. *Ethics*, II, Prop. 21, Scholium; 22; 29. *Chief Works*, ed. Elwes, II, 102-103, 106.

11. *Meditation* III, opening paragraphs, and *The Passions of the Soul*, passim. *Philosophical Works*, trans. Haldane and Ross. I, 157-159; 331-427.

12. *Ethics*, III, Prop. 9, Scholium; Prop. 39, Scholium; IV, Preface. Elwes edition, II, 137, 156, 189.

13. Spinoza was of course too much of a realist to go to this extreme, though he was later charged with being a Quietist. His ethical evaluations of the everyday problems of personal and social life constitute a great part of the appeal of the *Ethics*.

14. See for example, Gerhardt, VI, 488-489, 492.

15. On the influence of Leibniz's theory of feeling upon eighteenth century aesthetics see Ernst Cassirer, *Leibniz's System in seinen wissenschaftlichen Grundlagen* (Marburg, 1902), pp. 469-472.

16. Leibniz's earliest suggestion of this was in the "Fundamenta Praedemonstrabilia" in his *Theoria Motus Abstracti* (1671): Gerhardt, IV, p. 230; especially the seventeenth predemonstrable principle.

17. The influence of Ockham is widely considered to be the source of this view, though its role on the Continent, for example in Paris, Padua, and the German universities, did not go so far. A better Scholastic example of extreme "nominalism" is the Oxford Dominican John Crathorn, who reduced knowledge to arbitrary *termina ad placitum*, holding that certainty in the knowledge of independently real objects must rest on the verity and goodness of God alone. Johannes Kraus, "Die Stellung des Oxforder Dominikanerlehrers Crathorn zu Thomas von Aquin," *Zeitschrift für katholische Theologie*, 35 (1935), 66-68. How this position was transmitted to the seventeenth century, when Thomas Hobbes adopted the same view of the arbitrariness of thought, is still an unanswered question. The work of Marius Nizolius in Italy, for a later edition of which Leibniz wrote an introduction in 1670, would no doubt be a link in the historical chain of influence.

18. *Meditation* III; *Philosophical Writings*, trans. Norman Kemp Smith (New York, 1958), p. 194.

19. Spinoza, *Ethics*, II, Prop. 49, corollary. Elwes trans., vol. 2, 121) and Leibniz's notes on Thomasius, (Academy ed.), VI, i, 45, n. 15; letter to Magnus Wedderkopf, May 1671 (Academy ed.), II, i, pp. 117-118 (Loemker, rev. ed., pp. 146-147).

20. *New Essays*, chap. 28, sec. 10. Langley's translation, pp. 262-263.

21. For Leibniz's comments on Shaftesbury's *Characteristics of Men, Manners, Opinions, and Times* (1711), see Gerhardt, III, 423-431.

NOTES TO CHAPTER 6

1. Quoted in the translation of J. F. Anderson, *An Introduction to the Metaphysics of St. Thomas Aquinas* (Chicago, 1953). pp. 65, 47.

2. *Ethica Nicomachea* I, 6, 1096b, lines 8-15, as interpreted by Léon Robin, *La théorie platonicienne des idées et des nombres d'après Aristote* (Paris, 1908), pp. 131-172, 554-560.

3. Duns Scotus introduced the transcendentals as attributes of God, the infinite, as opposed to the ten categories which apply to finites. *Philosophical Writings*, ed. and trans. by Allan B. Wolter (London, 1962), pp. 2-9.

4. Ernest Moody, *Truth and Consequence in Medieval Logic* (Amsterdam, 1953), p. 28. Also *The Logic of William of Ockham* (New York, 1935), pp. 45-46.

A clear statement of the doctrine of transcendentals in Plato's Dialogues (especially the issue of the relation of being to unity) is given by Gottfried Martin, *Wilhelm von Ockham: Untersuchungen zur Ontologie der Ordnungen* (Berlin, 1949). The theme is continued in all of Martin's later writings.

5. Allan B. Wolter, "The Transcendentals and their Function in the Metaphysics of Duns Scotus," *Franciscan Institute Publications*, Philosophy Series no. 3 (St. Bonaventura, 1946).

6. Gottfried Martin, *Wilhelm von Ockham*, passim; also his *Allgemeine Metaphysik* (Berlin, 1965), especially pp. 82-92.

7. Martin, *Wilhelm von Ockham*, Preface, p. x.

8. Comenius, *Prodromus Philosophiae*, sec. 71, pp. 104-105.

9. For Campanella's doctrine of the primalities see B. M. Bonansea, *Tommaso Campanella*.

10. Johannes Sperling, sober atomist and foe of obscurantism, ended the dedication of his *Dissertatio de principiis corporis naturalis* (Wittenberg, 1647) with the salute: "Vale, Vir clarissime et ex physica physicum, non ex physico physicam agnoscendam, statue." This principle could be generalized.

Giordano Bruno had stated the case for regulative principles strongly, if somewhat scurrilously, in *Spaccio de la bestia trionfante*, Book II. *Opera Italiana*.

11. Especially *Disputatio* 43, sec I, parts 1-6.

12. *Meditations on Knowledge, Truth, and Ideas* (1684), Gerhardt, IV, 422-426.

13. Alsted, *Encyclopaedia* (Herborn, 1630), Book 25, sec. 1, chap. 1.

14. See Alsted, *Methodus metaphysicae*, pp. 108-117. In the *Metaphysica tribus libris tractata* (Herborn, 1613), Book I. Alsted had given a much more eclectic and abstruse enumeration of the transcendentals.

15. Compare, a century later, Jonathan Edwards's doctrine of Excellency, which had the same source in the Reformed tradition as Alsted's.

16. For Leibniz's reading notes, see the Academy ed., VI, i, pp. 151-160.
Bisterfeld's works underwent a posthumous revival after his death in 1655, largely through the publication through Adrian Heereboord and others, of the *Philosophiae primae seminarium* (1657) and the two volumes of *Opera: Bisterfeldus Redivivus* (The Hague, 1661).

17. *Bisterfeldus Redivivus:* "Artificii definiendi catholici liber tertius," secs. 38-57. Bacon's use of perception is in the *De Augmentis Scientiarum*, Book IV, chap. 3 (ed. Spedding, Ellis, and Heath.), I, pp. 610-611.

18. Gerhardt, VII, 87-88.

19. The old studies by Hans Emil Weber, *Die Philosophische Scholastik des deutschen Protestantismus im Zeitalter der Orthodoxie* (Leipzig, 1907); Paul Althaus, *Die Prinzipien der reformierten Dogmatik* (Leipzig, 1914); Max Wundt, *Die deutsche Schulmetaphysik des 17. Jahrhunderts* (Tübingen, 1939); Peter Peterson, *Geschichte der Aristotelischen Philosophie im protestantischen Deutschland* (Leipzig, 1921) trace this development.

20. *Advancement of Learning*, Book II, chap. 17, sec. 12, on Method. For Aristotle's original intent see W. D. Ross, ed. *Aristotle's Prior and Posterior Analytics* (Oxford, 1949), pp. 520-522.

21. *Prodromus Pansophiae*, sec. 86 (Precept IV); secs. 107-111.

22. For the manneristic elements in Descartes, examine his descriptions of art (for example in *Meditations*, Part I), his use of dreams, the deceitful demon, and other figures. In Pascal, the figures of terror, the great wager, etc. suggest a manneristic mood, as does his individualistic style.

23. Again we are reminded of the primalities of Campanella's thought; his influence may be seen in their prominence in Spinoza, Leibniz, and others.

24. See the essay on Wisdom, Gerhardt, VII, pp. 87-88. Campanella's primalities find repeated statement in Leibniz; for instance in a fragment printed in Bodemann, *Die Leibniz-Handschriften* (IV (Phil.) Vol. III, sec. 5, Bl. 27), (Hanover, 1895), p. 70.

25. "On the Correction of Metaphysics and the Concept of Substance" (1694) Gerhardt, IV, 468-470 (Loemker, rev. ed., pp. 432-434.)

26. *Nouveaux Essais*, IV, v, secs. 2, 11 (Langley's translation, pp. 451-452).

27. Karl Heniz Haag, *Kritik der neueren Ontologie* (Stuttgart, 1960), pp. 7-8.

28. Martin Heidegger, *Die Kategorien- und Bedeutungslehre des Duns Scotus* (Tübingen, 1916), p. 78.

29. Leo Spitzer, *Classical and Christian Ideas of World Harmony: Pro-*

legomena to an Interpretation of the Word "Stimmung" (Baltimore, 1963), pp. 132-138.

30. Gerhardt, VII, 352 (Loemker, rev. ed., p. 675).

NOTES TO CHAPTER 7

1. Aristotle, *Parts of Animals*, I, i, 639a, b, and elsewhere. For the sources in Zabarella see chap. 2, note 18.

2. *De methodis*, I-III, *Opera Logica*, 3rd ed. (1597), cols. 133-140. These conclusions have shifted somewhat in Zabarella's later defense of his position against Piccolomini, the *De Doctrinae ordine apologia*. Here he holds that the resolutive order applies to operative sciences, the compositive order to contemplative sciences only. However, see also the *Liber de ordine intelligendi*.

3. Not until a more subjectivistic period, after Descartes, did the meaning of *invenio* shift to its present sense.

4. Descartes, *Discourse on the Method of Rightly Conducting the Reason*, In *Philosophical Works*, trans. Haldane and Ross. I, p. 92.

5. Joachim Jungius, *Logica Hamburgensis* (Hamburg, 1638), IV, chap. 17.

6. Leibniz, Academy ed., VI, i, 279-280.

7. Arnauld and Nicole, *La logique ou l'art de penser*, 5th ed. (Paris, 1683), IV, chap. ii.

8. Jean Fernel, *De abditis rerum causis* (Lyon, 1605), pp. 16-17.

9. For Hobbes on method see *De Corpore*, I, chap. 6.

10. Max Caspar's detailed introduction to his recently reprinted German translation of Johannes Kepler, *Harmonice Mundi* (Darmstadt, 1967), explains Kepler's investigations carefully.

11. Galileo, *Dialogues concerning Two New Sciences* (New York, 1914), "The Third Day's Dialogue," pp. 153-243.

12. The well-known *Primae veritates*, from which Couturat derived the logical basis of Leibniz's system. Louis Couturat, *Opuscules et fragments inédit de Leibniz* (Paris, 1903), pp. 518-523 (Loemker, rev. ed., pp. 267-271.)

13. Leibniz, *Nouveaux essais*, IV, xi, 14. For Leibniz's theory of verification of truths of fact, see Loemker, "Leibniz und die Grenzen des Empiricismus," *Kantstudien*, 56 (1966), 315-328.

14. Letter of March 24/April 2, 1699. Gerhardt, II, 168, 169 (Loemker, rev. ed., 515, 517.) Newton also used the geometric mode in writing his *Mathematical Principles of Natural Philosophy*; his remark about the cause of gravity, "Hypotheses non fingo," is well known.

15. *Advancement of Learning*, II, xii, 1 (The World's Classics, p. 40.)

16. Léon Brunschvicg, *Le progrès de la conscience dans la philosophie occidentale*, 2nd ed. (Paris, 1953), II, p. 157.

17. See the letter of Leibniz to John Frederick of Hanover in the fall of 1679, in which he discussed his revived project for the *Demonstrationes*

Catholicae, and described his motives for studying mathematics in Paris. Academy ed., II, i, 487-488. For the outline of the *Demonstrationes Catholicae* see Academy ed., VI, i, 494-500.

18. Leibniz, *Nouveaux essais*, IV, x, and the corresponding sections of Locke's *Essay*.

19. Leibniz, *Nouveaux essais*, IV, xi, 13; xii, 4-13.

20. Gerhardt, IV, 354-392. See especially the animadversions on I, 1, 2. (Loemker, rev. ed., 383-384.)

21. Arnauld and Nicole, *La logique ou l'art de penser*, IV, vi, 427.

22. Loemker, "On Substance and Process in Leibniz," in Reese and Freeman, eds. *Process and Divinity: The Hartshorne Festschrift* (LaSalle, Ill., 1964), pp. 403-425.

23. R. M. Yost, *Leibniz and Philosophical Analysis* (Berkeley, 1954). Heinrich Scholz, however, argued that the separate fields in which Leibniz developed logical orders (or "Leibniz languages") can be subsumed logically in one inclusive order.

24. See note 13 above.

NOTES TO CHAPTER 8

1. For a recent discussion of this conception, in connection with the Leibnizian ideal of harmony, see Franz Vonessen, "Reim und Zahl bei Leibniz," *Antaios*, 7 (1966), 99-120.

2. See the paper by Hans Aarsleff, "The Study and Use of Etymology in Leibniz," in *Studia Leibniziana*, III (Wiesbaden, 1969), 179-180, and the sources cited by him.

3. The medieval theory of music was based upon St. Augustine, *De musica* (Migne *Patrologia Latina*, vol. 22), and Boethius, *De musica* (*Patrologia Latina*, vol. 63). Both distinguished the science of music ("the science of good modulation") from musical taste, instinct, or skill; as one of the quadrivium it belonged to the a priori forms of numerical order. For a brilliant account of the role of cosmic considerations, both in medieval music-theory and in the earliest Gothic architecture, and the relation of both to Christian Platonism as taught in the School of Chartres, see Otto von Simson, *The Gothic Cathedral* (New York, 1956; Harper Torchbook edition 1962), especially chap. 4.

4. *Harmonie universelle* (Paris, 1636-37). For the discussion of patterns of musical harmony in the sixteenth and seventeenth centuries see Claude V. Palisca, "Scientific Empiricism in Musical Thought," in H. H. Rhys, ed., *Seventeenth Century Science and the Arts* (Princeton, 1961), pp. 91-137.

Alsted's *Encyclopaedia* (1630) offered a comprehensive summary of the state of musical theory in the early seventeenth century (Vol. I, Book 20, pp. 1195-1211).

5. For examples in Gothic architecture of the combinations of the tetradic number order and the Golden Section, the reader is referred to von Simson, *The Gothic Cathedral*.

6. Robert Fludd, *Monochordium mundi symphoniacum*, (Frankfurt, 1623).

7. For the tradition which treated the Mosaic tabernacle, the temple of the harmony of the divine plan of creation and redemption, see von Simson's *The Gothic Cathedral.*

8. For the details of this and other matters, see Max Caspar's detailed introduction to his (recently republished) German translation of Kepler's *Harmonice Mundi: Weltharmonik*, (Darmstadt, 1967). It is interesting that in his *Musurgia universalis* (II, p. 376) the imaginative Jesuit Athanasius Kircher, who was himself far from being a model of scientific sobriety, found Kepler's work so dark and mystical as to be incomprehensible.

9. For a historical development of these points see Palisca's article, cited in note 4.

10. On this point see Ernst Cassirer, *Leibniz' System in seinen wissenschaftlichen Grundlagen* (Marburg, 1902), pp. 458-472.

11. Lewis W. Beck has given, in a "fanciful" but pertinent figure, a brief description of the development of Leibniz's system as a fugue in which the same themes arise in different contexts at different times, yet "at every moment, a cross section of all his thoughts shows a marvelous harmony." *Early German Philosophy* (Cambridge, Mass., 1969), p. 203. I should supplement this by crediting Leibniz at many points with the greater harmony which results from the resolution of transient disharmonies, such as are inevitable in all polyphonic music in the form of canon or fugue.

12. In his *Paragranum*, Paracelsus treated the health of the body as a harmony of its parts and functions.

13. This theme was developed in the short "Discours sur les beaux sentiments," published in Jean Baruzi, *Leibniz* (Paris, 1909), pp. 365-368.

14. *Harmonice mundi* (Caspar's German translation, Munich, 1939), pp. 175-195. Jean Bodin's discussion is in the *De Republica Libri VI* (Paris, 1586), Book VI, chap. 6. The source of this numerical conception of justice is Aristotle's *Magna Moralia*, 1182. In his *La vérité des sciences contre les sceptiques ou Pyrrhoniens* (Paris, 1625), II, chap. 10, p. 419, Mersenne attributes this serial interpretation of the three forms of political order to Boethius and also criticizes Bodin's theory.

15. A decisive passage to this effect is the selection from his early notes for the *Elementa juris naturalis* at the head of this chapter.

16. The ideal of "la réduction de tout aux harmonies ou nombres, idées et perceptions" (Gerhardt, IV, 523, in refuting Pierre Bayle) is frequently affirmed by Leibniz.

17. *De Umbris idearum* (1582), *Opera Latine Conscripta*, ed. Fiorentino (Naples, 1879), Vol. II, Part i.

18. *Ibid.*, "Second Intention of Shadows," p. 22.

19. Compare Leibniz's later appetite and perception.

20. *De umbris idearum:* "Seventh Intention of Shadows," p. 24. See also the following Intentions, especially 11 and 12.

21. Intention 13, p. 28.

22. *De umbris idearum* p. 81 (Part III, sec. 8).

23. *De umbris idearum*, Intention 7.

24. Alsted, *Encyclopaedia*, Vol. 4, Book 21.

25. Leibniz's notes and comments on the *Philosophiae primae seminarium* are in the Academy ed. VI, i, 151-161. The table appears in the *Alphabeti philosophici sive philosophiae praecipiorum libri tres*, p. 59.

26. The *Alphabeticum philosophicum* (compare note 25 above) is found in *Bisterfeldus Redivivus*, 2 vols., a posthumous edition of Bisterfeld's works edited by Adrian Heereboord. Vol. 2, 1-132.

27. For the later Puritan elaboration of this doctrine see Jonathan Edwards's discussion of excellence and mutual consent in his early *Notes on the Mind* and the discourse on *The Divine and Supernatural Light*.

28. Bisterfeld followed Bacon's usage in designating all true propositions as axioms. Primitive propositions are principles.

29. *Alphabeticum Philosophicum*, III.

30. *Alphabeticum Philosophicum*, V, p. 28.

31. *Ibid.*, II, xxxv, xxvi. The metaphysical theory that consent is the basis of society (in the preceding quotation) anticipates a theory of the general will.

32. *Artificii Definiendi Catholici Liber*, vii, in *Bisterfeldus Redivivus*, I.

33. For example, Kenelm Digby's sympathetic powder, Robert Fludd's attribution of virtues or powers to bread and honey. Note Scaliger's attacks on sympathism; also Jungius, *Physica* II, i, chap. 1.

34. *Sciagraphiae symbioticae seu Compendii symbiotici*, Libri II, in *Bisterfeldus Redivivus*.

35. The phrases come from Book IV of *The Harmony of the World*.

36. The term "harmonie préetablie" first appeared late in 1695, in the context of the discussion aroused by the *Systeme nouveau*. See Kurt Müller and Gisela Krönert, *Leben und Werk von G. W. Leibniz: eine Chronik* (Frankfurt, 1969), pp. 134-135. The term *harmony* without the adjective, by contrast, occurs frequently in Leibniz's writings from the very beginning.

37. Academy ed., VI, i, p. 438 (1669 or 1670).

NOTES TO CHAPTER 9

1. Contrast *Metaphysics* V, iv, and *Physics* II, viii, 198-199, with *On Generation and Corruption* II, vi, 333b.

A disputation, earlier than Boyle's, about the ambiguity, and therefore the invalidity, of Aristotle's definition of nature is found in Johannes Sperling's *Dissertatio de principiis corporis naturalis* (Wittenberg, 1647). Sperling, a pupil of Daniel Sennert, was an anatomist and atomist who defended a traducian theory of human reproduction and heredity, and therefore extended natural causality into many previously occult explanations.

2. Hermann Siebeck, "Ueber die Entstehung der Termini Natura

naturans und Natura naturata," *Archiv für Geschichte der Philosophie*, 3 (1890), 370-378.

3. Renaissance medics were led by their experiences with sickness and health to distinguish three types of events—those *secundum naturam* (health, for example), those *praeter naturam* (illness and its causes), and those *super naturam* (incurred by divine infusion).

4. Gaston Grua, *Textes inédits de Leibniz* (Paris, 1948), p. 854.

5. *A Free Inquiry into the Vulgarly Receiv'd Notion of Nature*, in *The Works of the Honorable Robert Boyle*, ed. Thomas Birch (London, 1772), p. 166.

6. *Some Motives and Incentives to the Love of God* (London, 1670), popularly referred to as *The Essay on Seraphic Love* or as *The Christian Virtuoso* (a title which could be modernized as *The Christian Scientist*) and *The Excellency of Theology* (London, 1674) both attest Boyle's concern in protecting the superior certainty of the Christian revelation, by spiritual insight, from encroachment by the new science. Locke apparently was influenced by Boyle's conviction of the higher certainty of the knowledge of God (See the *Essay*, IV, x) but based this certainty upon reason rather than immediate revelation.

7. Robert Boyle, *A Free Inquiry*, p. 163.

8. These notions are obviously not without interdependence. Boyle explores their ambiguities and suggests replacements for all but the last two, which he rejects entirely: "Employ them not at all."

9. The full title is *De ipsa natura, sive de vi insita actionibusque creaturarum, pro dynamicis suis confirmandis illustrandisque.* Gerhardt, IV, pp. 504-516.

10. For this exchange see Louis Dutens, ed., *Leibniz, Opera Omnia*, II, 2, pp. 97-101. Also the Rektoratsrede of Johannes Steudel, *Leibniz und die Medizin* (Bonn, 1960).

11. This Leibniz had learned from Boyle. See Chapter 4 above, especially n. 21.

12. As published by Samuel Clarke in *A Collection of Papers, which passed between the late Learned Mr. Leibniz and Dr. Clarke in the years 1715-1716, relating to the Principles of Natural Philosophy and Religion* (London, 1717).

13. Thus the effect of Newton's work was to strengthen a metaphysical dualism, and this is reflected in Locke as well. But it is difficult to define the place of the free man in the rigid Newtonian determinism. It may be suggested that although the alienation of modern man from his physical and social environment was given its intellectual foundations only after the critical work of Immanuel Kant, Newton made a first break in the harmony inevitable. This is shown in the French libertine movement, particularly in Voltaire. To this extent Leibniz's bitter remark (in the opening letter of his controversy with Clarke) that atheism had been increased in England by the new mechanical philosophy may have been perceptive.

14. Gerhardt, IV, p. 108; quoted by Joseph Moreau, *L'univers Leibnizien* (Lyon, 1956), p. 49.

15. For another seventeenth century criticism of the deification of nature and an attempt to restore its role as divine revelation, see Gerhard Vossius, *De Theologia gentilis et physiologia christiana, sive de origine ac progressu idolatriae, deque naturae mirandis quibus homo adducitur ad deum.* (Amsterdam, 1700). On the early history of the deification of nature see E. R. Curtius, *European Literature and the Latin Middle Ages* (New York, Bollingen, 1953), pp. 319-370.

16. Edgar Wind, *Pagan Mysteries in the Renaissance* (New Haven, 1958), discusses this tradition of esoteric mystery symbolism and the objections to it.

17. The short titles of Vanini's works are: (1) *Amphitheatrum aeternae providentiae,* and (2) *De admirandis naturae, reginae deaeque mortalium arcanis libri quattuor.*

18. Robert Boyle, *A Free Inquiry,* pp. 165-166.

19. *Ibid.,* p. 170.

20. Richard Popkin has shown that the tradition of skepticism (and therefore implicitly of much libertinism) in the seventeenth century contained two distinct strains, the one attacking reason in defense of revelation, the other skeptical of revelation and reason alike.

21. Leibniz, "Dialogus inter theologum et misosophum" (Leibniz had first written "scepticum" and then substituted "misosophum"), Grua, *Textes inédits,* pp. 18-20. Grua dates the dialogue 1677-79.

22. *Traité de la Nature et de la Grace* (Paris, 1680).

23. Leibniz, *Discourse on Metaphysics,* secs 7, 16. Loemker, rev. ed., pp. 307, 313. It is true that Leibniz's discussions of miracle are in some ways ambiguous. He uses the notion negatively in his criticism of occasionalism, for example, as the three explications of his system written in 1696 show (Loemker, rev. ed., pp. 459-460). Here miracle is interpreted as an intervention by God in "natural and ordinary matters," and is rejected. In his fifth letter to Clarke (secs 107-116) they are events "surpassing the powers of creatures."

24. *De abditis rerum causis libri septem* (1548), p. 13 of the edition of 1605.

25. *De rebus naturalibus* (1597) chap. 1, cols. 234-235.

26. Otto Casmann, *Nucleus mysteriorum naturae enucleatus* (Hamburg, 1605), I, 2.

27. For the early history of the problem see A. G. van Melsen, *From Atomos to Atom* (Pittsburgh, 1952).

28. Boyle's theory echoes in a tentative way the discussions by the Spanish Jesuits of a *vinculum substantiale* called upon to explain the unified mass, force, etc. of composite bodies. This theory was revived in the correspondence between Leibniz and Bartholomew des Bosses. Boehm, *Le Vinculum substantiale chez Leibniz* (Paris, 1938).

29. For a recent edition of a paper of Leibniz on the subject see Pierre Costabel, *Leibniz et la dynamique* (Paris, 1960), pp. 57-95. Also the *Specimen Dynamicum* of 1695, Part II. Loemker, rev. ed., pp. 444-450.

NOTES TO CHAPTER 10

1. Walther von Tschirnhaus, *Medicina mentis* (Amsterdam 1687).

2. It would exceed the limits of this study to describe the brilliant mathematical analogy which Leibniz seems to have conceived as a justification of this structured order of unique individuals in classes. This analogue can be described as a matrix or determinant of order infinity (its columns the ideas or perfections of God; its rows the various finite degrees of the perfections in creation). Such a determinant could be broken down, step by step, into determinants of lower finite order, each of which would be marked by a parameter defining the class of individual combinations included in it. The final reduction would be in the many unique combinations of perfections (complete notions of individuals) no two of which would be alike, but each of which would enter into many different classes, depending upon the parameters determining them.

The individual terms into which such a determinant is resolved would be the analogue to the individuals (and classes) constituting all possible worlds. It would require further calculation of maxima and minima to determine those compossibles which would be the best of all possible ones.

3. The concept of a substantial plurality of attributes is a development of Platonism which reached Northern Europe through Bruno and others. A source for Leibniz and possibly for Spinoza was the *Philosophiae primae seminarium* of John Bisterfeld, which Leibniz annotated in his university years. In commenting on Bisterfeld's classification of attributes he noted: "Bisterfeld asserts in the P. P. S. that the attributes of being are infinite" (Attributa entis esse infinita autumat Bisterfeld in *Philosophiae primae seminarium.*) (Academy ed., VI, i, p. 24.) The editors of VI, ii, (p. 543) print the source which evoked this comment in Bisterfeld's works: "To the extent that a being is more simple and more excellent it will be more composite. The thing itself teaches that a being, insofar as it is more outstanding (*praestantius*) has to that extent more attributes and can have more externals (relations?). Thus God can, as it were, have innumerable attributes."

4. A letter to De Volder, Jan. 21, 1704, contains what may be Leibniz's most succinct definition of substance (Gerhardt, II, p. 264): "That there is a certain persisting law which involves the future states of that which we conceive as the same (or self-identical)—this itself is what I say constitutes the same substance."

5. In Disputation 5 of the *Disputationes Metaphysicae.*

6. De corpore, II, chap. 11, sec. 7. *Opera Latina.* ed. Molesworth, vol. 1, 120-123.

7. That is, in the absence of further statements by Spinoza about personal individuality or identity. See *Ethics*, II, Definitions 3, 4, 7; Axiom 5; Propositions 9, 11, 12.

8. *Nouveaux Essais*, I, xxvii. (Langley translation, pp. 238-257).

9. The reader may recall the discussion of Descartes's conception of ideas in Chapter 5.

10. The label "super-nominalist" freely renders Leibniz's *plusquam nominalis* as he described Hobbes in his Introduction to Nizolius (Academy ed., VI, ii, p. 428). Leibniz was aware of the difference between Ockhamism and an extreme terminism such as the Dominican John Crathorn had advocated. See the *Zeitschrift für katholische Theologie*, 35 (1935), pp. 66-87, for similarities between Hobbes and this radical thinker of the fourteenth century. (See also Chapter 5, n. 17.)

11. Alsted's history of the study of the affections in his *Encyclopaedia* (*Pathologia*: chap. III, p. 3364 ff.) begins with Plato's *Theaetetus*; includes Aristotle, *Ethics*, II; Galen; Boetius, *De Consolatione*; Azorius, *Moral Institutes* Bk. III; Fracastoro, *De sympathia* chap. X; Cardan, *De subtilitate*, Exer. 14; Luis Vives, *Peregrinus*; Gutberleth, *Pathologia*. Alsted follows Vives in rejecting the Stoic *apathia* on the ground that human motivation and action are impossible without the affections.

12. Both Spinoza and Leibniz regarded the will as "nothing but intellect." (Cf. *Ethics*, II, Prop. 49, corollary and the Academy ed., VI, i, p. 45, note 151.) Yet both also treated volitional acts as reflectively ordered appetites and therefore essentially emotive.

13. As his theory of the "beast-machine," his fantastic proposal for mind-body interaction through the pineal gland, and his voluntarism show.

14. Couturat, *Opuscules et Fragments* (1903), p. 10. The fragment is from 1676.

15. For his early comments see the fragment on dreams in the Academy ed., VI, ii, pp. 276-279.

16. Cassirer et. al., *The Renaissance Philosophy of Man* (Chicago, 1948), pp. 387-393.

17. *De Concordia et Discordia, Opera Omnia*, V, pp. 194-197, 227, 281-282, and Books I and IV passim.

18. *De Pacificatione, Opera Omnia*, V, 421.

19. An example is Leibniz's correction of the definition of substance in his notes on Spinoza's *Ethics*; substance is, as Spinoza said, that which is *in* itself, but it is not conceived through itself (Gerhardt, I, pp. 131, 139).

20. *Bisterfeldus Redivivus: Artificii definiendi catholici liber tertius*, secs. 38-57. For the reference to Bacon see Chapter 6, n.17.

21. Academy ed. VI, i, p. 482.

22. Leibniz's reaction to this controversy as it was carried on between Bossuet and Fénélon is given in the Preface to his *Codex Juris Gentium Diplomaticus* of 1693; reprinted in Gerhardt, IV, pp. 460-463 (Loemker rev. ed., pp. 421-424).

23. See the *Discourse on Metaphysics*, secs. 35-37; Gerhardt, IV, pp. 460-463.

24. "Interest" was used by Leibniz and others in the seventeenth century as meaning self-interest.

25. See especially the *De Rerum originatione radicali* (1697), Gerhardt, VII, pp. 302-308.

26. For example, Walter Lippmann, *Essays in the Public Philosophy* (Boston, Little Brown, 1955).

27. Leibniz's notes on Shaftesbury's book (Gerhardt, III, pp. 423-431) show his sense of the validity of felt moral convictions, and the underlying Platonism of both men's views. What Leibniz rejected in Locke's ethical views was his inclination to base moral judgments upon public opinion.

28. See Loemker, "Das ethische Anliegen des Leibnizschen Systems," in *Studia Leibniziana Supplementa, IV* (Wiesbaden, 1969), 63-76.

Bibliography

Aarsleff, Hans. "The Study and Use of Etymology in Leibniz," *Studia Leibniziana Supplementa*, III, 173-189. Wiesbaden, Steiner Verlag, 1969.

Alsted, John Henry. *Clavis Artis Lullianae, et verae logices duos in libellos tributa*. Strassburg, 1609.

————*Diatribe de mille annis apocalypticis*. Frankfurt, 1627. English Translations:
The Beloved City or the Saints Reign on Earth a Thousand Years— faithfully Englished with some Occasionall Notes (by William Burton). London, 1643.

(Anonymous), *The Worlds Proceeding Woes and Succeeding Joyes: in Cruell Warres and Vehement Plagues, in Happy Peace and Unity amongst all Living Creatures, or the Triple Presage of Henry Alsted*. London, 1642.

Christlicher und wohlgegründeter Bericht von der künftigen tausend jährigen Glückseligkeit Kirchen Gottes auff dieser Erden—treulich verdeutscht durch Sebastianum Frankum. Schleusingen, 1630.

————*Encyclopaedia VII tomis distincta*. 2 vols. Herborn, 1630.

————*Logicae systema harmonicum: in quo universus bene disserendi modus ex authoribus Peripateticos juxta et Rameis traditur*. Herborn, 1614.

————*Metaphysica tribus libris tractata*. Herborn, 1613.

————*Philosophia digne restituta: Libros IV praecognitorum philosophicorem complectens*. Herborn, 1612.

————*Summa casuum conscientiae*. Frankfurt, 1628.

Althaus, Paul. *Die Prinzipien der reformierten Dogmatik in Zeitalter der aristotelischen Scholastik*. Leipzig, Deichert, 1914.

Ames, William. *Conscience, with the Power and Cases thereof*. London, 1639.

Arnauld, Antoine. *Oeuvres philosophiques*. Edited by Jules Simon. Paris, Charpentier, 1843.

————and Pierre Nicole. *La logique ou l'art de penser*. 5th ed. Paris, Desprez, 1683. (Original ed. 1662).

Arnisaeus, Henning.*Disputatio metaphysica de Deo continens naturalem Dei cognitionem*. 1604.

Aubrey, John. *Brief Lives*, edited from the original manuscripts with an introduction by Oliver Lawson Dick, 2nd ed. London, Secker and Warburg, 1950.

Augustinus, Aurelius. *De Musica*. In Jacques Paul Migne, *Patrologiae cursus completus series Latina*. Vol. 22. Paris, n.d.

————*On Free Will*, in *Library of Christian Classics*. Vol. 6. *Augustine: Earlier Writings*. Philadelphia, Westminster Press, 1953.

281

Azor, John. *Institutionum moralium, in quibus universae quaestiones ad conscientiam rectè aut pravè factorum pertinentes breviter tractantur.* 3 vols. Leiden, 1600-1611.

Bacon, Francis. *The Advancement of Learning and New Atlantis,* with a preface by Thomas Case (The World's Classics), London, Oxford University Press, 1951.

_____*De Dignitate et Augmentiis Scientiarum,* in the *Works of Bacon.* Edited by James Spedding, R. L. Ellis, and Douglas Heath. Vol. 1. London, Longman & Co., 1861-1879.

_____ *Works.* Edited by William Rawley. London, Robinson, 1879.

Baker, Herschel. *The Dignity of Man.* Cambridge, Harvard University Press, 1947. Reprinted as *The Image of Man,* New York, Harper Torchbook, 1961.

Baron, Hans. *The Crisis of the Early Italian Renaissance: Civic Humanism and Republican Liberty in an Age of Classicism and Tyranny.* 2 vols. Princeton, Princeton University Press, 1955. Revised edition in one volume with an Epilogue, Princeton, 1966.

Baruzi, Jean. *Leibniz, avec de nombreux textes inédits.* Paris, Bloud, 1909.

Beck, Lewis W. *Early German Philosophy: Kant and His Predecessors.* Cambridge, Mass., Harvard University Press, 1969.

Bentley, Richard. *The Folly and Unreasonableness of Atheism—in Eight Sermons Preached at the Lecture Founded by the Honorable Robert Boyle.* London, Mortlock, 1693.

Bethell, S. L. *The Cultural Revolution of the Seventeenth Century.* New York, Roy Publishers, 1951.

Bisterfeld, John Henry. *Bisterfeldus Redivivus, seu Operum Joh. Henrici Bisterfeldi . . . posthumorum. Edited by Adrian Heereboord. The Hague, 1661.*

_____*Philosophiae primae seminarium.* Edited by Adrian Heereboord. Leiden, 1657.

_____*Phosphorus Catholicus, seu artis meditandi Epitome, cui subjunctum consilium de studiis feliciter instituendis.* Breda, 1649.

Bodemann, Eduard. *Die Leibniz-Handschriften in der königlichen öffentlichen Bibliothek zu Hannover. Hanover, 1895.*

Bodin, Jean. *Colloquium Heptaplomeres, de rerum sublimium arcanis abditis.* Paris, 1857.

_____*De Republica Libri VI, Six Livres de la republique.* Paris, 1586.

Boehm, A. *Le Vinculum substantiale chez Leibniz: ses origines historiques.* Paris, J. Vrin, 1938.

Boethius, Anicius Manlius Severinus. *De Musica.* In Jacques Paul Migne, *Patrologia Latina.* Vol. 63. Paris, n.d.

Bohatec, Josef. *Die cartisianische Scholastik in der Philosophie und reformierten Dogmatik des 17. Jahrhunderts,* Part I. Leipzig, Deichert, 1912. Reprinted, Hildesheim, Olms, 1966.

Bonansea, B. M. *Tommaso Campanella: Renaissance Pioneer of Modern Thought.* Washington, Catholic University of America, 1969.

Bossuet, Jacques Bénigne. *Discours sur l'histoire universelle.* Paris, 1681.

Bouillier, Francisque. *Histoire de la philosophie cartésienne*. 3rd ed. Vol. 2. Paris, Delagrave, 1868.

Boyle, Robert. *The Christian Virtuoso*. In *Works*. Edited by Thomas Birch. Vol. 6.

———*The Excellency of Theology, compar'd with Natural Philosophy, as Both are Objects of Men's Study*. London, 1674.

———*A Free Inquiry into the Vulgarly Receiv'd Notion of Nature, Made in an Essay Addressed to a Friend*. London, 1685.

———*The Origine of Formes and Qualities, according to the Corpuscular Philosophy*. Oxford, 1666.

———*Some Motives and Incentives to the Love of God, pathetically Discours'd of in a Letter to a Friend*. London, 1661; 5th ed., 1670.

———*Tractatus de ipsa natura, sive libera in receptem naturae notionem disquisitio ad amicum*. Geneva, 1688.

———*The Usefulness of Natural Philosophy*. In *Works*. Edited by Thomas Birch. Vol. 2.

———*The Works of the Honorable Robert Boyle*. Edited by Thomas Birch. 6 vols. London, 1772.

Browne, Sir Thomas. *Religio Medici, Urn Burial, Christian Morals, and other Essays*. Edited by John Addington Symonds. London, Walter Scott, 1886.

Brucker, Johann Jakob. *Historia critica philosophiae mundi incunabulis ad nostram usque aetatem deducta*. 4 vols. Leipzig, 1742-1744.

Bruno, Giordano. *Concerning the Cause, Principle, and One*. Translated by Sidney Greenberg, in *The Infinite in Giordano Bruno*. New York, King's Crown Press, 1950.

———*The Expulsion of the Triumphant Beast*. Translated by Arthur D. Imerti. New Brunswick, Rutgers University Press, 1964.

———*Opera latine conscripta*. Edited by Francesco Fiorentino, F. Jocco, H. Vitelli, V. Imbriani, and C. M. Tallarigo. 3 vols. in 8 parts. Naples, 1879-1891.

———*Opera italiane*. 3 vols. Bari, Laterza and Figli, 1907-1909.

———*De Umbris idearum*. In *Opera Latina*, vol. 2, part 1.

Brunschvicg, Léon. *L'éxperience humaine et la causalité physique*. 3rd ed. Paris, Presses Universitaires, 1949.

———*Le progrès de la conscience dans la philosophie occidental*. 2nd ed. Paris, Presses Universitaires, 1953.

Burckhardt, Carl J. *Gestalten und Mächte: Reden und Aufsätze*. Zurich, Fretz and Wasmuth, 1941.

Burckhardt, Jacob. *The Civilization of the Renaissance in Italy*. London, Allen and Unwin, 1944.

Burnet, Thomas. *Telluris theoria sacra orbis*. 2 vols. London, 1681; Frankfurt, 1691. English translation: *The Sacred Theory of the Earth*. London, 1695.

Burtt, E. A. *The Metaphysical Foundations of Modern Physical Science: a Historical and Critical Survey*. New York, Harcourt, Brace, and Co., 1925.

Butterfield, Herbert. *The Origins of Modern Science, 1300-1800.* New York, Macmillan, 1962.

Campanella, Tommaso. *Atheismus Triumphatus.* Paris, 1636.

Cardan, Jerome. *De subtilitate rerum libri XXI.* Nuremberg, 1550.

Carré, Meyrick H. *Phases of Thought in England.* Oxford, Clarendon Press, 1948.

Casmann, Othonus (Otto). *Christianismi integras adversus pseudo-evangelicos, eius mutilatores.* Frankfurt, 1607.

———*Nucleus mysteriorum naturae enucleatus laboribus aliquando Scholasticis ex solertissimorum ac sagacissimorum seculi nostri interpretum naturae scriptis.* Hamburg, 1605.

Cassirer, Ernst. *Das Erkenntnisproblem in der Philosophie und Wissenschaft der neueren Zeit.* 3 vols. Berlin, B. Cassirer Verlag, 1922-23.

———*Freiheit und Form: Studien zur deutschen Geistesgeschichte.* Berlin, Cassirer Verlag, 1918. Reprinted, Darmstadt, Wissenschaftliche Buchgesellschaft, 1961.

———*Individuum und Cosmos in der Philosophie der Renaissance.* Leipzig and Berlin, Studien der Bibliothek Warburg, 1927. Reprinted, Darmstadt, Wissenschaftliche Buchgesselschaft, 1963.

———*Leibniz' System in seinen wissenschaftlichen Grundlagen.* Marburg, Elwert, 1902.

———*The Philosophy of the Enlightenment.* Translated by C. A. Koelln and J. P. Pettegrove. Princeton University Press, 1951.

———*The Platonic Renaissance in England.* Translated by J. P. Pettegrove. London, Nelson, 1953.

———Paul Oscar Kristeller, and John Herman Randall, Jr., eds. *The Renaissance Philosophy of Man.* Chicago, University of Chicago Press, 1948.

Castiglione, Baldesar. *The Book of the Courtier.* Translated by C. S. Singleton. Garden City, Doubleday and Company, 1959.

Charbonnel, J. Roger. *La pensée italienne au XVIᵉ siècle et le courant libertin.* Paris, E. Champion, 1919.

Charron, Pierre. *Trois vérités contre tous les athées, idolâtres, juifs, mahométans, hérétiques, et schismatiques.* Bordeaux, 1583.

Chastel, André. *L'art italienne.* Paris, Larousse, 1956. German translation: *Die Kunst Italiens.* Translated by Herman Buse. 2 vols. Munich, Prestel Verlag, 1961. Reprinted, Darmstadt, Wissenschaftliche Buchgesellschaft, 1961-62.

Clark, G. N. *The Seventeenth Century.* 2nd ed. Oxford, Clarendon Press, 1947.

Clarke, Samuel. *A Collection of Papers, which passed between the late learned Mr. Leibniz and Dr. Clarke in the years 1715-1716, relating to the Principles of Natural Philosophy and Religion.* London, J. Knapton, 1717.

Clauberg, John. *Differentia inter cartesianam et aliis in scholis usitatam philosophiam;* with a supplement, *Dissertationes communicatae de libertate philosophandi.* Berlin, 1680.

_____ *Logica vetus et nova modum inveniendae ac tradendae veritatis, in genesi simul et analysi facili methodo exhibens.* Duisberg, 1656. 2nd ed., Amsterdam, Elzevir, 1658.

_____ *Opera Omnia philosophica.* 2 vols. Amsterdam, 1691.

Clavius, Andreas. *Philosophiae antiquissimae et recentissimae prodromus; definitiones notionum universalium et principiorum . . . ex entis actualis essentia demonstrata.* Celle, 1740.

Clavius, Christopher. *In sphaeram Joannis de Sacro Bosco commentarius.* 4th ed. Paris, 1608.

Cognatus, Joannes (Jean Cousin). *Fundamenta religionis, hoc est de naturale dei cognitione, de animi immortalitate, et de justitia dei, adversus politicorum seu atheorum errores.* Douay, 1597.

Cohn, Norman R. *The Pursuit of the Millennium: Revolutionary Millenarians and Mystical Anarchists of the Middle Ages.* Rev. ed. London, Secher and Warburg, 1957.

Comenius, Amos. *The Analytical Didactic of Comenius.* Translated by Vladimir Jelinek. Chicago, University of Chicago Press, 1953.

_____ *Sapientia reserata sive pansophiae christianae seminarium.* Oxford, 1637. Later editions entitled *Prodromus pansophiae.* Latin-German edition: *Vorspiele: Prodromus pansophiae, Vorläufer der Pansophie.* Düsseldorf, Stern Verlag, 1963.

The Conway Letters. Edited by Marjorie Nicholson. New Haven, Yale University Press, 1930.

Costabel, Pierre. *Leibniz et la dynamique: les textes de 1692.* Paris, Hermann, 1960.

Costello, William T. *The Scholastic Curriculum at Early Seventeenth Century Cambridge.* Cambridge, Mass., Harvard University Press, 1958.

Crenius, Thomas (pseud. for Thomas T. Crusius). *De eruditione comparanda in humanioribus, vita, studio politico, cognitione auctorum . . . item peregrinatione tractatus.* Leiden, 1699.

Cronin, Timothy J. *Objective Being in Descartes and Suarez.* Analecta Gregoriana, vol. 154. Rome, Gregorian University Press, 1966.

Curtius, E. R. *European Literature and the Latin Middle Ages.* Translated by Willard R. Trask. New York, Bollingen, 1953.

Descartes, René. *Oeuvres.* Edited by Charles Adam and Paul Tannery. 11 vols. with supplement. Paris, Leopold Cerf, 1897-1909.

_____ *Philosophical Works.* Translated by Elizabeth Haldane and G. R. T. Ross. 2 vols. Cambridge, Cambridge University Press, 1935.

_____ *Philosophical Writings.* Edited and translated by Norman Kemp Smith. New York, Random House, 1958.

Dibon, Paul. *La philosophie néerlandaise au siècle d'or.* Vol. 1. *L'enseignement philosophique dans les universités a l'époque precartésienne (1575-1650).* Paris and Amsterdam, Elsevier, 1954.

Digby, Kenelm. *Two Treatises, in the One of which the Nature of Bodies, in the Other, the Nature of Man's Soule, is Looked into, in Way of Discovery of the Immortality of Reasonable Soules.* Paris, 1644 (Also London, John Williams, 1645).

Duhamel, Jean Baptiste. *Philosophia Vetus et Nova ad usum scholae accomodata, in Regia Burgundia olim pertracta.* Nuremberg, 1682. (Based on the Paris edition of 1651).

Duhem, Pierre Maurice Marie. *Etudes sur Léonard de Vinci.* 3 vols. Paris, Hermann, 1906-1909.

Duns Scotus, John. *Philosophical Writings.* Edited and translated by Allan B. Wolter. London, Nelson, 1962.

Dutens, Louis. *Recherches sur l'origine des découvertes attribuées aux modernes, ou l'on démontre que nos plus célèbres philosophes ont puisé la plupart de leurs connoissances dans les ouvrages des anciens.* 2nd ed. Paris, 1766.

Edwards, Jonathan. *The Nature of True Virtue.* Ann Arbor, University of Michigan Press, 1960.

Eglin, Raphael. *Prophetia halieutica novae et admirandae.* Zurich, 1598.

Erasmus, Desiderius. *Moriae encomium, id est, stulticiae laudatio.* Basel, 1540. English translation by White Kennett, *The Praise of Folly.* Chicago, Covici, 1925.

Eschweiler, Karl. *Die Philosophie der Spanischen Spätscholastik auf den deutschen Universitäten des 17. Jahrhunderts, Spanische Forschungen der Görresgesellschaft* I (1928). Münster, Beyerle-Finke-Schreiber, 1928.

Fayol, Jean Baptiste. *L'harmonie celeste, découvrant les diverses dispositions de la nature . . . pour discerner les erreurs de M. Descartes.* Paris, 1672.

Feller, Joachim Frederick. *Otium Hanoveranum sive Miscellanea ex ore et schedis illustris viri . . . Godefrois Guilhelmi Leibniz.* Leipzig, 1718.

Fernel, Jean. *De abditis rerum causis libri duo.* Lyon, 1605.

Fleckenstein, J. O. *Gottfried Wilhelm Leibniz: Barock und Universalismus.* Thun and Munich, Ott Verlag, 1958.

Fludd, Robert. *Monochordium mundi symphoniacum.* Frankfurt, 1623.

Friedrich, Karl J. *The Age of the Baroque.* New York, Harper and Brothers, 1952.

Galileo Galilei. *Dialogue on the Great World Systems.* Salusbury trans. rev. G. Santillano. Chicago, University of Chicago Press, 1957.

———*Dialogues concerning Two New Sciences.* Translated by Henry Crew and Alfonso de Salvio. New York, Macmillan, 1914.

———*Discoveries and Opinions of Galileo.* Translated and edited by Stillman Drake. Garden City, Doubleday and Company, 1957.

Gassendi, Pierre. *Abregé de la philosophie de Gassendi en VII tomes,* by F. Bernier. 2nd ed. Lyon, 1684.

———*Animadversiones in decimum librum Diogenis Laerti qui est de vita, moribus, placitisque Epicuri.* Lyon, 1675.

———*Exercitationes paradoxicae adversus Aristoteleos.* The Hague, 1624.

Gebhardt, Carl. "Rembrandt und Spinoza," *Kantstudien,* 32 (1927), 161-181.

Gerland, E. *Geschichte der Physik. I: Von den ältesten Zeiten bis zum Ausgange des 18. Jahrhundert.* Munich and Berlin, Oldenburg, 1913.

Glanvill, Joseph. *Plus Ultra, or the Progress and Advancement of Knowledge since the Days of Aristotle.* London, 1668.

———*Saducismus triumphatus, or Full and Plain Evidence concerning Witches and Apparitions.* 3rd ed. London, 1689.

———*The Vanity of Dogmatizing.* Reproduced from the edition of 1661. Edited by M. E. Prior. New York, Columbia University Press, 1931.

Goclenius, Rudolph. *PSYCHOLOGIA: hoc est de hominis perfectione, animo, et in primis ortu huius . . . commentationes ac disputationes quorundum theologi.* Marburg, 1590.

Gooch, G. P. *English Democratic Ideas in the Seventeenth Century.* 2nd ed. Cambridge, Cambridge University Press, 1927.

Graf, Pablo. *Luis Vives como apologeta: contribución a la historia de la apologética.* Madrid, Graficas versal, 1943.

Gruber, Johan Daniel, ed. *Commercii epistolici Leibnitiani: Tomus prodromus, qui totus est Boineburgicus.* Hanover and Göttingen, 1745.

Gueroult, Martial. *Descartes selon l'ordre des raisons,* 2 vols. Paris, Aubier, 1953.

Haag, Karl Heinz. *Kritik der neueren Ontologie.* Stuttgart, Kohlhammer, 1960.

Hazard, Paul. *La crise de la conscience Européenne, 1680-1715.* 3 vols. Paris, Boivin, 1935. English translation by J. Lewis May. *The European Mind (1680-1715).* London, Hollis and Carter, 1953.

Heidegger, Martin. *Die Kategorien- und Bedeutungslehre des Duns Scotus.* Tübingen, Mohr, 1916.

Heimsoeth, Heinz. *Die sex grosse Themen der neueren Metaphysik und der Ausgang des Mittelalters.* 4th ed. Darmstadt, Wissenschaftliche Buchgesellschaft, 1958.

Herbert, Edward, Baron of Cherbury. *De religione gentilium, errorumque apud eos causis.* Amsterdam, Wolters, 1700.

———*De Veritate, prout distinguitur a revelatione, a verisimili, a possibili, et a falso.* 3rd ed. London, 1656.

Hobbes, Thomas. *Elementa de Corpore.* In *Opera philosophica quae Latiné scripsit omnia.* Edited by William Molesworth. London, 1839-1845. Vol. 1.

———*Leviathan.* Edited by Michael Oakeshott. Oxford, Blackwell, n.d.

Hocke, Gustav René. *Der Manierismus.* 2 vols. I: *Die Welt als Labyrinth: Manier und Maniè in der europaischen Kunst von 1520 bis 1650 und in der Gegenwart.* II: *Manierismus in der Literatur: Sprach-Alchimie und esoterische Kombinationskunst.* Hamburg, Rowohlt Verlag, 1957, 1959.

Hönigswald, Richard. *Denker der italienischen Renaissance: Gestalten und Probleme.* Basel, Haus vom Falken, 1938.

———*Geschichte der Erkenntnistheorie.* 3 vols. Berlin, Junker und Dünnhaupt, 1933.

———*Die Philosophie von der Renaissance bis Kant.* Berlin, de Gruyter, 1923.

Hontan, Baron de la. *See* Lom d'Arce, Louis Armand a, Baron de la Hontan.

Hume, David. *A Treatise of Human Nature.* Edited by L. E. Selby-Bigge. Oxford, Clarendon Press, 1896.

_____*Dialogues Concerning Natural Religion.* Edited by Norman Kemp Smith. Oxford, The Clarendon Press, 1935.

Jones, Richard Foster. *Ancients and Moderns, A Study of the Rise of the Scientific Movement in Seventeenth-Century England.* 2nd ed. Berkeley, University of California Press, 1965.

Jordan, G. J. *The Reunion of the Churches: a Study of G. W. Leibnitz and His Great Attempt.* London, Constable, 1927.

Jungius, Joachim. *Logica Hamburgensis, hoc est Institutiones logicae in usum scholae Hamburgensis conscriptae.* Hamburg, 1638. Latin-German edition, ed. Rudolph W. Meyer, Hamburg, Augustin, 1957.

Kaser, Max. *Das römische Privatrecht,* 3 vols. Munich, C. H. Beck, 1955.

Keckermann, Bartholomew. *Opera omnia quae extant.* 2 vols., Geneva, 1614. This work contains the *Praecognitorum logicorum tractatus primus; Systemata logicae plenioris; Systema logicae minus; Systema physicum septem libris adornatum; Scientiae metaphysicae brevissima synopsis et compendium.*

_____*Systema S. S. theologiae tribus libris adornatum.* Hanau, 1602.

_____*Systema systematum.* Edited by J. H. Alsted. 2 vols. Hanau, 1613.

Kepler, Johannes. *Harmonice mundi.* Edited by Max Caspar. In *Gesammelte Werke.* Edited by W. von Dyck and Max Caspar. Vol. 6. Munich, C. H. Beck, 1937-1939. German translation by Max Caspar. *Harmonice mundi: Weltharmonik.* Darmstadt, Wissenschaftliche Buchgesellschaft, 1967.

_____*Mysterium cosmographicum.* Edited by W. von Dyck and Max Caspar. In *Gesammelte Werke.* Vol 1.

Kiefl, F. X. *Der Friedensplan des Leibniz zur Wiedervereinigung der getrennten christlichen Kirchen.* Paderborn, Schöningh, 1903.

Kircher, Athanasius. *Ars magna lucis et umbrae in X libros digesta.* 2nd ed. Amsterdam, Jannson, 1671.

_____*Ars magna sciendi in XII libros digesta.* Amsterdam, Jansson, 1669.

_____*Musurgia universalis, sive ars magna consoni et dissoni in X Libros digesta.* 2 vols. Rome, 1650.

Kneale, William, and Martha Kneale. *The Development of Logic.* Oxford, Clarendon Press, 1962.

Knox, R. A. *Enthusiasm: a Chapter in the History of Religion, with Special Reference to the XVII and XVIII Centuries.* Oxford, Oxford University Press, 1950.

Koyré, Alexandre. *From the Closed World to the Infinite Universe.* Baltimore, The Johns Hopkins Press, 1957.

Kraus, Johannes. "Die Stellung des Oxforder Dominikanerlehrers Crathorn zu Thomas Von Aquin," *Zeitschrift für katholische Theologie,* 35 (1935), 66-87.

Kristeller, Paul Oscar. *Renaissance Thought: the Classic, Scholastic, and Humanistic Strains.* New York, Harper, 1961.

———*Renaissance Thought II: Papers on Humanism and the Arts.* New York, Harper, 1965.

Kvacsala, John. *Johann Amos Comenius: Sein Leben und seine Schriften.* Berlin, 1892.

———"Irenische Bestrebungen zur Zeit des dreizigjährigen Krieges," *Acta et commentationes Imperialis Universitatis Jurievensis* (formerly Dorpat), 19 (1894), pp. 1-24.

———"Johann Heinrich Bisterfeld," *Ungarische Revue,* 13 (1893), 40-59, 171-196.

———"Die pädagogische Reform des Comenius in Deutschland bis zum Ausgang des XVII. Jahrhunderts," *Monumenta Germaniae Pedagogiae.* Vols. 26, 27. Berlin, Hofmann, 1903, 1904.

———"Thomas Campanella, ein Reformer der ausgehenden Renaissance," *Neue Studien zur Geschichte der Theologie und der Kirche.* Edited by G. N. Bonwetsch and R. Seeberg. 6 (1900), pp. 1-154.

Lalande, André, ed. *Vocabulaire de la philosophie.* 9th ed. Paris, Presses Universitaires, 1962.

Lasswitz, Kurd. *Geschichte der Atomistik vom Mittelalter bis Newton.* 2 vols. Hamburg, 1890. Reprinted, Darmstadt, Wissenschaftliche Buchgesellschaft, 1963.

Leibniz, Gottfried Wilhelm. *Deutsche Schriften.* Edited by G. E. Guhrauer. 2 vols. Berlin, 1838-1840.

———*Elementa philosophiae arcanae de summa rerum.* Edited by J. Jagodinski. Kasan, 1913.

———*Leibnizens nachgelassene Schriften physikalischen, mechanischen, und technischen Inhalts.* Edited by Ernst Gerland. Leipzig, Teubner, 1900.

———*Mitteilungen aus Leibnizens ungedruckten Schriften.* Edited by G. Mollat. Leipzig, 1893.

———*Nouveaux essais sur l'entendement humain,* Academy ed., series VI, Vol. 7. English translation by A. G. Langley, *New Essays concerning Human Understanding, together with an Appendix consisting of Some of his Shorter Pieces.* Chicago, Open Court Co., 1916.

———*Oeuvres complètes de Leibniz, publiés pour la première fois d'après les manuscrits originaux.* 2nd ed. 7 vols. Edited by Foucher de Careil.

———*Opera Omnia.* Edited by Louis Dutens. 7 vols. in 6. Geneva, Fratres de Tournes, 1768.

———*Opuscules et Fragments.* Edited by Louis Couturat. Paris: Alcan, 1903.

———*Philosophical Papers and Letters of Leibniz.* Translated by L. E. Loemker. Rev. ed. Dortrecht, D. Reidel, 1969.

———*Die philosophischen Schriften.* Edited by C. I. Gerhardt. 7 vols. Berlin, 1875-1890.

———*Sämtliche Schriften und Briefe,* ed. Deutsche Akademie der

Wissenschaften (formerly Prussian Academy). Berlin Akademie Verlag, 1921.

———*Textes Inédits de Leibniz*, publiés par Gaston Grua, 2 vols. Paris, Presses Universitaires, 1948.

Leiwesmeier, Josef. "Die Gotteslehre bei Franz Suarez," *Geschichtliche Forschungen zur Philosophie der Neuzeit.* Vol.6. Paderborn, Schöningh, 1938.

Lenoble, Robert. *Mersenne ou la naissance du mécanisme.* Paris, J. Vrin, 1943.

Lewalter, Ernst. *Spanisch-Jesuitische und deutsch-lutherische Metaphysik des 17. Jahrunderts, Ibero-amerikanische Studien,* 4. Hamburg, 1935. Reprinted, Darmstadt, Wissenschaftliche Buchgesellschaft, 1967.

Lieder, F. W. C. "Friedrich Spe and the Théodicée of Leibniz," *Journal of English and Germanic Philology,* 11 (1912), 1-50.

Locke, John. *An Essay concerning Human Understanding.* Edited by A. C. Fraser. 2 vols. Oxford, Clarendon Press, 1894.

Loemker, L. E. "Boyle and Leibniz," *Journal of the History of Ideas,* 16 (1955), 22-43.

———"Das ethische Anliegen des Leibnizschen Systems," *Studia Leibniziana Supplementa,* IV (Wiesbaden, Steiner Verlag, 1969), 63-76.

———"Leibniz and the Herborn Encyclopedists," *Journal of the History of Ideas,* 22 (1961), 323-338.

———"Leibniz's Doctrine of Ideas," *Philosophical Review,* 55 (1946), 229-249.

———"Leibniz und die Grenzen des Empiricismus," *Kantstudien,* 56 (1966), 315-328.

———"On Substance and Process in Leibniz," Reese and Freeman, ed. *Process and Divinity. The Hartshorne Festschrift.* Lasalle, Ill., Open Court Pub. Co., 1964, pp. 403-425.

———"The Origin and Problem of Leibniz's Discourse of 1686," *Journal of the History of Ideas,* 8 (October 1947), 449-466.

Lom D'Arce, Louis Armand de (Baron de la Hontan). *New Voyages to North America, containing an Account of the Several Nations of that Vast Continent.* 2 vols. London, 1735.

Ludwig, Josef. *Das akausale Zusammenwirken der Seelenvermögen in der Erkenntnislehre des Suarez.* (Inaugural dissertation.) Munich, 1929.

Lukács, Georg. *Die Zerstörung der Vernunft.* Berlin, Aufbau Verlag, 1954.

Lullus, Raymundus; see Alsted, John Henry. *Clavis Artis Lullianae.*

Mahnke, Dietrich. "Die Rationalisierung der Mystik bei Leibniz und Kant," *Blätter für deutsche Philosophie,* 13 (1939), 1-73.

———*Unendliche Sphäre und Allmittelpunkt.* Halle, Niemeyer Verlag, 1937.

Maier, Anneliese. *Die Vorläufer Galileis im 14. Jahrhundert.* Rome, Edizione de Storica et Litteratura, 1949.

Malebranche, Nicholas. *De la recherche de la vérité.* Edited by Genevieve Lewis. Paris, J. Vrin, 1945.

___*Oeuvres complètes*. Edited by A. Robinet. 21 vols. Paris, J. Vrin, 1962-1970.

___*Reponse de l'auteur de la Recherche de la Vérité au livre de M. Arnauld, des vrayes et des fausses idées*. 2nd ed. Rotterdam, 1685. Also in *Oeuvres complètes* de Malebranche, VII.

___*Traité de la nature et de la grace*. Edited by Ginette Dreyfus. Paris, J. Vrin, 1958.

Marshall, John S. *Hooker and the Anglican Tradition*. London, Adam and Charles Black, 1963.

Martin, Gottfried. *Allgemeine Metaphysik*. Berlin, de Gruyter, 1965.

___*Wilhelm von Ockham: Untersuchungen zur Ontologie der Ordnungen*. Berlin, de Gruyter, 1949.

Melsen, A. G. van. *From Atomos to Atom: a History of the Concept Atom*. Pittsburgh, Duquesne University Press, 1952.

Merguet, H. *Handlexikon zu Cicero*. 1905. Reprinted, Hildesheim, Olms, 1961, 1962.

___*Lexikon zu den philosophischen Schriften Ciceros*. 3 vols. 1892-1894.

Mersenne, Marin. *Correspondence de P. Marin Mersenne*, publié par Mme. Paul Tannery. Edited by Cornelis de Waard. 10 vols. Paris, Presses Universitaires, 1932-1967.

___*Harmonie universelle, contenant la théorie et la practique de la musique*. Paris, 1636.

___*L'impiété des deistes, athées, et libertins de ce temps, combattué et renversée*. Paris, 1624.

___*Questiones celeberissimae in Genesim, cum accurata textus explicatione; in hoc volumine athei et deistae impugnantur et expugnantur*, Paris, 1632.

___*La vérité des sciences contre les sceptiques ou Pyrrhoneans*. Paris, 1625.

Metzke, Erwin. "Erfahrung und Natur in der Gedankenwelt des Paracelsus," *Blätter für deutsche Philosophie*, 13 (1939), 74-90.

Meyer, Lodewijk, *Philosophia scriptura interpres: Exercitatio paradoxa in qua veram philosophiam infallibilem s. literas interpretandi normam esse, apodictice demonstratur, et discripantes ab hac sententia expenduntur ac refelluntur*. Eleutheropolis (Amsterdam), 1666.

Mittelstrass, Jurgen. *Die Rettung der Phaenomena*. Berlin, de Gruyter, 1962.

Montaigne, Michael, Seigneur de. "The Apology for Raimond de Sebond." In *Essays*, translated by Charles Cotton, 2 vols., pp. 365-573. London, n.d.

Moody, Ernest A. *The Logic of William of Ockham*. New York, Sheed and Ward, 1935.

___*Truth and Consequence in Medieval Logic*. Amsterdam, North-Holland Pub. Co., 1953.

More, Henry. *Antidote against Atheism*. London, 1662.

___*Divine Dialogues, containing Sundry Disquisitions and Instructions* *concerning the Attributes and Providence of God.* 3 vols. London, 1668.

——*Opera omnia: tum quae Latine, tum quae Anglice scripta sunt.* 3 vols. London, J. Martyn, 1679.

——*Philosophical Poems.* Cambridge, 1647.

Moreau, Joseph. *L'univers Leibnizien.* Lyon, Emmanuel Vitte, 1956.

Mornay, Philippe de, Seigneur du Plessis-Marly (Mornaeus). *De la vérité de la religion chrétiénne contre les athées, Epicuriens, payens, Juifs, Mahumedistes, et autres infideles.* Antwerp, 1581.

Müller, Kurt, and Gisela Krönert. *Leben und Werk von G. W. Leibniz: eine Chronik.* Frankfurt, Vittoria Klostermann, 1969.

Newton, Sir Isaac. *Mathematical Principles of Natural Philosophy and . . . System of the World.* Translated by Andrew Motte. Revised and edited by Florien Cajori. Berkeley, University of California Press, 1946.

——*Observations upon the Prophecies of Daniel and the Apocalypse of St. John.* Edited by B. Smith. London, J. Darby and J. Browne, 1733.

Nicholas of Cusa. *Idiota de staticis experimentis.* Edited by Ludwig Baus. In *Opera Omnia,* Heidelberg Academy ed., Vol. 5. Leipzig, Meiner, 1937.

Nisard, Charles. *The Gladiators of the Republic of Letters in the 15th, 16th, and 17th Centuries.* Paris, Michel Léroy Frères, 1860.

Olschki, Leonardo. *The Genius of Italy.* New York, Oxford University Press, 1949.

Ong, Walter J., S. J. *Ramus and Talon Inventory.* Cambridge, Mass., Harvard University Press, 1958.

Palisca, Claude V. "Scientific Empiricism in Musical Thought." In H. H. Rhys, ed. *Seventeenth Century Science and the Arts.* Princeton, Princeton University Press, 1961.

Paracelsus (Theophrastus Bombastus von Nettesheim). *Sämtliche Werke nach der huserschen Gesamtausgabe . . . in neuzeitliches Deutsch übersetzt.* Edited by Bernhard Aschner. 4 vols. Jena, Fischer, 1926.

——*Selected Writings.* Edited by Jolande Jacobi. Translated by Norbert Guteman. Bollingen Series XXVIII. Princeton, Princeton University Press, 1955.

——*Sozialethische und sozialpolitische Schriften.* Edited by Kurt Goldammer. Tübingen, Mohr, 1952.

Pascal, Blaise. *Pensées.* Paris, Didot Frères, 1865.

Perrault, Charles. *Parallèle des anciens et des moderns en ce que regarde les arts et les sciences: dialogues avec le pöem du siècle de Louis le Grand, et une epistre en vers sur le geniè.* Paris, 1688-1690. 2nd ed. 1692.

Peterson, Peter. *Geschichte der Aristotelischen Philosophie im protestantischen Deutschland.* Leipzig, Meiner Verlag, 1921.

Peuckert, Will-Erich. *Die grosse Wende: das apokalyptische Saeculum und Luther; Geistesgeschichte und Volkskunde.* 2 vols. Hamburg, Claasen und Goverts, 1945. Reprinted, Darmstadt, Wissenschaftliche Buchgesellschaft, 1966.

Philagrius le Roy (pseud.). *Philosophia radicalis eclectica, inter peripateticos et antiperipateticos media, compilata et nova methodo juxta ordinem alphabeticum digesta in Tractatus II.* Antwerp, 1713.

The Phoenix: or a Revival of Scarce and Valuable Pieces from the Remotest Antiquity to the Present Times, being a Collection of Manuscripts and Printed Tracts . . . London, 1707, 1708.

Pico della Mirandola, Giovanni. "Oration on the Dignity of Man," translated by Elizabeth Forbes. In Ernst Cassirer and others, ed. *The Renaissance Philosophy of Man.* Chicago, University of Chicago Press, 1948, pp. 224-225.

Pintard, René. *Le libertinage érudit dans la première moitié du XVIIe siècle.* Paris, Boivin, 1943.

Popkin, Richard. *The History of Skepticism from Erasmus to Descartes.* Rev. ed. New York, Harper, 1964.

Rader, Ralph. *The Man of the Renaissance: Four Lawgivers.* New York, Viking Press, 1933.

Ramus, Petrus (Pierre de la Ramée). *Dialecticae Institutiones.* Paris, 1647.

Randall, John Herman, Jr. *The Career of Philosophy.* Vol. 1. New York, Columbia University Press, 1962.

_____ *The School of Padua and the Emergence of Modern Science.* Padua, Editrice Antenore, 1961.

Reiser, Antonius. *De origine et progressu antitheismi seu atheismi epistolaris dissertatio.* Strassburg, 1669.

Rhys, H. H., ed. *Seventeenth Century Science and the Arts.* Princeton, Princeton University Press, 1961.

Rémusat, Charles F. M. de. *Histoire de la philosophie in Angleterre depuis Bacon jusqu'a Locke.* 2 vols. Paris, Didier, 1874.

Riedl, John O. *A Catalogue of Renaissance Philosophers (1350-1650).* Milwaukee, Marquette University Press, 1940.

Rigault, Hippolyte. *Historie de la querelle des anciéns et des moderns.* Paris, Hachette, 1856.

Ritter, Gerhard. *Via antiqua und Via moderna auf den deutschen Universitäten des XV. Jahrhunderts. Sitzungsberichte der Heidelberger Akademie der Wissenschaften,* philos.-hist. Klasse, 7 (Heidelberg, 1922). Reprinted, Darmstadt, Wissenschaftliche Buchgesellschaft, 1963.

Robin, Léon. *La théorie platonicienne des idées et des nombres d'après Aristote: Étude historique et critique.* Paris, 1908. Reprinted, Hildesheim, Olms, 1963.

Rosenberger, Ferdinand. *Die Geschichte der Physik in Grundzügen.* Brunswick, 1882.

Ross, W. D., ed. *Aristoteles, Analytica priora et posteriora, recensuit brevique adnotatione critica instruxit W. D. Ross.* Oxford, Clarendon Press, 1949.

Ryan, John Kenneth. *The Reputation of Saint Thomas Aquinas among English Protestant Thinkers of the Seventeenth Century.* Washington, Catholic University of America Press, 1948.

Saame, Otto. *Der Satz vom Grund bei Leibniz: ein constitutives Element seiner Philosophie und ihrer Einheit.* Mainz, Hans Krach, 1961.

Saavedra-Fajardo, Diego de. *Respublica literaria, or the Republick of Letters, being a Vision Wrote in Spanish by Don Diego de Saavedra.* Translated by J. E. A. B. London, 1727.

Santillana, Giorgio de. *The Crime of Galileo.* London, Heineman, 1958.

Scaliger, Julius Caesar. *Exotericarum exercitationum libri XV de subtilitate ad Hieronymum Cardanum.* Hanau, 1634.

Schelhammer, Gunther Christopher. *De natura sibi et medicis vindicata, sive de natura liber bipartitus.* Kiel, 1697.

———*Naturae vindicatae vindicatio, qua ea quae de libro de natura olim fuerunt asserta . . . respondetur.* Hamburg, 1702.

Schneider, Hans-Peter. *Justitia Universalis: Quellenstudien zur Geschichte des "christlichen Naturrechts" bei Gottfried Wilhelm Leibniz.* Frankfurt, Klostermann, 1967.

Scholz, Heinrich. *Mathesis Universalis: Abhandlungen zur Philosophie als Strenger Wissenschaft.* Edited by Hans Hermes, Friedrich Kambartel, and Joachim Ritter. Darmstadt, Wissenschaftliche Buchgesellschaft, 1961.

Schüssler, Hermann. *Georg Calixt: Theologie und Kirchenpolitik; eine Studie zur Oekumenizität des Luthertums.* Wiesbaden, Steiner Verlag, 1961.

Selden, John. *Table Talk: being the Discourses of John Selden Esq. or his Sense of Various Matters of Weight and High Consequence relating especially to Religion and State.* 3rd ed. London, 1716.

Shaftesbury, Anthony Ashley Cooper, third Earl of. *Characteristics of Men, Manners, Opinions, and Times.* 3 vols. London, 1711.

Shearman, John. *Mannerism.* Harmsworth, Penguin Books Ltd., 1967.

Siebeck, Hermann. "Uber die Entstehung der Termini Natura Naturans und Natura Naturata," *Archiv für Geschichte der Philosophie,* 3 (1890), 370-378.

Sigwart, Christoph. *Kleine philosophische Schriften.* 2 vols. 2nd ed. 1881.

———*Die philosophische Weltanschauung der Reformationszeit.* Leipzig, 1874.

———*Ulrich Zwingli: der Charakter seiner Theologie mit besonderer Rücksicht auf Picus von Mirandola.* Stuttgart, 1855.

Simson, Otto von. *The Gothic Cathedral: Origins of Gothic Architecture and the Medieval Concept of Order.* New York, Pantheon, 1956.

Smith, Norman Kemp. *New Studies in the Philosophy of Descartes.* London, Macmillan, 1952.

Sperling, Johannes. *Anthropologia physica.* Wittenberg, 1647.

———*Antiparasceve pro traduce.* Wittenberg, 1648.

———*Dissertatio de principiis corporis naturalis.* Wittenberg, 1647.

Spink, J. S. *French Free-Thought from Gassendi to Voltaire.* London, Athlone Press, 1960.

Spinoza, Baruch. *Ethics Demonstrated in a Geometric Manner.* In *The Chief Works.* Translated by R. H. M. Elwes. Rev. ed. London, 1887.

Spitzel, Gottlieb (Spizelius, Theophilus). *De atheismo eradicando . . . ad Antonium Reiserum Epistola.* Augsburg, 1669.

———*Examen vaticinii cuiusdam Anglicani de ultimo Romae excidio anno MDCLXVI.* Augsburg, 1666.

———*Scrutinum atheismi historico-ratio-logicum.* Augsburg, 1663.

Spitzer, Leo. *Classical and Christian Ideas of World Harmony: Prolegomena to an Interpretation of the Word "Stimmung."* Baltimore, The Johns Hopkins University Press, 1963.

Sprat, Thomas. *The History of the Royal Society of London, for the Improving of Natural Knowledge.* London, 1667.

Steiner, George. *The Death of Tragedy.* London, Faber and Faber, 1961.

Steuchius, Augustinus Eugubinus (Augustine Steuch of Gubbio). *De Philosophia perenni sive veterum philosophorum cum theologia Christiana consensu libri X.* Paris, 1577.

Steudel, Johannes. *Leibniz und die Medizin* (Rektoratsrede, Bonn, 15 Nov. 1958). Bonn, Hanstein Verlag, 1960.

Stöckl, Albert. *Geschichte der Philosophie des Mittelalters.* Vol. 3. Mainz, Kirchheim, 1866.

Strong, Edward W. *Procedures and Metaphysics: a Study in the Philosophy of Mathematical-Physical Science in the Sixteenth and Seventeenth Centuries.* Berkeley, University of California Press, 1936.

Sturm, Johann Christopher. *De natura sibi incassum vindicata.* Nuremberg, 1698.

———*Idolum naturae similiumque nominum vanorum . . . dissertatio.* Nuremberg, 1692.

———*Philosophia eclectica.* Altdorf, 1686.

———*Physica eclectica sive hypothetica.* Vol. 1. Nuremberg, 1697.

Suarez, Francisco. *Metaphysicarum disputationum in quibus et universa naturalis theologia ordinate traditur . . . Tomi duo.* Mainz, 1600.

Swift, Jonathan. *The Battle of the Books.* London, Chatto and Windus, 1908.

Thomasius, Jacob. *Schediasma historicum, quo occasione definitionis vetusta, qua philosophia dicitur GNOSIS TON ONTON varia discutiuntur ad historiam tum philosophicam, tum ecclesiasticam pertinentia.* Leipzig, 1665.

Thorndike, Lynn. "Censorship by the Sorbonne of Science and Superstition in the First Half of the 17th Century," *Journal of the History of Ideas,* 16 (1955), 119-125.

Toffanin, Guiseppi. *History of Humanism.* Translated by Elio Gianturco. New York, Las Americas Publishing Co., 1954.

———*Storia dell'umanismo.* Vol. 2: *L'umanismo Italiano (del XIV al XVII secolo).* Bologna, Zanchelli, 1950.

Traherne, Thomas. *Centuries of Meditations.* Edited by Bertram Dobell. London, Dobell Press, 1948.

Tschirnhaus, E. Walther von. *Medicina mentis.* Amsterdam, 1687. 2nd ed., Leipzig, 1695.

Tulloch, John. *Rational Theology and Christian Philosophy in England in the Seventeenth Century.* 2 vols. 2nd ed. Edinburgh and London, Blackwood, 1874.

Turnbull, G. H. *Hartlib, Dury, and Comenius: Gleanings from Hartlib's Papers.* London and Liverpool, University Press of Liverpool, 1947.

―――"S. Hartlib's Influences on the Early History of the Royal Society," *Notes and Records of the Royal Society of London,* 10 (April 1952), 101-130.

Ueberweg, Friedrich. *Grundriss der Geschichte der Philosophie.* 11th ed. Vol. 3: *Die Philosophie der Neuzeit bis zum Ende des XVIII. Jahrhunderts,* by Max Frischeisen-Köhler and Willy Moog. Berlin, Mittler, 1924.

Valla, Lorenzo. *De libero arbitrio.* Basel, 1518. English translation: *Dialogue on Free Will,* by C. E. Trinkhaus in Ernst Cassirer and others, *The Renaissance Philosophy of Man,* pp. 155-182.

―――*Opera Omnia.* 2 vols. Turin, Bottega d'Erasmo, 1692.

Vanini, Julius Caesar. *Amphitheatrum aeternae providentiae divino-magicum, christiano-physicum, necnon astrologo-catholicum, adversum veteres philosophos, atheos, epicureos, peripateticos, et stoicos.* Lyon, 1615.

―――*De admirandis naturae, reginae deaeque mortalium arcanis libri quattuor. Le opere.* Edited by Luigi Corvaglia. Milan, Società aninima editrice Danti Alighieri, 1933.

―――*Oeuvres philosophiques.* French translation by M. X. Rousselot. Paris, 1842.

(Villemandy, Pierre de.) *Philosophiae veteris ac novae parallelismus, in quo doctrinae parallelo et conciliatione . . . deducitur.* Amsterdam, 1679.

Vives, Juan Luis. *De Anima et vita libri tres.* Zurich, Gesner, n.d.

―――*De concordia et discordia in humano genere.* Antwerp, 1529. Frankfurt, 1576. Spanish translation by L. S. Gallego, *Obras completas.* Madrid, Aguilar, 1947.

―――*De pacificatione, Opera Omnia.* 8 vols. Valencia, 1784-1790.

―――*De veritate fidei Christianae libri V, in quibus de religionis nostrae fundamentis, contra ethnicos, Judaeos, Agarenos sive Mahometanos, et perverse Christianos . . . disputantur.* Cologne, 1568.

Voltaire, François Marie Arouet de. *Siècle de Louis XIV.* Paris, 1845.

Vonessen, Franz. "Reim und Zahl bei Leibniz," *Antaios* (Stuttgart, Klett Verlag), 7 (1966), 99-120.

Vossius, Gerhard Johannes. *De Philosophia et philosophorum sectis libri II.* The Hague, 1658.

―――*De theologia gentilis et physiologia christiana, sive de origine ac progressu idolatriae, deque naturae mirandis quibus homo adducitur ad deum.* Amsterdam, 1700.

Vreka, Anton. *Leben und Schicksale des Johann Amos Comenius.* Zunim, 1892.

Wade, Ira O. *The Clandestine Organization and Diffusion of Philosophical Ideas in France from 1700 to 1750.* Princeton, Princeton University Press, 1938.

Wade, Ira O. *The Clandestine Organization and Diffusion of Philosophical Ideas in France from 1700-1750*. Princeton, Princeton University Press, 1938.

Watson, Foster, ed. *Vives and the Renaissance Education of Women*. New York, Longman, Green and Co., 1912.

Weber, Hans Emil. *Die philosophische Scholastik des deutschen Protestantismus im Zeitalter der Orthodoxie*. Leipzig, Quelle and Meyer, 1907.

Weigel, Erhard. *Analysis Aristotelica ex Euclide restituta*. Jena, 1658.

―――*Cosmologia nucleum astronomiae et geographicae*. Jena, 1680.

―――*Idea mathesis universae, cum speciminibus inventionum mathematicarum*. Jena, 1687.

―――*Kurtze Beschreibung der verbesserten Himmels- und Erdgloben sambt dero nützlichen Gebrauch*. Jena, 1681.

―――*Universi corporis pansophici prodromus de gradibus humanae cognitionis ipsaque trina mentis operatione, generaliter agens, quem dicere posses pantognosiam*. Jena, 1672.

Whitaker, Vergil K. *Francis Bacon's Intellectual Milieu*. Los Angeles, University of California Press, 1962.

Wiley, Margaret L. *The Subtle Knot: Creative Scepticism in Seventeenth-Century England*. London, Allen and Unwin, 1952.

Willey, Basil. *The Seventeenth Century Background: Studies in the Thought of the Age in Relation to Poetry and Religion*. New York, Columbia University Press, 1940.

Willmann, Otto. *Geschichte des Idealismus*. 2nd ed. 2 vols. Brunswick, Bieweg Verlag, 1907.

Wind, Edgar. *Pagan Mysteries in the Renaissance*. New Haven, Yale University Press, 1958.

Wolf, Abraham. *A History of Science, Technology, and Philosophy in the 16th and 17th Centuries*. New York, Macmillan, 1935.

Wölfflin, Heinrich. *Kunstgeschichtliche Grundbegriffe*. 11th ed. Basel, 1948. English translation of 7th edition by M. D. Hottinger, *The Principles of Art History*. New York, Holt, 1932.

Wolter, Allan B. *The Transcendentals and their Function in the Metaphysics of Duns Scotus*. *Franciscan Institute Publications*, Phil. Ser. 3. St. Bonaventure, 1946.

Wood, Thomas. *English Casuistical Divinity during the Seventeenth Century, with Special Reference to Jeremy Taylor*. London, Society for the Propagation of Christian Knowledge, 1952.

Worthington, John. *The Diary and Correspondence of Dr. John Worthington*. Edited by James Crossley. *Publications of the Chatham Society*, II. Manchester, 1847.

Wundt, Max. *Die deutsche Schulmetaphysik des 17. Jahrhunderts*. Tübingen, Mohr, 1939.

―――*Die deutsche Schulphilosophie im Zeitalter der Aufklärung*. Tübingen, Mohr, 1945.

Würtenberger, Franzsepp. *Mannerism: The European Style of the Six-*

teenth Century. Translated by Michael Heron. London, Weidenfeld and Nicholson, 1963.

Yost, R. M. *Leibniz and Philosophical Analysis.* Berkeley, University of California Press, 1954.

Zabarella, Giacomo (Jacobus). *Opera Logica . . . quorum argumentum, seriem, utilitatem versa pagina demonstrabit.* 3rd ed. Cologne, 1597. Also 6th ed., 1604. Frankfurt, 1608. (Especially the works *de methodo, de ordine intelligendi,* and *de doctrinae ordine apologia.*)

———*De rebus naturalis libri XXX.* 3rd ed. Cologne, Zetzner, 1597.

Index

Absolutism, 4, 131, 223. *See also* Relativism

Act and potency, 90, 137, 138, 143

Activity and passivity, 90, 218-219, 222. *See also* Power

Adaequatio intellectus ad rem, 20, 108, 140, 206

Adequate knowledge, 122, 123, 127, 140, 158, 169-170

Advancement of Learning (Bacon), 7, 34, 78, 80, 89, 92, 121, 161

Aesthetics: styles, 21-26; Leibniz's influence on, 126. *See also* Beauty

Affections, 18, 33, 148, 185; amenability to reason and discipline, 234-236; in Descartes, 124; and evil, 240; and the good, 197; and human motivation, 235-236; as innate natural laws, 244; nature and power of (Vives), 124; and ideas, 124, 126; in Leibniz, 126; and the natural light, 67; social interdependence, 240; in Spinoza, 124-125, 197; in Stoicism, 124; and subjectivism, 234-237; Juan Vives's theory of, 69-70; and will, 124, 236. *See also* Perception and ideas

Alan of Lisle, 90

Alexandrian mathematicians, 101

Algebra, 101, 167

Alphabeticum Philosophicum, 191

Alsted, John Henry, 28, 29, 34, 35, 43, 69, 184; advice on educational peregrination, 259n46; on art and nature, 266n15; Azor's influence on, 82; and Bisterfeld, 144; Bruno's influence on, 189; educational application of harmony, 189-190; *Encyclopaedia*, 46-47; harmony in kingdom of grace, 191; and Hartlib, 80; history of the study of the affections, 279n11; on love, 249; mannerism in mathematics, 109; on symbiosis, 241; on transcendentals, 141-143

Ames, William, 82

Anabaptists, 60, 78

Analysis and synthesis, 38, 40, 158, 161-162, 235, 272n2. *See also* A priori and a posteriori

Ancients and moderns, conflict of, 39-42

De Anima et Vita Libri Tres, 124

Animal spirits (Descartes), 236

Animism, in prescientific thought, 88, 96-97

Antiparasceve pro Traduce (Sperling), 100

Apocalypticism, 78. *See also* Eschatology

Apologetic, philosophy as, 58-60, 136, 154, 196-197

A posteriori, *see* A priori and a posteriori

Appearance and Reality, *see* Phenomena, phenomenalism

Apperception, in Leibniz, 126. *See also* Perception, internal and external; Self-consciousness

Appetite, 190, 192, 248, 249

A priori and a posteriori, 103-104, 106, 162-166

Aquinas, Thomas, 58, 63, 67, 73, 134, 204

Archimedes, 101

Architecture, 24, 184-185, 202

Aretino, Pietro, 42, 91

Arguments for the existence of God, 70-74, 121, 262n34; from being (ontological), 71, 73, 122-123; from causality, 262n34; the cosmological argument, 72; from design (teleological), 73-74, 250; from interdependence of things, 72; from motion, 72, 262n34; by the natural reason, 63-68; from the nature of the soul, 72

Aristotelianism, 8, 231; and arguments for existence of God, 71; and atomism, 221; of Jean Fernel, 92; on mathematical objects, 105; on method, 160; and the "new way of ideas," 128;

Helmstedt, University of, 83
Heraclitus, 92
Herbert of Cherbury, 16, 64, 66-67,
    70-71, 131, 141, 244
Herborn philosophers, 141-145
The Hidden Causes of Nature
    (Fernel), 162
*On His Own Ignorance and that of
    Others* (Petrarch), 233
History, 74-77, 77-82, 207, 215
Hobbes, 57, 60, 108, 137, 167,
    193, 234; analysis of causes, 38,
    163; causal determinism in, 236;
    condemned as atheist, 60, 61-62;
    on conditions of a Christian com-
    monwealth, 56, 242; critical skep-
    ticism of, 9; individuation, princi-
    ple of, 229-230; and the isolation
    of man, 232; Leibniz's criticism
    of, 241, 249, 279n10; literary
    style, 41; on love, 241; on natural
    law, 244; nervous trace theory in
    psychology, 236; and "new way
    of ideas," 129; nominalism of,
    129, 159, 229-230, 232, 269n17,
    279n10; Puritan influence on, 78;
    and scientific method, 163, 195,
    266n13
Hofmann, Friedrich, 210
Honestas, ideal of, 6, 127; Bister-
    feld on, 192; and the courtier, 17;
    and freedom, 14, 246; on human
    nature, 222-223; and the ideas as
    forms, 118; and power, 13; and
    reason, 13-14; on satire, 43; on
    skepticism, 19-20; social implica-
    tion of, 17-18, 239-240
Hontan, Baron de la (Louis Armand
    a Lom d'Arce), 66
Huet, Pierre Daniel, 50, 59
Hugo of St. Victor, 90
Human nature, 222-223, 224-227.
    See also Man, nature of
Humanism, 6, 32-33
Humanism, civic and individual, 5,
    6, 86, 112
Humanities, their relation to sci-
    ence, 112
Hume, 106, 130, 201, 202, 215; on
    arguments for existence of God,
    73; and empirical criterion for

knowledge, 165; on sympathy,
    241; on unity of Republic of Let-
    ters, 51
Humor, 42
Hutcheson, Francis, 241
Huygens, Christian, 23, 94, 97, 247
Hypothesis, 111, 165-166

Ideal and real, confusion of, 152,
    154, 242, 247-248, 250
Ideas, 42, 167; as archetypes, 13,
    120; in Descartes, 42, 121-122; as
    determinants of classes and indi-
    viduals, 227-228, 278n2; as dy-
    namic, 13, 126, 127, 216, 221;
    eduction of, 118; as exemplary
    causes or forms (Suarez), 119,
    139; and God, 13, 105, 119, 139,
    198, 243; in honestas, 118; imma-
    nence of (in Scaliger), 118-119;
    innate (Bruno), 189; as laws, 101,
    102, 120; in libertinism, 118; ob-
    jective and formal meaning of,
    119, 120, 122; as objective es-
    sences or natures, 119, 122; the
    old vs. the new ways, 118-127;
    orders of, in Leibniz, 171-172;
    reality of, 117, 119, 120; regula-
    tive, 46, 196; relation to percep-
    tion in Leibniz, 125-126; role in
    harmonizing (Leibniz), 198; in
    Spinoza, 122-125; in Suarez, 73,
    119-120, 139; as *vis dei*, 221. *See
    also* Law, conception of ideas as
Identity, principle of, 171, 172,
    173-174; moral and metaphysical
    (Leibniz), 231
Imagination (Bacon), 46, 166
Immeation, 241
Immortality, 60
*Impieté des deistes, athées, et liber-
    tines combattué et renversée*
    (Mersenne), 59
Incarnation (doctrine of), in Vives,
    65
"Indefinite," 74. *See also* Infinite
Indians (American), their religion,
    63, 65-66
Individual, the, 22; and conceptions
    of substance, 227-228; in hon-
    estas, 10, 227; in Leibniz, 126,